Work, Aging, and Social Change

Work, Aging,
and Social Change

Professionals and
the One Life–One Career
Imperative

Seymour B. Sarason

With a Chapter
"The Santa Fe Experience"
by David Krantz

THE FREE PRESS
A Division of Macmillan Publishing Co., Inc.
NEW YORK

Collier Macmillan Publishers
LONDON

The Free Press
A Division of Macmillan Publishing Co., Inc.
866 Third Avenue, New York, N.Y. 10022

Collier Macmillan Canada, Ltd.

Library of Congress Catalog Card Number: 76-27224

Printed in the United States of America

printing number

3 4 5 6 7 8 9 10

Library of Congress Cataloging in Publication Data

Sarason, Seymour Bernard
   Work, aging, and social change.

   Bibliography: p.
   Includes index.
   1. Professions--United States. 2. Job satisfaction
   United States. 3. Age and employment--United States.
I. Title.
HD8038.U5S27   301.44'46'0973   76-27224
ISBN 0-02-927860-0

Passages from Seymour B. Sarason, *The Psychological Sense of
Community* (1974) have been quoted by permission from the
publishers, Jossey-Bass, Inc., San Francisco, California.

To Esther and Julie:

Each in her own way taught me more than
I wanted to know and much that I needed
to learn.

Contents

Preface

I must first explain why this is not the book I thought I would write. The story begins with a decade of responsibility taking care of aged, slowly dying parents, my wife's and mine. Watching loved ones approach certain death, having to exercise the most careful control over homicidal anger toward ignorant and insensitive medical personnel and evil proprietors of the death houses we call nursing homes or convalescent hospitals, and trying valiantly to maintain a semblance of normal family living, I decided to move into the field of gerontology. After all, I had learned a lot in discharging my willing responsibilities to parents, there was no doubt that aged people were coming into society's awareness, and I knew that my violent feelings toward medical and nursing home personnel obscured recognition of their victimization by their training (or lack of it) and by public policies that made health service a business. In moving into this problem area I was not departing too drastically from my past. My last three books (Sarason, 1974, 1972, 1971) dealt with the creation of new settings, the obstacles to changing existing settings, and the psychological sense of community which I regard as the overarching value by which to judge any social action or program. The field of aging contained all of these issues. So I and some superb undergraduate and graduate students immersed ourselves in the literature, visited the major gerontological centers, and received valuable help and knowledge from diverse people.

There were some nagging thoughts, however, not the least of which concerned my capacity to remain relatively dispassionate in the face of massive injustice, societal indifference, and pathetically superficial thinking on the part of important policy makers. More upsetting, because it was inconsistent with what I teach, was the fact that we were slipping into the familiar clinical way of thinking: problems have to exist and *then* the clinician tries to repair the damage. I applaud clinicians precisely because they seek to help people with problems, and I support any effort to improve clinical outcomes. However, in the long run prevention is far more effective than our capacity to repair, and it is shortsightedness bordering on blindness to build up the clinical endeavor at the expense of the preventive one.

Sooner or later, the preventive approach is embedded or related to the developmental approach. A poet once said that life takes its final meaning in chosen death. As usual, the best poets can put into a few words crystallized truths of living. When an aged person looks back because there is more in his past than there will be in the future, that person ruminates, amongst other things, about choices made or not made, and how past choices seemed to lead to present conditions and color one's approach to the ever-shortening future.

The ultimately decisive factor for the direction I took, as well as for the shape and content of this book, was my struggle to comprehend why students of the late sixties were so cynical and looked so dysphorically toward their futures. Having myself been a militant and radical student, I could understand much of what was going on in our universities, except for the depth of the students' view of a future in which they saw themselves as trapped and stagnating. Many of them talked as if life had already passed them by and the future was a downhill course. There were few colleagues at Yale and elsewhere who did not share my perception. That really is not the point. What is the point is that two facts and a question came together in my mind. One fact was that by the end of the next two or three decades we will have more highly educated older and aged people than ever before in our society, perhaps any society. The second fact, contained in the first, was that the future aged would differ markedly from those who are currently aged. The question was: how will these highly educated (for the most part professional) people look to and experience aging? These facts and the question provided the specific focus for a developmental perspective, and that is why this book is so different from the one I thought I would write. The mode of inquiry changed, as did the kinds and ages of people who, without exception, shared with us their thoughts, feelings, dilemmas, and fears.

Writing this book presented special problems. There is a vast literature on work, but almost all of it has concerned blue- and white-collar workers, or professional–managerial groups in business, finance, or industry. My interest was in the highly educated professionals outside these settings, whose numbers have dramatically increased in recent decades (particularly within or around the fields of health and education). There is also a sizable literature on professions, but most of it has been directed to their histories, changes, and structure. It was not relevant to my purposes to get involved in the question of what is a profession, although to someone with different purposes that question would be crucial. There is no doubt that the number of professions has vastly increased; if there is any on that score, there can be none about the desire of people to regard themselves and to be regarded as professionals. In ordinary parlance the word "professional" has lost whatever conceptual boundaries it once had. In this book when I talk about highly educated, professional people, I mean individuals whose choice of work requires at least a college education giving them specific knowledge and skills, to be applied under supervision for a period of time, at the end of which they are entitled to a "label" which carries credentials for independent activity. With increasing frequency, the choice of work or career involves more than four years of college, even though it may not be required that the post-college years come immediately after graduation from college. In this book, all of the individuals we interviewed, formally or informally, had advanced degrees (mostly Ph.D., M.D., and J.D.), or were attending or applying to professional or graduate school.

This book is about the relationship between education and work. It is not written from the standpoint of how the former prepares one technically and conceptually for the latter, but rather in terms of how people's expectations from higher education have changed as a result of World War II and how these expectations, reflecting a reordering of values, have had pervasive consequences for the experience of work and the sense of the passage of time, one of the core ingredients of the sense of aging. The scope of this book, then, is more narrow than the title suggests, but the problems and issues it treats have enormous import for our society as it is and may become. I have tried to state and clarify matters, to focus attention on them, and to stimulate further discussion. Someone once told me that since everything is related to everything else, the first question a writer must answer before he writes a book is what he is *not* going to write about. I have found that very good advice, although it never really quiets the fear that one has left oneself open to allegations of ignorance or narrowness.

I do not treat in any scholarly fashion the literature on work, or aging, or social change, nor should this book be viewed as an effort in futurology. It represents my effort to think through some relationships heretofore only adumbrated in the scholarly and research literature, although novelists and playwrights have found the dilemmas of the professional fascinating fare. Almost all the readers of this book will be highly educated people, and most of them will have or be seeking professional status. Each will have a basis for judging the degree to which what I have to say strikes familiar notes in his or her experience. This is a book about our "inner lives" in relationship to social history, the force of culture, the process and effects of education, the experience of work, and our coping with mortality.

My debts are many and acknowledgment is paltry repayment. Esther Sarason and Peter Cowden were of inestimable help with interviews, discussion, and ideas. Robert McLellan and Victor Lieberman provided ideas and criticisms which were extremely valuable. Numerous graduate and undergraduate students, at Yale and elsewhere, contributed to our efforts in diversely important ways: Patricia Fountain, Priscilla Ellis, Ray Reisler, Julie Miller, Marnie Potash, Clifford Berken, Julie Sarason, and Kenneth Maton lightened my task and brightened my days. Nancy Carroll industriously and creatively waded through the data on career change. David Krantz of Lake Forest College contributed more than Chapter VIII to this book; he gave his friendship, and I am grateful. My friend and colleague, N. Dickon Reppucci, was a patient listener to my evolving ideas, and, as will be seen in Chapter X, his own research provided a solid basis for some of my surmises about what was happening to professionals in the public arena.

Terry Saunders, Leland Wilkinson, and Brian Sarata may be surprised to see their names here, but I can assure them they helped make this book. I profited greatly from discussions with Cary Cherniss, and I am deeply grateful to him for so graciously permitting me to use his data. My gratitude to Eleanor Smith, a superb and charitable secretary, is profound. Two friends, Burton Blatt and Wendell Garner, probably do not realize the degree to which our frequent personal discussions were a stimulus to my thinking. Elizabeth Meyer Lorentz played an indirect but important role in the writing of this book, if only as a dramatic example of the significance of personal growth as a value of living. I am indebted to Richard Hackman for his criticisms and encouragement. Similarly, a former colleague and close friend, Professor David Hunt of The Ontario Institute for Studies in Education, provided incisive suggestions and timely support. Jan Hunt knows how she helped, and I am indebted to her. Writing is a lonely profession and one needs good friends and colleagues to keep one going. I have been quite fortunate.

Consistency with the contents of this book requires that I acknowledge how crucially helpful it has been to be housed and materially supported by Yale's Institution for Social and Policy Studies. To grow requires a hospitable soil and this I found in ISPS, first under the leadership of John Perry Miller and more recently under Charles E. Lindblom. The Ford Foundation gave me an individual grant which helped me move in new directions. A grant from the small grants division of the National Institute of Mental Health made it possible to initiate and complete analysis of data on career change. My debt to Professor Saul Cohen of Clark University is very great, because he brought me into the orbit of his network project, funded by the Office of Education. Through this office, I came to know Drs. Morton Kreuter and Alan Entine (State University of New York, Stony Brook) who enlarged the scope of my thinking and knowledge about career change. Professor Entine's help is described in Chapter XI.

Work, Aging,
and Social Change

I
The Plan of the Book

WORK, AGING, AND SOCIAL CHANGE are all intimidating topics, any of
which should be approached with humility and caution. To treat them
in combination requires a kind of abandon, as well as acceptance of
the intuition that you will inevitably fall short of the mark. As I followed my thoughts and plans for this book, I was drawn to a view of
this combination, which had not been clearly formulated before or, if it
had, had not been given the importance I thought it deserved. Most
simply put, the question which gripped me was: to what extent, and in
the context of which social–historical forces, has the experience of
work of highly educated, professional people become problematic in
its satisfactions?

I can count on the reader knowing that dissatisfaction with work is
very frequent among blue- and white-collar workers as well as among
a large variety of highly educated, professional people in business,
finance, and industry. Indeed, scores of writers and investigators in
the administrative sciences have studied people in these settings in
ingenious, analytic ways, and our understanding of how organizational, situational, and personality factors combine to determine the
experience of work has been considerably increased. But what about
that very large number of professionals who are not in business, financial, and industrial organizations? In the past five decades the proportion of professionals in the population has increased (according to census data) at least four-fold, and in the past three decades the variety of
new professions has grown almost beyond comprehension. The
much-discussed knowledge explosion is mirrored by many of these
new professions, most of which offer legitimation by a system of credentials. These new professions vary considerably in size, institutional
relationships, visibility, and connection with other or older professions. It can be misleading to emphasize their newness, because many
of them have arisen within the context and traditions of older profes-

1

sions. For example, within medicine there are many new professionals who may or may not be physicians; we call them "specialists" of one kind or another, and although they are in the broad field of medicine or health, they can be foreigners to each other, and hostile ones at that. The new in the context of the old, plus the truly new, present us with a bewildering array of "professionals" that should caution us against making simple generalizations. So, when I raise the question about how professionals experience work, it is not with the expectation that an answer will be equally appropriate for all professions. To justify such an expectation would require, at the very least, the careful study of populations of professionals, taking into account a variety of variables, e.g., age, sex, educational background, expectations, geographical location, and marital status. It would also require the security that we know how to obtain the information that would illuminate and not obscure issues.

How we gain understanding of another person's experience of work should be no easy matter, except for those of that thoughtless cast of mind who turn complexities into banal simplicities, or cannot see substantive issues because everything is viewed as a technical problem. The experience of work, like that of sex, is so extraordinarily complicated and private, so determined by culture and tradition, so much the organizing center of our lives, and so much a developmental process that it is small wonder we as individuals have difficulty taking distance from "our work," i.e., from ourselves.

This is no less true, of course, for those who would study how "others" experience work. Indeed, one could argue that the extent to which we study how others experience work without coming to grips with our own experience of it makes it likely that communalities will be missed in our studies, and that our biased and ignorant perspective will produce the usual mischief of the dynamics of the self-fulfilling prophecy. You do not have to be a Freudian to recognize that one of Freud's major contributions was the fearless recognition and clinical demonstration that therapist and patient were not different from each other, that you did not need one theory for "them" and one for "us." (Freud's life is unusually instructive in that it illustrates changes in the experience of work over time, the dynamics of career change, and the degree to which our narrow conception of work denies the idea that the web of the experience is made up of "non-work" strands. These strands make a mockery of categories that have semantic clarity at the same time that they render pallid and segmented the stream and configuration of the experiences.)

The fact is that the highly educated professionals outside of business, finance, and industry have hardly been the focus of interest and study. We have hundreds, if not thousands, of studies of blue- and white-collar workers, and of managers and executives in business, finance, and industry, and yet that ever-growing group of professionals in other settings has virtually been ignored. This cannot be an oversight but rather, I assume, must be the result of a cultural and social–historical bias, a residue from earlier times in which the distinctions between labor and work, on the one hand, and social status, on the other hand, were highly correlated. That is to say, "to work" was to engage in activities stamped, so to speak, with a personal trademark, but "to labor" meant that the products of one's energies in no way reflected his personal stamp. However achieved, elevated social status exempted one from labor; in the past several hundred years, this status has become increasingly related to education. Law, medicine, and theology were the clearest examples of how professional status separated one from the mass of society. It has long been in the rhetoric of our own society that one should strive through formal education to avoid a life of labor, i.e., to escape from drudgery, cipherdom, and literally mindless activity. This did not mean, of course, nor was it intended to mean, that the goal of formal education was to attain professional status. The goal for most people was far more modest. Without education you automatically became a laborer; with some education you stood a chance of "bettering yourself." For a long time the phrase "get an education" applied to finishing elementary or high school. Professional status, requiring as it increasingly did prolonged formal education, was not for the masses but for the few. The professional was one with a "calling," someone whose personal and intellectual gifts were recognized by forces, divine or mortal, steering him (and it was not *her*) toward a life quintessentially meaningful in the most personal ways. However much the Reformation legitimized business and commerce and gave to such activities the characteristic of a divine mission or calling, it never quite succeeded in establishing parity of nobility between material acquisition and the altruism of the traditional professions.

The point is seen most clearly, even today, in orthodox Judaism, in which biblical study is literally a holy activity, and those individuals showing signs of the "calling" are given special status and provided with the material means to permit them to devote their entire lives to an ever-fascinating, challenging, wisdom-attaining, totally absorbing activity. The orthodox Jew who is a worldly "success" may be respected, but he is simply not the equal of the scholar. How can one compare the mind-expanding work of the scholar to the mundane activity of the businessman? Indeed, the ultimate value of the businessman's activities lies in the extent to which he makes it possible for the biblical scholar to be unconcerned with earning a world living. For Judaism no less than for Christianity, the Age of Enlightenment, exemplified most clearly in Voltaire's life (e.g., Besterman, 1967), witnessed an assault on religion and ritual and a glorification of the life of the mind and the rule of reason. One of the long-term effects of the Enlightenment stemmed from the belief in the perfectibility of man, a perfectibility which would require a mind liberated from the shackles of superstition and exposed to the wonders of nature, the crowning jewel of which was the human mind (Becker, 1932). Perfectibility, of course, would require education. Ironically, the Enlightenment, as did Judaism, put scholarship at the pinnacle of valued work, albeit devoid of the traditional religious justification. Science spawned new knowledge and new fields, the universities slowly began to accommodate to the new forces, and the seeds of new professions began to take root.

Our culture has a long history, which is not understandable if one ignores how entrenched became the belief that the good life—which did not include business, finance, and industry—required prolonged education and professional status. Beginning in the latter part of the last century and continuing to the present day, the person of means who made a substantial gift to a university received a quality of praise more valuable than that accruing by virtue of having amassed a fortune. The university was and is viewed not only as a repository of past knowledge and wisdom or the generator of new knowledge, but as the selector of students who will continue the traditions, i.e., that select few who in some way will use their education and professional training in the service of others.

It is no wonder that highly educated people were seen as privileged, exposed as they had been to the panorama of man's past accomplishments and future possibilities, as well as having acquired special knowledge and skills guaranteeing a lifetime of personal and intellectual challenge and fascination. And if society did not always match income to professional status, it was argued that the good fortune of being able to pursue one's chosen destiny was no mean form of compensation. Given the choice of working for less or laboring for more, what highly educated person in his right mind would opt for laboring? Both society and the highly educated agreed on the sensible answer.

On what grounds, then, is it warranted to assert that the experience of work by highly educated, professional people may have taken on some of the features, if not of labor, then of despair, disappointment, boredom, and conflict? But the title of this book raises at the outset still another question that inordinately complicates discussion: What are the relationships between work, aging, and social change, and have these relationships changed for the highly educated segment of the population? This question in turn stimulates a third: with which one of the triad should one begin? To handle them in some concurrent fashion proved quite unwieldy. What finally made sense to me was to focus on the relationships between work and social change, because as they became clarified their significances for aging would emerge. I say this because the experience of work is one of the major determinants of how one experiences the passage of time, and one way to look at aging is in terms of how the sense of the present invades and colors past and future. As one experiences changes in work, one's view of himself in the stream of time is altered.

Although I do not deal directly with aging until later in the book, it is an implicit (and sometimes explicit) factor in discussion. *Within the next two or three decades we will have the most educated aged population ever. Almost all current thinking and programming for aging people is in terms of those who are now elderly.* If only because our society will in the future be dealing with quite a different population than it is now, it is essential that we try to understand work-aging relationships.

In Chapter II I discuss two points which I believe to be crucial in opening up the discussion. The first point is an obvious one which our language tends to obscure: the experience of work cannot be understood by what a person overtly does or what he says he does, nor by focusing primarily on those internal cognitive processes required to deal with the external tasks. In making a distinction between a specific job or a task, on the one hand, and work, on the other, one concedes that "working" is a more complex and differentiated experience than "performing a task," and is not bounded by space or time. The experience of work is comprised of people, events, and relationships far afield, in a literal sense, from the physical arena of work. I quote extensively in that chapter from John Dewey's *Art As Experience*, because he states so clearly the criteria of the concept of experience, illustrates it with compelling examples and, in the process (in typical style), instructs us in the dangers of confusing different labels with different processes. The second major point in Chapter II is that our society builds great expectations into our psychological stance. It is no less American than apple pie. Great expectations from life have long been characteristic of our culture and set us apart (from our perspective as well as from that of most of the world) from other societies. If social realities for most people make a mockery of this rhetoric, it is nevertheless true that the power of great expectations is not easily diminished. But for those in the more distant past who were privileged to receive prolonged education, the stance of great expectations was realistic, and this was no less true for those millions who in the last four decades poured into our colleges and educational system. What happened in our society after World War II, largely because of that war, was a reinforcement of the rhetoric of great expectations, all the more powerful because the Great Depression had become weak in memory and a new peaceful world seemed struggling to be born. The GI bill for veterans, the consequences of which have hardly been studied even though their dynamisms are readily acknowledged, gave a substantial base for great expectations to millions who ordinarily would have lacked such a base. The importance of higher education (the more the better) was conveyed to everyone through all the media. Education was the road to salvation-success. As a student of mine once said: "College became the equivalent of the Old Testament, and graduate school was the equivalent of the New Testament. Science, research, and professionalism were the new Trinity to which we all prayed in the church of education." If my student was a little too entranced with his analogy, he nevertheless conveyed how the post-World War II period was characterized by great expectations and a creeping cynicism.

⨏ Chapter III is devoted to World War II and its immediate aftermath, a period of a few years during which enormous changes occurred that set the stage for the emergence of new values which lent a distinctive quality to the entire postwar period, up to the present day. The dynamics and requirements of this war (the first "real" world war), starting with the draft, which began before we formally entered the war, changed the lives of individuals and families in the most drastic ways. This was as true for the educated as for the less educated, albeit in different ways. It is easy to overlook the fact that for millions of people World War II required a career change, a fundamental change in the experience of work. The consequences were not necessarily negative. Who poured into higher education, and why, requires recognition of the different ways individuals experienced their work in the armed services. Similarly, in order to comprehend the postwar era from the perspective of highly educated people, the relationship between the war experience and the emerging strength of certain values has to be clarified. These values were an intrinsic part of what I call the Age of Psychology. The millions who came to our colleges and universities were predisposed to hear and accept the new messages for living and the implicit and explicit values contained in them. If the experience of work has changed for highly educated, professional people, in no small measure this was due to the renewed strength of some old values. One might say that the rhetoric was taken quite seriously. Autonomy, new experience, authenticity, and personal growth—the labels might differ, but there was no mistaking how these values were supposed to govern living in general and work in particular. Whether one calls it the Age of Psychology or the Age of Mental Health is a matter of the esthetics of language, but in either case it was a new age: an age very much the offspring of the previous one had come into the world.

But the United States was not, and is not, the world, a theme on which I elaborate in Chapter IV. Some unfamiliar stirrings and writings from Europe a few years after the war received a mixed and puzzled reception, quickly followed by a warmer, if not enthusiastic, one. Europe was a shambles at war's end; out of that disaster emerged Sartre, Beckett, Genet, Ionesco, and Camus, with their tragicomic view of the absurdity of man's plight, quite in contrast to the regnant philosophies of our society. How do we account for the relative alacrity with which these new European philosophies became standard fare in college courses, and what does this signify about a changing conception of the role of work in life? And, it must be emphasized, these new philosophies were being taught almost exclusively to the highly educated, an ever-increasing segment of society. It was not a matter of "imposing" messages upon young people. There was, as always, a compliance factor, and in this instance the factor was not far from the surface of their thinking. I illustrate this point by comparing Arthur Miller's *Death of a Salesman* and Salinger's *Catcher in the Rye*; both were published shortly after the war and received wide acclaim, and yet they contain such contrasting views of society. Why was *Catcher in the Rye* more prophetic of how many educated people in our society were to feel about living and work?

If Europe was a shambles after the war, it was only a few steps from paradise compared with the holocaust which could overwhelm the world through atomic weaponry. The harnessing of atomic energy for destructive purposes introduced a truly new note into people's outlooks, if only because it made the denial of personal death more difficult than ever before. This is the focus of Chapter V, in which I give particular emphasis to how the possibility of world destruction had far greater impact on younger than older people, imprinting on the minds of the young qualities of cynicism, anxiety, and ambivalence about striving for a future. Changes in the experience of work have several sources; a major one in the past three decades has been the degree to which and the ways in which younger people perceived the consequences and probabilities of atomic destruction. Any factor or event that changes how people perceive and move toward the future (e.g., pollution, overpopulation, limited resources) must have an effect on how they approach and experience work. But younger people did not have only themselves to rely on in drawing gloomy conclusions about the future. There were many influential, older people, most of them in academia, who agreed with youth that if life was worth living, it was not worth as much now as before. For younger people to come to maturity and the world of work with some fear or dysphoria should occasion no surprise. We define our work and our work defines us, and both definitions emerge from categories of thinking, time perspectives, and cultural givens of which we are rarely conscious until events expose the fabric in which all of these were embedded. Such events have not been lacking for those who have grown up over the past several decades.

Chapter VI moves directly to the issue of the degree to which satisfaction from work has become problematic for professional people, drawing primarily on interviews and informal discussions with people in mid-life. There is, however, a prior problem: the extraordinary difficulty for such people to talk candidly about how they experience their work. We can call it a methodological problem, but it is rooted in the nature of our culture and history and contains a clash between great expectations and the values of contemporary society.

Professionals have long been high on society's pedestal. Indeed, their eminence largely accounts for the millions swarming for professional status. If the attainment of such status begins to lose its glamour and elements of boredom and lack of personal growth appear, if one's sense of autonomy founders on the realities of organizational bigness and external social-governmental controls, there are set into motion dynamics of conflict, guilt, and inadequacy against which the individual struggles in the most private way. To talk about such dynamics "out loud" is to compel one to confront the necessity for change, in order to experience that sense of rejuvenation which is required to avoid the prospect of pathetic aging. It is strange that on the surface at least, unhappiness in work makes the problem of candor particularly poignant for those professionals who have enjoyed their work and by conventional criteria have been successful. Why the problem of candor has to exist and how it can be circumvented, if only in part, are the major foci of Chapter VI. Once circumvented, the true circumference of the experience of work becomes apparent, as does the precarious balance between satisfactions and dissatisfactions.

In Chapter VII I discuss a cultural given, the force of which is no less consequential for its unreflective acceptance. I call it the one life–one career imperative: from early on in life through the college years, we are made aware of an ever-expanding smorgasbord of career opportunities, from which we are told we must choose the one dish of work to eat throughout our days. What is the *one* thing you want to *be*? I trace the force and effects of this cultural imperative from the time of birth through the years of college and beyond, and describe in a variety of ways the clash between the imperative and the values that became dominant after World War II. The significance of the imperative is not only in how it illuminates the agonizing conflicts in career choice or the work crises which now occur well before mid-life, but in the basis it provides for discerning how the status of the imperative in the present separates us from the past and points to a kind of future to which we have given little attention. The one life–one career imperative occupies center stage in the remaining chapters of this book.

Chapter VIII, "The Santa Fe Experience," is by Dr. David Krantz, who came to know scores of career changers and dropouts, almost every one of whom had been a highly successful professional, e.g., embryologist, museum director. Santa Fe is a magnet for such people; Dr. Krantz explains why. More important, however, is his description of these people, which illuminates the interaction between the one life–one career imperative and the dominant values discussed earlier affecting as these values do marriage, parenthood, and work—having explosive personal effects preceded by sustained personal turmoil. I am deeply grateful to Dr. Krantz for writing this chapter in a personal vein, revealing in the process the positive aspects of overcoming the problem of candor.

Because this book is about highly educated, professional people, and I am one of them, I could not maintain the fiction that I was writing only about "them out there" and not myself. At the very least, if I regarded myself as different from others, despite our sharing a common culture, I should describe and explain the difference. But the more I talked with others, the more I was impressed with communalities. The title of Chapter IX is *Career Change: An Autobiographical Fragment.* Frankly, I had difficulty keeping it a fragment, and I make no pretense that it is as complete or as compelling as it might be were it more than a fragment. If for no other reason, I consider it an important chapter because I use my career to raise questions about what constitutes a career change. These are questions we ordinarily answer in ways that obscure some of the most important aspects of the experience of work.

The health field constitutes one of the, if not *the*, fastest growing clusters of professional people. One segment of this health cluster is found in community mental health centers. It is a segment made up of a variety of professionals. In Chapter X, I describe why professionals in these centers are a frustrated, disappointed lot. Among the most important reasons is what I call the Federal, State, Local Complex (FSLC), a congeries of agencies and institutions related through legislation, containing and spawning controls that divest the professional of his sense of autonomy and authenticity. Community mental health centers are rather new in our society, and their birth was much heralded as a revolutionary departure from early ways of providing services which guaranteed unavailability to disadvantaged groups. Willingly, health professionals fought for these centers and sought support from the FSLC, and the support was provided. Little did the professionals know what consequences they would experience from such an alliance. Their idealism was a reflection of ignorance about the FSLC, an early victim of the realities of the public arena. I do not say this harshly or with any intention of assigning blame, but simply as a matter of fact. What has happened to these professionals is typical of what is happening to "public professionals" in general. Within the past few years a number of people have begun to study how these professionals experience their work, and the picture is an unpleasant one. I am grateful to some of these investigators, particularly Dr. Cary Cherniss at the University of Michigan, for allowing me to see and summarize unpublished data. If the experience of work by professionals has been a neglected area of research and discussion, there is good reason to believe it will not remain so.

What is a career change? How frequently does one or another degree of career change occur? The first question, as I indicated earlier, is raised in the autobiographical fragment. The second question, unfortunately, has no good answer, because the relevant data hardly exist. If we had good data, it would mean that attention had been given to how professionals experience work, but that is not the case. Ideally, one would want to have good base rate data, not only to judge frequency of career change, but also to see if there have been changes over time. The one life–one career imperative would suggest that career change would be low, but that an increase would have shown up in recent decades. There is also the problem of distinguishing between those who actively seek a change and those who would like to but take no action. That is to say, satisfaction in work cannot be judged by the fact that an individual stays in one career line. Chapter XI contains a discussion of these problems, as well as a variety of data (no one of which is adequate on research grounds) suggesting that career change is far from miniscule in frequency. I do not present these data because I think they prove a point, but rather because they suggest that the problem deserves the most serious study.

In Chapter XII I take up directly the issue of the psychological sense of aging, aspects and illustrations of which are contained in different parts of previous chapters. That biological and psychological aging are not synonymous goes without saying, but even a cursory perusal of the literature on aging belies the lack of seriousness with which the developmental aspects of the psychological sense of aging is taken. This was no less true in regard to biological aging until World War II when, in the course of performing countless operations on young men, it became obvious how many of them already manifested processes of bodily disease and decline. In this chapter, therefore, I stress how the psychological sense of aging develops relatively early in life, and the peculiar prod it receives from the dynamics of career choice and entry into professional work.

Needless to say, this psychological sense of aging has to be seen in light of the different and highly publicized threats to human existence. The psychological sense of aging emerges and is reinforced whenever the individual is confronted with the knowledge that time is limited, and that he or she is mortal, reaching for or being pulled by an ever-shrinking future. Those confrontations are many and start early in life, and the necessity of choosing how one is to fill in the future elicits, albeit fleetingly at first, concern about how one is experiencing the passage of time, the core ingredient of the psychological sense of aging. Few things bring this into the focus of awareness as poignantly as the experience of work.

The final chapter considers "solutions" and emphasizes how our usual ways of trying to solve social problems through changes in public policy have both intended and unintended consequences. "Problem creation through problem solution" almost has the status of a law, but that does not mean we take it seriously, and that is the case in the token attention we pay to the knowledge that we live in a society in which everything is becoming increasingly related to everything else. The second part of that chapter discusses an ongoing social phenomenon that undoubtedly will have enormous consequences for work, aging, and social change. I refer to the changing role of women. For example, as women continue to approach unambiguous equality of opportunity, the strength of the one life–one career imperative will further weaken. A major point, perhaps the most basic one, of the women's liberation movement is that its success will be as liberating for men as for women, and one way this may happen is by making it easier both for men and women to circumvent the economic obstacles to career change. In the last part of the chapter, I suggest that future changes in the experience of work and aging will depend on what happens to people's hunger for a sense of community. The idea of progress has three ingredients: in contrast to the past we know more, we can do more, and we are happier. I am no partisan of the idea of progress, because the evidence for the last ingredient is virtually nonexistent. Without a real sense of rootedness and belonging, the satisfactions we can expect from work or any other arena of social activity are perforce drastically curtailed. From the beginning to the end of our lives, we are social beings, and if the quality of our social relationships underlines our loneliness rather than our sense of belonging, it is hard to derive lasting satisfaction from our increased knowledge and capabilities. I close the book on this note—not from despair or a sense of hopelessness, but from the belief that not to recognize the bedrock significance of the sense of community is the most grievous error of all. Scores of people, from today and the past, have sounded this note of warning, albeit on different bases and for different goals. The problem lies not in people's unwillingness to listen to the note, but in the possibility that times and circumstances may dispose them to hear a melody that solves the problem by eliminating individuality. That, of course, would be the most unfortunate example of problem creation through problem solution.

II
Great Expectations and the Experience of Work

TO DISCUSS THE NATURE of work is to confront immediately inside–outside, subjective–objective, or part–whole issues. Shall we define work in terms of what we see an individual do, or what he says he does, or some combination of objective description and subjective explanation? If we wished to talk about the nature of work of a butcher, we could spend days watching, describing, and categorizing what we see him do. We would learn a lot about what he does, perhaps more than he could tell us if we had to rely on his own reports. But we would be uncomfortable stopping with such descriptions, if only because we would not understand why he does any or all of these things in the ways, sequence, and style we observed. We assume that what we observe is not random behavior, but that in some manner as yet unknown to us, it reflects a conception of what the tasks and problems of a butcher are. So when we talk to him about the nature of his work, it is because we believe that what he tells us can illuminate what we observed, i.e., we seek "inside" information to illuminate the "outside" or "objective" data. It is obvious, but it deserves emphasis, that in such an approach the anchor point is understanding what we have seen; the butcher contributes information and explanation which help us make sense of the "objective" data.

Imagine someone watching me watching and recording what a butcher does. He would be puzzled by some of the things he sees me do, but if he watched me long enough and could read what I was recording, he would gain some comprehension of what I was about. Still, he would undoubtedly be eager to ply me with questions to better understand what I was doing and why. If I told him that I was interested in the nature of the work of a butcher and, therefore, went about it in the ways he had observed, he would probably say that he now "understood" what the nature of my work is. He might say to me: "I could see what you were doing and I understood some aspects of it, but after talking to you I realize that what I saw were means to a goal. *Your* goal is to understand the nature of work of a butcher. But what did you learn about the goal of the butcher?" To which I would have to reply: "Why do you say that my goal is to understand the nature of a butcher's work? In a certain and very restricted sense you are correct, but you would be describing me wrongly to others if you told them that you met a psychologist whose work was to understand the nature of a butcher's work. Tomorrow you might watch me studying a lawyer, and at another time, it might be an accountant, or a podiatrist, or a taxicab driver. And if you were then to conclude that my goal was to understand the nature of work of a lot of different people, you would again be right and wrong. The fact of the matter is that I am interested in the nature of work as a means of understanding social history and social change, and if I didn't have the hope that this understanding would be deepened by focusing on the nature of work, I would be in a pretty bad personal fix. Without this hope, without the faith that my expectations will receive some satisfaction, how could I keep going? Now, if you asked me if I liked my work, I would not know how to answer you. Do you mean how much of a kick I get from studying butchers, lawyers, etc.—watching and recording and interviewing them? Frankly, it is sometimes interesting and often a bore. If I had to spend my life doing only that, I would go stark, raving mad. So, in that respect, I am not enthusiastic about my 'work.' But if you mean by work what you saw me doing, what I told you about it, and how I see it in relation to where I want to get some day—if that is what you mean by *my* work—then my answer would be infinitely more favorable. I have to be honest with you, though, and tell you that unless I felt that my work was respected by others—colleagues and family—I would be most unhappy. In a sense, my work is for them; it is like a gift I want them to like. Indeed, they frequently enter my experience of my work; they are *there* the way my pencil and recording pad are there."

It could be argued that my answer unnecessarily muddies the conceptual water by subsuming under the label "work" a mélange of subjective or inside variables, e.g., hope, faith, love, expectations and satisfaction. Granted that these and other variables get related to each other and to work, why confuse them with the different operations, overt and covert, which by common agreement or systematic study are the basis on which an individual and society either can judge the efficiency of performance, or seek ways to improve it, or to distinguish, as society must, among different types of work? In fact, if you enlarge the meaning or definition of the word "work," would you not have to invent another one to refer to what a person *does* and the mental *operations* which give rise to or accompany these overt actions? The issue which this question raises can be illuminated by the intelligence–personality dichotomy. For decades after Binet developed his scales, intelligence was defined by how an individual performed on the test, i.e., how he *did*, the items he passed, etc. There were many who believed that "intelligence is what an intelligence test measures." This view was hard to refute, if only because how people performed on the test had predictive power for what they would *do* on tests of academic achievement, and also because how they did was presumably helpful for administrative and personal decisions about school placement and career planning. There were two major objections to this way of defining or conceptualizing intelligence. The first was that intelligence tests sampled poorly the different "factors" comprising intelligence, an objection which challenged only slightly, if at all, the view that intelligence could be observed in what people did on tests. The task was to devise better tests, sampling more comprehensively the operations of intelligence. The second, more serious and radical objection was that it was a caricature of reality to separate intelligence from what might be loosely called "personality." No one denied that the experience of "doing" tests contained a variety of internal factors (attitudinal, motivational, affective) which played a role in what a person did, and bore a dynamic relationship to his past, present, and future experience. Therefore, to say that an individual's performance on an intelligence test was a measure only (or primarily) of intelligence was not only to distort the picture of how the individual experienced the testing—the organismic character of the experience—but also to do violence to an individual's right to be understood in his own terms.[1]

There are striking similarities in the ways in which work and intelligence have been discussed and studied. Let us indicate a few:

---

[1] It is ironic in the extreme, as Wolf (1973) has pointed out in her biography of Alfred Binet, that he went to great lengths to argue against such a separation! The American adapters of Binet's scale saw what he had *done* and ignored or were ignorant about the complexity of the "other part" of Binet from which his scale emerged. Intelligence became what intelligence tests measured, and that measurement was fateful for the lives of people. It all seemed so efficient, so quantitative, so much like physical science—so practical. And didn't it work? Did it not allow one to make judgments about people, to place this child in this class and that child in another class, to steer this person to this line of work and that person to another line of work, to say that this person is smarter than that one? Some people have claimed that the most solid achievement of American psychology has been the development of intelligence tests which permit one to predict future performance with a high degree of validity. But, as we shall soon see in the case of work, pride in such an achievement should be tentative, at best.

1. When an individual has taken an intelligence test, the most frequent question asked is: how did he or she *do*, by which is meant where does the score place him or her in regard to others and what bearing will this have on what we do in relation to the person? When we meet somebody, we may quickly find ourselves wanting to know what the person *does*, i.e., we want to know his label because if we know it we think we know a good deal about him or her. So, if the person tells us he is a physician, we automatically assume—a picture gets conjured up in our minds—that we know many of the things he does, with what, and where.

2. People are classified according to level and type of intelligence, depending on the "factors," abilities or discrete cognitive operations tapped by the tests. Some of these classifications can be quite elaborate. In the world of work, which consists of thousands of types of jobs, the classifications become far more elaborate, indeed overwhelming, as job descriptions become more detailed and analytical. Just as there are efforts to make distinctions within and among intellectual factors or operations, the same is done with work groupings. For example, there are scores of types of psychologists. There was a time, decades ago, when there were very few psychologists (and far fewer types), and very rarely were they found outside a university. Today, if you know that somebody is a certain type of psychologist, you have to ask many questions to find out what he or she does, and where, e.g., does the person work with children; individually or with groups; in a clinic, hospital, or private office; diagnostically, therapeutically, etc.?

3. It is difficult for any discussion of intelligence to proceed very far without the issue of "improvement" arising in the form of two questions. One, can an individual's intelligence be improved, i.e., to what extent can the person do better than he does? Two, what are the limits to the degree of improvement? Almost regardless of how people answer these questions, they agree that we need better means than we now have to describe intellectual performance and its concomitant mental operations. These same questions and issues have always characterized discussion and research on work, with the notable difference that improvement has tended to be seen less in terms of the welfare of the individual than in terms of how it benefits an organization. The enthusiasm for time–motion studies—the pride accompanying its promise to *really* record what people do—inhered in the material gains which would accrue to the business organization. If you had an indisputable, objective record of what people did in their work, you had a base for figuring out how to change and improve the quantity and quality of that work.

4. When one reads the literature on intelligence and work, particu-

larly up until World War II, one can note a tendency to try to get at the "essence" of intelligence and work performance by *eliminating* all factors, internal or external, which intrude on that essence. It was as if these factors were noise. In the spirit of laboratory experimentation, the goal was to isolate and study the phenomena one wanted to observe and, having done so, then to figure out how to alter or improve the essence. The possibility that the phenomena never existed in reality in the form studied, or could never exist in reality in that form, or that the noise, far from being noise, was an important part of the phenomena, was not seriously considered. Or, perhaps more accurately, if such possibilities were recognized, it rarely was reflected in what the investigators *did*.

It has not been my intention to derogate, let alone write off, much of what has been studied and thought about work. My aim, rather, has been to state and emphasize an obvious point: any conception of work that primarily or exclusively restricts itself to what people do and to the concomitant mental operations—restrictions reflected in methodologies for analysis of descriptive data and cognitive processes—simply cannot capture the complicated experience of work. Can we understand a dream without understanding the dreamer? The answer, of course, is that we have learned a lot about the characteristics of dreams (e.g., content, frequency, electrophysiological correlates), but have not lost sight of the obvious fact that whatever we have learned represents but a small part of the individual's experience of dreaming, i.e., its personal meanings and uses. Working, like dreaming, cannot be understood only by description, content, and even process. Freud's contribution was not in taking dreams seriously. From the dawn of history, people took dreams seriously. Although he illuminated the processes of dreaming and how they altered and patterned dream content—no mean achievement—his greater contribution was the pursuit of his conviction that dreams were, so to speak, the crater of an experienced volcano. It was not until he pursued this conviction in the context of his own dream experiences that he began to understand how organically related the dream was to the dreamer.

The point I have been stressing has long been obvious. Within the past hundred years, slowly but with ever-increasing frequency and strength, "workers" have resented and resisted the conception that they were *only* workers, i.e., that their worth inhered only in what they did and produced, and all else they might need, want, and hope for on and from their work were irrelevant, personal weaknesses or indulgences, if not flagrant examples of declining moral fiber—or sheer hubris. A twelve-hour day too long? Rest periods from monotonous, repetitive, bodily debilitating tasks? The right to discuss a variety of issues (pay, pension, vacation, grievances) with supervisors or employers? To ask, if not require, the boss to be more polite, understanding, sensitive? The right to feel secure through a union of peers? To the modern ear these questions may sound comically antique, but they make clear that what was at issue were two very different conceptions of how work was or should be experienced. It would be an oversimplification to say that these different conceptions were merely a consequence of conflicting economic interests, because that does not explain why in earlier times the different views were not all that different. Nor does it explain why once the divergence appeared, it took so long for it to spread throughout society. To explain the divergence in exclusively economic terms is no less a caricature of reality than it is to say that work is what people do, plus the concomitant mental operations.

What the worker was saying to the employer was: "I am more than you think I am. There is a lot more going on in my head and heart while I am doing my work for you. I have feelings, hopes, expectations, and needs. I am not you, I cannot be you, but I am not and do not want to remain what you think I am. I am far more than the doer you see. Although you and I may agree that I am a good worker in your terms, you cannot understand why I am not a satisfied worker. And when I tell you why I am dissatisfied, you tell me either that I *should* not feel that way, or that what I experience cannot be your concern. Should not feel that way? It is like commanding the ocean waves to stop. And if what I experience in my work cannot be your concern, are you at least saying, perhaps, that you concede that I experience far more in my work than you ordinarily recognize?"

The more benevolent employer might have replied: "You have been a good worker and I paid you for your work. But you have changed. You no longer are satisfied doing your job well, taking pride in the quantity and quality of your output. You have new expectations, new wants you not only wish me to recognize, but also to pay for. Of course, I am bothered by the fact that what you want will cost me more money, but that truly bothers me less than the fact that you do not see the radical implications of your thinking. Once I concede, even in the slightest, that you have a right to experience more from your work than you do now, where will it end? It would not be long before you would be telling *me* how *I* should experience my work."

What the worker was saying, and the employer correctly perceiving, was that the relationship between expectations and the traditional conception of work was being called into question. They were not new expectations in the sense that they had never been part of a worker's experience; they were now being articulated and pursued. The conflict was out in the open, and it is one which is far from over. Strangely, the semantics of the issue have not changed much. Work is still what a person does, as distinguished from working *conditions*. Although this distinction can be rationalized in terms of economic factors and collective bargaining negotiations, from a psychological standpoint it is another distorted fractionation of the work experience. As long as one stays within the economic framework in which profits, pay, and efficiency are major issues and goals, one is a hopeless prisoner of a perspective which automatically rules out the following questions: What is the meaning of work? How is it experienced? Within such a framework these questions are irrelevant.

When one considers how the work scene has changed in a century, how work and its conditions have changed and presumably "improved," why is it that so many people are unhappy about their work experience? No one would want to go back to the "good old days," yet many people today talk as if those days are not over. Our benevolent employer of a century ago would, if he could, say: "I told you so. Once you start giving in to what people want and expect, there is no end to it. Today they expect this, tomorrow that, and the pit of expectations is bottomless." Our prophet is right, for the wrong reasons. He is right in suggesting that if you look at work in other than a narrowly technical way and begin to consider seriously how much of an individual's experience is wrapped up in work, and how that experience is indissolubly a part of other "non-work" experiences, the nature of work will undergo pervasive change. He is wrong in seeing the issue only in terms of individuals, as if they do not exist in a society which has characteristics and dynamics of its own. Expectations exist in individuals, but rarely, if ever, do they fail to reflect what has happened in the larger society. If our benevolent employer had acceded even in part to what the workers wanted, he probably would have had no more difficulty with them, given the combination of the times and the demand. Having satisfied his workers, however, it did not follow that societal changes affecting those workers were thereby stopped and altered. Precisely because these were societal changes—the perceptible outcroppings of invisible system characteristics and dynamics resting on values and cultural history—one could have predicted that the expectations of the next generation would be different. So when our benevolent employer sees human nature as inherently greedy, requiring the most strenuous internal and external control lest its self-feeding and self-destructive dynamics be stimulated and reinforced—a view permitting him to say "I told you so"—he is quite wrong. But his view of certain aspects of his society is fairly correct, i.e., it has long been a generator of new and more expectations. And our benevolent employer probably never realized the extent to which, on the level of rhetoric, at least, he saw great expectations as a spur to his achievement.

Work and Experience

John Dewey's (1934) *Art as Experience* is one of those remarkable books that illuminate a particular sphere of human activity by demonstrating its kinship to other activities to which, by common consent, it has either no direct relationship or only a polarized one. The common tendency to think of work in terms of what someone does and the resultant products or consequences is, as Dewey says, a bar to understanding.

> The sources of art in human experience will be learned by him who sees how the tense grace of the ball-player infects the onlooking crowd; who notes the delight of the housewife in tending her plants, and the intent interest of her goodman in tending the patch of green in front of the house; the zest of the spectator in poking the wood burning on the hearth and in watching the darting flames and crumbling coals. These people, if questioned as to the reason for their actions, would doubtless return reasonable answers. The man who poked the sticks of burning wood would say he did it to make the fire burn better; but he is none the less fascinated by the colorful drama of change enacted before his eyes and imaginatively partakes in it. He does not remain a cold spectator. What Coleridge said of the reader of poetry is true in its way of all who are happily absorbed in their activities of mind and body: "The reader should be carried forward, not merely or chiefly by the mechanical impulse of curiosity, not by a restless desire to arrive at the final solution, but by the pleasurable activity of the journey itself."
>
> The intelligent mechanic engaged in his job, interested in doing well and finding satisfaction in his handiwork, caring for his materials and tools with genuine affection, is artistically engaged. The difference between such a worker and the inept and careless bungler is as great in the shop as it is in the studio. [p. 5].

Dewey is not creating an identity among a da Vinci, a Joe DiMaggio, a Willie Mays, a housewife, a spectator, and a craftsman. He is describing experiences, differing markedly in materials, activity, structure, and duration, but having several things in common. I can do no better than to let Dewey speak for himself:

> . . . we have an experience when the material experienced runs its course to fulfillment. Then and then only is it integrated within and demarcated in the general stream of experience from other experiences. A piece of work is finished in a way that is satisfactory; a problem receives its

solution; a game is played through; a situation, whether that of eating a meal, playing a game of chess, carrying on a conversation, writing a book, or taking part in a political campaign, is so rounded out that its close is a consummation and not a cessation. Such an experience is a whole and carries with it its own individualizing quality and self-sufficiency. It is *an* experience [p. 35].

For anyone concerned with understanding work as experience, Dewey's analyses help one to avoid confusing the product with the experience, the doings of the individual with the inevitable social experience of those doings, and the "here and now" features of work with its seamless incorporation of past and prospective experiences— the experience of work as a development, as a flow of experiences with distinctive albeit varying qualities, as a complicated and changing picture testifying to the continuous interaction between the individual and environmental conditions, and, fatefully, as a shaper of a life no less than the form of a "product" is shaped by its maker. The experience of work shapes the shaper, regardless of whether the shaper is today's Michelangelo, Einstein, mechanic, or house cleaner. If the assembly-line worker rarely or never has, in Dewey's terms, *an* experience in work, this says nothing about his capacity to have such an experience—as we would learn if we came to know him intimately—but it says much about his interaction with the work environment.

As Dewey cautioned, the lack of an experience in work is far from highly correlated with the value judgments society makes about different types of work. I am reminded here of Dr. Burton Blatt's comment about the "publish or perish" standard for promotion in the university. "There are two kinds of faculty: those who are promoted because they publish, and those who publish because they want to be promoted." This is an interesting and insightful comment because it speaks, as does Dewey, to the heart of the matter: work is always both individual and social; its antecedents and consequences are likewise always individual and social; and how these individual and social contexts fuse determines the degree to which work as experience contributes, in Dewey's words, "directly and liberally to an expanding and enriched life." Wrapped up in the phrase "expanding and enriched life" is both the fact that the experience of work is developmental in character (it is not a "here and now phenomenon" unrooted in a perceived past and future), and the value that it should be accompanied by the sense that one's understanding of one's self, materials, and world changes and grows. And, it should be emphasized, "enrichment and expansion" can be accompanied and even stimulated by failure and despair. To say that the experience of work should be enriching and expanding in no way implies a Panglossian vision of social living of which work is a part. What it does imply is that work is a kind of developmental drama performed on a stage onto which every major aspect of human behavior, aspiration, and feeling may be cast, fleetingly or otherwise, meaningfully or absurdly, at a point of expansion or constriction. To the spectator the drama may not be *an* experience. To those on the stage it is an experience, if it is only like that of Pirandello's characters in search of meaning.

Art as experience is work as experience. Once we can get beyond the cultural confusion in which labels are confused with things, products with processes, and processes with experience—"this is art and that is non-art;" "art requires creativity and non-art does not;" "the artist has and reflects a special human experience rarely found in or sought for by the non-artist"—once we comprehend the limitations of this Aristotelian way of thinking and categorizing, we can appreciate the significance of Dewey's attempt to demonstrate that far from being an atypical human activity, "artistic" activity is a typical one in that the desire to understand how one can shape and be shaped by materials and one's experience, how one's sense of change and growth heightens the vibrancy of living, and how one's experience of work can mire one in a past and infuse despair into a future, are common features of people's work when the appropriate conditions exist. Obviously, "work" of all sorts varies considerably and significantly on all kinds of dimensions, but they all have in common at least two characteristics: they are *transforming* experiences, for good or for bad, in varying degrees; and again in varying degrees the experiences contain awareness that these are ongoing transformations, sought or imposed.

In 1947 Dewey wrote a foreword to a book *The Unfolding of Artistic Activity* by Henry Schaefer-Simmern (1948). "[Artistic activity] is not something possessed by a few persons and setting them apart from the rest of mankind, but is the normal or natural human heritage. Its spontaneity is not a gush, but is the naturalness proper to all organized energies of the live creature. Persons differ greatly in their respective measures. But there is something the matter, something abnormal, when a human being is forbidden by external conditions from engaging in that fullness according to his own measure, and when he finds it diverted by these conditions into unhealthy physical excitement and appetitive indulgence." When one reads this book, it is clear why Dewey was taken by it, because Schaefer-Simmern demonstrates and emphasizes, among other things, two points: the differences in the nature of process and product between *an* experience, and one in which process and product hardly reflect the individual's capacities; and second, the enormous differences in the transforming consequences of the two types of experience. Schaefer-Simmern is talking about far more than "art." That he is also talking about the nature and experience of work is a point most people will find hard to grasp because of their prepotent tendency, instilled in them by their culture, to pay more attention to what people do than to what they experience and how that web of experience may be genotypically similar in phenotypically different "doings." *To someone like Dewey, this is so obvious that in his preface he never mentions or even alludes to the fact that Schaefer-Simmern's book is about institutionalized mental defectives and institutionalized juvenile delinquents, as well as a wide array of other adults who had never considered themselves "artists."*

I had the good fortune to observe Schaefer-Simmern's work with mentally defective individuals, and rarely have I seen so clearly the identity between art as experience and work as experience. The products of these individuals were impressive enough (as the book's illustrations demonstrate), but no less impressive—in some ways more, because it contradicts traditional expectations about how such individuals work—were the sustained, organized, and deep qualities of their experience. To see these individuals in Schaefer-Simmern's "studio" and in the institution's industrial training site was to see the differences between experiencing labor and the experience of work—and to see what Dewey meant by art and work as an experience.

The people Schaefer-Simmern writes about never had great expectations, certainly not in the artistic realm. In this respect, they are quite different from the bulk of people in our society who from an early age are encouraged to develop great expectations, to strive for and to expect the satisfactions of working rather than the frustrations of laboring. For many people, these great expectations are dashed fairly early in life on the rocks of reality. For others, particularly those who reach our colleges and universities (and they are an ever-increasing proportion of their age group), these great expectations continue to be nourished, with very mixed consequences for students as individuals and the society as a whole. Great expectations may be as American as apple pie, but as a one-course menu for living and eating it is not sustaining.

Expectations in American Society

John Dewey had a long life. His adult years spanned the latter decades of the previous century and the first half of the present one. His mammoth impact on psychology, philosophy, and education rests on a corpus of work distinguished by a constructive criticalness, an analyticity which was both piercing and integrative, a sensitivity to the porous boundaries between the individual and his society, as well as between theory and practice, and, finally, an optimistic vision of what man could be and do. It was this last characteristic, I believe, which largely accounts for his popularity, and I do not use popularity as a criterion of the value of his substantive contributions, which rests on more secure grounds (e.g., see Bernstein, 1971). Dewey both reflected and reinforced the American belief and hope—honored more in the breach than in the practice, but honored nonetheless—that one could and should expect much from life. The idea that man's freed intelligence had found a hospitable home on this continent, that the litmus test of our democracy was in the degree to which an individual's capacities received opportune stimulation and practice, was long a part of public rhetoric. This was a "land of opportunity" in which the only major constraints on the individual were an impoverished imagination, a lack of boldness or initiative, and impersonal bad luck. Dewey knew otherwise, of course, but he also knew that there was some truth to the rhetoric in the sense that, comparatively speaking, there was opportunity and, absolutely speaking, that man's capacities for creative growth were not only part of his biological heritage, but also limited by a constraining society. Dewey did not justify high expectations only in terms of a basic *value* for the good society, i.e., only as a matter of fairness or justice. It would be nearer correct to say that the strength with which he held such a value was a consequence of how he understood the workings and possibilities of the human mind in its commerce with its environment. Let us recognize that it is academic snobbishness, mixed with an arrogant ahistorical stance, that has allowed Dewey to be dubbed as "only" a philosopher or an educator. That he was quite a general psychologist, and an even greater developmental psychologist (some of whose basic concepts are similar to Piaget's concepts of assimilation and accommodation) tends to be forgotten as a major source of Dewey's values.

Dewey's writings touched a responsive chord in various segments of our society. It was the sweet chord of expectation signalling the even sweeter melody of progress. Great expectations was one of the threads from which the American experience was woven. It is impossible to comprehend this experience without giving a prominent role to great expectations. The early settlers saw their coming here as no less than the result of divine guidance literally leading them to a new world, from which a new Eden would be fashioned. Even as the passing centuries saw the weakening and eventual breaking of the tie between religion and great expectations, it was religion and not great expectations that faded from the picture. Great expectations had a dynamic of its own, compounded of allure, the bounties of technology, seemingly unlimited resources, a constitutionally based respect for the individual (particularly of the "rugged" kind), infusions of immigrant populations fleeing oppression and poverty, and enough examples of rags to riches to prevent one from placing great expectations completely in the realm of fantasy. There were reasons in reality to believe in great expectations, if not for one's self, then for one's children. Within each of the different economically disadvantaged or oppressed ethnic and racial groups, there were those who were "models" of the American dream, i.e., those whose accomplishments demonstrated that if the streets were not paved with gold, they at least could take one far on the road of success.

The United States has always been a problem to left-wing ideologies and parties. From a Marxian perspective, our history could be written in somber tones, cataloguing injustice compounded by class conflict, economic oppression, racial degradation, and a particularly virulent strain of individualism. It would be a depressing history and by no means devoid of validity. Why, then, have those who have suffered the most been unresponsive to the radical's vision of the good society? There are many parts to the answer, but certainly one of them has been the depths to which great expectations have been embedded in us through the processes of cultural transmission, plus the fact that sufficient numbers have realized these expectations to lend some credence to the rhetoric.

It is hard to overestimate what a catastrophe the Great Depression was to most people. It caused personal turmoil, disappointment, and disillusionment from which many in the older segments of our society today still carry scars. One must bear in mind that, from its beginning in 1929 until a year or so after Roosevelt's inauguration in 1933, being out of work or hungry was an individual catastrophe and not a governmental object for action. And even when the federal government assumed responsibility, the programs were of the band-aid variety, leaving millions of citizens, young and old, dependent, anxious, and bewildered. It was not until World War II that the Great Depression ended.[2] And yet, throughout this period of social upheaval, the bulk of the people held to the belief that the situation would change for the better. They still nurtured hope and great expectations that in the not too distant future the land of opportunity would again be fertile.

[2] During World War II, things were accomplished which confirmed in people's minds the limitless possibilities of our society when the appropriate commitment was made. When President Roosevelt said we were going to build 50,000 airplanes a year, did we not do it, to the chagrin of some doubting Thomases? Did we not build warships and tankers beyond all expectations? Did we not demonstrate how to tap the unused capabilities of women, old people, and handicapped people in the war effort on the home front? And did we not demonstrate our scientific and technological genius in harnessing atomic energy? War, like the Great Depression, was a disaster for millions of Americans, but in its perversely dialectical way, the war broadened for millions horizons for themselves and their perceived world.

World War II and its immediate aftermath were further reinforcements to hope and great expectations. We were a decisive force in subduing a fascist enemy. A lasting peace seemed possible, not an ersatz one such as followed World War I. The obvious inadequacies of the League of Nations would be replaced by a viable United Nations. Colonialism was on its way out. Peace and justice seemed inexorable forces which would overcome the international conflicts breaking out soon after the war's end.

In our own society, the immediate post-war period was dominated by four developments which, over time, became intertwined. For our purposes, their significance lies in their illumination of the role of great expectations in our society. The first was the population explosion, which set in motion an economic expansion requiring material and human resources to a degree which could not be adequately dealt with. More of everything was needed, and new opportunities for work and advancement escalated. The Great Depression became an item in the history books, a relic of an unstable past from which the appropriate lessons had been learned, justifying a view of a stable future. The second occurrence was the rise of the poverty, civil rights, racial, and women's movements—all seeking to establish a durable foundation for their great expectations. They asked for no less than the opportunity to give expression to the great expectations which had long been their right but not their reality.

The third event, in point of time the first, was the passage of the World War II GI bill, which provided new opportunities for millions of veterans. For many of these veterans these were educational and career opportunities which they did not envision before the war. Education as a door-opening process to personal and material advancement took on a reality it had never had before. The fourth development was the culmination of what a small minority of people in Western society had been saying for several centuries: science and technology had the potential to solve all the important human problems and to allow everyone to realize their goals. This belief became general. What science had done in the past was nothing compared to its future potential (and the problem of death was no exception: witness the research on and potentials of cryogenics). Give science its head and follow it to a heaven on earth, if not for ourselves, then for our children or their children (Sarason, 1975).

For two decades after World War II, particularly for the adult population, the philosophy of great expectations was a factor in the experience of work. As increasing numbers of people poured into our colleges and universities—exposing them to knowledge and career possibilities that had not existed before World War II, inculcating in them the modern version of individual and social progress, and sensitizing them to the obligation of applying individual aspirations to the betterment of society—increasing numbers left these centers armed with hope and great expectations. Education was a door opener to opportunity; the more education one had the more doors would open, and widely. Gone were the days when a B.A. degree was a union card to a "good job." The dues had gone up, so to speak, and now one needed (and should want) advanced degrees for the "really" good jobs, i.e., jobs having high status, high pay, and high personal satisfactions.

It is hard to overestimate the significance of the fact that within the span of two decades increasing percentages of our population entered colleges and universities. From one standpoint, it could be argued that vast numbers of this population, herded as they were onto overcrowded campuses and attending overcrowded classes, hardly received an education. Education is not a passive process in which an instructor "puts" knowledge and wisdom "into" the mind of the student. Nor is it a process in which teacher and student never talk *with* each other. And the hallmark of learning is certainly not the degree to which a student can regurgitate on an examination what he has been told to read and what the instructor has said in lectures. Is it not a corruption of the traditions of a liberal arts education to transform college into a trade school? Was it justified to encourage students to seek a college education who had neither the appropriate motivations nor capacities to benefit from it? Worse yet, the argument goes on, how can one look approvingly at the proliferation of graduate degrees testifying largely to the payment of tuition? The tragedy of those years was not only that students were shortchanged, but that the function of the university to transmit and sustain the values of intellectual learning and inquiry—to "liberate" (through the liberal arts) the minds of people and at the same time instill an appreciation of cultural continuity—was transformed and degraded. Robert Nisbet's (1971) book *The Degradation of the Academic Dogma* represents one of the better analyses of this type of criticism. It is a bitter but not unsympathetic statement.

It is not to deny validity to these criticisms to say they becloud a most significant point: through a confluence of factors this "land of opportunity" suddenly opened wide the doors of higher education, which had been long accepted as a sure entry into a good life. If more people entered these doors than in any other society, past or present, it was not only because the doors opened wide, adorned with enticing welcome signs, but also because it had always been part of the transmitted culture that education was an instrument for personal progress, i.e., one should always strive and expect, and the more schooling one had the more one had a right to expect of life. The university, formerly the preserve primarily of the affluent, became more representative of the larger society. One can bemoan the untoward effects of such quick growth on the university, but one must not neglect to ask what was likely to happen to the new millions leaving our colleges and universities, armed with the hope that their experience of the world of work would confirm their great expectations.

Thus far, and in a necessarily sketchy fashion, I have emphasized several points:

1. The significance of work cannot be comprehended only or even meaningfully in terms of what people do. Work is always experienced in relation to a perceived past, present, and future, involving a variety of people differing in age, intimacy, status, and role. This seamless web of experienced relationships changes as a function of time, and it always reflects moods, forces, and events in the larger society. During periods of relative societal stability, the individual may not perceive any relationship between his experience of work and the nature and basis for that larger society, but when that stability ends or is threatened, the individual becomes poignantly aware of the underlying, unverbalized assumptions which gave direction and pattern to his life.

2. Deeply embedded in the minds of people has been the belief that ours is a society of promise and opportunity, possessing resources—material and human, scientific and technical—which justify belief in an "onward and upward" conception of progress for individuals and the society. A variant of this belief is the one which accepts as self-evident that the world should expect more from the United States than from any other country, i.e., that this country is a model which others would do well to emulate.

3. Education has been viewed as one of the most effective means of personal advancement. There were many ways of rising from the masses, and education was certainly one of the better door-openers (witness the number of colleges and universities which were created by business and industrial entrepeneurs, most of whom had no college education, but who perceived education as a significant force in society and the lives of aspiring individuals). Following World War II, higher education was made increasingly available to segments of society heretofore underrepresented in those centers, it being accepted as self-evident that the more education one obtained the better the chances to live the good life. Put in another way, the rhetoric of great expectations was given an eagerly accepted reality. In the span of two decades, we acquired more highly educated people than ever before in our society or in any other one.

To Labor and To Work

If the philosophy of great expectations from education suggests a reaching for a desirable state of affairs, however defined, it also suggests that there is a state of affairs to be avoided. The material and status benefits to be gained through higher education have always been obvious and emphasized to a greater degree than what may be termed intrinsic benefits—e.g., the increased understanding of, and fascination with, culture and history, one's perception of self-growth in regard to such understanding, and a never-ending sense of wonder about man and his works, possibilities, and dilemmas. Through education, one not only hoped to become a "better" person, but also to acquire interests and a style of thinking which would forever enrich one's life. These intrinsic, hard-to-define benefits were like a good diet: somehow they sustained one against debilitation, or at least they kept at bay some of the more insidious influences which make life difficult or unbearable. But there was little question that the most obvious benefit of higher education was that it led to a smorgasbord of career opportunities from which one could choose according to interests and talents, and one could expect one's choice to provide income over time to meet one's expectations. Material expectations varied considerably among the different career possibilities, but in no instance did one expect to find living an economic struggle. The public school teacher obviously expected less income than did the physician, but until recent years teaching was one of the more "noble" and obviously important professions, and if those who entered teaching were inadequately remunerated, the discrepancy between what they received and what they felt they deserved was far from enormous, and presumably there were other benefits which took the edge off the consequences of the discrepancy.

It is, I think, a mistake in emphasis to criticize our colleges and universities as having become more elevated forms of trade schools, pandering to materialistic students who tend to lack intellectual curiosity and appreciation of the intrinsic benefits of a higher education. From the traditional perspective of the faculties of the arts and sciences, the criticism is by no means without foundation. From the perspective of many students, any aspect of their education must meet the criterion of "relevance" for their future careers, and not many aspects do. The mistake in emphasis is one of insensitivity to the fact that at the basis of students' thinking was a distinction no less significant for its unclear articulation. The distinction was between *labor* and *work*. To labor is to be imprisoned in activity in which outcome or product has no personally meaningful relationship to the person's capacities and individuality, e.g., the assembly-line worker, garbage collector, pencil-pushing clerk, on the "organizational drone." To work is to have one's outcome and product bear the stamp of one's capacities and individuality. To labor is to be stamped by the activity; to work is to put one's stamp on the activity (DeGrazia, 1964; Green, 1968). Work, in Dewey's terms, contains the promise of *an* experience. Labor is devoid of such a possibility.

To deny that our society is one in which size of income and material possessions are criteria of "success" is a form of lunacy. As I have indicated earlier, the great expectations which have long been part of our ideology are largely defined in economic terms. It is not surprising, therefore, that following World War II, when millions of young people were able to obtain a higher education—during two decades of societal affluence in which advances in speed of communication and travel redefined the scope and substance of the good life—they saw education as ensuring some access to that good life. The society not only told them to expect, it told them what to expect. But that was never the whole story, because in some vague, inchoate way most of these young people were expecting their careers to have the characteristics of work and not labor. They may have left our colleges and universities seeking the highest bidder for their knowledge and skills; they may have chosen their first job because they could quickly move up the economic and status ladders; they may have gone on spending sprees for new homes, cars, TV sets, sailboats and other accoutrements of gracious living; and they may have easily cottoned onto the presumably painless use of bank loans and credit cards—they may have entered the world of work in all of these ways, but it is a mistake to conclude that they expected work to be an unfulfilling experience, to be a personal trap in which individuality and potentiality were the major victims.

I have deliberately restricted my comments to the two decades after World War II because most of that period has been characterized as somnolent, silent, and smug. Certainly, most of that period lacked the sustained overt emotionalism and upheaval of succeeding years. That turbulence did not begin on a certain day or in a particular year. Like all social upheavals, this one had its roots in the near and distant past. We think of World War II as turbulent, but the turbulence conjured up in our minds took place on battlefields, on the seas, and in distant lands. We tend not to think of the forces set into motion within our society, forces which began to alter that society radically, such as accelerated migration to industrial centers, new job opportunities for women and racial and ethnic minorities, an emerging civil rights movement (particularly in regard to segregation in the armed forces), rising affluence, mammoth disruption in family life, the setting of the stage for the future population explosion, and the beginning awareness that the postwar period was not and should not be a return to the good old days.[3] And if we think of the two decades after World War II as "silent" and "conformist," it is because we had no way of comprehending the significance of the availability of higher education to millions of young people. We were too busy enlarging and creating colleges and universities, too busy searching and garnering faculties to man them, too busy following up the wondrous scientific and technological advances spurred by World War II, to examine how this revolution in opportunity reflected past traditions and public rhetoric and what kind of harbinger it might be for different kinds of scenarios in the future. I do not say this in criticism. If we were unprepared to deal adequately with the problem in a logistical and architectural sense, we were even more unprepared to deal with its social history, institutional implications, and changing zeitgeist. It has been pointed out (Edwards, 1927) that national revolutions occur *after* rising expectations have been blunted. I am suggesting that the upheaval (not revolution) of the last decade stemmed in part from the earlier remarkable increase in the numbers of young people populating our colleges and universities. It was not only that they came in unprecedented numbers, but that they came with attitudes toward and expectations of our society which they had little or no reason to believe were unrealistic—until, of course, their later entry into that society changed their view of that society.

The relationship between education and work is complex, and the content and shape of that complexity varies over time within the life of an individual as well as over the course of a society's history. The major theme of this book is that in recent decades the relationship between education and work has changed. More specifically, we have become a society in which increasing numbers of its people have become and will become highly educated, and this, together with other societal changes, has created problems and raised issues to which insufficient attention has been given. It used to be that highly educated, professional people viewed themselves, and were viewed by others, as an elite fortunate in that they experienced work as fulfilling, challenging, and worthy, possessing few or none of the stifling characteristics of labor. Job dissatisfaction was not their problem, but that of the factory worker, clerk, and others in simple, routine jobs.

[3] Cabell Phillips's (1975) *The 1940s. Decade of Triumph and Trouble* will be rewarding reading for those who did not live through or are unfamiliar with the turmoil of that decade. Most revealing are his accounts of the deep changes taking place on the home front during the war years, but which did not come into societal awareness until years after the war.

There were, of course, highly educated people in business, finance, and industry and they had all sorts of dissatisfactions, but there was a question about their degree of professionalism and, besides, what could one expect as a small (or even a large) cog in the big profit-making competitive business organization? So, the argument ran, if these highly educated people chose a business career, it revealed something negative about their materialistic values. The "truly" professional person was first of all an individual—"his own person"—who determined when and how he would use the knowledge and skills acquired through general and special education to contribute to the enrichment of his "calling" and, directly or indirectly, to the improved welfare of people. To what degree this glorified professional experienced his work according to society's view of him, and his stated views of himself, is impossible to say, because those investigators who were interested in the nature of work were focusing almost exclusively on those who were in the business and industrial setting, and there was no dearth of fascinating problems to study there. What cause was there to study those in the more traditional professions who "had it made"? And if some did experience dissatisfaction with work, it was assumed to reflect idiosyncratic personal factors rather than factors peculiar to their profession.[4]

One does not have to resort to intuition, anecdote, or even personal experience to ask if the consequences of World War II would not radically alter the highly educated professional's experience of work, making his experience more problematic than ever before. For example, not only did the size of the existing professions increase enormously, but within each profession new specialties proliferated, leading to professions within professions. In addition, there was an equally striking increase in new professions which never existed before World War II. (Nowhere are these two facts clearer than in what is now called the "health industry.") But there was a third fact: the federal government encouraged and funded the creation and expansion of many professions. In one way or another, many professions and their members became related to and dependent upon the federal government, a departure from tradition whose consequences were not clearly seen. These three facts, involving as they did changes in public policy,

[4] It is remarkable that in the post–World War II sociological and social-philosophical literature on work and labor, the center of attention is "the worker" in the factory or low-level white-collar employees performing routinized functions. For example, Bell (1965) in the chapter "Work and Its Discontents" in his *The End of Ideology* has characteristically illuminating things to say about how modern society has increasingly and effectively imprisoned people in dissatisfying work, but he says nothing about how these same forces may have affected professional people. He makes some critical comments about professionals who study workers, but he never thinks about professionals in general the way he does about workers in general.

institutional size and structure, and financial underpinnings, should have suggested that the experience of work for highly educated, professional people would undergo a change.

There were other pervasive changes taking place in our society which left no doubt that work might become problematic for the new millions of highly educated people, most of whom desired to enter the different professions. In the next chapter, I shall discuss some of the changes which were less obtrusive or obvious than those I have already mentioned. Before concluding this chapter, I must remind the reader that my discussion has been in relation to the two decades or so after World War II. I have said nothing about the past ten years which witnessed upheaval, turmoil, and unrest. This omission was deliberate (but temporary), because I believe that these more recent developments, far from being discontinuous with the previous period, were a consequence of earlier changes. It is understandable if powerful forces in the present absorb our thinking and attention and shorten the time span within which we try to explain what is happening. We are the products of culture, but we are not schooled to understand how the dynamics of cultural transmission and change operate. Ordinarily, this is not a serious deficiency, but we are not living in ordinary times. And if we seek to shape a future different from the troubled present, our search had better be based on some understanding of how much of the past is still in our experienced present. Such an effort at understanding is justified, not on the basis that the past has "lessons" we can apply to present problems and possible futures, but in the hope that we can gain better insights into how much of that past remains in our ways of thinking. This is why the next chapter is devoted to World War II and its immediate aftermath.

III
World War II and Its Immediate Aftermath

OURS HAS BECOME a society with more highly educated people than ever before, more so than any society past or present. This fact has been noted and commented on from diverse perspectives: political, economic, sociological, and vocational. The size and relative youth of this population represent a dynamic in our society that will have widespread consequences, and it challenges our existing theories and knowledge to try to foresee at least the outlines of a different future. In trying to understand and meet the challenge, we must try to avoid the understandable but subversive tendency to see a future within a framework that bears the stamp of thinking insensitive to emerging cultural change, i.e., to new values and world outlooks which, precisely because they are vaguely sensed and articulated and are contrary to convention and tradition, can be underestimated in terms of their strength and future attractiveness. For example, before World War II it used to be said and believed—it was more than rhetoric—that when one got married, it was forever. And if it was not forever, it *should* be! Religion supported such a view and civil laws made the obtaining of a divorce a career in itself. But at the same time, there were divorces, extra-marital affairs, desertions, and other indications that there was a discrepancy between what people said and what they did, and between what they did and what they would like to do. If one went by marriage and divorce statistics, let alone the pronouncements of civic and religious leaders, one might have concluded that the traditional institution of marriage has a solid foundation capable of resisting change. However, if one went beyond the conventional statistics and took seriously how people experienced marriage, how they sought, successfully and unsuccessfully, both to maintain and circumvent its spirit and form, one might have been less secure about seeing mar-

35

riage in the future as a carbon copy of the present.[1] This is not to say that one could have predicted when and under what specific circumstances the institution of marriage would change discernibly, as it has. But one could have taken more seriously and validly the indications that in regard to marriage there was a discrepancy between appearance and reality, and one could have grappled with the kinds of societal events and changes that might unleash existing anti-marriage forces, e.g., a world war. At the very least, one would have avoided writing scenarios of the future that looked too much like the present. The problem with statistical projections is that they are based on two types of data: those data from the near or far past which are *now* seen as significant for the shape of the present and will be presumably for the future, and current data, usually of an aggregate or global nature, which are presumed to be better indicators of what the future will be. These types of projections can be valuable (e.g., demographic, ecological) but, more often than not, they founder because their assessment of the present either assumes a relatively stable set of forces and events, or there is a misweighing or ignorance of emerging and inchoate changes in values and outlooks that do not have the characteristics of social forces and movements, but that (together with societal events the timing, strength, and scope of which we can only poorly predict) will give shape to the future. It is these events that surface and give articulation to what previously had seemed atypical outcroppings of anti-traditional values and behavior, i.e., a view of self and the world at variance with what is customary.

Have those generations which came to maturity after World War II absorbed or created a new set of values and outlooks having direct consequences for how they look toward and experience work? Is it likely that in the process of providing higher education for millions of youth, they have been exposed to new values and possible life styles which, interacting with forces and events in their own and the world society, produced in many of them an outlook antithetical to the traditional view of the role of work over the life span? Is it possible that highly educated, professional people (young and old) no longer expe-

[1] If you go back to the novels, plays, films, and radio soap operas of the thirties, it becomes obvious how wide the discrepancy was between the public rhetoric about marriage and its realities. The discrepancy had existed for a long time, but with the growth of the mass media, particularly radio and film, the discrepancy became glaring. When the "dream" marriage between movie stars Mary Pickford and Douglas Fairbanks came to an end, it was front page news, testifying to how much people wanted to believe in the irrevocable ties of marriage, at the same time they knew how fragile the ties of marriage had become. Hollywood, as a cultural phenomenon and product producing center, contained in people's minds all of the ingredients of the war between virtue and sin, i.e., Hollywood was one big soap opera. From the vantage point of several decades, one could describe the current scene as another example of reality imitating "art."

rience the level of satisfaction from their work that they once did or were led to expect? Is it the case that the professional person experiences significantly less autonomy and sense of worth and status than in the past, that he is experiencing and will increasingly experience work as problematic? Have the contents of and the value bases for "great expectations" from work been changed in ways that make distinctions between work and non-work, between what people do and what they experience at work, increasingly untenable, misleading, and socially dangerous? If there has been such a change in expectations, might it not be in part a reflection of still another possible change which one can assume would be articulated among the highly educated segment of the population: a view of the future tinged with varying degrees of unease, foreboding, and fear of meaninglessness?

The point of these questions is less in their form or content than in the implicit suggestion that a change is occurring in the values, perspectives, and expectations of highly educated people; more correctly, I think, the change has already occurred and the question is how general it is and will become. Contained in this suggestion is the assumption that these changes can be most fruitfully pursued by adopting as a focus the role and experience of work. Work is one of the two major ways (our sex is the other) in which we define our personal identity and on the basis of which others presume to know what we are. The interaction between sexual identity and culture begins with the moment of birth, which is why its consequences are so difficult to change and overcome, as women well know. The relationship between work and personal identity, on the one hand, and culture, on the other, is in our society both less direct and understood. Indeed, our society encourages postponing the choice of a "work" identity for sixteen or more years, during which time the individual has the opportunity of being sensitive and responsive to the breezes, winds, and storms of societal change, and in ways which may make for a social meteorology quite different from that of older generations. If the optimist (the older generations?) says the bottle is half full and the pessimist (the younger generation?) says it is half empty, the optimist may win out in a public opinion poll if in the majority. But the victory may be a Pyrrhic one if the majority had been insensitive to the possibility (it may be a fact!) that the current minority will constitute the future majority.

But, it could be asked, why your emphasis on the highly educated segment of our population? Granted that this segment has become unprecedentedly numerous, granted that it is relatively youthful, and even granting that they approach the future with different values and outlooks, what special justifications are there for focussing on their relationship to work? Have their approaches to work changed in qual-

itatively different ways from other segments of the society? Have they
been more responsive to or affected by societal events than other
groups? Compared with other groups are they more cause than effect
of social change? Do the changes within this highly educated group
have an expecially significant import for the rest of society? These
questions will be explored throughout this book, and the reader will
be able to judge not only the legitimacy of the questions but the adequacy of the answers. There is, however, one answer which needs to
be presented at this point. Is it not noteworthy, if not strange, that
work—its nature, functions, consequences, and changing character—
has been studied and discussed primarily in relation to people with
less than a college education? From the time of Taylor's time–motion
studies to LeMaster's (1975) recently acclaimed book on *Blue-Collar
Aristocrats*, there have been thousands of studies on the nature of
work of "lower-level" workers. This, of course, should not be surprising because it has been in the economic interests of business and
industry, if only to improve profits and/or meet competitive challenges, to be concerned with the nature of work of those engaged in
production. But to pursue, especially in earlier decades, such concerns
required expertise in method and theory that business and industry
ordinarily did not have but which did exist in the university. Today it
is fashionable to say that our society has come to see the university not
as a frill or luxury, but as a creator of new knowledge which has or will
have the most practical and pervasive consequences for society.
Atomic physics, health, agriculture, child development, education—
these are only some of the university fields to which society looks for
answers to contemporary social questions. And society has poured a
fair amount of money into the university in the hope that it will generate the kind of knowledge that society can use. (What society expects
of the university is in large measure what the university has said society has a right to expect, assuming that society will provide the necessary financing, e.g., getting a cure for cancer.) Long before this type of
university–society relationship was forged (a direct consequence of
World War II), such a tie already existed between business and industry, on the one hand, and university individuals and departments, on
the other. Business and industry sought and could pay for such expertise. What seemed to go relatively unnoticed was not only that the *site*
for investigations and the *kind* of work to be studied were predetermined, but also *who* was to be the object of study. Initially, at least,
leaders in business and industry did not seek help for themselves—
they were not the problem—but for their workers, and help meant
improving the quantity and quality of products. It took a few decades
for acceptance of the idea that management itself was part of the problem, and because management increasingly consisted of college-

educated people, the relationship between education and the experience of work became prominent. The rise and expansion within the
university of schools of business and departments of economics were
not only testimony to how much the nature of work in business and
industry had changed and how strong their ties with the university had
become, but also to how problematic satisfaction with work had become for the highly educated segments of management, and the
amount of education and special training required increased steadily.
A good deal has been learned about the nature of work of
management-level people, and most of this has come from
university-based researchers and consultants. If what we have learned
is not cause for joy, if the stereotype of the college-educated business
executive as one caught in a competitive rat race destructive of morale
and morals is somewhat overdrawn, it has contributed to the belief
that these pitfalls only minimally existed for the highly educated, spe-
cially trained individual outside of business and industry. The physician, lawyer, college teacher, educator, dentist, clergyman, social
worker, and other professionals, presumably experienced their work in
significantly more positive terms, i.e., they did not encounter the psychologically debilitating constraints of those who were in the business
and industrial setting. This view is not held with the degree of assurance it once had. (Whether it ever should have been held with a high
degree of uncritical acceptance we shall never know.) This is not to say
that this change is large or small, but simply that the stereotype has
been called into question in recent years (e.g., Harris, 1975).

Surprisingly little attention has been given to the experience of
work of highly educated people who are not in business and industry.
In part, this is because there have been no forces outside the university
asking for and prepared to fund such investigations. And, equally important, these fields or professions, as they are represented organizationally within and without the university, have not seen the need for
such investigations. Professional fields, like individuals, tend to avoid
self-scrutiny. It can be an upsetting affair compelling one to redefine
reality and to change. If business and industry were forced to self-
scrutiny and the necessity for change, it was powered in part by the
need to survive in the economic market place. For other professional
fields, such survival has not been a major problem. That is to say, these
professions (as entities) were not threatened with extinction, bank-
ruptcy, or takeover. Indeed, their economic well being and public
status may be effective barriers to critical self-scrutiny.

As this book unfolds, I shall present a number of exploratory
studies that, at the very least, indicate that the questions I have raised
are legitimate and significant. But when one begins to grapple with
questions which have received relatively little attention, it is realisti-

cally modest to emphasize that not only should one not be too secure in how the questions are phrased, but also in the initial answers. Indeed, the first task is not a flight into data collection, but rather to try to understand how the different ways in which our society has changed permit one to raise issues receiving scant attention. If I am correct, even in part, that satisfaction from work has become problematic for highly educated professional people, this must reflect pervasive societal changes. By societal changes, I mean more than size of population, organizational complexities, wars, technological advance, international interdependence, the availability and allocation of resources, conflicts and realignments among social and racial groups, and significant alterations in the role of communication media. These are obvious and significant changes, but they are not of recent vintage; they do not represent discontinuities with the near or far past. Our society was not born yesterday. What is or may be distinctive is the degree to which and the ways by which increasing numbers of people are aware of and interpret these changes. It is not simply a matter of awareness or recognition, although undoubtedly there are some who see the new wine and put it into old bottles. It is that more people than ever before see these changes on the basis of new values, outlooks, and categories of thought, giving new qualities to the fabric of experience and thereby altering the experience of work (among other things). As we scan the post-World War II decades, can we discern the emergence of these new outlooks? Can we correlate them with obvious and significant societal events and forces? Is there reason to believe that these new outlooks and values found unusually hospitable soil in the colleges and universities to which people flocked in unprecedented numbers? These are some of the questions to which we will now turn in our endeavor to gain a social–historical perspective from which to view and study the possibility that work has become a problematic area for the highly educated segment of our population.

To attempt in the remainder of this chapter to discuss and answer the questions posed at the end of Chapter II is an impossibility. It is like trying to do justice to world history in one volume, even a large one. Something that on the surface seems as circumscribed in time and place as the American, or French, or Russian, or Chinese revolution turns out to be so fantastically complex and to have such deep historical roots, as to make a mockery of the boundaries of time and place. The last three decades are a case in point. What I shall do is focus on different and limited aspects of this period that I believe illuminate the thesis that work has become a problematic part of the lives of highly educated people. Such an approach runs the risk of giving too much weight to what one is paying attention to and underestimating the strength of what is outside this focus. When one is judging the presence and strength of a cultural change, which is precisely what I am trying to do, one tends to underestimate the force of traditional values. The assimilation of the dominant culture begins at birth. It is a process ordinarily carried out with such unreflective skill and depth, honed to sharpness by the weight of ideological tradition and cultural practices, that it is extraordinarily difficult for an individual to break out, if only transiently, from the mold. It is inherently and quintessentially a conserving process intended to insure continuity between generations. So if one believes that a cultural change has begun, one had better leaven this belief with a healthy respect for the forces behind continuity.

The Immediate Aftermath of World War II

By comparison with World War II, World War I was a minor affair.[2] World War II was truly global, and never before had so many people and institutions in our society been so meaningfully involved in or affected by a war. Millions of individuals literally stopped "working" and entered the armed services. The fabric of millions of families was altered as one or more of its members left for war. The frequency of new marriages among young people increased, as did the number of forced separations. Many fathers never saw their offspring until the war ended. Many never saw them because they died in battle. Many of these new marriages encountered all kinds of strains, not only because of the factor of forced separation, but also because of the fantasies and realities of infidelity. Women entered the work force in large numbers, a fact which had significance beyond the economic, because it provided them with a sense of self in a social context frequently, unexpectedly, satisfying. The war, as always, presented a bitter pill for parents having to withstand the real possibility that they would never see their children again, or that they would see them maimed. For the most part, wars are fought by young people, but the price paid by their parents (who are more numerous) is in its own way literally terrifying. For the United States the war lasted four years, although the draft was started in 1940. Five or six years in the life of a society are not long

[2] World War I was not a minor affair. It marked the end of one era and the beginning of another of which World War II was a part. From my readings, a good argument could be made that on a percentage basis more of the intellectual and educated stratum of Europe were killed in World War I than in World War II. More battles in World War I were in the nature of holocausts than in World War II, although none of them rival Hiroshima and Nagasaki for the speed of mass killing. Nevertheless, World War II was of such unprecedented scope (geographically, demographically, technologically, destructively) that one has to regard World War I as prologue to the later full-length drama.

except when they are accompanied by major changes in the accustomed way in which people experience their lives, their relationships to each other, and their traditional institutions. To live for and dream of a return to normalcy at the same time that one is adapting to a quite different state of affairs—and to live this way for several years, which in the life of an individual is a very, very long time—is an invitation to disillusionment.

There are many ways to characterize the war years. One is to say they were years of anxious waiting—waiting in terms of individual goals as well as of societal stability and world peace. The anxiety stemmed not only from ambiguity about whether the war would be won, but also from uncertainty about how and when it would end, and at what price. Bear in mind that for the first half of the war, Germany, Italy, and Japan seemed on the road to victory. Even near the war's end in Europe, when it seemed that Germany was on the way to defeat, it mounted a counteroffensive which came close to turning the tide. And if people greeted the atomic bombings of Nagasaki and Hiroshima with satisfaction and relief, it can only be understood in the context of an end to anxious waiting. From the vantage point of the postwar years, questions can be raised about the use of the atomic bomb. Some of these questions are legitimate, particularly those based on the assumption that means should have been taken to demonstrate to Japan the holocaustic consequences of the new weapon. But I have little doubt that if there had been a public referendum on the use of the bomb, the vote would have been overwhelmingly in favor of its use. Not that most people were bloodthirsty or desirous of inflicting a cruel revenge, but that if it meant an end to the fighting and the anxious waiting, they supported using it. And, of course, if the armed forces had been polled, the result would have been unanimous.

Another stimulus to the anxiety arose. From the very beginning of our involvement, casualties returned to civilian life, their numbers increasing as the war continued. The casualties were both psychological and physical in nature, and their difficulties in readjusting, as well as those of their families and friends, were common knowledge. But these reminders of what could happen were not essential for those experiencing prolonged anxiety. The dynamics of such waiting included the fear that separated people can and do change and that reunion at war's end might fall short of one's dreams. Regardless of circumstance some people manage to live in a fool's paradise, but for most people—wives, parents, older children—the reunion was seen as potentially dangerous.

I said earlier that millions of men stopped "working" and entered the armed services. For some this represented, of course, a massive, unsought interference with what they liked and wanted to do. For others, however, leaving their work was not intrinsically saddening because their work was not satisfying to them. They did not relish going to war, of course, and their reluctance had more to do with going to war than giving up interesting work. War has, as we know, perversely unexpected consequences. During World War II, some men and women in the armed services found themselves in jobs and positions of responsibility far above or more interesting than they experienced in civilian life. We are used to hearing either about the grime and tragedy of battle, and we cannot be reminded of it too often. We are also familiar with the confining, routine, and Catch-22 features of military living. But the fact remains that for some people, their military work was more satisfying than their civilian work. For these people, their numbers cannot be known but I assume they were not insignificant, the return to civilian life would pose difficult problems. Similarly, those who had been wrenched away from satisfying work and whose prolonged military experience was experienced as senseless futility and mind-breaking boredom would have their distinctive problems of readjustment. And let us not forget probably the largest group: those who left unsatisfactory work and experienced more of the same in the military. Their problems in readjustment were undoubtedly quite varied, but it is hard to see how they could return to civilian life with a positive conception of themselves.

An army needs officers, and the size of the military establishment during World War II required a staggering number. Traditionally, officers tend to come from the highly educated groups of the population and World War II was no exception. Medical, legal, business, educational, psychological, engineering, administrative, scientific— these were only some of the kinds of personnel that were required. Many who had already finished their education and were practicing their professions were drafted or volunteered for service. With the outbreak of war, it seemed as if our colleges and universities would be denuded of students (and faculty), who would be drafted *en masse*. But as it became clear that modern war required the kinds of knowledge and expertise represented in various university departments, and that to gain a minimum level of proficiency in these fields assumed a college education (e.g., physicians and engineers could not skip college) our colleges and universities became in part accelerated training centers supported by the military. In fact, government support of these programs made it possible for many people to receive a college education (however narrowed and accelerated) who ordinarily would not have, anticipating the GI bill. A sizable number of high school graduates who were college bound were drafted directly into the armed services, just as college students were drafted while they were still in school. Some of these people, either because they had been in college or had obtained high intelligence-test scores, were sent to officer candidate schools or selected for special training programs run by the military. Indeed, a good number of these young people were exposed to jobs and career possibilities which they pursued after the war. The correlation between education and officer status was lost on no one. If only occasionally, it gave rise to feelings of superiority and smugness among the educated; it very frequently was viewed with derision and hostility on the part of the less educated. Feelings aside, the significance of education in military *and* civilian life was established as never before.

It is hard to say how the experiences of the highly educated soldier influenced his adjustment to civilian work. Hordes of them flocked to the universities to finish their education or professional training, or as a way to reorient themselves toward the future. Those who had an established profession before entering the military had the difficult task of starting all over again, a task complicated by three factors. First, the returnees felt robbed by the years spent in service; those years may have had some value and interest in terms of work, but were not likely to have payoff for restarting a professional career. Second, they were aware that while they were in service those who remained in civilian life furthered their careers. Third, those who had remained in civilian life, however grateful they might have been to those who had been in the military, were not always prepared to welcome the new competition or to extend to them benefits they themselves did not have. Those who had remained in civilian life were not faced with a readjustment but with the linear pursuit of their work.

We must keep in mind that at the same time everyone was rejoicing at the war's near end, they were also anticipating that our society would soon be faced with massive economic problems, high unemployment, and social unrest. The change from a war to a peace economy has never been easy (for the victors, as well as the defeated), and given the length and the dimensions of World War II, it is not surprising that some grimly gloomy forecasts were made. The specter of the Great Depression, during which the veterans had come to maturity, seemed to be taking new shape on the horizon. From one depression to war to another depression? No one wanted to be on that road, but many feared they were. During the war the conflicts between industry and labor had largely been contained, but there was good reason to believe that as soon as the war ended that struggle would erupt again. The racial problem had already gathered momentum during the war, and it certainly would gather force and speed with the end of war. So, side by side with rejoicing at the approaching end of war was anxiety about the future of self and society.

One other factor must be mentioned, and again it is an example of the perverse dialectics of war. War is hell, especially for those in or near battle whose unseen but constant companion is death. But the conditions of war, as countless novelists have told us, also produce a social cohesion, a sense of community, a special freedom in thought, language, and behavior ordinarily missing in peacetime. Entry into service is an upsetting affair productive of loneliness, in which one actively seeks and needs to establish social roots. It is a socializing process in which internal and external pressures facilitate relationships and structured social living. One may experience frustration, loneliness, and despair—one can count on that—but one also can count on the sense of belonging which is a product of rigid military structure with its strong formal and informal codes of behavior. Life is structured and confined far beyond what one is accustomed to or desires, but the other side of the coin is that one knows one belongs. Griping and bitching are an important feature of military living (and why not?), as are the fantasies of freedom and pleasures when the war is over. However, for some soldiers the return to civilian life had some surprises, among which was a yearning for that strange amalgam of structure, freedom, and social cohesion they had so long dreamed of leaving. The people and world to which they were returning had, like themselves, undergone change. Unlike previous wars, our soldiers spent time in all corners of the globe in strange countries with strange customs, and some of the relationships, sexual or otherwise, they formed were not easy to give up or forget. Memories of war-time experiences were no less subject to the mechanisms of selective recall than were those of the civilian life they had left.

If the years immediately after the war did not produce economic chaos, they did exacerbate or produce personal turmoil. For at least a decade after the war, professional journals were full of articles about how the war helped set the stage for personal and familial conflicts. In fact, one characterization of those postwar years is as the Age of Psychology and Psychiatry. It is not fortuitous that not long after the war's end Leonard Bernstein composed the concerto, *The Age of Anxiety*. The federal government had begun a truly massive building program to care for veterans who had incurred service-connected disabilities, and a large fraction of the funds went to the development of psychiatric services. Indeed, between the Veterans Administration and somewhat later the National Institute of Mental Health, social science and psychiatry departments of the university were supported in training and research endeavors in regard to mental health. Mental Health! One might as well characterize those postwar years as the Age of Mental Health because it became a national concern. It was not only the veteran who needed help, but, it was argued, so did millions of other people. How could we educate and train enough psychotherapists to begin to meet the demand for help? What we really needed, said one eminent psychiatrist, were more five-dollars-an-hour therapists. The most obvious significance of these developments was the change it reflected in people's sense of autonomy, potency, and social connectedness, i.e., the ways in which they experienced and sought solutions for personal problems. One might also put it in this way: part of the change was in what people were advised to do when they had problems. The message from the burgeoning mental health professions was clear: if you have personal problems which are debilitating and interfering, you should not regard yourself as unique (far from it, you are but one of many), and you should not hesitate or feel guilty about going to the mental health professional. It was hard to avoid the ironic conclusion that it was normal to feel abnormal! In any event, however one characterizes individual experience or the professional message, there can be no doubt that in contrast to pre-World War II days increasing numbers of people began to purchase personal therapy. I use the work purchase advisedly because, aside from the service-connected disabled veteran, personal therapy had to be purchased, and the fee per hour guaranteed that the therapy could only be available to middle- or upper-class educated people. The restriction of the psychotherapies to such a narrow segment of the population did not receive critical scrutiny until the early sixties, although the issue had been joined in the earlier report by the Joint Commission on Mental Health (1961). One should not gloss over the fact that this commission had been created by federal legislation, a clear indication of the degree to which "mental health" had become a societal concern. It was also an indication that the existence and strength of traditional ways of viewing and dealing with personal problems had been further weakened and new instrumentalities had to be developed.

The age of psychology (or mental health or personal therapy) had some clear roots in World War II other than those directly traceable to personal, familial, and social instability. Before World War II, university departments of psychiatry were for the most part biologically oriented in theory and practice, and their ties with the social sciences virtually non-existent. Those were the days when psychoanalysis and other "dynamic" approaches to so-called mental disorder thrived outside of medical school departments of psychiatry. Although I do not pretend to have done an exhaustive survey, I could not come up with a single instance of a psychoanalyst who was a full-time member of a department of psychiatry. Undoubtedly, there were some, but their numbers must have been miniscule in the extreme. The situation in departments of psychology was different in that clinical psychology as a field and psychotherapy as practice were eschewed. The aim of graduate training in psychology was to produce scientifically rigorous, experimentally oriented researchers who (in typical reductionist style) would uncover the basic springs and mechanisms of human behavior. Then came World War II, and when the dragnet of selective service was cast, it pulled in psychologists and psychiatrists from within and without the university, the majority coming from without. Psychologists who had never seen a patient found themselves functioning as clinicians. Physicians who did not know the difference between psychotherapy and psychophysics frequently found themselves in the personal therapy or counseling role. As important as these role changes were several other factors: first, the exposure of these professionals to what happens to people under situational stress; second, the staggering number of individuals considered unfit to enter military life; third, the importance of psychological approaches in returning psychologically disabled soldiers to the battle front; and, fourth, the rise within the armed forces to positions of status and influence of psychoanalytically oriented professionals (e.g., the Menninger brothers). This last factor cannot be underestimated in trying to understand the dramatic changes which took place in departments of psychology and psychiatry after the war. *What it meant was that college students would be exposed to a conception of man and society, to an implicit and explicit set of values, discernibly different from that of previous generations. As we shall see later, this exposure, interacting with other societal changes, would have fateful consequences for the view these educated people would develop of the world of work.*

These changes within the university can only in part explain the response of college students to the content of the psychological and psychiatric fields. For example, beginning immediately after the war the number of students majoring in psychology on the undergraduate level and the number seeking to enter psychology as a profession increased amazingly. With the war's end, there were between 3,000–4,000 members of the American Psychological Association. Today the number is closer to 40,000—a rate of increase far beyond that of population growth. In fact, Edward G. Boring pointed out that if this rate of increase continued there would be more psychologists than there were people!

There can be no doubt that the college population (which included many veterans) "brought" with them some emerging, inchoate values and attitudes congruent with the Age of Psychology. What they brought was not of a piece; they and the times were too varied for that. Besides, if some new values and attitudes were beginning to sprout, one could expect that they would only barely be visible in the traditional turf. On the surface, there was what one would expect: a striving for material security and stability, a reaching for a future work niche, and traditional expectations regarding marriage and family. (For the highly educated professional who was a veteran there was lost time to be made up, and unlike those who were going to school there was little time for dispassionate reflection: one had to get back to the mainstream, and one had to act.) Those of us who lived through or remember those days will recall how one architectural feature of military life was transferred to some campuses, i.e., the Quonset hut, rows and rows of them accommodating the veteran and his family, inevitably taking on the appearance of a budding slum or, as some said, a concentration camp. Privacy was a luxury, if not an impossibility. Such living was but another motivational goad to complete one's education and begin "really" to live. University faculty who taught these veterans look back nostalgically on those days because the veteran was so mature and motivated. Although I think there is some basis for this nostalgia, I do not think that high motivation was absent in non-veteran students, who sometimes took the veteran as a model or even viewed him with envy.[3]

On August 10, 1975, on national television, the wife of the President of the United States explicitly sanctioned pre-marital sex. Such a statement would have been unthinkable before, during, and for a long time after World War II—or, if it had been made, its political repercussions would have been both obvious and incalcuable. (Even as late as the fifties, the fact that Adlai Stevenson was divorced was considered a liability in his presidential candidacy.) One of Mrs. Ford's justifications for her position was that it might make for more lasting marriages. That there is little or no evidence to support such an expectation is less interesting than the recognition afforded to changing sexual practices and male–female relationships. What we today call the sexual revolution started a long time ago. It was going on long before World War II, accelerated during the war, and really picked up steam with the war's end. Historically, wars have accelerated such changes. Questions of generality aside, the college campuses provided many recruits to the revolutionary army. The change was one of degree (as was the divorce rate), and it was powered by values and ideas which did not attain clarity until a decade or so later.

To label these values and ideas is a dangerous affair because labels tend to lend an air of specificity and a boundary which is neither intended nor warranted. In addition, labels tend to convey an impres-

---

[3] I noted a similar attitude in students who came to college after the turbulent sixties. They would listen with rapture and envy to the older students, who would regale them with stories of what it was like in those days of excitement. It was as if the latecomer felt robbed and deprived, robbed of the opportunity to have participated in a legendary past and deprived of the prospect that such days would return. I cannot say how general this reaction was in the postwar years. The sixties were not the murderous hell of the war years, but as the war novels began to be published the twinning of death and heroism appeared, as it almost always does.

sion of self-contained dynamics propelling individuals independent of the social–cultural matrix of forces. Take, for example, the label of tolerance or acceptance of diversity in the behavior and values of other individuals and groups, i.e., the value that you have to go your way in your own way and accept the same in others. Acceptance of the idea of relativity in values was certainly not a new idea, but in the aftermath of the war it started to gain an unprecedented currency, not paraded or heralded but rather subtly becoming the "natural" way of viewing the world. People *were* different, there was no one way of living a life, God (if you were a believer) was not a dogmatist, our past customs and practices had gotten us into some gory messes (witness the past and previous wars), the eternal verities (at least those who proclaimed them) were shams. The war had been fought to create a new world, not to perpetuate the old one. It was to be a new ballgame with new rules. Individuals owed it to themselves to create a new world, not to be imprisoned in the old one. I must emphasize that acceptance of these ideas and values was not obvious, or announced, or pronounced. They were, so to speak, in the winds created by the swirling forces of total war and in the air people breathed. There was no "movement" with the slogan "each must do his or her own thing," or for each of the diverse groups comprising our society to go its particular way. It was rather that shape was being given to the idea that not only did you have to find your way, but in doing so, you were not bound by past custom. The sexual revolution was a more surface phenomenon reflecting an emerging conception of life style. That a new life style was emerging should occasion no particular surprise when one considers that the war came upon the heels of the Great Depression, i.e., a decade-and-a-half of frustration, deprivation, and a deepening reservoir of hope and dreams.

Still another feature of those early postwar years was the search for novelty or, better yet, the idea that in what was obviously not the best of all possible worlds one had to get as much as one could. It was more than mere hedonism in that it referred also to career choice and expectations as well as to what one wanted one's young to experience. There were new professions or work frontiers, and there were so many places to enter and experience them. One no longer felt bound by one's childhood environment, and in many instances one very consciously did not want to stay in the home town. The flight from rural and farm areas accelerated, and we probably became more mobile than any previous society. It was a matter of being pulled, as well as feeling pushed. For millions of people, the opportunity to see this country (to see the world came later) became a real possibility. A new Westward Trek began and California was Mecca. That state's amazing population growth, which began to zoom with the war's end, had many sources: estheticism, recreation, career opportunities. The California college and university systems seemed to grow in size like the red-woods; underlying the California mystique were visions of a new life, new experiences, a new paradise. California was not Hollywood, as many people found out, but even when it fell short of the mark it promised new experiences and life styles. The significance of the California migration was that the attitudes it suggested were general in regard to a desire for new experience and life styles.

I said earlier that the search for novelty or new experience was "more than mere hedonism in that it referred also to career choice and expectations as well as to what one wanted one's young to experience." The growth of interest in the fields of child psychology, child development, and child psychotherapy is not explained by the population explosion; certainly the substantive foci of these fields are not so explained. We have long been a child-oriented society, and the popular and professional literature never lacked for suggestions about how to rear a healthy child. Breast vs. bottle feeding, ad lib vs. scheduled feeding, permissiveness vs. firmness, rooming-in with the mother vs. the neonate in the hospital nursery, early vs. late bowel training—popular magazines and the professional literature were full of discussion and controversy about these and similar issues. After World War II there was an exponential increase in interest in the dilemmas and opportunities of child rearing. As in the case of adults, children as a group seemed to manifest more problems, and parents as a group seemed to spend a good deal of time scanning their horizons to find those who could provide answers, reassuring or otherwise. What emerged, particularly among the highly educated, was the firm conviction that what happened in the earliest years was forever fateful for the rest of a child's life. It is beyond my purpose to go into these matters in any detail except to note one frequent feature of parental behavior: the importance of stimulation, novelty, and varied experience for a child's growth. You did not leave such matters to chance. It was a major parental responsibility to figure out ways in which a child's curiosity could be stimulated and broadened. This said as much about the significance of such a value and attitude in the lives of parents as it did in those of children. I intend something less than caricature when I say that many parents seemed to set about to produce children who were a modern edition of Renaissance Man. The more objects or situations to which a child was exposed, the more likely that all his capacities would be tapped, but to accomplish that end required parents to provide the novelty and stimulation to elicit and quicken expression. What parents want for their children inevitably reflects something about what parents want for themselves and, I am suggesting, the desire for new and stimulating experience had become after the war stronger in parents who were highly educated. Such a desire can be expressed in different ways, e.g., fantasy, the acquisition of material possessions, new and more social relationships, travel, and psycho- therapy. Of the many forces which impel an individual to seek psychotherapeutic help, not the least are curiosity and the desire to become a new person (and it is both the strength and unrealism of this desire which in part account for the prolongation of the therapy).

In trying to identify some of the major emerging values and at- titudes characterizing the college population (and many older edu- cated people) in the years immediately after the war, a set of factors emerge which for want of a more apt label I shall call "sensitivity to authenticity." Here, too, one is not dealing with a new phenomenon, especially when one is trying to understand the phenomenology of younger people. If it increased in strength, events in the world pro- vided a good deal of the power because events internal and external to our society were constant reminders that if war is the continuation of politics by other means, peace can be the continuation of war by other means. Having witnessed or engaged in a global war to defeat war- mongering fascist dictatorships, having been convinced that the bitter lessons of World War I had been well learned and were not going to be repeated in or after World War II, having come to believe that the impotent League of Nations would be supplanted by a viable United Nations, having come to see (or to have been told) that the aloofness of the United States from global affairs had contributed to World War II and that future world peace depended on this country's involvement and leadership—having forged these beliefs during a prolonged war, is it any wonder that people in general and educated youth in particu- lar began to develop a hypersensitivity to the difference between ap- pearance and reality, between rhetoric and action, between change and progress as the years immediately after the war exposed the fragil- ity of peace and international cooperation? However one explains the cold war or views the uses of the atomic bomb and the development of the hydrogen one; however one judges the disintegration of the British empire, the struggles of colonial peoples and the Chinese revolution; however one interprets the United States' use of its power and leadership—the fact remains that as soon as the war ended there began a succession of events and controversies which indicated that hopes for a better world had been allowed to run roughshod over reality. The United States had long been viewed by other countries, particularly the European ones, as naively moralistic and idealistic in its approach to foreign affairs. The immediate aftermath of the war (the years from 1945–1950) moved many Americans closer to the European view of man and world affairs. International crises were many, confrontations between Russia and the United States became standard fare, culminating in the Truman Doctrine about our international leadership and goals. If anything, domestic crises were more frequent and paralyzing, if less dangerous. Those were the years when labor, big labor, really came of age and took on the giants of industry. The strikes were long and costly. The stakes were, after all, very high.

Hypersensitivity to authenticity does not, of course, exclude cynicism or disillusionment. If I emphasize authenticity as a value—that one should be true to oneself regardless of role, status, and narrow self-interest—it is because I believe it has been underestimated as a nascent value in those years. My meaning is well illustrated by the presidential campaign of 1948. It says a lot about those pot-boiling years that up until the Democratic convention in Philadelphia it was not at all certain that President Truman would be renominated. There were efforts to dump him and nominate General Eisenhower (who declined). One thing seemed as certain as the sun's rising: if Truman were nominated, he would be massacred! On the basis of some early campaign polls, one noted polling specialist (Elmo Roper) said that in light of the wide margin which Dewey had over Truman, he saw no point in further polling, and he left *that* scene. How does one explain Truman's victory, perhaps the most astounding in our history? Many books have been written about the 1948 campaign, and the one point I shall be stressing should not obscure the many complex issues and forces entering into that campaign. Nor should my point be seen as *the* major or crucial one in it. The point is important in that it indicated how strong the value of authenticity had become and what it might portend for the future. Briefly put, the point is that "plain speaking, give-em-hell Harry" whistle-stopped (the phrase originated in that campaign) around the country as no president had ever done and, in his phrase, "told the people the truth." Truman was a politician but dissimulation was not one of his characteristics. His social and geographical origins did not predispose him to be a fervent fighter against racial and religious bigotry, but he took up those cudgels when they were not fashionable and even split his own party. The fact is that people saw him as authentic, as truthful as allergic to hypocrisy.

The 1948 campaign was a societal event. In terms of individuals, another phenomenon (to which I have already alluded) which bears on authenticity occurred, and that was the increase in the practice and use of psychotherapy. Whatever else psychotherapy is as a process, and however controversial may be its efficacy, one of its bedrock values is to seek truth. People enter psychotherapy for a host of reasons, realistic and illusory, but in one way or another, it becomes a quest for what one "really" is and wants, the so-called authentic self obscured and distorted by life experiences. At its best, it is a process quintessentially geared to help someone "find him or herself," to separate fact from fiction, to explore the perceived gulf between the possible and the impossible, and to act consistently in terms of new self-knowledge. It deserves reiteration that psychotherapy was primarily a vehicle sought by educated people, including many young people who were in our universities in the early postwar years. A pioneer in the use of psychotherapy with the college population was Carl Rogers, who not only received wide attention and response through his book *Counseling and Psychotherapy* (1942), but also fathered a generation of psychologists who employed his non-directive approach in scores of college centers. The label "non-directive" was most apt and illuminating, because it conveyed Rogers' emphasis on the importance of not steering the client to a predetermined goal, but rather to build on the client's own capacity to articulate his authentic self as a stimulant to growth-producing action. The important point is that Rogers became a household word on college campuses. What he stood for obviously struck a responsive chord among students dissatisfied with themselves, disenchanted with the world, and seeking a moral basis for living. Be true to yourself was the clear message. Authenticity, sensitivity to what one is and needs, was a prized value. It would be caricature, illustrated in countless jokes about Rogers' non-directive technique, to say that he advocated "do your own thing," but it is not caricature to say that he provided the philosophical underpinnings for prizing the discovery of and confrontation with the "authentic self."

Relativity of values, the search for novelty, hypersensitivity to authenticity—these are some of the values, ideas, and attitudes (call them what you will) which took root in many people, especially among the highly educated, in the aftermath of World War II. Irving Kristol once said that the twentieth century began in 1945. It is a very astute observation, if somewhat too precise, not because the outlines of some inevitable future were clear or determinable—they were not—but rather because it so succinctly suggests how many new and different forces began to pick up strength. The seeds were planted, the social soil was variably fertile, but it was not yet clear what facilitating effects future fertilizers would have. The college population had changed dramatically, compared with the prewar years, in size, composition, and attitude. They brought with them a new and emerging set of attitudes and values which, so to speak, were under the table. On the surface, students did not appear all that different from previous generations: they were marrying, having children, choosing a life career, seeking the good life (quantitatively and qualitatively), and endeavoring to achieve stability in an unstable world. And there is no doubt that by traditional indices and cultural rhetoric one could put up a case for "the more things change the more they remain the same." But, as I have suggested, there was reason to believe that breezes of change were not absent. And if one has doubts about the degree to which young people were bringing new values and attitudes to the campus, there can be no doubt that they encountered a setting markedly changed from the prewar years.

Changes in the University

As one would expect and hope, new ideas and fields should characterize the university, and this was true in spades after the war. It is beyond my purposes to detail these changes. Suffice it to say that universities, particularly public ones, increased enormously in size, differentiation, and bureaucratism. I shall focus on aspects of change subsumed under the Age of Psychology; I have already touched on these in my remarks on the thinking and influence of Carl Rogers. But there was another development which was more pervasive and sustained: the legitimation in the university of psychoanalysis as a practice and a general theory of human development. Psychoanalysis had thrived outside the university, especially in our large urban centers where there were sufficient numbers of highly educated, middle- and upper-class people who could afford this expensive and prolonged form of therapy. To be sure, psychology and psychiatry had long been aware of psychoanalysis, but it was an awareness marked either by ambivalence, or grudging recognition, or sardonic disdain for its language, sexual emphasis, and lack of conceptual and methodological rigor. Jastrow's (1932) book is a good example of what I mean. It became a different ballgame after the war. Within the university, foundations, and funding agencies of government, psychoanalysis was accorded an unprecedented degree of recognition and support. Its time had come.

What Freud said or meant has produced enough journal articles and books to fill most public libraries, and I have no intention of adding to that literature. Freud was one of those geniuses who at the same time that he had difficulty tolerating dissidents was himself changing his ideas and practices. Depending on what one wanted to prove and one's acquaintance with the enormous corpus of his writings, one could probably find some support for one's position. It is no wonder that when psychoanalysis entered the university, was taught at all levels, and became a stimulus for research projects, the subject matter took on a protean character. It is also significant that psychoanalysis did not become the sole possession of psychology and psychiatry departments. It began to permeate schools of education, anthropology, literature, and history departments. How prophetic that, during the war, it was a psychoanalyst who was asked to "analyze" Hitler as a way of determing how this type of personality might act under certain conditions of war (Langer, 1972).

Psychoanalysis conveys certain messages which tend to be independent of disagreements about it as a technique and theory. First, there is a part of us which is unknown or relatively unknowable and influences our conscious thought and actions—a part of us not governed by the ordinary rules of logic or ideational association. Irrationality is built into us. Second, we are fatefully the product of early experience, and we are largely unaware of the degree of this influence because of diverse ways in which the human mind inhibits, defends against, and resolves strong, early conflicts. Inhibitions are inevitable as are their foci around bodily parts and pleasure. Third, stormy conflict (internally and externally) between child and parent are also inevitable, the interesting question being who wins what battles and who loses what wars, at what price, and in what style. Fourth, neurosis is universal, but neuroses differ in how they adversely affect interpersonal satisfactions, self-image, and utilization of capacities. We can be more than we are. Self-deception to the point of self-defeat is frequent. Fifth, society can count on more than parents to instill a conservative, conforming force within it. Parents represent society, and rather well. Sixth, there are forms of treatment, based on a search for truth, procedures to dilute inhibition, which can help unravel the personal historical threads in the fabric of past experience and undo some of their baleful effects. There is hope, but it can only be sustained by seeking the truth and developing an authentic, trusting relationship with the therapist. In some general way, the therapist knows the truth, and his task is to engage the patient in the quest. Finally psychoanalysis is a powerful, upsetting experience which can have serious consequences for love, marriage, and work. During and after analysis, the patient is never the same as before; he obtains a new life compass pointing to new experiences and horizons. If one has not been reborn, at least one has a more secure sense of personal identity and capability.

From the vantage point of 1976, these messages are old hat. They were not in the years beginning in 1945. Some will maintain that the too easy propagation and acceptance of psychoanalysis resulted in distortions and bastardizations. That is beside the point. The fact remains that college students among others heard, absorbed, and acted upon these messages. Overall, psychoanalysis was heard as a message of personal liberation, authenticity, and exploration, and to many people it explained and excused a great deal—those were the days when "acting out" was a phrase which entered common (educated) parlance. I am not aware of any statistics bearing on the relationship between divorce and analysis or its therapeutic variants. Nor am I aware of correlational data between therapy and career change or some marked change in work style. But there is little doubt that in people's minds the deep effects of psychoanalysis were seen in terms of marital and work change. From its earliest days, psychoanalysis was viewed as advocating lust, licentiousness, and untrammelled expression of feeling. Its views on child development were seen as encouraging rampant indulgence and perverse sexual activity. Freud's (1955) famous case presentation was considered an infamous example of how debased a child can become in the hands of psychoanalysts (Freud and Hans's father). After World War II, the pendulum swung from disdain and rejection to acceptance and serious study. Marx, Darwin, Einstein—to the pantheon of greats of the past century was added the name of Freud. For a young professional to be admitted as a candidate to a psychoanalytic institute was a badge of honor. And if one were not a candidate but "only" in analysis, far from being a sign of weakness to be kept secret at all costs, it was often paraded as a sign of courageous avant-gardism. Those were also the days when artists of all kinds sought self-revelation and new springs of creativity on the couch.

The Age of Psychology was legitimated in the university, but it was taught to a college population predisposed to listen. There was, so to speak, a compliance factor at work. This does not mean that most students listened and absorbed the messages. Most listened, but probably far fewer were deeply affected then. The point is that the messages were gaining currency, a currency that was spent in different ways by different people. If the substance and implications of the Age of Psychology were vague and lacked the character of a movement, the answer *today* is not hard to fathom: *the individual was the focus of attention. The individual was concerned with himself and that was a concern tailor-made for the new psychology.* The world had changed and was changing. The consequences of the war had disrupted individual lives, and if individuals in the immediate aftermath of the war were concerned with themselves, it is small wonder. By circumstance, as well as by message, the solutions people sought were seen as largely within themselves. They knew, of course, that there was an external world which had almost gone to hell, and now, after victory, seemed to have developed other instabilities. But one had to take care of and strengthen one's own identity and security. Whether from Rogers or Freud, or any of their kin or offshoots, the substance of psychological theories and practices concerned the individual mind and not the societal fabric. Psychology was exquisitely interpersonal; the almost Talmudic devotion to the workings of the mind pushed questions about society far into the background.[4]

[4] I have discussed this in some detail in my book *The Psychological Sense of Community* (1974). The shift in psychology and psychiatry in the past two decades from absorption

As I indicated earlier, the thrust of this chapter was not to demonstrate a relationship between new values and attitudes among highly educated people, on the one hand, and an increase in their dissatisfaction with their work and careers on the other. My aim was rather to describe and characterize some connections between the war years and their immediate aftermath, suggesting in the process that new ideas or ways of thinking became more general. Implicit in this discussion was the hypothesis that these changes in values and outlook were both cause and effect of societal change, particularly in regard to marriage, family, and work. On the surface, at least, these changes were clearer in regard to marriage and family than to work. This may have had more to do with the fact that traditionally we studied more and collected more statistics about marriage and family than about the experience of work in this segment of the population. The highly educated, particularly those who entered one or another of the professions, were considered an elite who enjoyed challenge, novelty, and growth in their work. They did not labor. And there was some justification for this view, which two considerations might have tempered. First, to express dissatisfaction or boredom with, or a waning interest in one's work—particularly if one's work is judged by society as fascinating and important, as in the case of many professions—is no easy matter. To face up to such dissatisfaction is literally to question what one is and to have to justify continuing as one has. It is no less difficult, upsetting, and propelling than to come to the realization that one no longer wishes to live with one's spouse. Our experience suggests that to talk candidly about one's relationship to one's work is as difficult as talking about one's sex life. We define ourselves, and are defined by others, by what we do: our work. To question this definition produces internal conflict, in part precisely because we know that we have come to see ourselves quite differently from others. A second consideration which might have tempered this view is, as I emphasized in Chapter II, the absurdity, phenomenologically speaking, of defining work or a career as if it were or could be unrelated to other areas of living. Here, too, I am not suggesting cause-and-effect relationships, but rather that these different parts of our lives are experienced in relationship to each other. Strangely, this obvious fact has long been known and studied in the

with the intricacies of the individual psyche to a recognition of the individual in society has been enormous. I try to show the degree of that shift by discussing several pre-World War II books (e.g., Dollard, 1935; Plant, 1937, 1966) which had no impact but were signals of what today we regard as "natural." For a short while after World War II, "intra-psychic supremacy," a phrase coined by Murray Levine, was an apt way of characterizing the theoretical stance of psychology and psychiatry. Today Erik Erikson is an acclaimed representative of, and in part a cause of, that shift, and if now in orthodox analytic circles, he is viewed more favorably than in the past, this is an indication of how uncomfortable that fraternity was and is with the shift.

less-educated segments of society, but this knowledge was hardly generalized to the "more fortunate." From the vantage point of hindsight, one can say that awareness of the changes which were picking up steam after the war in regard to marriage, family, divorce, and the need for individual identity and security should have suggested that satisfactions from work and career would become more problematic for the educated elite.

In any event, the major significance of the changes I have discussed lies in the following interrelated questions. What social conditions and forces would facilitate a change in or confrontation with the attitudes and values of the individual focus of the new Age of Psychology? What might happen to students and faculty as the university became bigger and bigger, i.e., what would "work" in the university become? What might happen as millions of highly educated students, many of them professionals, entered the arena of work in which the constraints on individual autonomy (a basic professional value) became stronger and more obvious, i.e., as one became part of and subject to organizational dynamics? What kind of pendulum swing might occur as the shortcomings of salvation through individual therapy would become apparent?

Before taking up these questions, I shall in the next chapter shift the geographical scene from the United States to Europe. This shift is necessary because out of the disaster which World War II was for Europe came new voices expressing new values and outlooks which by the fifties were beginning to find a receptive audience among our educated people generally, and our centers of higher education specifically. Intellectually, morally, and philosophically, we continued to be importers of the ideas of the European intellectual–literary community. And, let us not forget that before, during, and after World War II, a sizable segment of this community had emigrated to the United States.

IV
The New Literature and
New Values about Work

IF EUROPE WAS an economic, political, religious, and philosophical shambles after World War II, there were good reasons for it. Beginning with the First World War, Europe had experienced one or another form of crisis, depression, and wholesale death. World War I alone killed off a large number of youth including many from or headed for the intellectual life. That Europe survived is less significant than how it survived, the price including the new era of total dictatorship, gas chambers, forced elimination and annexation of countries, and polarizations unbridgeable by any of the traditions of the Age of Enlightenment. When the Japanese bombed Pearl Harbor on December 7, 1941, we in this country glimpsed momentarily what Europe had long experienced. And Pearl Harbor was far from the continental United States.

Following World War II, the overall task in the United States was how to convert quickly from a war to a peace economy, there being no question that we had the wherewithal, from the standpoint of technology or resources, to accomplish the task. In Europe the task was more starkly simple: how to survive among impoverishment and ruins? We in this country tended to believe, rhetorically and actually, that "our" victory was another example of God's wisdom and mercy, and if one was not of a religious mind, the victory demonstrated that justice does win out. In Europe the question was: on what basis can one project transcendantal meaning into a world in which the innocent and the guilty suffer equally? How can senseless murder and death be given a meaning which can justify hope? On what basis can one believe or make choices in a world devoid of larger meanings, in a world of loneliness and inescapable privacy? Adrift in a chaotic sea, bereft of valid compasses, misled by our tradition-bound minds, how do we decide to continue when the ports we will find will have the names of

absurdity, meaninglessness, and eternal death? Will it be a rejuvenated Phoenix arising from the ashes or another imprisoning, deluding
image? God is dead, thank God, but how do we decide why to live,
how to live? Terror, anxiety, and death are the individual's inheritance, plus the unenviable capacity for choice. What is man, what
is he like phenomenologically as he faces or (more likely) ignores the
nature of human choice?

In the intellectual community of the United States after the war,
these disturbing questions were hardly heeded; they were likely to be
viewed as questions raised by disturbed people, or as another stage in
Europe's convoluted philosophical tradition which had long stifled the
emergence of the scientific mind by its obsessive concern with strange
categories of the introspective, self-absorbed mind. This is not to say
that these issues were greeted with wild enthusiasm in Europe, but
only that they rooted there more quickly and received more attention.
Writers like Sartre and Camus were read more widely and became
centers of controversy in Europe more than in the United States. As a
philosophical tradition, existentialism was far from new in Europe,
and so when, in the writings of people like Sartre and Camus, the
age-old questions of the nature of human choice, anxiety, responsibility, and the structure of being were reraised, in the context of devastated societies and bankrupt political and moral traditions, they
paradoxically served as stimulus to new intellectual activity, at the
same time they spotlighted an unglorious present and past and an
oppressive future.[1] Oppressive is a word which quickly comes to mind
in reading Camus' novels, i.e., the single individual oppressed by his
privacy and isolation, as well as by a world suffused with arbitrariness,
violence, insensitivity, and ludicrous order. The surrealistic quality of
individual consciousness is isomorphic with the outside world. What
came to full blossom in Camus and Sartre were the seeds planted by
Franz Kafka, whose writings two decades earlier—then considered
strangely compelling, literally fantastic, despairing, even schizo-
phrenic—were no less (and a good deal more) than a statement
of the individual vs. the monolith confrontation and disaster. If today
Kafka's *The Castle* has crept into our language and minds as the
metaphor by which to describe puny man overpowered by bigness,
bureaucracy and mind-boggling and mind-breaking stupidity (in the
guise of reason and justice), it was not always so in the United States. It
had long been so in Europe, and in saying that I intend no judgment,
but rather wish to emphasize why such metaphors had such cogency in

[1] The philosophical roots of modern existentialism have a long and fascinating history
critical to an understanding of modern living and its dilemmas. In my opinion, Barrett's (1962) *Irrational Man* contains the most illuminating discussion of these roots
and I urge the reader to consult that book.

Europe, particularly among Parisian intellectuals, among whom were many from other lands.

In terms of the substantive contents of philosophical, psychological, and psychiatric discussion, the United States and Europe differed blatantly after World War II. If optimism had nourishment in our society, pessimism was provided with appropriately nourishing ingredients in Europe. If we could hope for and even count on a somewhat predictable and desirable future, the European intellectual community tended to view us as, at best, naive, and, at worst, continuing to travel the very road which had led the world to disaster. When you have no food in your mouth, when the flush of victory is followed by the panic of staying alive with the memories of the dead, when you have to pick up the pieces at the same time you are not sure why or how, when despair makes a mockery of living for tomorrow, when life seems meaningless and lends a charade-like quality to the making of choices—when these thoughts insistently intrude into consciousness, is it surprising that life should be seen as absurd? To us progress was inevitable, albeit with interludes of stagnation and regression. Progress as a concept was as American as apple pie. To the European intellectual community, it was a poisonous dish. Caught between the Russian bear and the United States' bald eagle, where were they to go, and with what? The economic and, therefore, the political condition of Europe was so precarious, so pregnant with utter disaster and revolutionary potential, that within a few short years after the war the unprecedented Marshall Plan to help Europe recuperate was initiated. The United States recognized that if such aid was not given, the European mind and body would be forever transformed. Such were the fruits of victory for Europe. And, as is usual, it was from the intellectual–literary community—Beckett, Camus, Sartre, Ionesco, Genet—that the radical challenges to traditional world views emanated.

In one respect, however, there was a similarity between Europeans and my earlier description of the educated community in the United States. The individual mind became the primary focus. Sartre's tracts on his existentialism and Freud's analysis of the psyche can understandably arouse awe about the mind's complexities. But unlike Freud and his epigones, Sartre was a political animal. Nevertheless, the emphasis on understanding the single mind was clear. Although the recognition which psychoanalysis received in the United States after World War II was largely in terms of its ostensibly positive features (personal liberation, self-fulfillment, the search for truth, and the role of reason), and the analytic couch became the symbol of change and hope, this reception overlooked or ignored the pessimistic strain in Freud's writings. From the time of his shock at the carnage in World

War I, through the anti-Semitic holocaust of Nazi Germany in the thirties, Freud's view of man and his possibilities as a peaceful social being went downhill. Freud did not view psychoanalytic therapy as the jewel in the analytic crown. Far from it, he was too impressed with man's "death instinct," his presumed innate aggression and hostility, to overevaluate what therapy can accomplish, particularly in a world which constantly tempts the expression of man's destructiveness. But this part of Freud's thinking, one much closer to that of the European intellectual community after World War II (Freud and they did have similar life experiences!), received little attention in the United States. In Madison Avenue style, people were told what they wanted to hear, and what they wanted to hear was that there was a means for personal salvation. It took a while for the overkill to be exposed, for its limitations to be noted, and when this began to happen the French Connection became more attractive and legitimate. But eventual recognition required the further development of trends exacerbated by World War II.

My thesis has been that following World War II, the experience of work among educated people, its place in their lives, became related to some new and poorly articulated values, ideas, and attitudes. On the surface, at least, these relationships were neither strong nor discernible. Within a decade, however, a clearer picture was emerging in which the influence of the writings of the French literary–intellectual community could be detected. It is, therefore, important that some brief discussion be devoted to some of the themes and forms of these writings. The theatre of the absurd provides a most illuminating basis for such discussion.

The Theatre of the Absurd

One of the consequences of a culture and a tradition is the way it provides what appears to us as a "natural" amalgam of form, substance, and expectation. So, if we go to a baseball game we know what to expect; it never occurs to us to expect that the shape of the playing field will be different, that the number of players on each team will be more or less than nine, that after two strikes you are out, or that spectators will be wandering around the diamond. Indeed, if all of these and similar "crazy" things were to go on, we would protest, demand our money back, and petition the incarceration (to jail or the mental hospital) of those responsible for such irresponsible behavior. That ain't baseball and we will have no part of it! Whatever this new game is, we do not like it or want it. We cannot comprehend (we do not want to comprehend) the kind of mind which can so alter our expectations of form and substance. If it happens once or twice in different places, it may appear in the news media as the most recent example of human goofiness. If, however, it appears to be catching on, it seems more than a passing fad, our resentment may turn to puzzlement. Why do people go? What kinds of people? Is our world really going to hell? How do we protect our world against such absurdities? In our less apoplectic moments, we may realize that this is the way man has always responded to tamperings with the established order of things, and we may conclude that in light of the fact that most of these tamperings have been truly nonsensical and had extremely short lives, we are undoubtedly correct in assuming that the latest tampering will pass away too. But, comes the nagging thought, what if this latest tampering is one of those instances which reflect what some people vaguely think and feel, and of which these new "happenings" are an appropriate expression?

In the preface to the second edition of his stimulating book *The Theatre of the Absurd,* Esslin (1969) states:

> On 30 December 1964 *Waiting for Godot* was revived at the Royal Court Theatre in London with Nicol Williamson as Vladimir. The production was extremely favourably received by the critics. As to the play—the general verdict seemed to be that it was a modern classic now but had one great fault: its meaning and symbolism were a little too obvious. . . . When the same play made its first appearance in London in August 1955 it had met with a wide measure of incomprehension. Indeed, the verdict of most critics was that it was completely obscure, a farrago of pointless chit-chat [p. IX].

Esslin tells the following fascinating story. In November, 1957, several months after the first production of *Waiting for Godot* in this country (in Miami), the San Francisco Actors' Workshop presented the play to an audience of fourteen hundred convicts at the San Quentin penitentiary. The director was apprehensive. "How were they to face one of the toughest audiences in the world with a highly obscure, intellectual play that had produced near riots among a good many highly sophisticated audiences in Western Europe?" The audience stayed, loved, and understood the play in their different ways. They seemed to understand waiting, waiting, waiting. They also seemed to grasp that if Godot had come it would only be a disappointment; hope may spring eternal, but it falls inevitably to its death; "there is no place to go"; the future is nothingness, the present is grotesque comedy compounded of terror and loneliness, and the past a nightmare of foolish expectations.

When the play opened on Broadway to critical acclaim—starring one of the century's great comic buffoons, Bert Lahr, who said *he* was not at all sure what the play was about—at least two things received a kind of legitimation. The first concerned content: man as a comic–tragic figure, alone in an uncaring world, imprisoned by language which facilitates people's talking over, past, and beyond others rather than with them, and having to deal with unfathomable anxiety and the ineluctable fact of death, i.e., *Endgame* (Beckett, 1958). These were not new themes. What was new and portentous was a second factor: the form or structure and even the language of the stage was transformed so as to literally *show* the content, i.e., not to state the content, not to use elevated, poetic language to communicate it, not to develop a theme or plot to illustrate content, but to show it. How do you show "nothing happens"? The difference between Beckett and a sensation-seeking hack is the difference between elusive artistry and breast-beating mediocrity. And if the difference is elsewhere, the results are the same.

The initial reaction to the best in the so-called theatre of the absurd was not much more favorable than to the worst, and there was more of the latter than of the former. It was like the response to changing the game of baseball. But Beckett and Ionesco (and later Pinter and Albee) did not fade away. In fact, they caught on (sometimes for good and sometimes for bad reasons) as the absurd is the "in thing" in many countries. It is worthy of emphasis that the reaction was not local, even though, as Esslin is at pains to emphasize, there was no "movement," i.e., a group of writers who organize, put out their manifestos, and conduct a crusade. One cannot escape the conclusion that they were saying things in new ways which struck a responsive chord in many people grasping for metaphors, pictures, and concepts with which to give shape to vague stirrings within them.

The contrast between the European and American dramatist in those years after the war can be seen by examining briefly Arthur Miller's *The Death of a Salesman*, which received great critical acclaim in 1949. The salesman, Willy Loman, is a tragic figure: empty, unknown to himself, prototypically the outer-directed individual, enamored with all the trappings of material success, unaware of the disjunction between his reality and that of those he seeks to impress, and a parent who gave his sons a social inheritance unwittingly calculated to ruin their lives. Willy is also a psychologically and physically aging person who hides from himself the recognition that the meanings he gave to, and the expectations he had from, his work were deluding and defeating, i.e., a wine turned bitter and unpalatable. (If anything is clear in this play, it is how the experience of work is inevitably affected by and affects all other significant areas of living.) The substance of the play is not new to the American literary tradition. The hollow, hypocritical, depressed, anxious, morally rudderless man of business has long been a favorite of the novelist and dramatist. If Willy seriously contemplates suicide, it is from the kind of experienced terror, futility, and meaninglessness with which Beckett is obsessed. He has no place to go, there is no point in waiting, and the nothingness of death is preferable to the meaninglessness of life. Whereas Beckett shows this in a new dramatic way, Miller handles it quite conventionally through lofty language, connected sequences, and explicit moralizing. From the standpoint of drama, it is no new ballgame. What is going on and why, and where it will end, are known to the audience. Willy may be absurd, but life is not. If he is seen as hopeless, and is without hope, that says more, Miller is arguing, about a *type* of person than it does about people. From Beckett's standpoint Willy *is* man.

If there is any doubt about the different worlds of Miller and Beckett, it disappears when one looks at Willy's nephew Bernard, a peer of his sons. Unlike these sons, Bernard is the earnest, worried, hardworking boy intent on academic success as the means for upward career mobility. No fooling around for him, no skipping school or not handing in assignments, no distractions from the progression: school, college, law school, and arguing cases before the Supreme Court. Miller's play was not only a valid reflection of how people in the educated, intellectual community felt about materialism and the businessman's strivings and style, but it was also a valid indicator of how highly education and the professional life were valued. Don't be like Willy's son Biff; model yourself after Bernard.

My comments about Miller's play are in no way intended as criticism. Similarly, what I said about Beckett should not be interpreted as praise. The thrust of the comparison was to underline several points: the difference in the degree of radicalness in content and form, the way in which each of them reflected strong currents in their different societies after the war, and, significantly, the increasing acceptance of Beckett and his literary kin in this and other countries. That Beckett received the Nobel prize, which no one would have predicted in the decade after the war, and Miller did not (and will not, as seems most likely), may or may not be seen as just by future generations—prizes for literary distinction (like those for academic achievement) do not wear well with judgments over time (e.g., Hubbell, 1972). These artistic judgments aside, the citation accompanying the prize states a point I have reiterated: Beckett has given us a view of man's place in the world, and it is a view which despite its gloominess has served as a mirror for us to see ourselves; it has illuminated dark recesses of our minds and lives and has made death a plainer fact than in our daily lives we like to recognize. I cannot speak with assurance, but it is my impression that according the prize to Beckett was viewed with enthusiasm by the educated–intellectual–literary community in our country, and that obviously includes significant numbers of the faculty of our colleges and universities. I shall expand on the significance of this later. Suffice it to say here, the exposure of college students to the new "French mind," as well as their positive response to such exposure, coupled as these were with developments in the larger society, suggested that new values and *weltanschauungs* were transforming accustomed ways of thinking. If so, these transformations would ineluctably begin to affect the experience of work.

Before taking up such possible effects and their relationship to what was going on in our society, let us look at a literary work contemporary with *Death of a Salesman*, which sold and is still selling at a remarkable rate, and which differs from the play in most instructive ways. At the very least, a comparison between the two works illuminates the ideological cross-currents in the educated–intellectual community and cautions against glib, global generalizations about what people were thinking and feeling. The cross currents were many and the audiences too heterogeneous to permit painting a simple picture or to push the overarching importance of a particular hypothesis. We will be content with the more modest goal of identifying some themes which may over time supplant traditional values and attitudes. I am trying to determine if it is justified to consider the appearance of certain themes and values as valid indicators of change and, if so, what implications they may have (or have already had) for the way in which educated people approach and experience work. Changes in basis for and modes of thinking have diverse sources, but certainly one of the most potent has become those who make up the truly international artistic, literary, and university communities. This interconnectedness has accelerated in recent decades both within and between countries. Since World War II, our colleges and universities have sought to bring artists, writers of all sorts, and musicians (native and foreign) onto their faculties. As a result, there is a well-paved intellectual highway between the campus and other centers of creative effort. New ideas and values do not fly through the air waiting for the winds of chance to bring them to an appropriate location. The means for their dissemination have been programmed into the university.

The Catcher in the Rye

Salinger's novel was published in 1951, although small portions of it had appeared in 1945 and 1946.[2] Its sales fulfilled any novelist's and

---

[2] This novel, plus some of Salinger's short stories (1964), provide glimpses of the effects of the war on some in the educated stratum of society.

bookseller's dream. How do we account for this? Artistry is one part of the answer, but obviously, it was in the service of contents to which the reading public was prepared to respond.

Holden Caulfield is the central character and narrator. He is a seventeen-year-old from a background of means. Holden has been expelled from every prep school which he attended. Depending on one's criteria of normality, he will vary from being considered "seriously disturbed" to "borderline psychosis." He is entertaining, comical, tragic, romantic, impishly and dangerously impulsive, and an all-round failure to himself. He is the textbook adolescent with the serious exception that there are few if any signs that he wishes to or will break out of his privacy, fantasies, and terrifying loneliness. Many people cross his path, willingly or not, but except for his younger sister, the sense of human contact is absent. That younger sister, in addition to memories of a dead brother for whom he mourns, are his major sources of solace. There is an older brother out West selling his soul to Hollywood. From the time the novel begins to the time it ends, Holden's parents, like his literary brother, never put in a real appearance. Except for his sister, who already seems a younger edition of Holden, he is alone with himself, except that his own sense of identity, fractured and fleeting, is inadequate to constrain anxiety and ever-growing terror.

Except for a nuclear family which seems to have no center, what's new? (That's like saying that Holden is no Andy Hardy or the young boy in Eugene O'Neill's *Ah Wilderness*.) What is new is Holden's description of a crazy world. It is not a crazy description, but an astute and perceptive one of unrelatedness, senseless strivings, sordid greediness, misguided values, and bottomless gullibility. Whether it is a friend's mother he meets on the train, a prostitute in his hotel room, an uncomprehending taxi driver, a "friend" who is a doctoral candidate at Columbia, a former teacher married to an older woman, any of his class- or roommates, or two nuns he meets in Grand Central Station— Salinger gives Holden the capacity to spot their jugular, i.e., their shams, hostility, futility, or superficiality. Were it not for Holden's attachment to his sister and dead brother, he could be a character in one of Beckett's or Ionesco's plays. To Holden the world is absurd, and that is also the way he sees himself. Salinger's artistry consists in the fact that "crazy" Holden rings no less true than the craziness of the world he describes.

At one point in the novel, Salinger gives us Holden's stream of thought as he is walking to a bar to meet somebody. And what does he think about? War movies; his brother's strange, passive, isolating behavior when home on furlough; "cowboy generals"; soldiers who didn't know how to use a gun; the nightmare it would be if Holden had to be in the army with some of his peers, and how he would rather die before a firing squad than be part of the army in the next war, with its senseless marching and regimentation; who was the best war poet: Rupert Brooke or Emily Dickinson?; how could his brother hate war so much and still like Ring Lardner and *The Great Gatsby;* and wasn't *The Great Gatsby* really great? Salinger ends that stream of thought by having Holden express satisfaction that the atomic bomb had been invented because if another war comes he's going to be sitting "right the hell on top of it." The war was over, the atomic bomb had been dropped, but they were still there in young Holden's present (a point we shall return to in a later chapter).[3]

In this one paragraph, Salinger not only gives us a feel for Holden's style of thinking but he also artfully tells us about the different ways in which personal experience and formal knowledge are given shape, pertinence and quality by social history, better yet, the ever present past. Holden is truly a historical person, not a timeless one, because without it pedantically being forced into our awareness we know that much of Holden is a distillate of concrete events and forces of a particular time in our society. He is a war and postwar "child," but one in whom society has unwittingly planted attitudes that ultimately will be generally shared by his own and later generations with fateful consequences for the society. Holden does not have a long past on which to look back but it is one containing social upheavals with which as a society we are still struggling.

In a recent discussion with students about Miller's play and Salinger's novel, one of them said: "I have seen the play and I liked it. But I am not sure I would go see it again. I reread *Catcher in the Rye* about once a year, and I look forward to it each time. I felt sorry for Willy Loman but I really could not identify with him. Sure, I want to 'succeed' and reach the top of my field and get respect and recognition. Why did I choose to come to Yale and work like a dog to get good grades? And yet, Holden tells me more about how I think and feel about things than Bernard does. I suppose that also explains why I fell in love with *Catch-22,* and I reread that about once a year." The other students nodded vigorous consent. One of them sputtered: "I don't know how to put it into words, but to other people I must look like Bernard, while to myself I feel more like Holden."

[3] Gatsby and Holden share a number of characteristics. Both were constantly acting and dissimulating, changed their names (Gatsby a fateful once, Holden innumerable times), were generous with money, lived precariously vulnerable lives, and were alone, the more so as their sought-for encounters with others were almost always letdowns. Gatsby was obsessed by memories of a woman he loved, and the need to regain her became the end justifying any means. Holden's obsessions cannot be so neatly characterized, but his return to and his feelings for his dead brother are not unlike Gatsby's need for Daisy. Holden is haunted by a past he dimly senses but cannot articulate. Gatsby dies violently. It is an end we would expect for Holden, albeit not one in which he is sitting on top of an exploding atomic bomb.

Holden Caulfield is more like a younger Gatsby than he is a younger Willy Loman. Arthur Miller makes us feel sorry for Willy, not for the world; Salinger makes us feel more sorry for the world than for Holden who, unlike Willy, manages to see the world perceptively. Miller is optimistic because he tells us there are ways, Bernard's way, to live happily; Salinger offers no such optimism. Miller *blames* Willy (he also blames certain aspects of society); Salinger, far from attributing moral blame to Holden, is content to describe how crazy or illogical one can become in a crazy or illogical world.

Bernard's way! Miller's basis for optimism. Education. Holden Caulfield couldn't disagree more. He is not Willy's son Biff who glories in his athletic prowess, assumes his academic laziness will be overlooked, if not forgiven, dreams of fame and sexual conquests, and who cannot be bothered by the distractions of books and ideas. Biff was interested in the life of the body, not the mind. Holden is no intellectual weakling, he is a fairly well-read boy, he muses about ideas and life, and he has the courage to form and keep his own opinions despite the judgments of authorities. But he is also no Bernard who did his school work in the way he was told, strove to get the grades bright boys should get, used education "to make something of himself," and lived happily ever after (Miller never suggests another ending). No, Holden's allergy to schooling is not a derogation of education or the intellectual life. The allergy is to the *institution* of education: its arbitrariness, rigidities, pretentiousness, and lack of sensitivity to the individual. For the most part, his teachers are a sorry lot who strive valiantly to foist on helpless (and frequently hopeless) students senseless, stupefying collections of fact. Strangely, Holden has sympathy for these teachers because he sees them as actors playing a role, inexpertly and ritualistically.

Miller and Salinger, contemporaries, saw the individual in society quite differently. It is not a matter of one being right or the other wrong, because each was reflecting or picking up or sensing different attitudes and values among people. Clearly, Miller's messages were the more traditional of the two, i.e., they emphasized long-standing themes in American literature, which is but another way of saying that they were part of the ideology of a significant portion of intellectual and educated people (who do make up the bulk of the reading public or theatre audience). Although there are no data, I think it justified to assume that Salinger's novel as well as his short stories were read, and continue to be read, by more young people than was and is the case with Miller's play. The novel is standard fare in high school courses. At the very least, it suggested that there were new stirrings among younger people: a strange mixture of cynicism, longing for authenticity, disillusion with traditional authority and its major institutions, feelings of isolation and meaninglessness, and an acute sensitivity to cant and injustice. To the extent this is true, it helps explain youth's later receptivity to a host of writers, native and foreign, calling either for a moral revolution or new ways of experiencing the world or the recognition of life's inevitable foes: meaninglessness and death. It would be a mistake, however, to view this receptivity as a coalesced set of ideas and forces, as if those in whom these ideas were stirring were not at the same time possessed of traditional views and values. They existed side by side, although increasing numbers began to adapt life styles more rejecting of the traditional. I agree with Nisbet (1969) that it is fallacious to see history as a set of "pregnancies" inevitably leading to predictably new forms of thinking and living. That view of history may help us make sense of the past, but it is gross oversimplification of the natural history of social change, at least in the short run. For almost two decades after World War II, the old and the new were in conflict with each other in the minds of people. The forces of culture and tradition were (and are) not easily vanquished.

If what I have been describing and suggesting has some validity, one has to assume that it would have consequences for love–sexual relationships, marriage, and work. New values and world outlooks are not neutral affairs, they are dynamisms which alter one's perception of people, things, and society. Within a few short years after World War II it was obvious that significant changes had already occurred in marital and other love–sexual relationships. The "new freedom" was not all that new except for the fact that it came to center stage, for a while at least, as new values and world outlooks were surfacing. It occupied center stage for several months beginning in January, 1948, when Kinsey's *Sexual Behavior in the Human Male* appeared. If a continent had sunk into the ocean, it could not have received more public attention than that book did. Before it came out, when it came out, and for a time afterwards, all the news media seemed obsessed with reporting the book's aspects, reception, and implications. Pomeroy (1972) is not resorting to hyperbole when he begins his biography of Kinsey with these words:

> When Alfred Charles Kinsey died in August 1956 at the age of sixty-two, he was one of the most widely known scientists of this century, a household name in the United States and a familiar figure in the remainder of the civilized world. Many of his peers believed then, as they do now, that he ranked with Freud. Kinsey's two landmark volumes, *Sexual Behavior in the Human Male* and *Sexual Behavior in the Human Female*, raised one of the most violent and widespread storms since Darwin, not only in the scientific community but among the public at large. It is fair to say that Kinsey brought sex out of the bedroom and into the world's parlor. If he

did not succeed in making it completely respectable, he laid the foundation for the greater freedom of sexual behavior and the far better understanding of it that we have today [p. 3].

That first volume was both a cause and an effect of the so-called sexual
revolution. Kinsey tried valiantly to tell the reader that he was present-
ing research data in the best traditions of science and that the social
and moral values by which one judges the scientific facts are not in the
expertise or domain of the scientist. But given the times and the new
stirrings, particularly among younger people and so-called deviant
sexual groups (not so considered by Kinsey), the message was proof
positive of the built-in oppressiveness of society, its approval of sham
and hypocrisy, and its tyranny over individual expression. Miller's
Bernard and Salinger's Holden would not read the same messages into
Kinsey.

But what about the world of work and the goals of education? By
what conception of man and society can one assume that as new values
and outlooks begin to affect sex and marriage the approach to and the
experience of work will remain uninfluenced? When marriage becomes a tentative affair, when it is experienced as a producer of boredom and an obstacle to new experience, when its obligations are felt as
an increasingly heavy and dead weight, when marriage becomes a
barrier to explorations of new work possibilities—when these questions are asked, can the approach to and experience of work remain the
same? But one could as well reverse the direction of these questions: if
work is not fulfilling, if it is experienced as unchallenging, if one feels
one has made the wrong career choice, if there is a disjunction between
what one experiences in work and what one would like to experience,
how can intimate relationships escape from the net? If the new values
and outlooks did not show up clearly in the world of work, there are
several good reasons. I shall discuss these reasons in later pages, but
the most obvious reason can be stated now: the expectations, structure,
and organization of our economy make it difficult to approach work in a
tentative manner, i.e., changing work is no easy economic matter. Put
in another way: *our society has made it far easier to change marriage
partners than to change careers (partially or drastically), but the
dynamics behind both types of changes are similar, if not identical.*
There was a time when, on more than the level of rhetoric, marriage
was forever, and civil and religious law made it very difficult to undo a
marriage. That has changed with fantastic rapidity since World War II.
Insofar as work is concerned, and particularly with the highly educated in whom is ingrained the one career–one life assumption, change
has not and will not be so easy, psychologically and economically. But
more of this later.

Let us, finally, turn to one other "event" which was neither a novel nor a play, and in spirit and form far removed from the literary scene and the university. It was a momentous affair of worldwide import, and its special significance for us is two-fold: how it symbolized the changes wrought by World War II and, somewhat strangely, what it said about work and social change.

The Vatican Council

Pope John was elevated to his position on October 9, 1958, and three months later announced the convening of the Council. Both his elevation and announcement were surprises, the former because the College of Cardinals had been unable to agree on a choice, and the latter because it was opposed by the church's Curia which knew history well enough to know that such meetings can produce upsetting change. John had never been considered one of the hierarchy's shining lights, although his performance over the years in the diplomatic service was apparently more than creditable. It was he who after World War II became the papal nuncio to de Gaullist France, supplanting a person who was seen as a collaborator and against whom the younger clergy there were opposed. That younger clergy was viewed by Rome as radical, and one of John's task was to subdue and soothe them. John came to the Papacy knowledgeable about and sensitive to the upheavals of World War II, including the challenge to faith among the populace generally and the clergy in particular.

The Vatican Council, like the Constitutional Convention of 1787, did not occur because someone thought it was a good idea. It was a consequence of an approaching crisis within the church, just as our Constitutional Convention was an attempt to scrap or repair the glaring weaknesses of the Articles of Confederation which, far from being a confederating force, were producing and abetting divisions and vulnerabilities. For one thing, there were those within the church who felt that it was not blameless in regard to what had happened before and during World War II. If the church was the creation of God, how could it have either tolerated, ignored, let alone collaborated with evil? If the church is on the side of right, how can it sanction confusing might with right? In a world rife with poverty, intolerance, and injustice is there any doubt what the church must say and do? In a world which had been scourged by authoritarianism can the church itself remain authoritarian? After a war fought for international fraternal collegiality, could the church avoid changing in the direction of more collegiality in its governance? These and other questions arose to confront the church, and again it was in Europe, particularly in France and Holland, where the most explicit challenges to tradition and authority were phrased.[4] Authority, that was the concept which needed analysis and reformulation! In the United States we are used to hearing that one of the most important changes following World War II was disillusionment about and challenge to authority, particularly among our young. The change appeared earlier and more forcefully in Europe, and its appearance in religious circles (Catholic, Protestant, and Jewish), centuries-old institutions, signified the depth of the challenge. The winds of religious change were blowing in Europe, but in the first decade after World War II they were not strong enough to cross the ocean.

In the United States, as Wills (1971) has pointed out, the Catholic intellectual's dissatisfactions had a more traditional flavor, i.e., he did not think that his church's "behavior" truly reflected basic church doctrine. He did not question the doctrine; he wanted it to be reflected more sincerely, authentically, and literally than it was. The church could be the answer if it only was true to its origins and traditions. Wills described the Catholic liberal of the fifties with these words:

> But the liberal was not really fighting Rome. He opposed the American church because it was all too American. Its bishops had been shaped more by the ethos of the local chamber of commerce than by the American Academy in Rome. The pastor was obnoxious, not for his theology or his transnational ties, but for his lack of theology and parochialism. He was Babbitt in a biretta—as (conversely) Billy Graham was Fulton Sheen in a business suit. The liberal found it hard to talk with his priest, not in the sacristy, but on the golf course. While Paul Blanshard said that priets were foreign agents, the liberal sensed the more horrible truth, that they were aspiring nativists—heirs of their former persecutors, the Know-Nothings (about whom, with typical lack of historical perspective, Catholics knew nothing). The everyday church was narrowly American, its spirit more easily aroused by a Father Coughlin or Senator Joe McCarthy than by papal encyclicals.
>
> Faced with this phenomenon, the liberal outchurched his own parish church, which he thought of as a fund-raising operation, school board, and eucharist-dispensary. The liberal became a lay priest (he was often an ex-seminarian). He bought a priest's breviary, and learned to recite the divine office. He often found like-minded people to recite the "hours" with him. The mood was heavily monastic. In 1950, when Robert Hoyt and some friends founded a Catholic daily, the *Sun Herald* (code for Morning Star, a title of the Blessed Virgin), the staff attempted to communal life and said the breviary together. . . . The home, too, was to be a place for com-

---

[4] The war produced a crisis of faith in Protestantism and Judaism as well, in the latter case because so many people could not justify a belief in a God who would allow a holocaust. How do you pray to God who in His wisdom allowed one's family and relatives to die in gas chambers?

munal song and prayer. As monks in their house made up a spiritual "family," so the family would become a prayer enclave in the world, with Papa as the prior, presiding over liturgical dramas at the dinner table, Mama meanwhile doing all the work of "lay brothers" in a monastery (cooking, cleaning, preparing the sanctuary) [pp. 41–42].

It may not be a felicitous analogy, but it strikes me that Wills describes a type not unlike Arthur Miller's Bernard who is contrapuntal to Willy Loman and his sons. And if Holden Caulfield's perceptions of hypocrisy are not the same as those of the French intellectuals, religious and lay, they are kissing cousins.

The people who helped bring about the Vatican Council, as well as those who attended it (formally and informally, participants and staff), were, of course, highly educated people. They had made a career choice which required years of study. They had committed themselves to a degree and with sacrifices not matched in other lines of endeavor. What troubled them—and it troubled different ones for different reasons—was the increased tendency among the young priests in Europe to leave their careers. Why was this lofty career no longer attractive to the young? We are all familiar with what began to happen in the United States after the Vatican Council. Spurred by disappointment in the Council's achievements, morally ill at ease with the church's lack of leadership in racial matters and the Vietnam War, unable to accept the church's teachings in regard to birth control and the role of women, younger priests left the church in droves and the pool of recruits was drastically curtailed. Europe had witnessed this more than a decade before.

Why would so many people not consider becoming a priest? The answers to this question shed a great deal of light on how the educated young today, in contrast to earlier times, approach choosing any career. If I choose to use the religious career illustratively, it is because those who left the priesthood articulated their reasons, and why they left is quite similar to why young Catholics do not consider entering the church. But we are dealing with more than the religious work and career. One of the more obvious parts of an answer to why the priestly career is avoided is the reluctance to become part of the bottom layer of a large, hierarchically organized pyramid, from which one can rise, if at all, slowly. The structure of the organization when combined with tremendous size means that your life will be determined primarily by strangers far away. There is, therefore, the prospect that you will be trapped within narrow confines of activity for a long time, perhaps a lifetime. Bigness is impersonality, impersonality lends itself to arbitrariness, and arbitrariness is the kiss of death to self-realization.

But all of this speaks largely to the conventional criteria for success and advancement that have so frequently been found self-defeating. Beware of the Bitch Goddess of traditional success! (That, of course, is precisely what the young priest used to be willing to eschew.) More important than "success" is authentically being one's own person, i.e., to be "true" to oneself, to realize one's "potentials," to be able to move in "new" directions, and not to contribute to man's inhumanity to man. Individual self-interest and organizational self-interest are predisposed to be in conflict (the possible validity of this the young priest of earlier days would not accept). Who shall speak for man? Certainly not institutions which in their self-interest speak to only a portion of men and in so doing polarize humanity. The church, like General Motors, says it has the best interests of the people as its goal, but who is fooling whom? Why, to become a pastor for God, do I have to live an unmarried, childless life? Why can't I be true to God and still be a "whole" man? Why pay the price of personal frustration and deprivation? Why should my work carry such a lifelong burden? What are the inherent virtues, if any, of denying oneself this world? Early and final commitment to a career in the church may be the beginning of the process of dying, of the absence of challenge, renewal, and meaning. Stay as loose and as tentative as possible, be open to new experience and ideas, and beware of the signs of boredom and stagnation! Our world is not set up to be for us but against us. Beware of the conventional wisdom, particularly when uttered by older people, and conventional authority. The fear of entrapment, of being swallowed up, of boredom and stagnation, of moral pollution, of an early symbolic death, of being shut off from new experience and growth, of isolation in the midst of ever-growing population density—these are not new fears. They have long characterized young, thinking, educated people (albeit a minority of them), but now they were in tune with world upheaval, the content of education, and even the thinking of older influential people.

The answer may be overdrawn and its clarity exaggerated. But when one has talked with ex-priests, as well as with college youth looking forward to a career, the similarities are remarkable. But what permitted so many seminarians and ex-priests finally to change their "work," in numbers probably far beyond the percentage one would find in any other profession? What evidence is there that their moral and career crisis is atypical for many other professions? We have no data with which to answer the question, but I doubt that they are dramatically atypical. There is, obviously, one way in which they differed from all other professions: their career change did not have the obstacles, dilemmas, and obligations of marriage. This is not to suggest that the decision to change their careers was psychologically easy—far,

far from it. But could it be, as I shall argue later, that it is the marital–economic complex of factors which prevent more educated people in other kinds of work from making equally drastic changes?

I must remind the reader that my aim in this and the previous chapter was not to prove a thesis, but rather to suggest that events of the last four decades were so pervasive and upsetting that it would have been astounding—indeed, a negation of whatever we have learned about war and social change—if they did not produce changes in values and outlooks, i.e., in the "shoulds" and "oughts," the rights and the wrongs, the desirable and the undesirable, the perceived shape of the future in light of the experienced present. I have further suggested that these changes started to become a visible part of the social scene much before the turbulent sixties, and that it was among the ever-growing body of educated people that their conceptual rationale gained clarity. The role of work in this segment of the population has received relatively little attention. I have offered the hypothesis that social change in recent decades had a substance which could make satisfactions from work for the highly educated more problematic than ever before, or, more cautiously, more problematic than people liked to believe. As soon as one agrees that our society (the world society, really) has markedly changed in recent decades, he cannot avoid facing the likely possibility that the nature and functions of work have changed for *all* segments of society. And in seriously facing this possibility, he will have to pay special attention to the highly educated professional person, if only because such a person has been regarded as privileged in that his work and career lacked the characteristics of labor, i.e., his work bore his imprint, was highly valued, was intrinsically and endlessly challenging and interesting, and permitted him to attain new vistas and experience the sense of growth. I am not suggesting and will not suggest that this picture has been rendered invalid. I do and will suggest that there is reason to believe that the picture has changed and may well continue to change. Before going into these issues further, there is one more "event" which by its very nature changed the world and began to change the minds of people in it. It was so unprecedented and influential that special attention has to be given to its possible implications for the nature of work.

V
The Atomic Bomb, Work, and Attitudes toward the Future

To DISCUSS THE EFFECTS of harnessing the atom, either as a military weapon or source of industrial energy, on the attitudes and values of people requires more explicit recognition of age variables than I have given them thus far. In discussing World War II and its immediate aftermath, I talked primarily of younger people, specifically those around college age. For my purposes, I did not think it necessary to make fine distinctions among age groupings, e.g., those who were adolescent or younger during the war years, those who were then in college, those who reached maturity and finished college soon after the war, and, finally, that large swarm of children born after World War II and who reached college in the late fifties and early sixties. Obviously, each of these groups grew up in somewhat different worlds. Although I have restricted discussion to those in the highly educated parts of our society, even that restriction encounters issues, e.g., geographical, ethnic, racial, cultural variations. One can talk, as I have, about colleges and universities, but they are not of a piece. The new values and outlooks showed up more clearly in some centers than in others. The fact is, as I have emphasized, these new values and outlooks were not that clear or strong to justify trying to see how their manifestations varied in relation to other variables. Besides, my major aim was to suggest that the stirrings were there long before the turbulent sixties.

But when one talks about the attitudinal effects of the atomic and hydrogen bombs, variations in age cannot be ignored or glossed over: when the possibility of death is part of a society's ambience, when one's personal existence is presumably threatened, differences in age are crucial in determining how this possibility will be understood, absorbed, and reflected in behavior. Let me illustrate this point by a less somber phenomenon. In the early days of the space age everyone reacted with awe and pride to man in outer space. When man first set foot on the moon, which in this country was seen in the early morning hours, few people slept. In fact, many parents woke up their children so they could witness this unprecedented event. Some parents did not do this in case something went awry, and they did not want their children to observe death. And I doubt that there was anyone who in those exciting moments did not fear he might witness a disaster. For a few fleeting moments, each individual in the world who was watching knew that death was off-stage. But things went well, and everyone could once more forget the fact of his mortality. (I said this would be a less somber example, but is it not significant how the knowledge of death is always in the background, elicited in countless and unsuspected ways?) It was and is fashionable to say that we live in the Space Age, and that it began with the first Russian Sputnik in 1957. What do we mean when we say that? For me, for example, it has relatively little personal value and significance. In a purely cognitive and conceptual way, I can recite what the new age signifies and heralds, i.e., the wondrous possibilities it opens for human existence and, I have to add in light of human history, destructive possibilities as well. But in terms of my daily existence, my problems of living and aging, my social and interpersonal relationships, and everything else which fills and occupies one's days, the space age is of little or no account. I am what I am, and I will be what I will be, independent of the new age. Whether or not this is "objectively" true is not the issue—that is the way I feel. I am a product of another age, and I do not see myself in any way transformed by the new one. In the thirties I used to listen to Buck Rogers on the radio perform in outer space, but I knew it was all a fantasy. (He had *so* many enemies in outer space, and his enemies were our country's enemies!) Man in outer space is no longer a fantasy, but in terms of my life it may as well be.

But what about children for whom man in outer space is a reality before it can be a fantasy? In school and on TV they are being told what age they live in and what their future may look like. Without knowing how they absorb what they see, read, and are told, I assume the space age has a quite different meaning to them. Between a very young child and myself there are several generations, and one must expect that we have not absorbed the new age in identical or even highly similar ways. The future is history for all of us, but because each generation perceives a different future, their history will not be the same. My guess is that the youngest generations see a future space age of which they will be an integral part, not as passive viewers of a television set, but as active participants. For them there will be a space age. For me there will be none. In recent years I have been asking people of my generation three questions. The first is: has the space age changed you in any significant way? The answer was always no. The second question is: do you expect to be alive when the space age really gets going? That may seem to be an ambiguously phrased question, but no one had any doubt about what I was after. Without exception, they answered in the negative. The final question is: when the missions into outer space became increasingly frequent and adventuresome, did they in any way, if only fleetingly, remind you of the fact that you will die long before the space age matures, i.e., regretfully, it reminded you that your days are numbered, that you will never experience the wonders of that age? With only a few exceptions, each respondent answered affirmatively. For my generation the space age served to remind us of something we prefer to forget. Much younger people, I assume, would find such a reaction quite strange. When we turn to the reactions of different generations to the actuality of atomic destruction, we again get a contrasting picture.

The Conceivable and the Inconceivable

Some time in 1961 my wife and I were having our annual discussion about moving to a different house. (In 1976 we still conduct such discussions.) Julie, our daughter, who was then in her sixth year, was listening intently and at one point said: "Why don't we move to Ireland?" Since parents are not supposed to ignore children and their questions, however foolish, we asked her why Ireland? To which she replied: "We were told that when they start to drop atom bombs, Ireland is not one of the countries they will drop them on." I was amused at her reply but did not probe further. Every now and then I would remember her reply, wondering if she really believed that atom bombs would be used in future wars. I had become aware that a number of young people truly believed that atom bombs would be used, i.e., the probabilities were high that they and millions of other people would be wiped out. The United States, Russia, China, and France were testing their bombs, and each test received extended play from the mass media. These tests were protested by various groups: college students, women's organizations, and other groups. Younger children, especially those of the protestors, were certainly reminded repeatedly of what was at stake.

Within the past few years I have had occasion to discuss Julie's question with small groups of college students and younger faculty members. And I put it to them in the context of the question: was it a real possibility to her that the bombs would drop and she would be killed? Was she anxious about her own death? Their response, both from the college students and younger faculty (who were thirty-five years of age or less), was uniform and can be paraphrased: "You're damned right it was real to us. In grade and high schools it was quite frequently discussed in class, i.e., what might happen when the bombs dropped, what we should do, the importance of knowing and having bomb shelters. And don't you remember how many families were building bomb shelters? Don't you remember Governor Rockefeller's state program for bomb shelters? We were scared and frightened for our lives."

Behind my questioning was the realization that I considered it inconceivable that leaders of nations would be crazy enough to use the bomb, that they would risk endangering the existence of the human species. Whether this view is or will be "objectively" invalidated is not at issue, but rather the fact that I have a view of the future rooted in a past in which endangerment of the human species was inconceivable. Progress was not only conceivable but obvious! Endangerment of the human species was not only inconceivable, but it was a fiction of depressed and disturbed minds, the always-present prophets of gloom and doom that all societies have had. My generation, of course, had its threats: hunger, depression, and war. But the conditions causing hunger in *me* passed, the college education *I* thought inconceivable was attained, the foreign threats to *my* existence as a person and a Jew were eliminated, and my fears that I would not be able to pursue my interests proved erroneous. So if I lived my days certain that there would be a future, far better than the present and certainly the past, it said as much about the values and outlooks of those days as it did about me as a person. The fact is that I am not atypical of my generation. Now we *know* that the future is not a certainty, that the dice of luck can throw us deadly snake eyes, but most of us do not *believe* it will happen.

It is quite otherwise with younger people who were born in or reached maturity after World War II. And not only because of the atomic bomb. There was Korea, the Russia–United States confrontation over missiles in Cuba, assassinations of relatively young leaders of youth (the Kennedys, Martin Luther King), Vietnam, the China–Russia frictions latent with awesome destructiveness, countless little wars (civil or otherwise) around the globe, wholesale death through famine. But the atomic bomb, like pollution of natural resources and the atmosphere, is of a different order. Its effects are not local or bound by the present. When it is dropped we will be surprised, there will be no warnings, and we will literally be devastated. It will not be a different ballgame; there will be no ballgame. What is for me and many in my generation inconceivable is, for younger people, quite conceivable.

Death Anxiety, the Future, and Work

In 1973 Ernest Becker's *The Denial of Death* was published, unfortunately posthumously. It is truly a magnificent book in terms of scope, integration of viewpoints, and creative insights. It is not a pleasant book because it is about what all of us, from very young children upward, know but do not want to face: the fact that we will die. In the most clear and compelling ways (he writes beautifully about a deadly subject), he describes the inevitable origins of the knowledge of mortality in very young children and the vicissitudes this knowledge undergoes over the life span. We live each day—it is as if we *have* to live each day—as if we are immortal, but there is always a part of us that knows this is not true. We protect the inviolability of a never-ending future by a lifelong denial of what we know unless, of course, external events and bodily status force us to give up the fiction. With a foreshortened future, or a future we see as not one to strive for, the present can be bitter fruit. If death is put in the context of an ending signifying a new beginning, as is held in religions, it performs the function of providing us with an endless future, albeit mystical and unknowable. But increasing numbers of people no longer accept such a possibility, and they are left with the problem of how to give meaning and purpose to a life which will end in nothingness. Unless one's sense of the future is a force pulling one to it, we live in and for the moment or day with no experience of change or growth. To want change or growth requires a perceived future justifying planning, delay of gratification, and appropriate action. If a person has no faith in such justifications, if the absurdity of the ending makes today a treasure and concern for tomorrow a ridiculous indulgence of hope, change and growth are not in the picture. However you define the future you reveal your implicit or explicit view of your mortality.

Becker never mentions the atomic bomb. It is not in the index, and though I have gone through the book several times I find no mention of it. For Becker's purposes to establish and describe the many ways in which all people everywhere struggle with the knowledge of their mortality, and seek in countless ways to justify their lives by visions of immortality that defeat the possibility of nothingness, this omission is not significant. For my purposes, however, Becker's presentation provides a solid basis for understanding why so many of today's younger people have such a different view of the future than that of older generations. They came to maturity during times when events, of which the bomb is the most flagrant, exacerbated what in less troublesome times is experienced as a life and death struggle in fantasy and fact. The death anxiety elicited by the bomb, pollution, and other kinds of contemporary standard fare has been a form of adding injury to insult.

Older people have difficulty comprehending young people's reactions to knowledge of their mortality. We like to believe that young people, whatever else they may be concerned with, give short shrift to thoughts of their death. Justification for this view is provided by young people themselves. When queried, relatively few will admit to brooding about death, a fair number will say that they think about it from time to time, and a few will say that they never think about it. But what happens when you ask them this question: "Suppose that you get up in the morning and you become fortuitously aware that you have a lump or some kind of growth in the neck region. What are your immediate thoughts likely to be?" I have put this question to many of my students. Except for a handful, their reactions were far from neutral. The most frequent response was (paraphrased): "I bet it is cancer. I am going to die. I had better see someone quick!" As one student remarked in discussion: "Isn't it strange that it takes an experience like that to remind us of the obvious?" It is not, as Becker makes clear, strange at all because that knowledge was there all the time waiting, so to speak, for reality to produce its reemergence, e.g., a lump in the neck, or the possibility of atomic death, or the threat of war. I have been told by physicians associated with college health services that the number of students who react with anxiety and panic to bodily illness is not inconsiderable. One physician with whom I have discussed this issue stated: "Between what they read, and what is drummed into them through the mass media, they know a lot about what can happen to the body. As a group, they are somewhat better than first- or second-year medical students who interpret each of *their* bodily symptoms as a sign of fatal disease." Although I have no evidence, it seems a reasonable hypothesis that concern about death is more frequent among the highly educated in comparison with the less-educated groups. Supporting this hypothesis are the following: college students are among the most vocal and active anti-pollution groups; they are also among the more obvious proponents for new diets; and they probably represent the largest fraction of those who walk, jog, and bike regularly for health reasons. I am a very early riser and go to my office at what my students consider an ungodly hour. I also live in a white, middle-class, suburban neighborhood in which the level of education is quite high. On the way to my office I can always count on seeing neighbors doing their morning jogging. As I get to the Yale area, the number of people jogging dramatically increases. Most of them, of course, are students. Would I see people jogging in neighborhoods of different socio–economic–educational status? I made it my business to drive at the same hour in other neighborhoods. I never saw a jogger.

Consider the different meanings which can be attached to the degree to which transcendental meditation and biofeedback methods have swept the college campuses. Obviously, their popularity has diverse roots, and it is not my intention to resort to ridiculous reductionism when I suggest that one of its roots is the desire to increase the life span by self-control of thought and body that keeps out or dilutes the insidious social world. Concern with increasing the life span, of course, is another way of saying that one, directly or indirectly, is grappling with the fact of one's mortality. There is no way of demonstrating that educated youth of today, in contrast to those of several decades ago (leaving aside war periods), show signs of greater anxiety about death. A case can be made for such an hypothesis, especially if one takes seriously what has been told in the most serious and portentous tones: between the atom bomb, air and water pollution, ecological imbalances, and overpopulation there is a good chance that the human species can vanish from the earth. On the day I wrote these words there appeared on the editorial page of the *New Haven Register* (September 5, 1975) a three-column article about the pros and cons of United States policy on the use of nuclear arms. The article begins as follows:

> Washington—The Ford administration's refusal to rule out firing strategic nuclear weapons at the Soviet Union during a conventional war has sent chills through arms control circles and many Capitol Hill offices.
>
> Secretary of Defense James R. Schlesinger argues that the contingency to launch before the Soviet Union unleashed its nuclear arsenal is necessary to deter attacks on the United States and its allies.
>
> But critics of this strategy are concerned that the policy—coupled with a Pentagon decision to aim accurate nuclear warheads at Soviet missile silos—would put a hair trigger on nuclear war, lowering rather than raising the nuclear threshold as Schlesinger claims.

Similar articles appear frequently in newspapers, magazines, and policy-oriented journals. They vary only in the degree to which they describe possible future holocausts. Their significance lies in two factors. First, they reflect the degree of anxiety experienced by many older people. Second, many university faculty members (because of either their own or their field's historical ties to the development of atomic weaponry, like the physicists, or simply because the nature and future of society are a central professional concern) are engaged in policy formation and policy controversies and bring these issues into the seminar room. Over the past two decades the college student has been reminded on countless occasions of the gloomy future which may be in store for him.

If educated people in general and younger ones in particular see a problematic future in which their hopes and lives may be destroyed, we should at least recognize that it is a view which has a basis in reality and which has been communicated to younger people. But, as I have emphasized, reminders of personal death via senseless use of atomic energy is only one source of anxiety; there are many other reminders which (like pollution of water and air) are more "silent" and ongoing.

The generations which came to maturity since World War II, in contrast to those before them, view the future with greater dysphoria. This is a momentous change because it is a view which robs the present of unbridled optimism about and faith in societal stability and personal fulfillment. It introduces a note of tentativeness and transiency, a wariness that pinning a great deal of hope on a fantasied future of personal satisfaction is too tempting to the gods who play with human fate. Young people have never been noted for their willingness or capacity to plan over the long term. They may have said that they were planning to be teachers, doctors, or lawyers, and they knew what they had to do to become one of these professionals. You went to college, the appropriate professional school, and received your credentials for entry. They were not concerned with what "becoming" would do to them, i.e., how it would inevitably change them as people, change their picture of themselves in the future, and how fateful some of their decisions were for that future. It was a process of "becoming" in which they learned that "becoming" did not end with obtaining their entry credentials but continued into the indefinite future. Indeed, by the time they obtained these credentials most of them were beginning to understand the difference between the short and the long term, between the very structured future of the student and the more ambiguous future of the new professional, between choosing among alternatives predetermined by others and the situation in which they have to assess for themselves what the alternatives may be, between teachers who are out to save their souls (there *are* many) and those in the "real world" who are out to imprison them, between being in love and being married, and between being married and being a parent. If it is in the nature of things that one cannot understand a process until one has experienced it, that nature in no wise predetermines how one approaches the process or the variety of ways it can be experienced. In earlier times there were several factors which made the process seem "natural" and, with one exception, the student did not have to think about them. The first, so deeply ingrained that it did not have to be verbalized, was that they could count on a desirable future; they would be alive in that future, there would be a place for society, its authorities and conventions. Perhaps a better way of putting it is that they did not question the underlying assumptions, values, and structure of society. Of course, they were aware of injustice and inequity, but that was because "the game" was not being played by agreed-upon rules. It was a good game, and it could be a better one if only the players and the referees were better, and could one doubt that such improvement in the future was inevitable? Was it not a worthy goal for us, the fortunate and educated elite, to make it a better game and future? The third factor, and this was articulated, was that Lady Luck was an important factor in life and that somehow, sometime, she would show us her favor by suddenly opening up closed or even unknown doors to personal satisfaction and achievement. By her very nature, Lady Luck was inscrutable and unpredictable, but a very favorably disposed figure. And if we were unsure about when she would look in our direction, there was no doubt she had already bestowed her brand of fortune on people we knew. We saw Lady Luck as accepting and overlooking "the game," and she was not bound by the usual rules. Lady Luck was a companion to all of us, but it was young people who courted her most abjectly.

This picture of earlier generations of educated youth is, of course, overdrawn and incomplete. One could add to, amend and qualify it, depending on which of these earlier generations one focuses. Even so, one would emerge with a picture dramatically different from that of the current scene. The future is, at best, seen as traversing an obstacle course in which each obstacle produces a scar which does not heal and may even prevent one from reaching the next obstacle. At worst, the future is seen as slowly vanishing or dissipating in a miasma of stupidity, absurdity, and nothingness. Unlike the biblical portrayal of Armageddon in which the forces of good and evil are arrayed against each other and God will insure the victory of the virtuous, this future contains the possibility of an ending brought about by senselessness, insanity, and a sizable degree of self-destructiveness—the while we are breathing lethal air, wracked by fatal irradiation, and killing each other for scraps of food to fend off starvation. Far from desiring to play "the game" contemporary youth are reluctant participants, or avid dropouts from society, or seekers of new life in rural or city communes. More important, they question or simply do not accept traditional authority and institutions, and they have a healthy respect for those with the courage militantly to oppose tradition and to experiment with new life styles or old ones heretofore in disrepute. As for Lady Luck, they are more impressed with Evil Fate. To depend on Lady Luck is either to deny reality or to indulge silly fantasy.

This picture, too, is incomplete and overdrawn, but the contrast between recent and past generations is unmistakable. There are, as always, youth who play the traditional game. They may, in fact, be in the majority, but it is a shaky majority, not only in terms of numbers but in the shakiness of the underpinnings for their values and out-looks. They are quite aware of the growing numbers of their peers who are not playing the game or playing it with an explicit tentativeness; they look back with envy to when the college campus was a more exciting place; they continue to hope that there will be a place for them in society; and they have begun the process of lowering their sights. The thinness of their values and hopes is best revealed by their reaction to the economic downturn of the last three years. The disillusionment, anger, and cynicism surfaced as they had to change their view of the future. As several students put it to me: "We are the unlucky generation. We missed the excitement of the sixties and we have to face the limited opportunities of the seventies." There is in many of them the nagging thought that absurdity may well be the condition of their lives. They play the game, they want their hearts to be in it, but their minds are wary and suspicious.

Very few educated people of all ages have been immune to these changes in values and outlooks. On a superficial level the older segments of our population know and have observed these changes, whether they like them or not. Their heads may not be in the sand, but rather at some high elevation from which they look down at what is for them a changing and deteriorating world. But it is precisely this kind of knowledge and observation that engenders in some the depressing thought that their lives have been in vain, that their hopes for their children have not been realized, that they are approaching the end of their lives without the sense of accomplishment, that things simply did not work out as they hoped and expected. And, as we shall see in later chapters, when such knowledge interacts with work dissatisfaction and/or marital instability, it is no wonder that their view of the future bears some striking similarities to that held by the younger segments of our population. They are different generations grappling in different ways with the same problems. The younger segment asks: on what bases can I put meanings and hopes into my life? The older segment asks: on what bases can I extract meaning and value from my life? The younger segment asks: what should I live for? The older segment asks: what did I live for? These questions would have little urgency were it not that both the younger and older segments know that they will die, and most of them also believe that, however much they would like it otherwise, there is no life after death. A poet once said: life takes its final meaning in chosen death. The younger segment is sensitive to this message, more sensitive, perhaps, than earlier generations in our society, and this in part accounts for the anxiety and bewilderment so many of them feel in making decisions and plans. The older segment agrees with the poet, but for many of them it is a grudging agreement because of the mistakes they believe they made in their plans and decisions.

I have suggested that death, and therefore the meaning of life, has become a more conscious concern of recent generations of educated people. Pronouncements about the death of God, the realities of atomic destruction and pollution, mass starvation due to overpopulation, novels and plays stressing life's absurdity, emptiness, and isolation, and, of course, the fear of criminal assault on personal safety—by what psychology can one avoid raising the possibility that the heretofore well-fortified walls around the denial of death, particularly among younger people, have begun to show cracks? Not gaping holes, just cracks. To the skeptical reader I offer the following considerations to ponder. It is my impression that in the past decade more books have been written on death than in the previous three, and if one adds articles in professional journals (let alone those in the mass media) the increase is astronomical. In colleges around the country courses in thanatology are no longer rare. I have sat-in on one such course in a high school. I am told that such courses are not rare occurrences! And unless my experience is very atypical one cannot but be impressed by the number of students and faculty who, from service or research interests, are involved with the dying patient, the dependent aged, pre-retirement and retirement problems, and the scandals of what we euphemistically call nursing or convalescent hospitals. And, finally, is not the number of educated youth who have committed themselves to one or another of the Far Eastern religions a reflection, in part at least, of a deep need to give life some transcendental meaning?

One has to view my conclusion from a historical perspective, if only to see that there is little new about it and that it was in broad outline predicted by people two or more centuries ago. The critics of the challenge to the Catholic church; those who opposed any tampering with the established order of social class and privilege; those alarm viewers who regarded democracy as the death of traditional authority (from the ashes of which, they said, only anarchy would arise); the decriers of the Industrial Revolution, which was seen as a despoiler of humanity and a disintegrator of family bonds; the analyzers of a capitalist society who saw it as a pernicious economic–political vehicle for isolating people from each other, as well as alienating the individual from his "true nature"—at the core of all these stances, albeit from different motives, partisanship, and solutions, was the knowledge that when man has no moorings or place in an established and predictable order of things, or a sense that his life has transcendental meaning, the fact of his mortality will overwhelm and destroy him. Man is an earthly, social animal who, precisely because he knows that one's future is finite, is disposed to see forces in the world that can unnaturally foreshorten that future. Young people today, precisely the most educated among them, perceive such a foreshortened future. It would, perhaps, be more correct to say that they vaguely sense this, like a recurring nightmare which comes between intervals of experience that only in the most disguised ways reflect the anxieties of the nightmare.

But this is not only a problem for youth, nor does it originate with them. They are, after all, living in a certain part of society where they hear and read a great deal. Critics may argue that students do not read enough, or they read too much of the wrong things, but the fact remains that by virtue of their education they have a level of interest in and knowledge of the world far beyond those with less formal schooling. They are aware that many of the books they read were written by members of university faculties, and that these books are discussed in their classes. Although they may not know it in a statistical sense, the fact is that in the past fifteen years there has been an exponential increase in the number of books and articles dealing with the possibilities or realities of a bleak future. These publications vary considerably in the degree of depression with which the authors view the future and wish to communicate to the reader, e.g., students. Indeed, an argument can be made that the generation gap of recent decades was less than has been assumed, and that the values and outlooks of youth bear a startling resemblance to those which have been written about by some of their elders. For example, Robert Heilbroner has long been a highly respected economist in university circles. He never has been a member of the university establishment of economists (if there is such a group), and his books, which have been widely read, bear the stamp of an independent, critical, analytical mind. He has long challenged the adequacy of traditional economic theory, but his criticisms were sobering, lacked stridency, were reasoned and original instead of dogmatic and parochial. In 1974 he wrote *The Human Prospect*, a thin volume first published in the January 24 issue of *The New York Review of Books*. Listen to the first three paragraphs:

> There is a question in the air, a question so disturbing that I would hesitate to ask it aloud did I not believe it existed unvoiced in the minds of many: "Is there hope for man?"
>
> In another era such a question might have raised thoughts of man's ultimate salvation or damnation. But today the brooding doubts that it

arouses have to do with life on earth, now and for the relatively few generations that constitute the limit of our capacity to imagine the future. For the
question asks whether we can imagine that future other than as a continuation of the darkness, cruelty, and disorder of the past; worse, whether we do
not foresee in the human prospect a deterioration of things, even an impending catastrophe of fearful dimensions.

  That such a question hovers in the background of our minds is a propo-
sition that I shall not defend by citing scattered evidence. I will rest my
case on the reader's own response, gambling that my initial assertion does
not generate in him or her the incredulity I should feel were I to open a
book whose first statement was that the prevailing mood of our times was
one of widely shared optimism. Thus I shall simply start by assuming that
the reader shares with me an awareness of an oppressive anticipation of the
future. The nature of the evidence on which this state of mind ultimately
rests will be the subject of the next section. But the state of mind itself
must be looked into before we can proceed to examine the evidence, for
our initial perspective enters into and colors the assessment we make of the
"objective" data. Let us therefore open our inquiry into the human prospect by taking stock of our current anxiety [p. 21].

Professor Heilbroner then proceeds to buttress his view of the future which, while he does not predict the end of the world in the near
future or even over many decades (unless, of course, as he says, the
spread of nuclear arms among new and old countries produces a con-
flagration), seriously questions man's survival on this planet. It is not a
polemic he gives, or an argument devoid of data, or a glib rehash of the
gloom-and-doom variety, or a simplistic set of solutions reminding one
either of Dr. Pangloss or Dr. Billy Graham. In fact, if one comes to this
book after familiarizing himself with Professor Heilbroner's earlier
works, one may be struck, as I was, by two things. First, here again is a
first-rate mind trying to pierce and map the core of the problem, always aware that there is a difference between the facts and the truth,
and never forgetting that economics in action is always at root a reflection of values and a philosophy. The second reaction to the book is that
this is a pained and perplexed man who, against his predilections and
conscious will, is forced to ask: will man survive? because he finds
himself for the first time in his life beginning to answer the question in
the negative.

  The present generation of adults has passed its formative years in a
climate of extraordinary self-confidence regarding the direction of social
change. For the oldest among us, this security was founded on the linger-
ing belief in "progress" inherited from the late Victorian era. For the
middle-aged, educated as I was in the 1930s, this Victorian heritage was
already regarded as a period piece, battered first by World War I, then dealt
its death blow by the Great Depression. But its comforting assurance had
been replaced by the equally fortifying view that history was working like

a vast organic machine to produce a good socialist society out of a bad capitalist one. And for the younger adults who formed their ideas in the 1940s and 1950s when this Marxian vista was itself regarded as an antique, reassurance was still provided by a pragmatic, managerial approach to social change. This was a time when one spoke of social problems as so many exercises in applied rationality: when economists seriously discussed the "fine tuning" of the economy; when the repair of the misery of a billion human beings was expected to be attained in a Decade of Development with the aid of a few billion dollars of foreign assistance, some technical advice, and a corps of youthful volunteers; when "growth" seemed to offer a setting in which many formerly recalcitrant problems were expected to lose their capacity for social mischief.

Today that sense of assurance and control has vanished, or is vanishing rapidly [p. 21].

Professor Heilbroner's analysis and projections are of a kind which lead him seriously to raise the question of whether democracy, with its emphasis on individual freedom, *should* survive in its present form. He finds himself forced to reexamine the "humanitarian's" view of human nature because of "its inability or unwillingness to come to grips with certain obdurate human characteristics."

It is not at all crucial for my purposes to attempt to evaluate Professor Heilbroner's analysis or conclusions. Although his view may be extreme and his conclusions unduly pessimistic, the significance of his book is in the tone of his writing, his despairing outlook, and his belief (quoted earlier) that the reader will share with him "an oppressive anticipation of the future"—and his is only one of scores of serious books of its kind to which students have been exposed. If the student is predisposed to view life and the world as absurd—the kind of view which in the fifties began to "take" to the theater of the absurd and to a variety of literary Holden Caulfields—Professor Heilbroner's book will be taken as proof positive of the validity of such a stance. And the proof is not being supplied by the young but by their elders. It is interesting to note that Skinner's *Walden Two*, published in 1948, was (and still is) widely read by college students, and that was a book which like Heilbroner's not only paints a bleak future for society but argues against the traditional view of the adequacy of democracy. There is nothing in Skinner's (1971) *Beyond Freedom and Dignity* which is not contained in *Walden Two*, and with both books the critics have usually not disagreed with Skinner's analysis of society and its future but with his amazingly oversimple "behavioral engineering" and claim that he has solved the problem of the nature of behavior and behavior change. I do not think I have to elaborate further on the point that the bleak future which in recent decades so many young people have projected was influenced by what many older peole were telling them. When Heilbroner says at the outset that he is assuming that he can count on the reader sharing with him "an oppressive anticipation of the future" he is referring to more than one generation of readers.

A dysphoric view of the future is a way of describing the present. The future is not "out there" in front of us, but it is rather a creation of the present, coloring and justifying it. So, to the extent that young people have a dysphoric wariness about their futures it must be reflected in their experience of choice in the present. Society, through various of its agents, institutions, and customs requires that choices of all sorts be made over the life span. From the standpoint of the individual, these may not be seen as the requirements they are but rather as opportunities to move from a present to a desired future. Society literally requires that all children go to school, but most young children see it more as an internally determined and desired step rather than as the legal requirement it is. As they grow older some of them become quite aware of the legal requirement and, as we have seen in recent years, their reactions can cause quite a stir. As a result, school systems have developed alternative schools and programs to give students a choice, but a choice set within the boundaries of compulsion. Going to college is not a legal requirement. Pressure from parents, the knowledge that college has financial payoff, and the fact that students may know that if they desire to be a certain kind of professional they *must* first go to college—these may have the same consequences as legal compulsion even though the students may initially experience their decision to go as one stemming from internal choice. The more education a student seeks, the more choices he has to make, and they are always made in large part in relation to a perceived future which is ordinarily an extrapolation of the perceived present. If they are living at a time, as was the case for twenty years after World War II, when engineers were in demand and paid high starting salaries, many will "choose" engineering. If, as was also the case in that period, there is a shortage of experts in various foreign languages, some will opt for those fields. However, if, as is currently the case, there is a surfeit of all kinds of professionals, the experience of choice changes dramatically.[1] The question for many students becomes not "What should I be?" but rather "What can I be?" As one student put it to me: "Why try hard to be anything if there is a good chance that in the future you will find you are out in the cold?" The economic factor does not operate in isolation, and its greatest significance lies in its interaction with a host of other factors sometimes incompatible with each other, e.g., desire for growth, the value of authenticity, the need for new experience, fear

[1] There is, of course, a surfeit if one accepts the characteristics and values of our economic system, having as this system does the characteristics of a yo-yo. So, today we have too many teachers. Ten years ago there was a shortage and requirements were drastically altered to entice people into teaching.

of early death and a world holocaust, impotence to control one's fate, and the need for community. It is a strange picture of the future that they glimpse, containing as it does optimism and idealism in the foreground and anxious clouds of disaster in the background. The clouds are not passing natural phenomena but the consequences of man's creativity and capacity for self-destruction. And if they are told or believe that the forecast is for good social weather, there is a part of them that knows what a dismal science this kind of forecasting is. Their education and life experiences—World War II, the cold war, nuclear explosions, assassinations, racial conflict, mini- and maxi-wars in different parts of the globe, pollution, overpopulation, the hopes and disappointments of the social programs of the sixties, the lost battle to reform the quality of education, the puniness of the individual in the face of anonymous bigness, Watergate, an economic turndown raising the spectre of the Great Depression, the feet of clay of so many public leaders—with the knowledge of all these factors is it any wonder that their view of the future is symptomatic of their experience of the present? Is it not puzzling why so many of them are not more wary, cynical, and despairing? Or is it that far more of them do feel in these ways but, like the fact of one's death, it cannot be allowed to occupy center stage in the theatre of their thoughts? We shall have more to say about this in later chapters, but what needs to be emphasized here is that however vaguely sensed this picture of the future may be it arises from the experience of the present. *If true, it must be reflected in how these young, educated people approach the choice of career, marriage, and parenthood; and one would expect that wariness and tentativeness would be important ingredients in their approach.* If the future created in the present is seen as strewn with booby traps, total commitment to *a* course of action that assumes a well-paved, protected road is not possible. When working for a future satisfaction is perceived as a gamble requiring sustained delay of gratification, the delay can at best be an ambivalent one and at worst relinquished in the face of unpredictable obstacles. If the scramble to enter one's chosen work increasingly takes on the worst competitive features of Darwinian natural selection, some will withdraw, a few will participate and "win," and most will go on living knowing that they "lost." A future empty of one's original goals pushes one back into the present and away from the future. To come to maturity committed to the values of self-realization, authenticity, and the challenge of growth and novelty, and then to see these values submerged if not drowned by forces beyond them, is not easy to adapt to, especially if adaptation strengthens on a symbolic level that vague sense that one "has had it," that one has grown prematurely old, that the endless future does have boundaries.

In saying the above, there was no intention to describe a gloomy picture. I must remind the reader that my major aim has been to describe a period in our society in which traditional values and outlooks began to change, especially among those with the most education. It has not been a steady or linear change nor has it been a coherent one. The transformation of values or world outlook never takes place in one day or year or even decade. It is not a conscious or deliberate process in the sense that a people make the decision and herald a new world. For a period of time the old and the new can coexist so that within the groups where the new is taking hold the old is still there. And let us not underestimate either the force of older cultural values or the strength of the societal structure to which they are related. The values and structure of a society, unlike the walls of Jericho, do not crumble at the sound of a trumpet.

We become aware of social change after the change hits us in the face, so to speak, and ordinarily that is a long time after the seeds of change were planted. Then we are aware that those who reflect the change most clearly were born in that new soil and in which the new values and world outlook they sprout seem "natural." Precisely where we are in this process of change I do not know. I am convinced that change is already apparent, but that is not to say I can judge accurately its pervasiveness, strength, and future course. I must also emphasize that I have tried not to judge the change, and if it appears that my assessment has introduced such factors as death anxiety, a dysphoric view of the future, and a wariness and tentativeness about moving to the future, I must remind the reader that side by side with this I have stressed the strength and significance of the values of self-realization, authenticity, and the need for the sense of growth, challenge, and novelty. It is not an orderly picture: logically arranged, the content clear, and bounded by a recognizable frame. Just as to many older people modern art is an abomination, a travesty of traditional (and, therefore, "correct") modes of handling form and content, to others (especially the young generations) it is a source of esthetic pleasure.

The gist of what I have been saying has been put well by Joyce Maynard (1974) in her book *Looking Back: A Chronicle of Growing Up Old in the Sixties*. The title is a pithy summation of her message, but the reader is urged to read the book to get the flavor of the phenomenology of an articulate, educated nineteen-year-old. I have chosen three representative paragraphs:

> Pollution and overpopulation have built up slowly, but our awareness of them came all at once, in 1969. Suddenly the word *ecology* was everywhere. We were juniors the year we all read Ehrlich's *Population Bomb* and felt again the kind of fear that hadn't really touched us since the air-raid drills of 1962. Not personal, individual fear but end-of-the-world

fear, that by the time we were our parents' age we would be sardine-packed and tethered to our gas masks in a skyless cloud of smog. Partly because the idea of pollution hit us so suddenly, and from behind (just when we were alerted to the possibility of quite a different kind of shock, and expending our fury over the war), the realization that our resources were disappearing hit us hard. We were a generation unused to thinking ahead, incapable of visualizing even our twenties, and faced suddenly with the prospects of the year 2000 and forced, in youth, to contemplate the bleakness of our middle age [p. 121].

The words *ambitious, up-and-coming, go-getting* used to be the highest compliment awarded to a bright young man just starting out on his career. Back in those days, the label *businessman* held no unfortunate connotations, no ring of war-mongering or conservatism or pollution. The future may have been uncertain, but it was certainly considered, anyway, and the goals were clear: a good marriage, a good job, a good income—that was a good life.

My generation's definition of The Good Life is harder to arrive at. Our plans for the future are vague, because so many of us don't believe in planning, because we don't quite believe in the future. Perhaps we make too much of growing up with tension, from as far back as the Cuban Missile Crisis, but the fact is that the tension of the sixties put us in a kind of suspension. There were always fallout shelter signs, always secret servicemen and always, when the words "we interrupt this program to bring you . . ." flashed on the screen, the possibility of an assassination. When a plane flies low I wonder (just for a second)—is it the Russians? The Chinese? [p. 153].

Ms. Maynard's outlook is similar to that of other people her age who have written about their disillusionments. Indeed, she is far more cautious than most in her predictions:

It's impossible not to wonder where the young hip kids of today will be twenty years from now. Their parents say they'll settle down ("We were wild in our day too . . .") and some of them will—some will later join their parents' establishment world just as, for now, they've joined a group that is itself a kind of establishment. But there's another group, involved in much more than a fad, and their futures are less easy to predict. They've passed beyond faddishness, beyond the extreme activism of the late sixties and arrived at a calm isolationist position—free not just from the old establishment ambitions and the corporate tycoon style, but from the aggressiveness of the radical tycoon. The best thing to be, for them isn't go-getting or up-and-coming, but cool. Broad social conscience has been replaced by personal responsibility, and if they plan at all, their plans will be to get away. The new movement is away from the old group forms of moratorium crowds and huge rock concerts and communes. Young doctors who once joined the Peace Corps are turning more and more to small-town private practices, Harvard scholars are dropping out to study auto mechanics or farming. Everybody wants to buy land in Oregon and Vermont. If we have any ambition at all now, it is not so much the drive to get ahead as it is the drive to get away [p. 154].

For how many of her generation of educated people Ms. Maynard speaks cannot be determined, but their numbers are not miniscule. What neither Ms. Maynard nor others who write along similar lines seem to recognize is the possibility that for two generations before them (e.g., their parents) similar values and outlooks were aborning but were more shapeless and less a goad to overt action. It is interesting that Ms. Maynard (like the others who have written) tells us little or nothing about her parents. She tells us a good deal about the boredom and trivialities of schooling, the importance of a car at sixteen, her deep addiction to TV and the Beatles, peers and peer-group pressures, the Bomb, and a whole host of other developmental figures and occurrences—and she tells it with charm and seriousness. But it is as if adults generally, and her parents in particular, were off at a party on another planet. I cannot resist the temptation to characterize her book as an unusually clear example of the egocentricity of youth. This would be a carping *argumentum ad hominem* were it not for Ms. Maynard's assumption that the special group she describes as "free not just from the old establishment ambitions and the corporate tycoon style, but from the aggressiveness of the radical tycoon" is a new phenomenon. Further, for her to say "If we have any ambitions at all now, it is not so much to get ahead as it is the drive to get away" is to ignore the history of the stream of American expatriates which reached a peak after World War I and resumed its climb after World War II, fleeing from what they perceived to be the American (Air Conditioned) Nightmare. And by no means all who have gone to Vermont or Maine (or Oregon, California, or New Mexico) are of Ms. Maynard's generation. In Santa Fe or Taos, for example, two favorite "drop-out" centers, Dr. David Krantz (see Chapter VIII) has interviewed and described scores of "fleers" who are of Ms. Maynard's parents' generation, educated people who for the most part were very "successful" in their work, but who gave up one life style for a new one. In Michener's (1971) *The Drifters*, one finds again that not all drifters were young. They had many older kin. As I tried to show in earlier chapters, the generations which came to maturity in the forties and fifties were hearing messages about life's absurdity, the futility of planning, the senselessness of waiting for a Godot, and the death of God and tradition. Ms. Maynard's description of her school years, and they are perceptive and choice, reminds one of Salinger's Holden Caulfield, the social analyst, who preceded her book by more than two decades.

I would be in agreement with Ms. Maynard if she had said that, in contrast to previous generations, more of her generation articulated and accepted the future outlook she describes, and that their attitudes toward work, marriage, and parenthood have a more crystallized base of dysphoric wariness and superficial commitment. *If I stress continuity among generations, it is less because on the surface they were strikingly similar (they were not), and far more because the social conditions making for changes in values and outlooks were similar and picking up strength.* For example, within the past decade increasing numbers of college students have taken a year off from their studies to travel, work, gain new experiences, and "find themselves." Many colleges and universities have (if only for economic reasons) set up their own "year abroad" programs. The motivations behind this desire of students to leave their campuses are varied, but there can be no doubt that in many instances they involve boredom, an unwillingness or inability to make a career commitment, a thirst to explore the world and themselves, and a fear of being captured by an enveloping present and future. (And among those who cannot take such a step during their college years, there are many who take it between graduation and entrance to graduate or professional school.) On the level of action and institutional practice, this is quite a change from previous decades when in order for a student to take a year off he had to run an obstacle course to prove that the year off he sought was either necessary for health reasons or was directly related to his academic career. His motives were held suspect; he was guilty until he could prove the innocence of his motives. So, far fewer took a year off. But in no way can this be interpreted to mean that they did not harbor many of the same feelings and attitudes about their education and future than those of Ms. Maynard's generation. They, too, wanted to see the world, and many of them did just that during the summer. They, too, were not gyrating in enthusiasm about their exciting college experience, and many of them were uncertain or fearful about choice of career. It was during the so-called somnolent fifties that college students began to become involved in the civil rights controversies, and although it was a trickle compared to the later flood of students who left their campuses to enter the fight, the "movement" had already begun: the college experience was discernibly beginning to be influenced by new values and outlooks. And, let us not forget, this change did not emanate *sui generis* from the minds of the students. Stimuli for and support for the change were coming from some faculty and parents. Students on their own never create a change; external forces always help to plant ideas and even to provide leadership. The word change is shorthand for new ideas and values which impel to action. When they will be clear in action is not predictable, unless one is of that cast of mind which sees dates, or a decade, or the end of a century as a characteristic of the social process when in fact they are like mileage markers on an interstate highway. Rome "fell" in 410 A.D., but it was one of the longest falls in history.

In Chapter VI, I shall take up directly the implications of the changes I have been discussing for the experience of work or career among educated people. As I indicated in earlier chapters, those who have entered or are entering the professions have always been viewed as a privileged elite who by virtue of their education and special training will find their chosen work self-fulfilling—not only rewarding in a financial or status sense, but in a personal–intellectual one as well. If the considerations I have been discussing up to now have even partial validity, they suggest that this educated elite, younger and older, may well be finding their work and career sources of disappointment, i.e., there is an increasing discrepancy between what they expected and are experiencing from work. When changing values and outlooks are by their very substance a redefinition of the future, from a time when the individual can count (rightly or wrongly) on stability to one when (rightly or wrongly) dysphoric uncertainty and pessimism become the norm, the experience of work will not be immune to the change. Here again, as I pointed out in Chapter II, the experience of work cannot be understood in terms of a narrow conception of work, as if what we see people doing, and what they say they do, can illuminate how the experience of work rests on values and outlooks rooted in the present and projected into the future, influencing and influenced by personal relationships and obligations, and answering, however vaguely, the question of how one justifies existence. We define our work and our work defines us, and both definitions emerge from categories of thinking, time perspectives, and cultural givens of which we are rarely conscious, until events expose the fabric in which all of these were embedded. Such exposure has taken place in our society in the last three decades, and its reverberations for the experience of work among the highly educated are beginning to be sensed.

VI
The Professional and the Problem of Candor about Work

OVER THE YEARS there have been scores of studies demonstrating a substantial positive correlation between level of education and work satisfaction. Among those groups with the highest levels of education and professional training, there is some variation as to which report the most satisfaction, e.g., doctors, lawyers, and college professors usually report high levels of satisfaction. In almost all of these studies, the data were obtained by asking one or several or more questions (via questionnaires, telephone-public opinion polling, and occasionally informal discussion and interviewing). These types of studies can be faulted on several grounds, but their agreement on the correlation between education and reported work satisfaction forces one to accept the fact that when these types of methods are employed, the responses will have a predictable order having a surface plausibility. The question I raise is not whether the correlation is a meaningful or reliable one, but whether the methods by which it is obtained are appropriate to the possibility that the experience of work has become more problematic for highly educated people. For example, if we were to employ the usual methodologies with one hundred physicians and an equal number of garbage collectors, is there anyone who would predict that garbage collectors would report a higher level of work satisfaction than physicians? And if the members of each group were asked if they would rather be members of the other group, the outcome would not be in doubt. But what if we asked the same questions of different kinds of physicians, e.g., pediatricians, internists, opthalmologists? We would not expect the different groups to report the same high level of satisfaction, although the largest difference between any two groups would not even approximate the size of the difference between garbage collectors and physicians. If we were then to ask each member of the different medical groups whether they would rather be a member of another group, what might we expect? Would similar numbers of general practitioners and neurologists, for example, opt for internal medicine? Would similar numbers of orthopedic surgeons and pediatricians choose psychiatry? I am not aware of studies which have focused on these questions among physicians, but I have spent years in and around medical centers, and unless my experience is grossly atypical, physician groups would differ markedly in the degree to which they would remain in their present groups. This conclusion does not stem from my asking physicians about the level of their satisfaction or desire to shift to another specialty. If as an outsider I had asked them these questions, I have no doubt they would have reported the usual high level of satisfaction, and few would have said they would prefer another kind of medical work. (Why this is so is taken up later in this chapter). Let me give three examples of some of the conditions in which physicians voiced views of themselves in relation to their work and career that ordinarily are not articulated by them in response to direct questions by "investigators."

1. I had just been examined by a locally well-known and highly respected surgeon to whom I went whenever I wrenched my vulnerable knee. He conducted his examination and prescribed a course of treatment. I started to leave his office and in a perfunctorily courteous manner I asked, "How has life been?" To my surprise he did not respond "routinely" but sighed and said: "I do not know why I allow myself to be so busy." His tone of voice suggested that he wanted to talk and so we did, in the course of which I told him about my current interests in the increasing frequency with which people seem to be changing careers. He then said to me: "Surgery *is* interesting. For a period of years it did fascinate me. I *am* a good surgeon. In fact, I'm a damn good one. So I'm good, so what? What I really want to do is to get into the history of medicine." He went on to relate how so many of his days were filled with uninteresting problems (like my knee), and only occasionally was he faced with a challenge which made his day.

2. In the course of a social evening there was discussion of the mixed consequences of technical and scientific advances, the so-called knowledge explosion. Three of the five people in the group were physicians, and they were the most articulate in describing the depth of their feelings about knowing less and less about more and more or, as one of them put it, "that mixed feeling of anger and futility that you will never escape from your ever deepening despair that you are a scholarly fraud. The more my patients treat me as a god the more hypocritical I feel." Given the opening, I indulged my own interests

by saying: "You guys don't sound terribly fulfilled in your work."
There was an embarrassing silence of several seconds during which I
felt remorse at having asked the question. The silence was broken by
all three physicians talking at once. Paraphrased, they said: "How can
you say that? I get a lot of satisfaction in treating and helping people,
although I do not pretend that I help as much as I would like, nor
would I say that my work is always interesting either personally or
intellectually." To which I replied: "I in no way meant that you did
not get satisfaction in your work. It seemed to me that what you were
saying was that you no longer felt the excitement of growth and learning, and this was getting you down as you realized that that is the way
it was always going to be." Their response was: "But isn't this true in
every or most professions? Maybe it is worse in the practice of
medicine because the demands for your service make it extremely
difficult to give high priority to *our* needs." The possibility that the
situation may be worse elsewhere (the grass was browner elsewhere)
allowed these physicians to admit, albeit indirectly, that there was an
aspect to their work that was deeply troublesome to them. The significance of the conversation lies not only in the degree of poignancy
these physicians (all in their mid-forties) experienced about a source of
dissatisfaction, but also in the suggestion that responses to questions
about work or career satisfaction almost always reflect a relative judgment which is rarely articulated.

3. In any fair-sized community, particularly one in which there is a
medical school, there are a few internists to whom other physicians
gravitate as patients, i.e., a doctor's doctor. I knew who some of these
physicians were in New Haven, and through the good offices of my
own physician I was able to interview one such doctor, the understanding being, of course, that nothing personal or identifying would
be discussed. I explained to this physician that I was interested in
pursuing some "intuitions" reflected in two questions: What are the
rarely articulated work and career problems of physicians? To what
extent are they serious problems? Approximately forty per cent of his
practice were physicians from all specialties, the modal age being
between forty-five and fifty-five years. (In a large number of instances
wives were also patients of this doctor.) I began the interview with this
question: Is there any dominant impression you have about these
physicians? His answer was: "In the last five years ninety per cent of
what I deal with is depression." He was not using the term depression
in any technical sense, but rather to convey a very noticeable and
articulated sense of unhappiness, or frustration, a puzzlement that life
was not working out as they had expected. "In some instances their
children are causing them all kinds of worry, and it really affects the
satisfactions they get from their work. Or there are marital problems

which they feel are destroying them. It is as if they find themselves asking: is it all worth while? Was it all worth while? Where this fits in with what I think you are after is that it exacerbates their feeling that medicine is like being on a treadmill, but you can't stop it, and you don't know who is at the controls. Some doctors don't mind the tread-mill because they are being paid rather well to perform on it. But they are a minority for whom being a physician was probably always a means to other ends, e.g., a nice house, big cars, frequent vacations, and a lot of status. I call them the businessmen. But the majority wanted to be healers, not only to understand how the body works, but to contribute to that understanding in some way. In my own case, medicine was a 'calling' in which you took on the obligation to learn, to do your best regardless of what it took out of you, to put the interests of patients at the top of the priority list. But that is maladaptive today because of scads of patients, more and more and more specialization, and most important of all the economics of becoming a doctor and becoming a prisoner of a high standard of living. Medicine has be-come a business and business has become the tail that wags the dog." I told him that although I understood what he was saying, I somehow felt that something was missing, i.e., that there was a disproportion between the degree of frustration he was describing and the factors he was listing to explain it. He replied: "Let me put it to you this way. The public sees us as master of our fate and captains of our soul, in addition to being their life-savers. The fact is that we are not only not life-savers, but we know that we cannot practice medicine by the highest standards. Inside us we judge ourselves much more nega-tively than the public does. We know, like no one else knows, what a jungle the practice of medicine has become. And we know one other thing: as individuals we have surprisingly little control over how we practice medicine. We are being hemmed in and challenged on all sides, and it will be worse in the future. What the public doesn't understand is that in the current downgrading of physicians they have touched an open nerve, but how can we say that out loud?" Towards the end of the interview, I asked: "You have said in a number of ways that these mid-career physicians are quite aware of their dissatisfac-tion, and they cannot talk about it openly. That's a rough feeling to deal with, especially if you see yourself as having that feeling for the rest of your life. How do they cope with it?" His reply: "Psychoanalysis, alcohol, women, and sometimes drugs."

These anecdotes, which can be multiplied, run the risk of convey-ing a distorted impression in which the "inside story" is really the exact opposite of that conveyed in public rhetoric. For all I know, that may not be far off the mark, but I think that such a sweeping conclusion too easily discounts the strength of the satisfactions, intrinsic and extrinsic, which physicians report. I presented these anecdotes primarily to indicate that work or career satisfaction is no easy matter for professionals to talk candidly about, *especially if the profession is seen by others as an endlessly fascinating and rewarding line of endeavor*. To proclaim one's dissatisfactions or doubts is tantamount to questioning the significance of one's life and future, to appear to others as "deviant," and to raise questions in their minds about one's personal stability. How can you say you are frequently bored in, or feel inadequate about, or unchallenged by your work when the rest of the world sees you as meeting and overcoming one challenge after another, as a fount of ever-increasing knowledge and wisdom, as a person obviously entranced with his career? And it is not made easier when to proclaim such feelings to one's colleagues is perceived as sensible as Macy's telling Gimbels its problems.

Now let us listen to a surgeon who has become a well-known essayist and short story writer. In a short piece in *Harpers* (October, 1975) Dr. Richard Selzer asks: why should a surgeon write?

> All through literature the doctor is portrayed as a figure of fun. Shaw was splenetic about him; Molière delighted in pricking his pompous medicine men, and well they deserved it. The doctor is ripe for caricature. But I believe that the truly great writing about doctors has not yet been done. I think it must be done by a doctor, one who is through with the love affair with his technique, who recognizes that he has played Narcissus, raining kisses on a mirror, and who now, out of the impacted masses of his guilt, has expanded into self-doubt, and finally into the high state of wonderment. Perhaps he will be a nonbeliever who, after a lifetime of grand gestures and mighty deeds, comes upon the knowledge that he has done no more than meddle in the lives of his fellows, and that he has done at least as much harm as good. Yet he may continue to pretend, at least, that there is nothing to fear, that death will not come, so long as people ask it of him. Later, after his patients have left, he may closet himself in his darkened office, sweating and afraid [p. 30].

This is unvarnished candor, the substance of which few physicians allow themselves to voice in public. It is not the voice of a physician derogating all that he and his peers have done or denying the validity or sincerity of those occasions in which, in John Dewey's terms (Chapter II), he has had *an* experience, i.e., the sense that all that he is has in some way made commerce with the world outside of him. But, again in Dewey's terms, these experiences are not always positive; they may be those soul-riddling experiences of failure or despair which bring one down to size and are reminders of one's puniness and mortality.

No, it is not the surgeon who is God's darling. He is the victim of vanity. It is the poet who heals with his words, stanches the flow of blood, stills the rattling breath, applies poultice to the scalded flesh.

Did you ask me why a surgeon writes? I think it is because I wish to be a doctor [p. 34].

This is a revealing ending to Dr. Selzer's essay, because it underlines the unrecognized strength of the need to feel that one is making a (healing) difference, a *permanent* difference, unimpeded or contaminated by man and society's unseemly qualities. It is an ending which seems to be denying that there are or should be endings. One should and need not find himself closeted "in his darkened office, sweating and afraid." There is "work" which is more creative, more transcendental, with more staying power than surgery, and that is the work of the poet. The grass is indeed greener elsewhere! Poets will applaud Dr. Selzer, but if they were as candid as he, we might find them saying much the same things about their stock-in-trade, except, of course, some of them would draw from a deep well of bitterness filled with the ingredients of lack of income and recognition, as well as the resistance and inadequacy of language to the poet's need to translate ideas and imagery into an external form—or, more frequently, the searing knowledge of the poet's inability to bend language to his purposes. It is one thing to say that every line of work has its obstacles, frustrations, and drawbacks (just as it is probably true that every line of work has some occasional satisfactions). It is quite another thing, however, when the frustration is festering and continuous and centers around one's sense of personal purpose and change, that sense which alone allows one to meet the future and not to avoid it. When Dr. Selzer asserts that the surgeon is not "God's darling, he is the victim of vanity," he is failing to recognize how the desire to be God's darling has been built into our society, particularly among those of us, the most highly educated, who have been encouraged to discover, so to speak, God's ways and works, and thereby gain something of God's immortality. And so when we find out that we are not God's darlings, it is a narcissistic wound we are loathe to talk about—unless like Dr. Selzer, we think we have found a new and better poultice to cure the wound!

Every physician I have described or alluded to thus far was in mid-life. This was not fortuitous selection on my part. Work or career satisfaction varies as a consequence of a number of factors and time is certainly a major one, not because of time per se, obviously, but because we use the passage of time as a criterion by which to judge the success of our plans and the fulfillment of our hopes. When a person enters a professional field, his endless future has markers denoting in an approximate way what he would like to or should accomplish at those points. That road to the future also has markers which we distinguish from the professional ones by calling them personal or social or familial: marriage, children, their schooling, their careers, etc. This distinction, as I pointed out in Chapter II, may fit the needs of theoreticians and specialists who understandably are loathe to deal with messy totalities, but we should not take the distinction too seriously. As more than one of my informants indicated (especially the doctors' doctor), the personal and professional are constantly interacting in terms of satisfaction, i.e., the experience of each inevitably contains and affects the other. For example, how do we explain a physician (or anybody else) whose satisfaction in his work evaporates following the death of one of his children? Or a physician who says his world is falling apart following the arrest of his child for possession of hard drugs? Or the one who cannot concentrate on his practice because his child has just informed the family she does not wish to go to college? And what about the physician who is seen as sacrificing his work as he gives increasing attention to the practice of love? These are not isolated instances nor, obviously, are they peculiar to one group of people. We work for a number of purposes, but not all of them are contained in the structure of work (narrowly defined), and the outcomes of our plans and hopes in our work and personal lives are not insulated from each other. If we are ordinarily not aware of their interrelationships, it is not because they are nonexistent, but for reasons of good fortune or stupidity. There is no doubt that different levels of satisfactions in different areas of experience can compensate for each other or multiplicatively and adversely exacerbate each other.[1]

What we learned about these mid-career physicians, and it is by no means peculiar to them, is that mid-life is a confrontation between myth and reality. It is more like a war in which many battles or skirmishes are being fought. Death starts to take away parents, colleagues, friends, and loved ones. Marriage may become an imprisonment. Children may not "turn out well," or they will leave for distant places, leaving emotional vacuums. And, of course, one begins to reevaluate whether one wants the future of one's career to be a continuation of its past, and in that battle is the question: what are my alternatives? I am touching on issues here I deal with at greater length in Chapter IX. *I mention them here in order to emphasize that for the professional person mid-life is, like the beginning of adolescence, experienced as an eruption of internal stirrings which had best not be articulated.* To

---

[1] We are all familiar with individuals who bury themselves in their "work" as a means of self-defense against disasters elsewhere in their lives. Such a defense, however, exposes how the fabric of the work experience inevitably contains threads from elsewhere. They are background, not figure, in the fabric, but nonetheless, they are as important and inevitable as background in visual perception.

say them out loud, to communicate them candidly to others is not made easy for us in our culture. Indeed, we are made to feel gauche or strange if we admit publicly to the strength of these stirrings and their anxious and painful contents. They are viewed and experienced as private problems. So private, they can only be voiced to one's physician or psychotherapist.[2]

But, one could ask, is what you are saying about mid-life any less true for the lesser-educated segments of society? Are their problems in social living, working, and aging qualitatively different? I assume they are, if only because this group are more economically vulnerable in the market place and less protected, again economically, against the ravages of illness and aging. Like everybody else, however, they cannot escape questions about the meaning of their lives, the fate of their hopes, and their worth as they and others judge it. But I am assuming that there is one important difference: in contrast to the lesser educated, the highly educated professional now in mid-life came to his career with greater expectations that he was embarking on a quest in which all of his capacities and curiosities would be exploited, the vibrant sense of challenge, growth, and achievement sustained, and his sense of personal worth and importance strengthened; the material rewards he would obtain would be as icing on a delicious cake. He may have harbored some doubts about the size of the cake and the healthfulness of the icing, or about the amplitude of his abilities, or talent for and luck in a competitive society, but these doubts were stilled by what he wished to believe and was encouraged by his education to believe. To start the race with these expectations makes one especially vulnerable to whatever suggests that they may have been unrealistic, and so when in mid-life these suggestions become varyingly insistent the resultant dissatisfaction is not easy to take. It is not easy to think about and less easy to talk about. Dr. Selzer can allude to it because, I presume, his second and concurrent career holds out for him all the great expectations he once had about surgery.

[2] This may be changing in our society. In the last fifteen years, gays and women have come out of their closets and impressed on society experiences heretofore kept private. For society even to begin to try to listen to their innermost turmoil and feelings of degradation was made possible only by their collective persistence. Similarly, the flourishing group-dynamics industry (which has a bewildering array of responsible and irresponsible components) thrives in part because it provides an outlet for many highly educated, professional people to give voice to their inner turmoil about work and social living. I was able to obtain what I believe is a reasonable estimate of the age, education, and work of people who attended four such week-end group sessions. Two were held in the Midwest, one in the South, and one in the East. Thirty to forty people were in each group. They were overwhelmingly highly educated people; the modal age was between thirty and forty; and about half were professional people. The outpouring of feeling in these groups bore a striking similarity to what the doctors' doctor related to me about his physician patients.

But how many are there in mid-life who can substitute one set of great expectations for another?

Now let us turn to another mid-life physician whose book talks directly to the question: has work become more problematic for the professional person? Thus far I have only indicated that it is more problematic than society recognizes or the professional will admit. Dr. Harris (1975) minces no words:

> As we struggle to attain a higher plane of social organization, the physician becomes increasingly subordinate to organizations, governments, institutions, and men of neither license nor tradition in medicine, who have vaulted into positions of power in the newly created health syndicate: businessmen, lawyers, accountants, car salesmen, bankers and the new breed, the hospital administrator; paper doctors who treat paper. They see to the health of the by-laws, procedure manuals, bills, accounts, debits and insurance forms, beguiled by the delusion that if the records are neat and orderly, institutional care of the patient is neat and orderly.
>
> The doctor, as their hireling, is forced to use the tools and services they provide, which may not be the best available; urged to consider the community as a whole when treating his patient; coerced into violating the confidentiality of the doctor–patient relationship by monitoring the utilization of hospital beds by his colleagues.
>
> Nurses resent being "handmaidens" to the doctor, and strive to become an independent profession.
>
> There is a hue and cry for doctors to divest themselves of the elite position they have held so long in medicine. Who, then, should be the elite?
>
> Clearly the precious bond that exists between a patient and his doctor is being riven by unqualified intruders with unlimited power. The physician, in his spiritual and serving role, may be the commodity that is squandered in this struggle.
>
> The medical profession is increasingly in bondage. Like the point of an inverted pyramid it is being pressed deeper into the ground by the weight of an enlarging, expensive bureaucracy. If the profession of medicine is shattered by this burden, would it be asking too much for Aesculapius to be reborn? [pp. IX–X]

Sometimes as blisteringly, more often with controlled anger mixed with resignation, every mid-life physician with whom I have talked echoed Dr. Harris's themes. When they entered medicine after World War II, they pictured a future of autonomy, healing, and satisfaction, whether in the medical center or the private office. Within the medical fields, shaped like a pyramid, they were at the apex. They put themselves there, and they saw society as gladly having them. But today they see themselves dethroned as armies of new professionals have taken over and subordinate fields like nursing have asserted their independence of traditional authority. And the paper work, and the

ever-increasing and changing governmental regulations, and the imperialism of medical schools and the large medical centers—the physician currently in mid-life never anticipated challenges from these
sources. He never dreamed that he would some day be confronting the
organizational craziness and stifling bureaucratism of bigness.[3] There
is one other insult interacting with these other injuries: they sense a
real decline in society's attribution of God-like qualities to them. We
are all familiar with the increase in medical malpractice suits and the
refusal of some physicians to practice until the costs of malpractice
insurance were scaled down. The bitterness of the mid-life physician
toward these developments is very deep. The large majority inveighed
against avaricious and ambitious lawyers who prod clients to sue un-
justifiably; a much smaller number criticized physicians who will tes-
tify for such clients; and less than a handful stated that it was about
time that people woke up to the fact of how poor medical practice
could be and how frequent mistakes were in hospital care. What is
indisputable is their feeling that they have been tarnished, and they
are helpless to correct the situation. Helpless! That was the last word
in the language they would have thought of using to describe their
futures as they entered medicine.

During the 1975 strike of medical interns and residents in some of
the New York City hospitals I interviewed two physicians from that
city, both in their fifties and both in private practice with medical
school affiliations and responsibilities. One physician said: "Mark my
word. That is the most important strike which has ever taken place
anywhere, any time. In one respect I have no sympathy for them
because they are not dedicated to medicine. They don't work as hard
as we did, not because they are lazy but because they don't see the
point of breaking their necks, as we did, to learn as much as you can as
fast as you can. I always had the feeling I wasn't learning enough, that
they weren't teaching me all they could. My God, on my day off I
would go to the hospital if I heard that an interesting case was going to
be discussed. I worked like a dog, and they worked me like one, and
don't think I didn't resent it sometimes. But underneath it all I was
eating it up. For twenty-five dollars a month plus food and cigarettes!
Today they get anywhere from ten to fifteen or more thousand per year
and they are squawking. They want to be physicians and still have a
good time, and that's impossible if you are really dedicated. But in
another respect I sympathize with them. They work in these big, god-
damned hospitals where everybody is short changing everybody else
and where the individual doesn't really count. Hell, they have so
many bosses they don't know for whom they are working, and they

---

[3] Chapter X elaborates on this in terms of professionals in a relatively new type of
setting: the community mental health center.

usually don't know who makes what decision. About the only thing they really learn is what bad medicine is. If what is happening in medicine continues, we will all be forced to unionize, but against whom?"

The second physician gave a picture more in accord with what appeared in the newspapers: "A lot of those fellows are moonlighting and they want more time to do more of it and make more money. This business that because they work such long hours for several days the health of patients is endangered is baloney. Patients aren't getting better care today than thirty years ago. In fact, they may be getting worse care because everybody is out for himself, and no one really is in charge or wants to work. I wouldn't say this in public, but don't think that it doesn't worry me that I or some member of my family may get sick and go to the hospital. There are only two times you should go to the hospital: when you are well or you are dying. In the first case you don't need care, and in the second you probably will get care. If you are in between and you need human care, stay home and sweat it out."

A caveat is in order here. I am not trying to convey the impression that physicians currently in mid-life are weighted down with the burdens of despair, discouragement, and disappointment. These feelings are in the picture certainly, but I think that the strength with which they were conveyed was in part due to the fact that the physicians were verbalizing to me, sometimes for the first time, what they had difficulty facing in themselves. Therefore, these feelings came out with an intensity which can mislead one about the balance between satisfactions and dissatisfactions. And, we must never fail to remember, the strength of these negative feelings must always be seen in their experienced relationship to what has been happening in other areas of living that, though geographically separate and on the surface psychologically separate, are integrally part of the experience of work in two respects: the changing functions which work has for the individual over the course of life, and the role of work either in adversely affecting or compensating for what happens in different areas of relationships. Just as the physician is now aware of the fact that what happens in the larger society affects the field of medicine in very concrete kinds of ways, he, like the rest of us, knows that his experience of work very much affects and is affected by his experience outside of work. If our language differentiates between work and "nonwork," that is no excuse for assuming that the distinction is psychologically valid.

If my interviews demonstrated anything, it is how inordinately difficult it is for people to talk candidly about their experience of work, especially if their work is regarded by society, as it once was by themselves, as an endless challenge on the road to wisdom and growth. In this connection the following excerpts are revealing. They are from the pioneering study of medical students, *Boys In White* (Becker, Geer, Hughes, and Strauss), carried out in 1957 and published in 1961— somewhat after the mid-life physicians I interviewed had been in medical school. The two excerpts are presented by the authors as typical of statements made by the students describing medicine as a "peerless profession" or as the subtitle of their Chapter 5 says, the "best of all professions."

> After anatomy lab I stayed with Harvey Stone while he was scrubbing up. Harvey said, "You know we were talking it over at the [fraternity] house last night. We were wondering what it would be like to flunk out of medical school. I just can't imagine it because if you went back home everybody would say you had failed." I said, "Do you think it is more important than flunking out of other schools?" Harvey said, "Oh, yes. You know medical school is a kind of little plateau; it's the very tops in most people's minds. . . . I think it would be harder to go back and face all those people talking about you than it would be to stick it out here even if you were pretty unhappy here. I don't think many people have the guts to take social pressure of that kind. We've got so much at stake here it really isn't funny." [pp. 72–73]

> At dinner at his fraternity house Sam Watson said he liked to test his concepts by making pictures of them in his mind. I asked him how he would feel if he flunked out. He said, "Oh, I guess I would be very angry." Then he began to think about it and said, "Well, I guess it would be pretty hard to go back home and face the people. I think that would be very difficult." I said, "Do you think it would be more difficult than flunking out of any other school?" Sam said, "Yes, I do. You see medical school is like a dream. Now if you were in law school and flunked out you could very easily go into some business course and make out just as well, but once you started in medicine you couldn't work in any small part of medicine because you never would be satisfied. I have a picture for that. Medical school is like a stairway and I am standing on a stair and it is about three feet high and I am normal size, but I just look at this one stair. I can see the ones above but the thing I have to do is get up this step right now—this one step, and I can't really do anything about the ones above me. I think all of life is a stairway and I hope there will never be anytime when you come out on any platform at the top. I like to think that we could always look upward and never have to look down. I think we do. I think when you get to the top when you get your degree, you don't look back on what you have done, you look ahead again." [p. 73]

These are revealing statements which, taken together with the idealism the authors describe, define with crystal clarity what is meant by great expectations. Note, however, how difficult it would be for these students to tell others if they were unhappy or failed in medical school. If you believe you are in the best of all possible professions, and society says the same thing, how can you get society to understand your unhappiness or failure?

There is, two decades after the study was done, a dated quality to *Boys In White*. This is in no way a criticism but a consequence of the thoroughness and thoughtfulness characterizing the study. As one finishes reading the book one realizes how utterly unprepared these students (and their teachers) were for those societal changes which would change their lives. It is remarkable how insensitive medicine was to what was taking place in the world, and how unrelated it was to those changes. The students had a view of the future that was a replica of all past stereotypes: once they got out of the medical school rat race in which almost everything was prescribed for them, they would become autonomous, continuing to learn and grow according to their needs and interests, and not to what the medical faculty thought was appropriate. Money was important to them but by no means an overriding concern. Far more important to them was a continuing acquisition of knowledge and improvement of skills, constantly invigorating one's sense of self-satisfaction.

> At the Union I had coffee with Tom Arnold, Bud Jansen, and Harold Murphy. I asked them the question about the successful physician. Tom said, "Gee, I don't know what I think about that." Bud shook his head over it too but presently said, "I don't think it's the question of money but I just want enough to live on." Harold said, "You can make enough to live on in some other job. You don't have to come in to medicine for that." Bud said, "Sure, but I wouldn't be happy digging ditches, for instance. I think you have to have some kind of work that is satisfying. I think a physician's work should be self-satisfying to him; I mean he ought to enjoy what he's doing." Harold said, "I feel the same way: I think these guys that go into ditchdigging didn't really want to do that, but once they get in it they haven't much complaint. They might as well do that as something else. The thing I don't like is having to punch a timecard." Tom said, "I know one thing, I wouldn't want to drive a truck for a living, although you can make a lot of money and it's exciting sometimes." [p. 75]

The picture of the medical student one gets from *Boys In White* is remarkably similar to the retrospective accounts of mid-life physicians, i.e., idealism, autonomy, the satisfactions of learning and growth, and a comfortable living. If side by side with this sweet nostalgia is a bitterness with the changed scene and their unwilling envelopment in it, it is a mixture of feeling not unrelated to social reality. The wound is real and deep and festering, and the discomfort is compounded by the inability, difficulty, and fear of putting it publicly into words. Physicians have long been regarded, and have regarded themselves, as possessing knowledge and skills incomprehensible to ordinary mortals. If for a long time they have known the truth to be otherwise, they have kept it a well-guarded secret.

The Reactions to Candor

Physicians are by no means the only ones to feel unable or unwilling to talk candidly about their experience of work. Generally speaking, any professional whose work is viewed by society as important and interesting over the course of the career, and who entered the profession in part because he agreed with that opinion, will tend to refrain from utterances which deny the validity of that opinion. What happens when an individual disconfirms society's evaluation? How do people react when such a highly respected professional says: "I have had enough. I no longer want to do the same thing. I want new experiences and new challenges"?

Let us take an actual instance. Robert F., forty-two years of age, was superintendent of schools in a Midwestern suburban community containing a university. He received his doctorate from a prestigious university after he had spent several years as a classroom teacher. After receiving his doctorate he became a principal, and then he was offered a superintendency elsewhere, which he accepted. He had two children, three and six years of age. His salary was $42,000 a year. In the middle of the academic year, he applied to be admitted to the Yale mid-career program for school administrators. Ordinarily, this was a full year program enrolling a dozen or so big-city school administrators whose salaries were wholly or in large part paid by a special grant to Yale. In applying to come for only one (the second) semester, Robert would have to pay his own way because all fellowship funds for that year were exhausted. He also needed to be sponsored by a faculty member, and I was asked to see if I could do so after reviewing his file. His credentials were impeccable, which was probably less important than the fact that he knew of my work and wished to study with me. And he came. After chatting for a few minutes, I asked him how come his Board of Education gave him a sabbatical in the middle of the year? "They didn't give me a sabbatical, I resigned."

What emerged over the course of this initial conversation was almost identical, with one exception, to what the surgeon (page 100) had told me. Robert, by all criteria, was a very good superintendent and could stay on in that position for as long as he wished. His relationships with his Board, staff, teachers, and community groups were cordial and smooth. The community was suburban middle class, willing to support education rather generously, and quite articulate in their respect for him, his accomplishments, and goals. There were problems, of course; the job was demanding, but all in all it was a splendid situation for someone who had dreamed of such an opportunity. So why quit, and what were his plans? "For the past two years I came to realize that I had done what I dreamed of doing. And what I did, I did well. But I simply did not want to continue to do it year in, year out. Not that it is without its satisfactions. I had a wonderful bunch of people working with me, and I always get a kick out of helping people realize their goals. But I just didn't want to feel that I would always be doing what I have been doing. I wanted new experience and new challenges. I came to Yale to give myself a chance to think, figure out what I would like to do, and pursue some leads. I would like to be a college president or dean or something like that. The one thing I am sure of is that I want out from being a superintendent. And I realized that if I don't get out now I will never get out. *I* had to make the break, make the move, and start something new."

We had many long and searching discussions but among their most fascinating characteristics was Robert's description of people's reactions to his resignation. The chronology of their reactions went like this:

1. When he told his friends he had resigned, each of them assumed he had been offered and accepted a "better" superintendency.

2. When he said he had no other job, some of his friends thought he was being coy or secretive or that for some good reason he was not at liberty to reveal what his new job would be.

3. When it finally got through to his friends and colleagues that he really did not have a new job, and none was in the offing, their puzzlement was obvious and extreme. A few friends asked what the trouble was to drive him to such a rash decision. Indirectly, word came back to him that something strange had to be happening in his life to impel him to give up such a splendid job and career. His wife, of course, heard many of the same things and spent a fair amount of time reassuring friends that Robert had not gone off his rocker, and that their marriage was as secure as ever.

4. After a couple of weeks, a number of his friends, in individual discussion, expressed their admiration and envy at Robert's bold decision, bemoaning their inability or unwillingness to forge a new career. By the time he left to come to New Haven (at his own expense) almost all his friends and colleagues understood and approved what he was doing.

I could give other instances in which successful professionals had to contend with the puzzled reactions of others to a radical shift in work or career. They are reactions in all respects identical to our reactions when the marriage of friends, seemingly secure and happy by "objective" and traditional criteria, comes apart. We are surprised, puzzled, and curious; and in short order, we start intuiting what the sources of trouble might have been. It is another story, of course, if the marriage was obviously rocky and troublesome. *That* we can understand and we even feel relieved that the marriage partners will no longer suffer from the consequences of the mismatch. But when the marriage has been "successful," we are at a loss to understand. It is no different when someone like Robert F. starts divorce proceedings from his successful job and career.

Earlier in this book I pointed out that there has been a strange absence of studies on how highly educated, professional people experience their work over the course of time. I discussed three factors: society's positive judgment about such work, the individual professional's acceptance of society's view as he enters the profession, and the resistance of professional organizations to self-scrutiny. These and other factors which we will take up later make it inordinately difficult for the professional to be candid about feelings which go against society's stereotype of him and his work. As I pointed out, such feelings may engender others of guilt and peculiarity that are not wholly unrealistic in light of society's reactions, with which he has identified. If, for example, Robert's wife had reacted to his plans the way his friends initially did, and she had continued her protestations or went along with loud reluctance, he would have been far less secure about his decision. We have come across numerous instances of marriage break-ups or deterioration because the wife either prevailed in her objections, or, if she did not, the consequences altered the marital relationship or they could only resolve their differences through divorce. Today, of course, we are seeing the reverse situation: the "successful" housewife and mother who no longer wishes to remain in these roles, seeks new experiences and challenges in the world of (different) work, but whose husband and friends are uncomprehending of her experience and motives. In the past two decades numerous novels have been written on this theme, far more, I think, than were written in the past five decades about men.

Another major factor in the lack of studies is less obvious: *we have been far more interested in, and think we understand better, the consequences of failure than success.* If the individual is by conventional criteria doing well (e.g., he is gaining recognition, his income is increasing, he is respected for his knowledge and expertise, he has a comfortable home, travels, etc.), we unreflectively assume that his feelings about his work are isomorphic, so to speak, with these "objective" indices. (It is not unlike our reaction to the news that a multimillionaire has just killed himself. Why, we say to ourselves, would someone with so much money end his life?) There are no good data to estimate how many "successful" people experience their work in ways dicrepant with the favorable perception of others. Our interviews suggest that the number is not small, a conclusion confirmed by Gurin, Veroff, and Feld (1960) and by Kahn, Wolfe, Quinn, Snoek, and Rosenthal (1964, pp. 142–143) who obtained their data primarily through survey research techniques on national samples of differing occupational levels.[4] In Chapter X, we shall present data from the more recent studies by Cherniss and his colleagues indicating that the number of dissatisfied professionals is probably far from small. Because these earlier studies were actually carried out in the late fifties and early sixties, and taking into account all that has happened in our society since then, it is not surprising that ours and Cherniss's conclusions suggest that the extent of the problem has increased.

Candor about one's experience of work, as well as the reactions of others to it, are very much a function of the age of the individual, as well as the characteristics of the society at the time one is seeking information. Neither candor nor job satisfaction are, so to speak, platonic essences informed by or unrelated to the perception of society's status and direction, let alone their seamless relationship to marital status and marital–familial obligations. Candor about one's negative experience of work is intrinsically dangerous not only because of the surprised reactions of others, or the articulation of one's sense of guilt and peculiarity, but also because such candor confronts one with the need or necessity for action in new directions. It has been said that at least half of whatever efficacy psychotherapy has is a consequence of the individual's decision to seek help. That is to say, once an individual has the perceptiveness or honesty or personal strength to admit to himself that he must articulate to someone else his personal difficulties—he must act in order to gain relief from pain—he is on the road to change. And that decision is usually preceded by great turmoil. The professional who is dissatisfied with his work is in a similar (but not identical) situation: he knows he is dissatisfied, he knows he should do something about it, he is acutely aware of constraints on and obstacles to action, and he further knows that all that he knows is private,

---

[4] From a national sample of the different occupational groups Kahn, et al. (1964) found job satisfaction of respondents of high occupational status (e.g., professional, technical, managerial) to be significantly more labile than that of those of lower occupational status. They discuss this in relation to an earlier finding in a survey by Gurin, et al. (1960) in which respondents (in the higher occupational groups) who mentioned seeking only "ego satisfactions" in their jobs had the most ambivalence about job satisfaction. Kahn, et al. conclude: "Putting together these two positive associations—between status and ego satisfaction on the job, and between the seeking of ego satisfactions and ambivalence in job satisfaction—one would be led to conclude that the greatest ambivalence and instability in reported job satisfaction would be found among workers high in occupational status, a conclusion borne out by (our) data" [p. 110]. In light of such findings it is really puzzling why the experience of work of highly educated professional people has been slighted as an area of investigation.

and that once he says out loud to others he is dissatisfied he cannot escape the need to act. But the situation is even more complicated, because it is the rare professional who is without sources of satisfaction in his work and career, and, needless to say, it is the "successful" professional who no longer is challenged by his work who has special difficulties in being candid.

Let us return to the psychotherapy analogy. As I pointed out in Chapter III, before World War II people who sought psychotherapeutic help, then as now mostly highly educated people, tended to keep the fact secret, because if it became known, you would be regarded as strange, or perverse, or inadequate, or just plain crazy. However you were regarded, you were *different*, and it was a very pejorative difference. With the Age of Psychology ushered in by World War II there has been a dramatic change, by no means a total one. Through all the mass media, as well as in all parts of our educational system, people are encouraged to seek psychotherapeutic help for their personal problems: you are far from alone in feeling the way you do. You are not "crazy" if you feel this way or that way. You should regard your personal pain as no different from bodily pain; just take yourself to an appropriate mental health professional, and he will help you. What bothers you bothers millions of people. With messages like these, seeing a "shrink" became a public affair testifying to one's sophistication and aplomb. Candor was no longer a problem. Indeed, in some circles talking about one's psychotherapeutic or encounter experiences raised for some listeners the problem of how to be candid about their boredom. There is reason to believe that what happened to candor in relation to psychotherapy is happening in relation to the experience of work, particularly as regards those professionals in mid-life. In the course of a six months' period, I counted at least twenty newspaper articles directly concerned with mid-career changes among highly educated people, their contents usually containing capsule biographies of "successful" people who wanted to move in new directions. In that same period there were many additional articles in the publications of airlines. And with increasing frequency, popular-type books on the theme of "breaking out" have appeared.

Several years ago we became aware that counseling firms were advertising their services in the New York Times to professionals who were seeking new careers. We had a long interview with the head of one of the two firms who had advertised. He himself had been a minister who no longer was satisfied with his work and, being aware that he was far from alone in this respect, created the counseling service to serve other ministers. When he placed his advertisement in the New York Times, it happened to be put next to those for educational personnel, with the result that he became flooded with requests for service from both ministers and educators. His fee was not small, and he had a waiting list. But soon he began to get requests from a variety of professionals, and when we interviewed him he was in the process of setting up offices in several major cities around the country. To his knowledge, firms like his did not exist, or at least they did not advertise, until relatively recently. Perhaps the most telling "data" were provided us by Dr. Alan Entine, an economist at the State University of New York at Stony Brook, who has long worked in and written about occupational choice and change. His findings will be discussed at greater length in Chapter XI.

Do these accounts represent a trend which is picking up steam, and, if so, is it having the effect of facilitating the expression of hitherto private feelings and fantasies? The message from the popular media is clear: you should not feel guilty about changing the nature and direction of your work. Life is too short to feel confined by what you have done at the expense of what you can and would like to do. Look at these people, all with successful careers, who gave them up to pursue new challenges. It is not easy to do, but it can be done. The alternative is to live an increasingly hollow, dissatisfied life. This message is but another manifestation of the values and outlooks which began to take hold after World War II (Chapter III). Personal authenticity or self-realization, the need for new experience, the importance of growth— the language or jargon varied but their meanings were unmistakable—became overarching values informing personal living. They were values understandably eagerly accepted by the generations who came to maturity after World War II, but their significance and power did not become clear until those generations experienced work in our contemporary society. It is not fortuitous that so many of the capsule biographies of professionals who gave up their careers not only emphasize the dissatisfactions stemming from the creeping restrictions on the sense of autonomy but that the new directions they took were calculated to maximize autonomy. The feeling of entrapment, a kind of symbolic symptom of the dying, withering process, that these biographies describe are similar to what our interviews with professional people revealed.

A caveat is in order here. It has not been my intention to paint a gloomy, depressive picture of highly educated professional people in mid-life, nor have I wished to describe them as having little satisfaction in their work. For one thing, to generalize about such a mass of variegated people, even restricted to those in mid-life, is to indulge presumption. For another thing, as I have been emphasizing, the assumption that the highly educated segments of our population have been immune to the diseases of boredom, disinterest, and alienation from work has exempted them from close scrutiny (with the exception of those in business and industry, whose plight in bureaucratic bigness and the economic jungle was thought to be atypical of professionals in general). Finally, I have no firm basis from our own studies on which to base secure generalizations. My aims have been more modest but, nonetheless, important. At the very least, I have attempted to explore if and why candor about the experience of work is difficult. Our interviews and participant–observer role leave little doubt that candor about the experience of work and career among mid-life professionals is understandably difficult and dangerous, not only because of the economic–familial matrix in which work and career are embedded, but because the experience of work reflects an everchanging psychological fabric in which the hopes and plans of the past, and the perception of the future, give a pattern and dynamic to the living present that render it impossible to escape the question of life's purposes and meanings—and *that* question is the most insistent and important of them all. The difficulty is further compounded by society's view of the professional, and his early incorporation of that view, which, if and when they become discrepant, reinforces privacy rather than public expression of feeling. Another of my aims was to suggest that the mid-life professional who reached maturity in the forties and fifties, absorbing as he did certain values and outlooks about what was important in personal living, was unprepared for or ignorant of the fact that he was living in a society characterized by a dynamic of growth, bigness, and bureaucratization that would threaten those values and outlooks. It was not that the society changed but that it had been changing in these ways for a long time. If the professional knew but ignored this it was in large part because he assumed or was told that by having the elevated status of professional he would be exempt from evil consequences of the societal change. On a relative basis this assumption has validity, but I have suggested that this validity may be in the process of erosion, the pace of which is not determinable, if only because the problem of candor about the experience of work has been given scant attention.

Candor and Methodology

It should be obvious from this discussion that the problem of candor is not likely to gain much illumination by use of such impersonal means as questionnaires or survey research techniques. Such methodologies are not without value, because in the hands of sophisticated and ingenious people they can and have been productive in locating what may be the tips of icebergs. But if one sees the tip of the problem of candor and does not wish to skirt it but rather to estimate

the size and depth of what is below, the impersonal technique is insufficient. (We are not yet possessed of the equivalent of sonar in map-
ping the extent of the problem of candor.) It is noteworthy that among
the more revealing studies of the experience of work (Chinoy, 1955;
LeMasters, 1975) the investigator became part of the lives of the
people in whom he was interested. In Chinoy's case he began by working on the assembly line, got to know the people, established his
credentials as a sincere, responsible, and serious "academic," conducted his sometimes hours-long interview-conversations in their
homes, and essentially licked the problem of candor. LeMasters spent
several years becoming an acceptable part of the woodwork, as well as
an accomplished pool player, in a restaurant catering to his "blue-
collar aristocrats." It is impossible to read these books and question
seriously the degree of candor which these authors were able to elicit.
This does not mean that what their people said is unambiguous in
meaning or without any of the effects of the usual sources of distortions
or even dissimulation. In both studies, however, one rarely finds oneself unconvinced that what is being said by these workers has the ring
of truth, frequently the pain of truth. Far more important than the
questions asked, or where they are asked, or even who is asking them,
is the capacity to create a relationship in which candor is not only
possible but perceived as necessary for the enlargement of knowledge.
Let me illustrate with a personal example. When Dr. Alfred Kinsey
was interviewing males about their sexual lives and their development,
he came to Yale and gave a colloquium in our department. As Pomeroy
(1972) makes clear in his book, Kinsey was, to understate the case in
the extreme, a person dedicated to his research. He told us about his
research and why it was important for him to get 100 per cent samples,
i.e., he did not want a majority of the audience to volunteer, or almost
all—he wanted *all* in order to minimize criticisms about a selective
sample. I had never seen Dr. Kinsey before, but rarely before or since
have I met anyone who so combined the characteristics of Socrates
pursuing the truth and Billy Graham inspiring his audience to be
witnesses for Christ. Unlike Mr. Graham, however, one did not feel
that Dr. Kinsey would pass judgment on you. So I volunteered, feeling
safe that in "spilling my sexual guts," which is how I described the
interview when I was finished, I had contributed to the advancement
of knowledge. The best and briefest way I can communicate the
matter-of-fact manner in which the interview was conducted (by
Pomeroy, I think) and how I was responding about my most private
thoughts and behavior, is by telling what happened as I was departing.
Dr. Pomeroy handed me a self-addressed postcard on which I was to
send him the size of my penis on erection! Sure, of course, why not?
The point of this anecdote lies in the ability of Dr. Kinsey to set the

stage to make others feel that his request for candor made sense and that by your candor you and Kinsey were contributing to man's understanding of man. The most personal thoughts and behavior almost impersonally given and impersonally received!

The conclusions presented in this chapter are based on information obtained in two kinds of ways. The first was in interviews I or my colleagues initiated. They were either with people we knew or with people to whom others had vouchsafed for our sincerity and responsibility. The reason for the interview was always placed on the table immediately: "We are interested in how highly educated, professional people experience their work, how they chose their particular career, what changes, if any, in yourself in relation to your work you may have experienced, and how you view yourself and your work in the future. Strangely, we know a great deal in these respects about blue- and white-collar workers but precious little about people like yourself. We are interviewing all sorts of professionals." Usually we would start with the history of their work experience, but no two interviews went in the same way and we made no effort to stick to a predetermined sequence. We avoided, of course, putting words in their mouths, but on occasion, when the person was either not mentioning any dissatisfactions or giving what we thought was the socially expected or correct response, we would say: "In recent years some writers have said that work has begun to become problematic for many professional people and that it is not only the assembly-line worker who has problems. Other writers claim this is not the case. What do you think?" Still another question we might ask this kind of person was: "Do you think that others in your profession whom you know well feel the way you do about work?" It is noteworthy that the few individuals who reported themselves as having only minor dissatisfactions tended markedly to view others as far more dissatisfied.

What I feel most secure about are those other discussions which were not taking place about the problem of work but in the course of which the issue arose, directly or indirectly, and I took advantage of the moment to direct the conversation to my interest. These conversations, sometimes with one, two or more people, occurred on all kinds of occasions and in different places, but they all had two things in common: we knew each other in varying degrees, and the discussion was explicitly a two-way affair. That is to say, I was not an interrogator and the other person or persons were not "subjects"; in this sense we were equals pursuing an unplanned topic of mutual interest. It was on such occasions that the most spontaneous expressions of feeling occurred, i.e., they had the ring of candor, so that there were times when the uninhibited expression of dysphoric feeling was almost immediately followed by the facial signs of recognition that something painful and usually private had been made public. This should not be taken to mean that all the people reported dissatisfactions. As with some of our interviewees, some of these professional people unambiguously reported themselves as without significant dissatisfactions. Some of these people's assertions also had the ring of truth; others struck me as from people who *had* to present themselves to others as they believed others saw them. One could adopt the clinical stance and in the service of proving one's pet theories interpret any response or behavior as confirmatory. What is to the point is that my interviews, discussions, and observations compelled me to the conclusion that talking candidly about one's relationship to work was difficult and dangerous and not until we take this conclusion seriously will we be in a position to estimate the extent to which professionals now in mid-life experience their relationship to work as problematic. In later chapters I shall present conclusions about professionals arising from interviews which were far more structured and typically formal.

That candor about work has to be a problem for the mid-life professional can be deduced on different grounds from those I have employed in this chapter. Focusing primarily on individuals and methodologies in the usual psychological tradition can certainly be productive, but it can also have the consequences of tunnel vision, i.e., you do see something but it is very limited, and one has only the vaguest idea of what is in the background. Not surprisingly, if one looks at the cultural givens, those assumptions or institutional rationales which we accept uncritically as "right and proper" and timeless, we may become aware of a state of affairs in which there has to be a conflict-producing disjunction between these givens and a changed social scene, from which can be deduced the presence of conflict within certain categories of peoples. When there is a clash between a cultural given and societal change, it will be mirrored in some groups more than in others. I have already alluded to this clash, but in the next chapter it will be more directly addressed.

VII
The One Life–One Career Imperative

THE CONVENTIONAL CONCEPTION of career has long had a restricted scope: one life, one career, period. The developmental task of the individual is to decide from a smorgasbord of possibilities the one vocational dish he will feed on over the course of his life. This has been so accepted a view, reflected in institutional practice and rhetoric, that from the standpoint of the individual the choice of *a* career becomes a self-imposed, necessary, and fateful process. Whatever difficulties this may present, the force of culture transmitted through parents and schools leaves unquestioned in the individual's mind the conviction that making a single choice is a right and proper task. If, as we shall see later, the cultural imperative may not only be dysfunctional but is increasingly being questioned, the fact remains that for most people the imperative is ego syntonic, i.e., it should be obeyed. How this comes about could easily occupy another book, involving as it would the processes of socialization, the purposes of schooling, and the relationships among social history, economic structure, and cultural values. We will have to content ourselves with highlights or aspects of the process, at least to the degree where we can better articulate and formulate questions heretofore only vaguely conceptualized.

The Pre-College Years

The birth of a child changes and sustains parental fantasies about the child as a working adult, another way of saying that a significant aspect of the content of these fantasies is their orientation toward the future. The content of this aspect of parental fantasy varies enormously in specificity, motivational sources, and attention or time given to it. The clearest public example of what I mean is found in those occasional newspaper accounts telling of parents who have already sought to enroll the newborn in their alma mater, i.e., the infant is already seen as carrying on in the future a present and past family tradition. Parents tend to keep their fantasies to themselves, a tendency already reflecting the awareness that however differentiated their fantasies about the newborn may be, it is not "right" to appear to be already bending the child to one's desires. If, as sometimes happens, the parents are asked what they would like their child to be, the socially desirable response is to say: "Who knows what he (or she) will want to be? What we may want and what the child will want may not be the same. The important thing is that the child is happy in whatever choice it makes."

It is probably infrequent, although by no means rare, for a parent to nurture the hope that the child will choose the particular career dear to the parent. The parent may hope that the child will want to become a physicist or a lawyer but, true to the value of self-determination, the parent is prepared to accept other career choices. Ordinarily, the parent is unaware that he or she has clear limits as to range of acceptable choices. The professor of physics looking at his newborn son is not likely to think of him as a plumber, clergyman, or actor. Parents have no difficulty describing to themselves what they would *not* want their children to be. The higher the education and status of parents the more likely that the careers they fantasize for their children have clear limits of acceptability. It is also true that these fantasied careers may change over time depending on the child's perceived talents, personality, and interests. These changes can occur for positive and negative reasons: positive when the child manifests characteristics the parent sees as fitting a particularly desirable career, and negative when the talents and interests considered essential for a career are not evident.

I do not wish to convey the impression that parents, particularly when the child is not yet of school age, are concerned with or spend a great deal of time thinking about the child as a working adult. What I do wish to emphasize is that from early on parents do think of the matter in a fashion far from neutral, and their thoughts have two major characteristics: the first is that the child will, of course, receive as much formal education as possible, and the parental fantasy almost always assumes that, at the very least, a college education will be necessary for the fantasied career or cluster of possible careers. The second characteristic is also in the nature of an assumption but rarely, if ever, questioned: the child will one day be *a* thing, i.e., possessed of a label descriptive of *a* career which, however chosen, was *one* of many possible careers available to the child. The parent does not say his child will be a doctor *and* a physicist, or a lawyer *and* a microbiologist, or a teacher *and* an artist; on the contrary, it may be this *or* that, it cannot be both. On an abstract level, the parent may know or believe that the child can become a variety of "things," but this knowledge is followed by an assumption justifying a 'fact": the child will *have* to choose one career from a range of possibilities. Choosing in this way is seen as obvious and necessary, and it is precisely these feelings and attitudes which are the hallmarks of the cultural imperative because thcy tell us how people perceive and order their world without having to think.

From the time the child begins formal schooling, especially if the parents are highly educated, thinking about the child as a working adult becomes more frequent. Primarily, of coursc, they are vigilant to academic performance because of what it implies for access to college. And, of course, they are concerned with the child's happiness, but if the child seems happy enough at the same time his academic performance is poor or middling, the consternation of the parents can be considerable. These parents are concerned with the present and the not-too-distant future, but lurking in the conscious background of such concern are parental fantasies of the distant future that seem in jeopardy. The future may in fact be chronologically distant but in the minds of parents it is part of their living present. After all, as educated people (or parents setting a high value on education) they have read and been told how vital it is to monitor carefully their child's educational progress and to take whatever steps are necessary to insure that he will be in a position to choose from a wide, rather than a limited, number of future possibilities. And to choose means ultimately to be able to select *the* desired career; to be able to reject possibilities rather than to be in the unenviable position of having to choose only from among less desirable choices.

From the standpoint of the young school-age child, the sources, contents, and rationale for parental fantasies about his adult working life are not of great moment unless one of two conditions obtain: the child is not doing well in school and the future significance of this is communicated to him; or the parents, intent on shaping the child to what they want him to do as an adult, endeavor in diverse ways to influence him. But children do not live in social vacuums. One or both of their parents may work; they have relatives who work; and, of course, through reading and TV they are exposed to numerous types of work. If they say they wish to be astronauts, or baseball players, or detectives, or enter some other glamorous career, we smile indulgently and attribute such choices to the child's need for excitement, compctcncc, or powei—or we say that these choices reflect in large part what children literally *see*, however unrealistic these portrayals may be. Ordinarily, children in our society do not see their parents at work, but they certainly hear about parental work and attitudes in family discussion. What young children take away from these discussions, and the degree to which what they absorb has sustained or delayed effects, is difficult to say, but it would be a mistake to assume that the child's conceptions of and attitudes toward work are not influenced by these discussions.

There is, however, a type of childhood experience which on the surface appears far removed from the world of work but which I regard as important to the way some children will as adults view and choose a career. It is a frequent and important experience, the dynamics of which contain many of the features of beginning a career. I am referring to the relationship between what a child expects from schooling and what he feels he is getting.

Let us begin with the child's first approach to school. It is rare that a child approaches his first school experience without feeling the attitudinal mixture of anxiety and great expectations. As in the case of his first "real" job, he will leave home, spend a good deal of the day elsewhere, socialize with peers and authority figures, and his performance will be judged by himself and others. He is, so to speak, on his own, responsible for himself as never before. This independence may be experienced ambivalently but ordinarily it is subdued by the force of great expectations: satisfying curiosity about schooling, being with other children, playing, and, of course, learning skills and acquiring knowledge. In short, the child sees school as satisfying. Young children do not clearly make the distinction between labor and work—they do know the difference between play and non-play—but if they did, we would find that they approach school as a place not in which one labors but in which what one does bears the stamp of the child's desires, interests, and capabilities. Few children first approach school as if it were a factory or assembly line; that, for some children, comes later. If my work with elementary school children is any guide, the discrepancy between expectations and subsequent experience is slight in the early grades and increases in the later grades. But this conclusion must be tempered by the "work and candor" problem discussed in the previous chapter. Children know they are supposed to like school, and so when some adult (like myself) asks how well they like school, their replies should not be viewed as personal gospel. Similarly, when the adult asks the young child "What do you want to be when you grow up?", we are unaware of several things: that we are communicating the one life–one career rule, that we assume the child is disposed to tell us his hopes or fantasies, and that it is a meaningful question to the child.

In any event, I do not wish to convey the impression that most elementary school children, particularly those from educated family backgrounds, experience a poignantly sharp discrepancy between expectations and school experience. It is not likely to be a general phenomenon, because the beginning of each school year has its own novelties, challenges, and expectations: a new teacher, new children, new classroom, and the hope, sustained or renewed, for satisfaction. As they used to say about the Brooklyn Dodgers: wait until next year. One is justified in hoping when reality says that next season (the next school year) may be different. Schooling may be experienced as work or labor, and if it is the latter the new school year holds promise for change. I am, of course, suggesting that the child is learning, in his own ways of formulating experience, the distinction between labor and work in relation to schooling. It is a shifting distinction and, very likely, one that is largely private. It is not a once-and-for-all distinction, psychologically crystallized and impervious to change through experience. It is a distinction in process.

The transition to the high school years is a fateful one for internal and external reasons. Externally, and in the most explicit ways, the high school is so organized as to present the student with a series of "moments of truth," and parents play their role. For example, should or will the student be put into the regular or accelerated track? Which courses should be required in light of the student's college goals? What range of electives should be permitted? Which foreign languages should the student take in light of the kind of college he or she seems headed for? If anything is obvious in the high school years, it is the perceived relationship between choice of and entrance into college. Administrators, teachers, counsellors, and parents view the curriculum and the students' progress in it with great vigilance, because a choice has already been made: the student is college bound. The goal is to have the student in another situation of choice: acceptance by the preferred college. The importance placed on college stems less from considerations of its intrinsic educational worth than from its relationship to career choice. It would be unwarranted cynicism to say that schools and parents have little or no interest in the contribution of education to intellectual and personal growth. But it would take a monumental effort at denial of reality to ignore the degree to which schools and parents also view college in terms of its vocational significance, e.g., the increase in career options that completion of college brings about. If each year thousands of high school students apply to Yale and Harvard, it reflects not only a judgment about the quality of education in these types of colleges but status factors as well. And when we say "status," we mean that being graduated from these institutions "pays off" in terms of career choice and job options. The fact is that in recent years parents have been viewing the choice of high schools on the same basis as that on which they have always viewed college. As a result, there has been a surprisingly steady increase in the enrollments of private preparatory schools (*New York Times*, Oct. 19, 1975).

From the perspective of the student, the organization, pressures, and purposes of high school (and parents) have diverse internal consequences. He or she knows that two fateful choices are beginning to appear on the horizon: college and "What do I want to be?" High schools, especially in the last few years, have been concentrating on "career education," which aims at providing information about the spectrum of careers, arranging meetings with representatives from different career areas, and offering special courses. If the student has any doubts about the importance and necessity of thinking about *a* career, they are dispelled by these school efforts. It is hard for the student whose career interests have not even vaguely coalesced to avoid being overwhelmed by the near infinity of possibilities. The student who has already decided what he is going to be is spared the agonies of thinking and selecting, e.g., the student who knew from his earliest days that he was going to be a physician. Although no one expects the high school student to choose a career, and it is expected that even the choices he may express are tentative and subject to quick change, the student knows that the choice is in the future and there is no way around it. And that is the point: regardless of how he may view the prospect of college and career choice, he knows what is expected of him. The students who look to the future with eagerness, as well as those who do not, accept what society has told them to accept: to plan on being or doing "a thing" in life.

By the time the student is in high school, he knows the difference between labor and work. A large number of students experience school as labor: an imposed set of tasks, predetermined by others, that the student must perform. At the same time his output is accompanied by boredom and the sense of unrelatedness or indifference. Buxton's (1973) study of a very large number of high school students confirmed what many had long intuited: a large number of students, almost regardless of their level of performance or background, report a massive indifference to their school experience. Reading Buxton's book engenders a *deja vu* reaction, because so many of the high school students' descriptions of themselves are similar to those of factory workers. The force of Buxton's conclusions is confirmed by the more recent report of a committee of the President's Science Advisory Board, headed by Dr. James Coleman. The title of the report is *Youth: Transition to Adulthood* (1973). Their view of the high school scene leads them to recommend that the high school student should no longer be required to be in the school building each day for nine months of the year, but that he should spend a fair portion of the school year in an educationally meaningful work experience. This was not a recommendation for disadvantaged or racial or ethnic groups who find high school a trying and failure experience. On the contrary, it was a recommendation for all high school students because student indifference is so general.

We cannot avoid asking the question: is the trend toward disaffection among children from highly educated families a relatively recent development in our society, or has it long been the case that such students experienced high school as a monumentally boring experience? When I discussed the question with highly educated mid-life professionals, there was general agreement that their high school experiences in classrooms were far from satisfying or challenging. There was always a teacher or two they could recall whose class was distinctively interesting, but overall their memories were of routine and pressure relieved only by satisfying relationships with peers. As one person put it: "We were almost always learning what teachers said we should learn, what we *had* to learn if we were college bound. I think we did it willingly, not because it was interesting but because it would get us to where we wanted to go. I don't think it ever occurred to me to rebel, or even to question what we were doing, because that would mean questioning whether I wanted to go to college and obviously I wanted *that*. So when you ask me what kept me going in high school, it was that I wanted to be something and if sitting in dull classrooms was the price, I was more than willing to pay it. Like Latin, for example." Time and again what came through in these discussions was a belief in a desirable future or, perhaps more accurately, that if one played the game one could count on a desirable future.

In the past decade I have talked at length with many high school and college students. The question I put to them was: tell me what high school is like. (With college students in a seminar on education I routinely ask them to write a short paper on their high school experience.) There are marked similarities between what students and mid-life professionals report. But there are some obvious differences. First, the students challenged the wisdom and authority of school personnel, a challenge frequently expressed in action. They tended not to be passive accepters of traditional practice. Second, they expected high school to be personally rewarding, in that they would be allowed freedom to pursue their interests, and they bitterly resented "my imprisonment." In short, they were unwilling to accept high school as a necessarily boring interlude to a more desirable future. It would be wrong to see this as a youthful inability to delay gratification or as a hedonism antithetical to sustained work—although I have no doubt that this was the case with some students—because the foundations for their argument were surprisingly congruent with those of many scholars and critics. Third, there was an undercurrent of pessimistic anticipation that what they experienced in high school would not be dramatically different in college, although they clearly hoped this would not be the case. Fourth, they bitterly resented the pressures for grades and their panic-like reactions before, during, and after the college application period. They considered the college application process as demeaning and corrupting, the hallmark of a crazy society. They resented having to play the game, and many of them already knew that the process would be repeated in the future if their career goals required going to graduate or professional school.

One does not have to regard these students as sages and informed critics of schools and society to conclude that the college-bound student of recent years articulates values and attitudes differing from those of students two or more decades ago. Put more cautiously, they articulate and act on values which have been held by previous generations; they have fewer internal constraints against voicing these values, in large part because these values have been expressed by many people in the larger society. They have taken seriously what they have been told to take seriously. But what they have taken seriously runs headlong into an educational system which requires them to prize these values at the same time they feel they cannot act on them. They feel required to keep an eye on the future at the expense of satisfaction in the present; they are asked to labor now with work in the future as the lure; they are told of the limitless ways in which they could spend a rewarding working life.

After listening to young people talk about their high school experiences (and the picture of a civilized concentration camp is conjured up in one's mind), the question arises: what permits them to withstand the experience? For one thing, they believe that high school is a time-limited era in their lives and that once they are past this hurdle they will have more independence in college away from their families. Many of them will not look with enthusiasm at the prospect of further academic work and pressure, but the prospect of a new environment structured socially, academically, and architecturally quite differently from their high schools piques their curiosity and expectations. The transition from high school to college is like beginning a new career, containing as it does the dynamics of a rejuvenation, i.e., that congeries of feeling associated with youthful optimism and energy, and contrasting sharply with feelings of apathy, boredom, and confinement. A second factor which makes high school tolerable is one which will loom large and crucial in their future working lives: feeling part of an interpersonal network of peers, characterized by intimateness, openness, and the sense of mutual support. The network may be small or large, but it serves the purposes of diluting feelings of isolation, providing a sense of social worth, and influencing and supporting a shifting, coalescing sense of identity.

From the standpoint of the student, the *experience* of high school (like the adult's experience of work) is far from divided into two areas of experience: the academic and the social. On the contrary, the experience intimately involves the academic, the social, and the familial. That is to say, the "conditions of work" which we ordinarily and arbitrarily distinguish from "work" itself are always part of the fabric of the student's experience of high school. They are not background. Indeed, what the student complains about is that the high school's view of "work" violates his sense of and need for an integrative experience, rather than one which divides him in two: student and person. Whether or not this is a realistically based complaint, whether or not this is the young person's desire to shape rather than to be shaped by his environment, and whether or not it is a reflection of that youthful yearning for wholeness and growth, are important issues; but, in the long run, their significance resides in the fact that, for young people, the fragmentation of living into unrelated, and even antithetical, segments is, and will continue to be, unacceptable.

This, undoubtedly, is not a new phenomenon in our society. What is relatively new is the degree to which adult society has inculcated and reinforced in young people these attitudes and values in regard to the goals of living. If young people take a somewhat dim view of their schooling and society, it is in large measure a reflection of what they have absorbed from that society. If young people are more articulate than earlier generations about the authenticity and relevance of traditional institutions and their representatives, and if their view of their future has dysphoric hues, it is not because of any superior wisdom or insight, but rather their assimilation of, and accommodation to, messages from the larger society. To look at young people as if they live in a world apart from adults—as if, in fact, they have a "culture" different from that of those who surround them—is again to make arbitrary distinctions which have no justification in social reality. This is not to say that young people do not differ from older people, but the very fact that both groups are part of a common culture insures certain communalities and continuities. For example, young people do not (as the larger society does not) question in the abstract the value and goals of education; they question (as the larger society does) the adequacy and relevance of traditional ways of implementing these values and goals. They do not question that they should do or be "something" in life, but they may question when the fateful decision should be made. That is to say, they want to find themselves," to explore and sample in order to feel certain they have chosen their career well, but they do not question the need at some point to make the one life–one career choice.[1] The college-bound high school graduate looks to the future both in traditional and non-traditional ways. Much of him bears the stamp of the traditional culture; there is a small part of him which contains new seeds of cultural change, the growth of which will depend, as it always does, on external events and forces.

Earlier in this century it was safe to say that the directional seeds of change depended on what happened within the larger society, meaning within our national boundaries. This, obviously, is no longer the case, as it has become clear that changes elsewhere in the world quickly and inevitably affect our society. As individuals and as a national collectivity we know we are not, if we ever were, master of our fate and captain of our soul. *Indeed, the perception that this momentous change has taken place is one of the* major factors producing in young people a sense of *cynicism, resignation, anger, and rebellion.* After all, how can one reach out enthusiastically to the future, how can one unreservedly commit oneself to a long-term course of action, if there is evidence that one's future is as predictable as a snowflake's descent in a storm? The fact is that these disturbing thoughts are far from front- and center-stage in the attitudinal stance of most high school graduates. But these thoughts are in the drama, and their potential role in the evolving script cannot be lightly discounted—especially when one is not sure who or what will determine its future shape.

The College Years

If, in the last two years of high school, the major question is one of choice of and acceptance by colleges, the college freshman soon learns that all that has gone before was leading to an even more fateful question: What do I want to be? And how does that answer determine what courses I take and what major I should be thinking about? Two de-

[1] I cannot estimate their numbers, but there are some young people of high school age from educated backgrounds who would prefer to have nothing to do with schooling or making a commitment to the one life–one career imperative. Some do not go right on to college but work around for a time before returning to school; some never go on, to the consternation of their parents. Among college students the number of students who do or would like to depart from the conventions of schooling and *a* lifelong career is not miniscule (and neither is it for many older people in the society). In each instance there is no difficulty in pointing to psychological or personality factors as playing etiological roles, but to stop there as if such factors are unrelated to the socio-cultural context is a form of egregious psychologizing, especially if there is the possibility that what we are attempting to understand is a general or growing social phenomenon.

cades ago these were not such momentous questions, because the curriculum in the first two years was more prescribed and confining; i.e., there was little choice, and electives were few. Today, however, the freshman has far more choice. He is frequently given "credit" for some of his high school courses, and, depending on his scores on college entrance tests, he may be given "advanced standing." These changes in the early college years are, of course, a reflection of societal events and changes in societal values: challenges to traditional authority in all traditional institutions, the emphasis on personal expression and autonomy, as well as on the importance of experience both relevant to social issues and individual development. The need for authenticity is not only a private one; its fulfillment, ideally, has to mesh with the building of a more just society. What individuals want for themselves they require of society's institutions; authentic "wholeness" is not possible when mind and society are contradictory forces.

Colleges and universities—heretofore seen as islands of reflection and reasoned exploration, repositories of man's past wisdom and accomplishments, and the safeguards of man's potential for human progress—came to be viewed as Luther did the Papacy. Many universities had theses nailed on the doors of their administration building, and chief among them, Luther-style, was the demand for the elimination of bureaucratic obstacles between the individual and his relationship to intellectual salvation. As a consequence of that period students came to have more autonomy and, therefore, more choice. But gaining the opportunity for greater choice produced its own problems. On the one hand, by permitting the student to explore and sample, it enlarged his knowledge of the fantastic number of fields and careers potentially available to him, a consequence of how the post-World War II knowledge explosion got translated into the structure of the university. Increased choice piqued and reinforced curiosity, fulfilling one of the university's major aims to "liberate" the student's mind from the confines of parochialism, to help him perceive the many and wondrous ways in which the human mind attempts to understand man, his works, and society. (If not all students experience the liberation, there is no doubt that many of them do.) On the other hand, however, this expansion in possibilities dramatically increases the difficulty of answering the question: What do I want to be? The student is aware that there are many "things" he can be, that there are many directions he can go, that there are many areas he would like to explore but will be unable to within the confines of four college years. Two factors, one internal and the other external, set drastic limits on how he thinks about choice. The internal factor is that *he* feels he has to make *a* choice, that from the smorgasbord of possibilities he will be able to choose only *one* career dish. The external factor is that the college *requires* him at some point to make that choice, to commit himself to a "major," essentially to specialize. The opportunity to sample and explore is drastically reduced. From one standpoint, the student who knows when he comes to college or very early in college, what he wants "to be" is spared the conflicts explicit in choice. But even among these early deciders one frequently sees doubt and indecision as their experience and horizons force them to reconsider and justify their choice. It is not surprising, therefore, that in recent decades so many students take time out during college, or resist going on immediately to a specialized postgraduate program. Let me illustrate this point and obstacles to perceiving it by describing one of our interviewees:

Fred attended a small but prestigious liberal arts college. Both of his parents were highly specialized professionals. When he came to college he intended to be an English major because of his interests in creative writing. He had been editor of the high school paper, but his writing interests were in the creative rather than the reportorial realm. After his first semester he became very interested in botany, so much so that he decided to transfer to a large university which offered a much wider array of courses and relevant facilities. He pursued botany seriously, always doing extremely well in his courses, but during his third college year his interests enlarged to include the broader aspects of ecology, population dynamics, resource use and allocation. These were by no means separate interests. In some not so vague way he saw them all as interrelated. His parents hoped he would go on to medical school or, at the very least, gain a doctorate in a specialized area of interest. But Fred had one other interest: travel. Whenever he could, on his own or with parents, he would go off on a trip. He went to some lengths to emphasize that these were not vacations, escapism, or a pleasurable way of goofing off. As best I can gather, he had a list of places on this earth, derived from voluminous reading, that he wanted to visit and know. Some were in this country but others were in foreign lands. He had already been to some of the foreign spots with his parents. At the time I interviewed him near the end of his final year he was in a quandary about what to do or how to think about the following year. The contents of his quandary were not simple.

1. There is one foreign country he has longed to visit. If he doesn't do it now, he fears he may never do it, taken up as he will be either by graduate school or a job.

2. He feels unable to make up his mind about what kind of graduate program he would want to enter. Medicine is out. Botany does not encompass all of his interests, and neither does the usual program in ecology or population dynamics.

3. He would like to experience what the political arena is like, not because he has an interest in politics, but to get a better understanding of what happens when people try to have an impact. One of the things he has considered is getting some kind of job or affiliation with a legislator who has an interest in issues of energy resources and population growth.

4. He gets a profound satisfaction in doing things with his hands, e.g., carpentry, car repair. "I would like to try getting that kind of work and see how I feel about it." Apparently, this had nothing to do with the derogation of the intellectual life or an identification with values of "working" people. He just thoroughly enjoyed that kind of activity.

5. When it became known in his small town that he would be without a job after graduation, the principal of the high school asked him if he would like to teach a course on ecology, although he could only be paid a pittance. Fred was intrigued with the possibility, less because he had an interest in becoming a teacher but more because he felt it would be a very interesting experience.

6. Throughout college he had continued his creative writing, submitted several of his pieces to a variety of magazines, and one of them not only had been accepted but he had been paid for it! He wanted to continue writing, although he knew it would bring little or no income. When, at the end of the interview, I asked him what he would do if the world was organized to allow him to proceed as he wished, he replied: "I would like to try each of the things we talked about, although that might require a good part of my lifetime. And yet I want to settle down and I know I will have to."

If I presented all of my two-hour interview with Fred, there would be no difficulty in convincing the reader about several things: life had been easy for him (he recognized this); his parents up until two years ago were generally supportive of whatever he did in or out of school and encouraged him in his diverse interests; he loved his parents, felt guilty about his dependence, wanted to be autonomous, and yet felt (and wanted to feel) tied to them; Fred was embittered about the way the world was organized. In short, depending on one's personal and conceptual biases, you could conclude that Fred was an indulged, immature young man who did not want to face the realities of living and the need for choice, i.e., he wanted to eat his cake (with delicious icing) and have it. Indeed, Fred would agree partially with such a conclusion, if only because he was aware that this is how many people would view him. It would be the most senseless form of "sociologizing" to see Fred independent of personal–familial–developmental dynamics, losing in the process the distinctiveness of his personality, family, and home setting. But it would be equally senseless to indulge "psychologizing" to the point where one fails to see Fred other than as someone with a *personal* problem, i.e., as if *his* problem is his failure and in no way may signify a legitimate and positive response to the traditionally perceived future. But, it could be argued, nobody is blaming Fred alone. His family has played a role, as have his peers and the academic culture; and if I were to present the details of his love-life, one's penchant for psychologizing would be mammothly reinforced. Fred could easily be presented as a clinical "case," and not without some justification. However, all of this psychologizing too easily avoids several questions of potentially momentous significance for our society. Is Fred distinctive in having diverse interests and talents? Is he distinctive in wishing to test himself in a variety of careers? Is he incorrect in his belief that his unwillingness or reluctance to commit himself *now* to one career direction, far from reflecting a personal weakness, is adaptively preventive of future life problems? How would we think about Fred if his experience of conflict (within himself and between himself and society) about choosing a single career is not only general among young people but in a different form is a poignant problem for older generations? Has our society been changing in ways which have made dysfunctional the cultural imperative of one life–one career?

Fred was in no doubt about society's one life–one career expectation, but *he was unaware of the degree to which he agreed with society*. Fred wanted to settle down, he wanted to be able to commit himself to one career, but he felt unable to make the choice *now*. He fully expected he would be able or would be forced to make *a* choice in the not too distant future. In fact, it was because he felt he would have to make the fateful choice that he deeply wanted to satisfy his non-career interests: travel, carpentry. He never put it this way, but the thrust of his remarks was that the fateful decision inevitably would mean that parts of him would likely forever be in a state of "latency." It came as something of a revelation to Fred when I pointed out to him that his thinking and feelings reflected his agreement with society: he could be either *a* or *b* or *c*; he could not be two or three of them over his lifetime. Surprisingly, and unlike many others whom we have interviewed, he did not immediately raise all the realistic obstacles to what I said, but rather he felt relieved (and then excited) by the idea that he was not necessarily faced with something akin to a zero-sum condition, i.e., by moving in one direction he could never move in another.

In Chapter VI I described the guilt feelings in some highly successful professionals who wished to change their work, the guilt stemming from their perception of a discrepancy between their own and society's view of how they experience work. It was guilt mixed with a sense of personal weakness because they were not feeling the way they once did and always expected to feel. At a much younger age, Fred, accepting the one life–one career imperative, was having similar feelings. In part, Fred would agree that he was "a case," that the problem inhered only or primarily in him, and that once he "solved" the problem of choice, *that* problem would be forever out of the way. If that conclusion was not as valid as Fred would like or society asserted, he was in no position to make such a judgment.

One does not need a Fred to discover the one life–one career imperative, or that the problem of choice has deepened with the exponential increase in the number of possible careers, or that important choices are rarely, if ever, made without trace of doubt or reluctance, or even that individual needs and societal structure are frequently opposed to each other. The significance of a Fred is what he tells us about the power of this imperative and the foundation it provides for the way the educational system is structured, a power which transforms a social structural issue into a personal problem, i.e., it is a problem *in* Fred, some kind of failing on *his* part, and the validity of the imperative remains unquestioned. But a Fred suggests still another possibility which goes beyond, although it is contained in, the one life–one career issues: that is the emerging dominance of the value that one owes it to oneself to test and not to stifle interests and talents; to deny the priority of society's needs over those of the individual; to be true to what one can or wants to do and not what society says one can or should do. When Polonius told Laertes to "be true to yourself" he was talking about the ethical or moral domain of action. What I am suggesting that Fred is telling us is that he wants to be true to himself in terms of his interests and talents, that both he and society would be "wrong" to let parts of him go to seed.[2]

In at least one respect Fred is very atypical of many college students, which further illuminates how societal structure and dynamics aggravate the process of choice by further undermining whatever validity may have existed between opportunities for young people and the values they have absorbed. Fred's parents can and will financially support him in almost any career direction he chooses, probably regardless of how materially insecure that direction may appear. Fortunately for Fred, he not only seems to have the talents and academic record for his many career interests but these interests are in areas where employment is not hopeless. One does not have to be an economist to grasp the dimensions and consequences of what has happened in recent years in our society, and will continue for some time to come. Numerous career possibilities (e.g., languages, teaching at all levels) have virtually disappeared, and there are very few professions,

---

[2] After reading this chapter a graduate student said: "I think there is a clearer way of making your point. Why couldn't you say that more than ever before young people have been told that they are or could be Renaissance people. We were told in six thousand different ways all the things we could experience and be, and not only was this world a new one but it was also *ours*. And weren't we told (broad smile!) that we were brighter, wiser, and more sophisticated than previous generations? And we should get as much out of life as possible, and how much we got would depend on us? That the worst thing that could happen to you is for your grasp to be less than your reach?" If this student was agreeing with me it was, I hope, less because I was directing his dissertation and more because what I had written made sense out of his own experiences.

old or new, which do not have a surfeit of candidates. The effects on the college population have been profound, and it would be an egregious mistake to see them solely in terms of economic security. On the surface, of course, they are anxious about earning a living; that is the immediate problem. But not far from the surface is a cynical despair, a semi-articulate anger, and a bewilderment about a situation in which they have been made impotent, forced to give up cherished values about work and living, and, fatefully, robbed of the opportunity to choose according to such values as authenticity, personal expression, and multifaceted experience. The smorgasbord of career possibilities has become a sparse cooking table and the agonies of choice (tinged now with the delight of nostalgia) have been replaced with accommodation to the one life–one career dish, assuming one is lucky. How long this depression-like economic period will last is a worrisome matter because its length will determine how many millions of young people will come to view their short pasts as a "come on," as a cynical mind-expanding invitation to a mind-confining future.

The present economic situation is, unfortunately, a splendid example of how a society can ignore its historical realities until events force it to recognize them, i.e., it operates in a realm of values and action until it is, so to speak, hit over the head by those realities. Since World War II we have proceeded, and we have certainly transmitted the message to our young, as if our society had learned to avoid its economic yo-yo tendency, the Great Depression being a relic in the museum of conquered and extinct horrors. Today, an addition to the museum is required. Analogously, our society has proceeded as if the one life–one career (like the one life–one marriage) imperative is and has been normative and adaptive. That the cultural and educational rhetoric has long considered it normative cannot be disputed; that this rhetoric is being seriously questioned is also beyond dispute. Take, for example, the very recent (Wirtz, 1975) report "The Boundless Resource" by the National Manpower Institute (that was given such a big play by James Reston and the editorial board of the *New York Times* on Dec. 7, 1975). If I am critical of certain features of the report, this should in no way dissuade a potential reader, because it is an important, refreshing, and even eloquent statement, and it summarizes a variety of data in a compelling way at the same time that it emphasizes the mischievous inadequacy of reams of available educational and employment statistical data.[3]

[3] *Work in America* (1973, 1974) is another book that deservedly received a good deal of attention and acclaim because it so thoughtfully summarized a vast literature and emphasized the weaknesses of certain methodologies used to obtain people's feelings about work. But like the Wirtz book, *Work in America* pays little attention to the highly educated groups I have been discussing. The omission is a culturally significant one because of what it implies and reinforces about the experience of work of highly

At the beginning of the report there is a statement of a value which epitomizes what young people in recent decades were told and accepted:

> An education–work policy is not one that misconceives of education as having for its purpose the preparation of people for work. Rather, it includes this purpose as part of education's function of preparing people for life, of which work is one part; it takes full account of learning as a human value in itself. Nor is education conceived of here solely in its institutionalized sense.
>
> "Work" is similarly used—not in any narrow vocational sense, although, again, it *includes* vocational values as an important aspect of work. It refers not to a given but to a changing function, and it refers to labor not only as a unit of production but as a human value.
>
> The other point to make clear is that the prospect suggested here is not fully perceived in terms of what it takes to make a system or society function. Such perception is essential, but as a means not an end. To identify the human resource as an essential ingredient of systemic growth is in no way to confuse the priorities of individual and institutional interests. The superior claim on reason of this different growth concept is that to develop people's capacities more fully inevitably increases their prospects for *a higher, better, and more satisfying life experience*.

Several pages later this value is stated somewhat more concretely:

> A next order of business is working out the arrangements—by no means simple, yet not all that hard—for permitting and even encouraging those young people for whom it makes sense to build a considered break into their academic sequence; so that they move out of school for a year or two, occasionally even longer, and then move back in. One of the most interesting recent developments, its implications still little recognized, is the tuition-refund practice being followed by more and more large corporate employers. Under this practice, employers reimburse workers for the tuition costs of work-related study.
>
> A more basic change is called for in the nature of the adult experience. To an extent considerably exceeding our realization of it, most of us take work as a given, something that exists and develops as the consequence of forces outside our control. In this sense we think of it differently from the way we think about education. Education we recognize more as within our jurisdiction, and so to be adjusted to work. This concept of work is wrong to begin with, and stands in the way of fully rational education–work policy-making. Because the changing nature of work is insufficiently recognized, the tendency is to develop vocational and even career educational planning around meanings that work may already have lost.

---

educated, professional people. Percentagewise these people are a minority and economically advantaged, but if as a group they are experiencing satisfaction from work as problematic, the consequences for the rest of society are or will be disproportional to their numbers in society. This is a major conclusion I illustrate in Chapter X, where I discuss the professional in community mental health centers.

The short of it is that some kind of provision for interspersing the earning and learning of a living, for interweaving employment and self-renewal, is going to have to be recognized as the essential condition for an effective career as worker, citizen, or human being.

These prospects are only barely suggested by what has been thought of so far in terms of adult education. There are, to be sure, impressively large figures, in the tens of millions, for the numbers of adults taking courses of one kind or another that come within this description. A significant amount of this is going on, and here again it will be this already developing experience that offers the basis for future building. But on closer scrutiny it turns out that the very large part of what is covered by these impressively large figures is either (1) training taken to improve people's competence in whatever they are already doing, or (2) some comparatively narrow and superficial exposure to essentially peripheral interests. Both are important. But they don't even touch on the really basic elements in this situation.

. . . We haven't the vaguest notion of the number of people (only that it is exceedingly large) who come—someplace between the ages of twenty-five and fifty—to a point of significant realization that they ought to be on a different career course, not just as a matter of boredom or frustration or some kind of whim, but as a calculated judgment about improving their worth both to themselves and to the whole system. Sometimes this conclusion is the dictate of external circumstance: A machine is doing now what the individual had been doing before. Sometimes it is merely the delayed effort to find out more than was clear the day after graduation (or some less dignified academic exit) what the individual's real capacities—and interests and desires—are. Perhaps even more frequently it is a case where years of on-the-job experience have brought a person to the point that a year or so of special training would mean an enlargement of his or her value.

It is a strange system that makes no provision for the educational renewal opportunities which would give these midcareer decision-points the meaning and significance they ought to have. Nor is there any good or sufficient reason for this. In other comparable countries there are now fairly full developed arrangements, provided by both practice and law, for promotional leaves of absence for those who have spent some considerable time in the work force. There is precedent elsewhere, too, if there are to be periodic cycles of unemployment, of institutionally arranging for an expansion of educational and training programs during periods of recession and of contracting these programs when the demand for labor increases.

It is hard to imagine anyone disagreeing with the way this value is put. Numerous studies are cited justifying the need to recast the one life–one career imperative, but throughout the report there is a healthy awareness that available data are either ambiguous in their meanings or downright misleading because of the superficial context of concepts and values that gave rise to them. But there is one major blind spot in the report that I will point to in light of the following statement from it:

Most of the change described here has been viewed from the standpoint of forced job shifting or of reentry into the labor force. This is an obviously limited, and therefore limiting, perspective. For many of us, the most important aspects of lifetime change result from other forces than the pressures and stresses of a churning economy. Once we lift our sights to accommodate this reality, the present structure of lifetime educational opportunity in this country emerges clearly as not only inadequate but primitive. For, besides help in adjusting to a changing job "market" or in getting around blocked avenues of job progression or in making the jobs they've got more gratifying, we need the kind of help that will enable us to make the most of the *positive* changes in our lives—most notably the availability of increased leisure time in our middle and later years. The time has come to enlarge the perspective of the present adult education system in the United States to take in this larger horizon.

According to conventional wisdom, youth is the appropriate time for instilling in civilization's contemporary representatives all that is worth knowing from the storehouse of knowledge accumulated by representatives past. This premise needs to be reexamined. The broader knowledge base the society desires to impart, and may require for its survival, has been loaded so much on the youth years—one year of learning after another—that for many young persons education becomes a chore of life, a mean obligation more than the grand opportunity. In consequence, more and more people are concluding that a spacing out of education should be available to the young who are, in their own current terminology, being "spaced out" by overdoses and that "stop-out" privileges should be offered along the way. But it is equally important that consideration be given to adulthood's stifling monotonies. Stop-out opportunities for youth make sense. So does the option to "stop back in" later, as adults.

The assumption implicit in the defense of basic educational values has always been that living in the present is enhanced by an understanding of the wisdom of people who lived before or who have lived longer or have simply thought more. Putting all "utility coefficients" aside, this assumption is valid for people seventeen, thirty-five, or fifty-five, if it is valid at all. Whatever its hour, life is always precious. Advanced insight into why things are as they are, why individuals are as they are, what life offers and how it is secured, how other peoples and races live and think—such capacity for cooperation. It doesn't diminish this ideal to recognize that the growth potential of the society and its economy seems encouragingly less finite in this context than it does if we concentrate our thinking solely on the earth's available physical resources and consider the exponential rate at which they are being consumed.

One would expect or hope in light of these words that this very important report would have looked searchingly into *all* occupational levels or categories, from the lowest to the highest. But there is hardly a word devoted to the highly educated, professional segment of our society, obviously a very large and growing one. What the omission does is reinforce the view that it is only among blue- and white-collar workers that the one life–one career imperative is no longer functional or adaptive. How can one fault a report which talks so eloquently and cogently about the self-defeating divorce between the worlds of work and education, about the plight of disadvantaged groups, about the dead-end work situations of so many millions of our citizens? And when one reads the concrete and long-overdue recommendations at the end of the report (leaving no doubt as to what segments of the population the report is concerned with), one can easily feel guilty about pointing to this omission which, after all, involves those who by objective economic and educational indices seem "to have it made." One should not feel guilty. The omission indicates, at the very least, an incomplete understanding of how our society has changed so as to affect the nature of work for everyone. As long as we see the problematic nature of work primarily in terms of social class we are misreading the pervasiveness of social change in our society. And that is what is at stake: The validity of our understanding of what our society has been, is, and may be, and the nature of the dynamics powering social change. The report is quite correct in its criticisms of society's toleration of economic, racial, and sexual inequalities and how they dilute and frequently extinguish the individual's sense of productive and meaningful living, infecting the entire society with a creeping malaise. But the report is singularly lacking in its analysis of what has created this malaise and how this has affected *all* major segments of society. There is the implication in the report that unless we drastically recast our view of the relationship between work and lifelong education for the less privileged parts of society, the quality of life in our society will further deteriorate. There is, of course, truth to this assumption, but it is not the whole truth. If, as I have argued, work has become problematic for highly educated, professional people—and taking into account their influential role, their effects on the entire society, and their present and future numbers—we must be wary both of solutions which virtually ignore these groups and of the social analysis from which such solutions derive. I shall return to this point in a later chapter, where I shall suggest that to the degree that work has and will increasingly become problematic for these groups, everyone else in society is adversely affected, i.e., they have been negatively affected by societal changes and in turn they have become a cause of or contributor to the malaise. I must emphasize that my criticism of the report is not that it pays only glancing attention to certain groups but that the neglect suggests a superficial understanding of the social forces (within and without our society) powering social change. Despite this, the report deserves the highest praise for the clarity with which it articulates and justifies the personally and socially self-defeating consequences of the one life–one career imperative.

Attitudes about Career Choice and the Subsequent Enlightenment

The assimilation of culture, starting as it does from one's earliest days, provides us with knowledge and values essentially defining us as individuals as well as the nature of "reality." All of this takes place with an efficiency of which we are unaware and prevents us from recognizing that what we regard as "natural" in the social order and social life is an achievement of culture and not the culmination of the wisdom of the ages or the only and best of all possible worlds. One should not be surprised that the one life–one career cultural imperative should appear "natural" and that its constraining consequences for individuals (as in the case of a Fred or older professionals I have described) so easily get transformed into guilt or self-criticism. The significance of the report of the National Manpower Institute is that its articulation and questioning of the imperative strongly suggests a social change leading to its weakening. This, of course, is not the first time the imperative has been questioned; but it is, to my knowledge, the first such statement to have the imprimatur of well-known public figures, and to appear with such public recognition. If only because the report pays such slight, substantive attention to the highly educated segment of our society, I turn now to observations of and conclusions from our interviews with college students grappling with career choice, as well as interviews with those who, professionally oriented, have made a choice and are receiving professional training. I make no pretense of discussing all aspects of such choice, but rather those which illuminate the cultural imperative. What I will describe and discuss derives from well over a hundred interviews in three colleges. Two of them are liberal arts colleges, drawing students from similar high socio-economic backgrounds but differing markedly in size, setting, prestige, and location. As measured by conventional academic and intellectual criteria, their students would by group averages differ, but the degree of overlap is sizable. Different interviewers were used in the two settings. With the few exceptions I shall note, the contents of the student reactions to our questions were remarkably similar.

The third college was quite different: primarily non-residential, drawing largely from the local community, and tailoring its programs to young men and women coming from essentially working-class backgrounds. It could be called a private four-year "community college" struggling to maintain academic standards, and at the same time trying to exist by adapting to the needs and capabilities of what may be described (non-pejoratively) as a serious, not well prepared, pool of non-liberal arts students. I shall discuss this third college after the first two.

A number of students had already taken a semester or more off or were planning a hiatus before applying to graduate or professional school. In almost all instances where "time out" had already been taken, the reasons had a surface plausibility in that the experience was clearly educationally enhancing. But also on the surface were three considerations: it was an experience very much desired in its own right, it was seen as a way of crystallizing and narrowing the choices for a career, and it was powered by what I can only describe as an "If I don't do it now, I'll never do it" attitude. In fact, it was the last attitude—reflecting a kind of thirst for new, stimulating, self-illuminating experience—which seemed unusually strong. Take it when you can get it before the world starts closing in on you—this was the impression one got from listening to some of the students. I do not wish to convey the impression that as a group (they were a minority of all the students interviewed) they were a worried, unhappy lot viewing the future with marked concern (although some did), but rather to suggest that they had more than an intuition that options for self-determined experience would diminish in the future. There was in their report of themselves the belief that if they could maximize *now* the range and depth of their experience, their more restricted future would be made more tolerable. (When I offered this interpretation to my college seminar, one of the students looked at me as if I was from another world and said: "But isn't that what we are always being told, that we had better take advantage of life *now* before we *settle down,* making it sound as if when we go into the real world we won't settle down, we'll start to *sink?*")

Statistics are not required to prove that in the last fifteen years the "time out" phenomenon during the college years has increased exponentially. Boredom, poor performance, lack of interest, and disdain for college life are a few of the negative reasons—negative, of course, from the perspective of the college and larger society. And there are, as I indicated above, positive reasons. Although the reasons, positive and negative, are quite diverse, these are, for the most part, students trying "to find themselves." Is it not ironical that the phrase "to find himself" or "to find myself," suggesting as it does the search for *the* essence, for that psychological core which when found gives one *the* answer to *the* road one must take, was uttered by so many young people at that period in their lives when society was requiring them to make *a* choice? It is more than a coincidence; it indicates how well the

culture has instilled the imperative at the same time it suggests that
the potential for recognizing and resisting the imperative is there. But
what light is shed by our other interviewees, the large majority of
whom never took time out? With few exceptions, they longed to be
able to take time out in order to pursue their interests and dreams, to
take distance from themselves and schooling, to reflect on where they
are and where they should go, to experience the presumed joys of
self-determined activity, to say "no" to the "rat race," and to postpone
having to make final choices. Here again I am not trying to conjure up
a picture of depressed youngsters, bemoaning their fates, or beating
their breasts in misdirected fits of frustration (although a few fit the
picture). The dysphoria was of a muted sort kept in check by hope, the
satisfactions of comradely living, the occasional vibrant experience of
personal and intellectual growth, and the less frequent sense that the
vague, amorphous future was taking shape and, like a magnet, drawing the student to his destiny: to the work which would give meaning
to living.[4] This caveat, however, does not lessen the significance of the
enormous value students put on "self-realization." They fear entrapment: as life goes on their options for new experience will drastically
decrease, as will their ability to withstand being narrowly molded by
society's demands.

It was striking how "natural" it was to these students to give the
highest priorities to autonomy, self-realization, and personal authenticity. My noting this may seem strange to some people who would
say: "Isn't that exactly the way you would want them to scale their
values? Wouldn't it be strange if they thought otherwise?" The point is
not a "should" or "ought" one, but rather that such priorities are on a
collision course with the one life–one career imperative (and, I must
add, the one life–one marriage rhetoric) and, more obviously, the increasing bureaucratization of professional work. For example, one of
the interview questions was: "Have you ever considered a career in
business, finance, or industry?"[5] The fact is that the students' spontaneous answers to the question were quite similar and unambiguous:
you would be a small cog in a wheel, it takes a long time to get to the
top; it can be morally corrupting; it is hard to be yourself. That the
large bulk of these students had never contemplated such a career is
less noteworthy than the vehemence with which some of them dero-
gated the possibility. But the significance of their replies lies in a
confusion between a fact and an assumption, or between hope and

[4] The interviews were conducted between 1973–1974, before the *full* impact of the
worst recession since the Great Depression seeped into student consciousness.

[5] In the more prestigious college almost all the interviewees were headed for careers in
medicine, or law, or to careers requiring an advanced degree; this was less the case in
the other liberal arts college.

reality. The assumption is that their criticisms of careers in business, finance, and industry are not valid for careers elsewhere. The fact is, as so many of our midlife professionals related, that professional careers are increasingly lived in large, bureaucratized organizations, and individual practitioners find themselves hemmed in by rules, regulations, and forces beyond their control. One can argue about the *degree* of discrepancy between assumption and fact, but one is then conceding that our students' perception of what has happened in our society contains a large dose of ignorance. I shall return to this issue later when I discuss our interviews with medical, law, and graduate school students.

Why are so many of our interviewees seeking careers in medicine and law, and what light does this shed on the one life–one career imperative? Almost without exception, these careers were viewed as increasing options and flexibility as to life's work. From one perspective, their choice was similar to that of "choosing" to go to college: they were approaching medicine or law as a cluster of known and unknown career possibilities from which they would make a final choice. Entering law or medical school essentially postponed the final adaptation to the one life–one career imperative. In a number of instances, the students verbalized the virtue of postponement; medical or law school was another refuge in which they would have time to wrestle further with what they wanted "to be." (This stance was more frequently verbalized by those planning to go to graduate school.) But what was behind the very frequent assertion that going into medicine or law gave them great flexibility as to what they could do over a lifetime? "In medicine (or law) you have a variety of ways you can use your training"—this typified what students meant by flexibility. Is one justified in interpreting this as a dim awareness that in whatever aspect of medicine or law they might start they may not want to continue and would look to a new career or kind of work, albeit under the rubric of medicine or law? On the most cautious level of interpretation, one could say that as a group they were prepared for the possibility that they might wish to do a lot of different things over the span of their professional lives, a preparation opposed to the one life–one career imperative. If one views career in terms of labels, then this interpretation is not justified. However, if one ignores labels and pays attention to what people do, how they think and feel about what they do, and how all of this relates to fantasied and actual change which will or does require them to see themselves differently, to be doing new and different things and to be occupied with new and different problems and people—this perspective, I think, comes much closer to what these students meant by flexibility. In this connection the replies of our interviewees to another question are relevant. The question was:

Have you heard or read about the "mid-career crisis"? Without exception, the students knew about the mid-career crisis, and in the case of the prospective law and medical students, they assumed they would be able to deal with it by moving in one or another new direction in these fields. They all hoped they would be lucky and avoid it, but if it occurred, they would shift their directions. Not surprisingly, the depth of their understanding of the mid-career crisis was not great, but it was a concept or possibility in their consciousness. It was a concept quite explicitly related to their fear that they would be entering fields which would require an enormous amount of further education, time, energy, and money; that they would be subjected to a finely honed molding process; and that in the process they might change *as individuals* in undesirable ways. It was rarely clear what these undesirable ways might be, except that they would become different kinds of people who essentially (and unwittingly) "sold out." (Their relative inarticulateness on this score is in striking contrast to their articulateness about why they never considered a career in business, finance, or industry!) From these interviews, it is hard to avoid the conclusion that many of these students were already anticipating threats to their personal authenticity, autonomy, and growth. Here must be noted a feeling expressed by a number of all of our students from these two colleges. There was anger, resistance, and bitterness at being "forced" to make career choices at this point in their lives. Even some of those who, in the initial stage of the interview, spoke with certainty about their career choice would, later, voice doubts and resentment at the lockstep educational process which too easily restricted their range of experience. On the surface, the bulk of our students did not sound like Fred; the more one probed, the more their similarities to Fred appeared. Directing blame onto society was undoubtedly facilitated and exacerbated by their anxiety about getting into medical, law, or graduate school. There was more than anxiety; there was a bitterness at the competitiveness, the waiting, the injustice inhering in a situation in which they might be blocked from pursuing their goals—not because they lacked the credentials, but because of the scandalous discrepancy between the numbers of openings and applicants. They were, so to speak, beginning to become experts in some of the dimensions of the individual vs. society polarity. I have no doubt that if we had asked the students directly how they felt about the one life–one career imperative (i.e., whether they agreed with its rationale, or if it was the basis on which they constructed their lives), they would have denied its validity, both on a personal and a general basis. And yet, faced with the possibility that their entry to a particular career would be blocked, many of them felt their worlds were coming to an end. We did end the interview with this question: "Imagine that you will live for the next one hundred years, and you had a choice of dividing it into four careers. What would they be?" First, I must note a kind of joy (it was not amusement or fantasy play) with which they took to the question, as if they recognized instantly that they wanted to be more than one thing, that there were different ways they could experience life. It was surprising how many of the students did not include on their list the career choice they were decided on and were already preparing for. What was not surprising was the number of choices in which the element of competition was small or non-existent and in which the experience of novelty would be frequent. For example, and again reminiscent of Fred, a career which maximized travel was very frequent. Travel came up spontaneously in one other question which had to do with the satisfactions the students expected from pursuing their career. Having the means to travel, particularly among the prospective physicians, was a frequent response. I do not think I am far off the mark when I suggest that these students see themselves as they see the world: a wondrous complex of stimulating possibilities to be explored, experienced, and savored. My travel agent has the slogan: See the world before you leave it (which is why, I presume, he is seldom around). The students seem to be saying: I want to experience *all* aspects of *me* before it is all over. Is it any wonder that so many of these students view the future with a subdued dysphoria, as if they have already had the best years of their lives, as if they must now give up exploration of themselves and the world and "settle down"?

A puzzling finding. *Not a single pre-medical student said he was going into the field to help people, and very few of the other students expressed such a motivation.* Our questions as well as the ambience of the interviews permitted such idealism to be expressed, but it was conspicuous by its absence. It could be argued that far from being puzzling it was a symptom, and an inevitable one, of the change which occurred in the society at large and among young people in particular as a reaction to the turbulent sixties and the demise of the hope that "we shall overcome" social inequities, cant and rhetoric, and stifling tradition. There is, of course, truth to this interpretation and, in fact, a few of the students expressed disappointment that they had missed those exciting times. It follows from this interpretation that the students are being "realistic," that they are living in times inhospitable to movements for social change. This interpretation is, I think, too simple, if only because it assumes an identity between personal and social idealism. Compared with students in the sixties, the current crop is seemingly less concerned with remaking society, but if one examines the personal values powering student activity in the sixties, one finds little or no difference between the groups. The rhetoric of the students in the sixties abounded in themes of new life styles, personal autonomy and growth, and authenticity. Let us not overlook that although in those times some students sought a fusion between personal and social idealism, there were others who, on the basis of the same values, opted out of society. Indeed, those who sought personal salvation other than through participation in social–political activities were not small in number. From this perspective, the differences between the student generations have been exaggerated, and a case could be made that the personal values which came to full public view in the sixties are no less present today. Precisely because of the changed societal picture, conflict with society has sharpened, albeit in a less public way. Once these personal values become detached from social reform, the antithesis between these values and social organization—one manifestation of which arises in the process of career choice—takes new shape. Put another way, the social idealism of the sixties had behind it a personal idealism; it was not only pointed to changes "out there" but to desired changes within, to new opportunities for self-exploration and self-development. If "stay loose" was a guide to action, it was also a perception that committing oneself to one lifelong pursuit was a trap and a kind of symbolic form of death. Our interviewees also want to stay loose on the basis of values similar to those held by students in the sixties. From this perspective, the degree of difference between student generations in the expression of social idealism is not so puzzling, because then, as now, they were struggling in phenotypically different ways with genotypically similar values. If today's students are more explicitly concerned with these values and, therefore, with themselves, one should not make the mistake of concluding that the conflict between them and society has disappeared, a victim of the need to accommodate and survive. There is that aspect to the current scene but, at the same time, such needs exacerbate the conflict between both society's demands and its restricted range of opportunities, on the one hand, and the individual's struggle to see a future amenable to a multifaceted existence, on the other. As I pointed out earlier, the loud sixties amplified the muted themes of the so-called silent fifties. Those themes are no less present today, and how they will be re-expressed in the future is not predictable in its details. One can assume, however, that it will involve contradictions between individual dreams and impersonal social reality, and between a differentiated set of self-defined potentialities and the confining societal opportunities for their expression.

Now let us turn to the community-college students who differ in so many ways (e.g., background, academic potential, intellectual orientation) from the students in the first two colleges. Although not all of them came from modest or impoverished backgrounds (they were, as in the other two colleges, primarily white), the bulk of them came to college after several years of blue- or white-collar work. Several of them had committed crimes and had been in jail. None had anything like a distinguished high school record. The impression one gets from their reports of their pre-college years is that they not only did not know where they were going, but also that they did not know where they were. The reasons for finally deciding to go to college were diverse, ranging from insights gained while in jail, to acceding to parental wishes that they "become something." Unlike the modal students from the first two colleges, these students came to college to acquire marketable vocational competencies, e.g., in business administration, law enforcement, applied psychology, health services, hotel management. One could snobbishly call this college a "trade school," but that would be unfair both to the college's intentions and the students' expectations. In fact, it is their awareness of how much weight society puts on degrees and professional labels that, in large part, powers their desire for a college education and sustains them in the liberal arts courses they are required to take. One can characterize these students as those who "want in" on the so-called good life, and they want in rather desperately. Many of them had far more than a semester or a year of "time out," and their reasons were quite different from those of the students I saw previously. They are ready to "settle down"; they are more than willing to do so, if society will only have a niche for them. Their career goals are modest and narrow, and yet they expect from these careers everything the other students hope for. The one life–one career imperative, directly or indirectly, is not a concern. The bulk of them did not know what the mid-career crisis was, and they had difficulty (when it was explained to them) thinking about what they would do in such a situation. If I earlier characterized the first group of students as naive about certain aspects of societal realities, I would have to say that the community-college students were even more so. They are seeking status, autonomy, and a sense of growth. They are unaware that their undergraduate program, comprised as it is of vocational and liberal arts courses, will not be viewed with enthusiasm by a society increasingly credentialized, ever responding to the pressure to "raise standards." Consider two facts: some of these students are in college only by virtue of federally funded programs for disadvantaged youth, and a fair number of students are in programs gearing them to positions in one or another of the program descendants of the war on poverty. What happens to these students when they find no position in a time of economic retrenchment and are forced to take positions similar to those they had before college? Or, if one's temperament is on the positive side, what will happen to those who obtain positions and then find themselves second-class citizens in the professional community? We are discussing students whose expectations have been raised, and we are not talking about small numbers. In the past two decades, as a matter of public policy, there has been a deliberate attempt to make higher education available to such students, promising them in the most explicit manner that only through such education will they be able to partake of the good life. The rhetoric was exemplary and it was powered by federal monies in what seemed to be a society of endlessly expanding opportunities. Today the rhetoric is less shrill and federal monies less flowing. When expectations have been dramatically raised for a large segment of the population who heretofore had few reasons to hope, then frustrated, there is a tendency for these expectations to be transformed into a social dynamism producing social change. And history provides no assurance that social change is always for the betterment of man.

Most of our community-college students, even though all were white, were kin to that much larger pool of youth about which the report of the National Manpower Institute is so concerned, and for whom it pleads so eloquently for society to recognize how this "boundless resource" must no longer be viewed within the one life–one career imperative. If policy makers are showing signs of recognizing this, one must hope that they will also recognize how well our culture has instilled the imperative in those it seeks to liberate.

Before going on, a caution is in order about some of the generalizations I have made. Any conclusion or generalization must be of a limited nature, if only because the college population is heterogeneous on many internal and external factors. To a certain extent, a conclusion is time-limited in its applicability as a major change in the larger society occurs, e.g., a serious economic downturn. Precisely because the college students are at that point in their lives when they are about to enter society, they are sensitive to the winds, indeed, the breezes of change. There is a more subtle limitation which the reader may have picked up, particularly in the discussion of the students in the first two colleges. The picture I painted contains some seemingly contradictory elements. If not contradictory, there are discordant tensions among them. For example, most of my interview with Fred led to the conclusion that he objected strongly, both to constraints on his interests and talents and to the requirement that he "declare" himself and make *a* choice. It was not until the end of the interview that he spoke about the part of him that wanted to settle down. Similarly, again in the initial phases of the interview when we focused on the different career possibilities students had considered in college and their current career plans, we would get a statement of intention which far more often than not contained no doubts, giving us the impression that the one life–one career imperative had been learned well. As the interviews went on, however, the doubts and anxieties about the choice tended to emerge, not, as I have emphasized, with forthrightness or agonizing breast beating (although that occurred in a few cases). A final example: I characterized these students as (amazingly?) naive about both the bureaucratization and bigness of the fields they were planning to enter, and how these could be obstacles to meeting their goals and being consistent with their values. And yet they knew about the mid-career crisis and were sensitive to the fact that the force of a society is to mold them in accordance with its conventions, values, and style. In short, depending on what part of the interview one read, or the particular bias one had, one might come away with a slant somewhat different from mine or that of others who conducted interviews. It is relevant here to report some of our reactions of "surprise," not only to our interviews with students but to all other individuals and groups interviewed by our project team. The first surprise reaction was to the ease and duration of interviewee response. They talked, and only occasionally did we feel that some thought, feeling, or idea was being suppressed. Frankly, we expected some people, perhaps half, to be open with us, and the remainder to be on guard or reticent. We were not prepared for the uniformly spontaneous and revealing talk. The second surprise reaction was to the way almost every interviewee (student or otherwise) thanked *us* at the end of the interview, a typical concluding remark being, "This has been very helpful. It forced me to think about things I have not thought much about. I really pulled a lot of things together." The fact is that we were never helpful in the sense of giving advice, providing information, giving reassurance, or alleviating anxiety—although at times we were sorely tempted to do so. It would be sham modesty to deny that we were skillful interviewers and very good listeners, although the skill inhered not in how we asked our simple open-ended questions (which many elementary school children could easily have done) but in getting elaborations and clarifications. That is only a part of an explanation, and not a terribly important one. Another part is that all our interviewees were volunteers (we were rarely turned down) who were told: "We are interested in how students make career choices [or in the case of older groups we would say we were interested in how they experienced their work]. There is no hidden agenda." I have no doubt that the major factor making for openness and candor was that we were asking them to talk about something of enormous personal importance. Indeed, I think even with less skilled interviewers a good deal of the information would have been obtained. Obviously, I am suggesting that to the extent that there appear to be some inconsistencies among some of our conclusions about the students, I do not think they are, except minimally, an artifact of the interview or interviewers, but rather an accurate reflection of where these students are in their lives. These are students who quintessentially have incorporated the old and the new values of their society. On the one hand, they have been taught and learned well the one life–one career imperative, and, on the other, they have been exposed to and incorporated values in conflict with the imperative. Those are not new values in our society, but following World War II they, so to speak, came into their own. The conflict has many aspects, only some of which the students can articulate. In a cultural-history sense the students are young; in the sense of being products of a particular culture, they are also old. What is culturally new in them confronts institutional traditions and practices which, at the same time that the confrontation exacerbates and even sharpens conflict, produce the agonies of ambivalence, the fear of being courageous, and a degree of understandable fuzzy thinking. There is never a one-to-one relationship between values and actions. It is relatively easy to get agreement on a verbally stated value (e.g., "One should realize one's potentialities") but the high degree of agreement quickly dissipates when you try to get agreement about what actions are consistent with such a value. Between values and actions is a universe of alternatives, and choosing among them is the most fertile ground for controversy. As a group the students have little difficulty explicating some of their values and their conflict-producing relationship to the very narrow range of alternatives society permits them. To a degree they can articulate certain values, particularly the "new" ones, but they are less able to articulate the "older" values our society has inculcated in them from the day of their birth. The old and the new are in our society and, inevitably, they are in the student, to a far greater degree than in older segments of society. If the students feel in conflict with themselves and with society, it is also true that, in relation to values, our society is in conflict with itself and, not infrequently, with college students.

Medical, Law, and Graduate Students

Now let us turn to our interviews with medical, law, and graduate students from various departments in the university. Our interviews came from students in three medical schools differing in size, academic reputation (i.e., research reputation of the faculty), internal competitiveness, and location. We also conducted interviews in two very different law schools. However, the observations and conclusions I will present are based on far more than these interviews, because in the past several years I have made it my business to keep in touch with undergraduates who went off to medical, law, or graduate school. In addition, in the course of my visits to different universities I have met and talked with scores of post-undergraduate students, and whenever possible (it was not difficult) I steered the discussion to the subject of how they were experiencing school and what they were planning. Far from infrequently, students indirectly brought up how they were seeing themselves as budding professionals, at which point we were off and running.

Medical and law students cannot be grouped with graduate students for at least one major reason: when a student decides to go to graduate school he not only applies to *a* department in that school but almost always to *a* particular program in the department. Many graduate departments ask (which has the effect of requiring) the student to declare the program of his interests. The student does not have to stay in that program, but if he or she has begun work with a faculty person in that program, and especially if the student is receiving financial support *because* he is in that program, switching to another one is psychologically and diplomatically no easy affair. In contrast, medical and law students are admitted to a school, not a department. A few may feel certain about the aspect of law or medicine in which they will specialize; some "think" they know; many admit they do not know. This is in keeping with their belief that one of the virtues of these professional schools is that you are exposed to experiences in many fields and even if you make a particular choice, you are able later in life to shift to another aspect of law or medicine. Graduate students, in contrast, are aware (and many were aware as undergraduates) that although they can "practice" their specialties in several different settings, shifting to another special aspect of the field will be very difficult. For example, the student who is headed for graduate work and a career in mathematical psychology knows before he begins that if he ever decides to shift into clinical or social or child psychology, he will be starting a new career. I am reporting what students think and feel. Medical and law students are comforted by the belief that, in their training and beyond, they will have more career options and flexibility than those in most other fields—and people in those other fields tend to agree. The degree to which this is objectively the case is quite another matter, as we will soon learn.

Medical and law students, unhesitatingly and despairingly, declare that the most overwhelming feature of their experience is the necessity to acquire information—facts laid upon facts glazed with more facts. One might call it knowledge, but the important thing is the students' dawning awareness of the difference between knowledge and wisdom, and in some instances this awareness is terrifying, not only because all this is a continuation of their undergraduate experience but also because they fear "this is the way it will always be." Students' sense of competency is only minimally bolstered by how much they know in a book, classroom, or laboratory sense, if only because they know of the wide discrepancy between what they know and what they need to know. Far more important to the sense of competency, stimulated by all kinds of fantasies from the communications media, is how well one performs in the role of physician or lawyer, a role they really never experience in training. Surprising to us was the frequency with which students reported belittling behavior by faculty and more advanced students. For example, a number of medical students told us something akin to the following: "When I began to go on the wards and to the clinics, I was made to feel as if I was in the way, or that I didn't exist. And when I was allowed to *do* something with a patient, the intern or resident would usually say something critical, making you want to disappear." Law students similarly reported how fearful they were to engage faculty in discussion, particularly in class, because of the tendency, witting or unwitting, on the part of some teachers to demonstrate how illogical, superficial, and hopeless were the students' ideas. (This is in startling contrast to reports of the experience of graduate students.) The reader may wish to discount these student reports by a large fraction, but what cannot be discounted, in my opinion, is the increasing sense of incompetence which students experience, judged by *their* perception of what they know and can do, on the one hand, and what they feel they should know and be able to do. From one point of view this would be viewed as a healthy state of affairs, i.e., one could say, "Thank God they know they know so little." But what students are saying has relatively little to do with "healthy" modesty or humility and more to do with a serious narcissistic wound to their hopes, expectations, and values. Autonomy, exploration, curiosity, authenticity—these were their cherished values, and instead they feel dependent, steered, and fraudulent. In the case of medical students, they expected to be exposed to many new experiences and challenges culminating in the sense of competence and approximating society's reverence for the healer, and they were, but the consequences were different from expectations. In the case of law students, they early on become quite knowledgeable about the differences between law and justice, facts and truth, as well as about the amazing capacity of the human mind to be inconsistent and to twist facts so as to conform to self-interest. As one student put it: "The body of law is impersonal, and our job is to make it meet our client's personal needs, regardless of our personal needs and values." Whether or not this is a fair or wise statement I cannot say, but it does point to the law student's fear of inauthenticity, i.e., that the pressures to force him to act against his own values, confirming one part of society's ambivalence toward lawyers, are real and strong. The chances of "selling out" are not seen as miniscule.

There are exceptions to what I have described, and for many students there are gratifications and satisfactions. One of these satisfactions paradoxically confirms the general picture the students paint at the same time it explains why depressive hues are relieved by more pleasant ones. More characteristic of medical than of law students is social encapsulation, by which I mean the formation of peer groups (of varying size) the members of which work and socialize with each other, providing all sorts of supports, not the least of which is toleration of the frustrations and fears of its members. "Socialize" is an appropriate term, but it does not convey the fact that almost always (and the wives of married medical students will say *always*) the social function becomes a protracted discussion of "work": now and in the future. It is on these occasions that all the agonies and ambiguities of career choice are re-experienced; the one life–one career imperative reasserts itself. The students tend not to be aware of the reassertion as they think of the onrushing future. Depending on what year they are in, they have been exposed to diverse aspects of their field, but the exposure to any one sub-field has not been extensive, albeit it was sufficient for many students to decide what sub-fields they will not go into. Phenomenologically speaking, law and medicine are not really seen as "fields" or careers but rather labels covering an array of specialties, any one of which can become a career. They are studying law and medicine but, early on, external pressures interact with internal ones to require a decision about what kind of lawyer or doctor one will be, and those pressures are based on the imperative that one should make that decision because one cannot be A *and* B—more correctly, one may be A and B but the chances are very high that you will be a poor A and a poor B. Students are aware, of course, that you can be A and *then* B but this tends to be put in the realm of fantasy when they consider how much time it will take just to be an acceptable A. What I am suggesting, of course, is that what has died is the myth that law and medical schools vastly increase your options and flexibility. In one sense this is true in that the student is exposed to new knowledge and new fields, but it is far less true in regard to choice of field or career.

The pressure to choose is rarely a matter of interest alone: "Am I more interested in A, B, or C?" The complicating factors are reflected in these kinds of questions: "Will I be as good in A as in B or C?" "If I go into B and for one or another reason it doesn't pan out, will it be harder to get out than if I go into A or C?" "Should I forget about A, B, and C and go into D, where the chances of getting a good placement are higher?" And in a few cases this question is clearly articulated: "I really don't like medicine (or law). Rather than thinking about A, B, or C, maybe I should get out and try something else, or just get any kind of job which gives me time to think. The longer I stay here the harder it is to get out." There are students, I assume, who make a choice relatively unbothered by indecision, reluctance or subdued fear. I say "assume" because, as in the case of the undergraduate, the longer one talks with them the more their fears for the future emerge. In most cases, however, the process of choice is a bothered one. However, their anger or resentment or anxiety are far more controlled than was the case with the undergraduates. There is, rather, what I can only call a kind of subdued sadness in some, an anxious vigilance in others, and a passive resignation in still others—reactions which can stand side by side with and be obscured by high hopes and belief in lucky stars. That is to say, they want to feel they are on the right road and that they will make the right choice, and when they make that choice the disturbing thoughts are pushed well into the background, albeit temporarily. A former student of mine, now a lawyer, to whom I had sent an article of mine (Sarason, 1975) in which I said that our society has made it easier to change marriage partners than to change careers but the dynamics are the same (if not identical), wrote me the following which I quote with his permission:

> . . . The marriage–career bit is interesting and certainly true in my case. But have you forgotten our discussions when I was a Yalie and then at the law school and I was trying to decide whether I should marry _____ ? I bring this up because I think what you are saying is just as true for your first marriage as it is for your career choice. Sure I loved _____ but what drove me (and you?) crazy was that I felt I could probably love a lot of other girls. I knew that if we got married it wouldn't be a smooth course, and I remember how guilty I felt by that occasional thought that if it didn't work out, we could end it. Law was a final choice, not marriage. There was so much about _____ I loved but there was always that nagging doubt: would it work, would we be happy? You were the one that pointed out to me that that was the same kind of problem I was having about what I wanted to do in law. I am sure you remember [my mind is a blank on this : SBS] how much I was like one of Neal Miller's rats in an approach–approach conflict. I wanted to go into constitutional law, but I was also enthused about labor law, and in the background was my feeling that if I really wanted to help people I should go into what today they call consumer law. In those days I called it fighting injustice. I haven't changed my field, although I'm tempted to, but _____ and I did split.

My former student is illuminating more than the differences in strength of the cultural imperative as between marriage and career. In Chapter II I indicated the unreality of conceptualizing the experience of work as if it were not part of a life fabric, as if an individual's experience of work did not contain in the most conscious ways what was experienced in other areas of functioning. That is to say, if we define work or a career in terms of labels denoting what people do or how they think about what they do, we can never recognize how much of the experience of work we are overlooking. For example, I have been using the labels "medical and law students," and I assume that the reader has some knowledge of what these students *do*. It would take a large volume to describe in detail what these students do and the changes which occur as they move through their training programs, but I am safe in assuming that by using these labels the appropriate imagery is conjured up in the minds of readers. My former student's letter should caution us that we are leaving something out, and that is love, e.g., for parents, someone of the opposite sex, or a friend, or children. Many of our students were married, or living with someone they loved, and it was not infrequent that both man and woman were pursuing different career lines. How these students experienced their "work," the personal significance it had for them, their approach to their careers, the location of their first job—in regard to each of these, the student's love relationship with another person was a factor, part of that seamless web which is obscured by dividing experience arbitrarily into separate components. In some instances the process of career choice seemed uncomplicated by the intimate relationship (which is not to say that the choice was uninfluenced by it). In other instances the nature of that relationship—its tensions, conflicting interests, attitudes toward style and level of living—very much complicated the student's approach to choosing a career. As one student put it: "I'm glad I'm married to _____. I love her. She has done a lot for me. But, frankly, I did not realize how being married to her would enter as it has in my deciding what to do." Or, as one of the women medical students said: "I have been having troublesome thoughts. You see, when I began living with Perry, I hoped we would get married some day, and I know he felt the same way. That was when I thought I would become a pediatrician, go into practice with somebody so I could have time for a good family life. I would have a good income which would take the heat off Perry because as a _____ his income would obviously be O.K., but nothing to write home about. Then things began to happen: I was as good a student as anybody, I got interested in _____, and two of the professors said I should go into that field. I'm toying with that, and were it not that it probably would mean I would have to go for training where Perry would have a rough time getting located, I think I already would have made up my mind. Really, I don't know. One day I'm going into _____, the next day I'm backing off, and Perry is always in the picture, although he is only part of my indecision." This young woman is not only illustrating the workings of the one life–one career imperative, as well as the way in which intimate relationships are part of career choice, but the ever-increasing frequency with which professional women are experiencing the travail in career choice. The growth and articulateness of the women's liberation movement have made this a well-known problem.

I would suggest that in similar ways men have long experienced the problem. That is to say, the experience of career choice has rarely been independent of the influence of love relationships. If we have thought otherwise, it is because of what we wanted or were told to believe, as well as of those internal and external contraints which have made men less than candid and researchers more than naive.

For those medical and law students who envisioned their professional lives as characterized by autonomy and never-ending professional growth, the years they spend in training make it difficult to sustain such a view. Briefly, they are brought up short by the facts of organizational bigness and complexity, on the one hand, and the ever-increasing societal constraints on the individual, on the other. They are unaware of how quickly they gave up the fantasy of the individual practitioner, but they are not unaware that they entered fields which, if not jungles, are arenas of competitiveness, "image making," and status seeking, in which it will be a long time before they have other than a bit role. If they had no real understanding of "organizational man," they rather quickly gain it. And if it ever occurred to them, they would admit that they had a good deal in common with those who entered business, finance, and industry. If they thought that the competitiveness and anxiety connected with getting into medical or law school were a one-time insult to personal integrity and the canons of justice, they find themselves in two or three years re-experiencing those days, now in connection with getting into a "good" law firm or a good internship. Far from having their need for autonomy satisfied, they continue to find themselves in states of dependency, and they begin to sense that this may always be the case. For most students these problems are not momentous; they are nagging notes in the background that occasionally intrude into the foreground of thought. But they are there. For other students the intrusion is frequent and poignant, accompanied by the sense that one "has had it," leading in some to self-blame and in others to a derogation of their profession or a sick society, or both. It is among these latter students that the one life–one career imperative can be extraordinarily difficult.

If you listen to medical and law students, they leave little doubt in your mind that they feel they have grown and changed. This feeling has little to do with possessing greater factual knowledge or technical skills (of which, objectively, they have few) but rather with the sense that they understand, as they never have before, some of the workings of society and what is required to withstand, or defeat, or avoid entrapment in that society. They see themselves as pragmatists by necessity, not by choice. They are still hopeful that luck will be on their side. They look to and reach for the future, frequently with some eagerness, but with a degree of anxious vigilance far greater than that which they brought with them to their professional training. Every student is aware of the disjunction between his or her sense of competence and what they are expected to do or to be like in their professional roles, a disjunction making for "privacy" because "success" is not attained by, and society looks unkindly on, professionals who proclaim their ignorance and limitations. Candor becomes an easy victim, and the separation between public and private "image" starts to widen, as our mid-life professionals reported.

Let us turn now to our graduate students who are very heterogeneous, coming from such fields as psychology, biology, history, political science, etc. They were all pursuing their doctorates. This heterogeneity makes generalization difficult and dangerous, but several generalizations can be made with a fair degree of security. One such generalization is that for about a third of these students graduate school had been a kind of "holding pattern": it would give them time to "really" decide what they wanted "to be." This is not to say that they had been uninterested in the graduate field, but rather that they were unprepared to make a lasting commitment or had not been able to start in the career of their first choice. The majority of students, however, were in graduate school because it was their first choice.

Unlike medical and law schools, which are professional schools, graduate schools are research training centers (although less than in earlier decades), the Ph.D. certifying that the individual has met the criteria for doing independent research and scholarship. The dream of the overwhelming number of graduate students is to do significant research which would be recognized, thereby facilitating appointment in a college and university where they can continue their research and teach the coming generations. To be a professor means that one has something to profess, and the Ph.D. is the union card which is necessary for a possible faculty appointment. The dream founders on certain realities. First, there is the frequent conflict between the research a student would like to do and that which his faculty advisor or other teachers think he ought to do. That is to say, a professor is not likely to commit himself to a student whose research interests are tangential to his own. This may be because the professor recognizes his lack of expertise in regard to the student's research interest or, more likely, he gives priority to students whose interests are more similar to his own. It is by no means infrequent that a student cannot find a faculty member whose interests are similar to his. The situation can, indeed, get complicated if the student is being paid to participate in the faculty member's research project and finds himself uninterested in what he has been asked to do. There are, of course, students who experience none of these conflicts in their research experience and training, but they are a minority. Most students experience some degree of conflict between what they would like to do and what they are "told" to do, or "advised" to do. If many graduate students feel alienated from their research, it is in part a consequence of these kinds of conflict. Not only is the student's need for autonomy frustrated but the cherished values of authenticity and growth continue their search for expression.

Medical and law schools have done a good job in convincing themselves and their students that their programs require a fantastic amount of the student's time, more than in other fields. Medical students, in particular, can go on at length about the duration of their working days and weekends. If this is true, it is less true than is thought, as many graduate students will attest. Someone once described graduate school as a road mined with a series of obstacles where at any one point there is not one but several. There are courses and there are short and long papers for each course; there are qualifying and comprehensive examinations which require encyclopedic knowledge (not possessed by the students or most faculty members); there are language requirements which almost all students see as the exam tail wagging the graduate dog; and in lieu of these language requirements some departments graciously allow substitutes no less time-consuming and anxiety-arousing; then, of course, there are the literature reviews for the write-ups of research projects; and, finally, there is the doctoral dissertation which is a career in itself—so that one of my colleagues, when a student comes in to discuss his prepared dissertation project, routinely says: "And now we will take up the differences between a dissertation and a career." I have no desire to challenge medical and law schools' belief in how extraordinary are the time demands on their students. For all I know, they may well be tied for first place, but I am suggesting that whoever is in second place is not far behind. The point, of course, is that graduate students spend a good deal of time satisfying the demands and requirements of others, with the result that many of them ask themselves: Is it worth it? When does it end? Will there be an end? These questions take on added force as they learn about the culture of the university, e.g., the promotional ladder which frequently does not exist, the publish-or-perish dictum, the omnipresent internecine warfare, the way universities vary in the non-research burdens put on their faculties, and the modest income of young faculty members. It is no wonder that the future plans of graduate students can change radically in short periods of time as their eyes are opened to the realities of university life and organization. As the eyes open to the realities of their training in particular and the university in general, some of the students for whom graduate school was a holding pattern leave, if they have a viable alternative; for the others feelings varying from concern to obsessiveness mount as they approach the job finding stage. "Will I find the kind of job which will allow me to do the kinds of things I *have* to do if I am to be happy?" At this stage students find themselves thinking about and accommodating to job possibilities other than the university, a bitter pill for most to swallow.

What happens when catastrophe strikes? When the possibilities are high that you may not even have the opportunity to conform to the one life–one career imperative because of a severe economic downturn? Medical students articulated how comforting it was that they would have no problem earning a decent living in medicine, which is why some of them finally chose that direction. Law students were less relaxed, nervous but nevertheless on the relaxed side. With graduate students the situation is seen as calamitous, as indeed it is. Some leave graduate school as they see their field shrink before them; others seek to prolong their graduate training in the hope that the black clouds of economic disaster will lift; all are bitter and resentful that they were, so to speak, fired from society before they could resign. As one insightful student put it to me: "At age 26 I know what forced retirement must be like."

In reviewing what I have said about medical, law, and graduate schools, and in thinking about how to summarize, a question intruded into my thoughts, and the more I toyed with it the more helpful it seemed to become. Have I not been saying that what happens to these students is analogously similar to what happens to children who are seeking and are provided answers to sexual questions? More specifically, when as a result of the child's curiosity he or she asks sexual questions (e.g., about birth, origins of sex differences), the answers which are provided are both satisfying and unsatisfying, in the sense of Murray Levine's dictum about "problem creation through problem solution." By providing an answer, new questions are stimulated. But more than cognitive questions are stimulated as the child's concrete imagery enlarges and transforms the nature and scope of what he is interested in. Exposure to biological realities is never an emotionally neutral experience to children and, precisely because of the way children think, the exposure has upsetting consequences as they wrestle with the personal–familial imagery which the new knowledge has stimulated. As we know both from research and clinical experience, many children react strongly against the new knowledge. Outright rejection of the new knowledge; excessive curiosity and/or obsessiveness about the answer and its implications; anger, resentment and bitter disappointment about self and parents—these are only a few of the strong reactions of children. One might say that in the pursuit of knowledge and bodily pleasure their eyes (literally and figuratively) have been opened up to a complexity for which they did not bargain. The little boy may want to be a boy in a bodily sense, but he may also want to be like girls in a psychological sense, and this is no less true for girls; neither boy nor girl can comprehend the overt and covert pressures requiring them to be only one thing both in a bodily and psychological sense. The cultural imperative regarding sex-role typing is potent indeed.

The students I have been discussing have had their eyes opened to the realities of the university in society, and as they approach the end of their training, they know they will be dealing directly with a complex, personal and impersonal society. They have had many of their questions about the university and society answered, and if some of the answers were satisfying, others clearly were not. They also received answers to questions they did not ask, either because it did not occur to them to question what seemed obviously true, or because they quieted earlier fears by depending on hope and luck. A prime example of this is the answer or message conveyed to them in numerous ways: decide what your "specialty" will be—or worse yet, decide which problem in that specialty you will concentrate on—because professional security and success depend in large measure not on competence but on *special* competence. There is another part of the message: of course you should learn and know as much as possible about all aspects of your field—you must avoid the trap of knowing more and more about less and less—but you must also face the reality that what makes you marketable is your specialness. Shades of the double bind! The double bind is not only a characteristic of the external message; it becomes a feature of the individual's psychological makeup steering him in two desirable but incompatible directions. There is always a part of the individual that desires to accede to the one life–one career imperative, and there is also that part of him that finds it constricting; the conflict sharpens as the institutional and societal pressures pose another kind of choice: decide within your field on that part of it which will give you your professional identity, that will allow you to say to yourself and to society, "I am A. I am not B, C, D, or Z." In modern society the route of the one life–one career imperative, and its offspring of specialization, is efficiency, just as in business and industry the value of efficiency of operations is wedded to "rationalization of roles and functions" to produce the most complicated tables or organizations on which each person can find his little box (with help).

If anything can be concluded with assurance, it is that by the time the student has finished his special training, the soil for career development already contains the seeds of desire for career dissatisfaction and for career change. When and in what ways these seeds will show themselves are not predictable, depending as that does on a host of internal and external factors; nor does this mean that when the combination of these factors rechallenge the validity of the one life–one career imperative, the consequences for the individual are always psychologically debilitating. Adverse consequences should be expected to be the rule, if for no other reason than that the longer one has been embedded in a career and a social–familial–economic context, the harder it is to face and make the difficult decisions, as our mid-life professionals have told us. To extricate oneself from the confines of any cultural imperative is never easy; on the contrary, these imperatives, powered as they are by society's conservative tendency to maximize continuity and minimize change, have been so well learned by the individual that *his* internal makeup contains the major barriers to actions counter to these imperatives. This is true for our students, but it appears to be less true than it was for previous generations.

The next two chapters are concerned largely with people in midlife. The distinctiveness of Chapter VIII, by Dr. David Krantz, lies not only in the career changers or career dropouts he describes but in the locale: Santa Fe, a magnet for such people. Chapter IX is a fragment of my autobiography, presented not for its importance but as a means to raise questions about how we ordinarily define and view a career.

VIII
The Santa Fe Experience

In Search of a New Life: Radical Career Change in a Special Place

David L. Krantz

A FEW WEEKS AGO, a local newspaper carried this item: Prominent New York Banker Turns Waiter. The story was brief. It told of the banker's meteoric success and his present job as a waiter in a ski resort hotel. The item's placement indicated that it was not of great moment. It was tucked away on a back page as a filler. Its sole value seemed to reside in that it was not a blank space in a sea of newsprint. Although such items now appear infrequently, there are good reasons to expect that they may become more of a commonplace in the future. Here are a few of the trends that lead me to this futuristic prediction:

Since World War II there has been an explosion of new fields and career possibilities. These fields have created a burgeoning group of professionals in our work force. Yet, for all these possibilities, individuals remain generally fixed in the societal prescription of "one life–one career." What happens to the individual who gets bored or seeks to broaden his one career option? Change is not easy. Increasingly, these new career options require more specialization and training. Even if the individual should seek further education, he would likely find that the available training facilities are already oversubscribed. And this very insufficiency of training opportunities may have been one basis for his seeking a career change; being unable to initially obtain the necessary education, the individual may have had little choice but to settle for his second or third career option. Working a lifetime in a less than acceptable career choice is truly problematic.

165

Another impact of increasingly educating our work force is a heightening of expectations. Higher education tends to underline such values as: work should be meaningful; the individual should experience satisfaction and fulfillment through his work. The absence of these values has provided one major source of dissatisfaction among blue- and white-collar workers. Although it is often believed that the highly educated professional is immune to the dissatisfactions of his less well-trained colleagues, there are indicators that the professionals' world of work contains similar difficulties. That the professional experiences such problems is suggested by the increasing trend of his changing careers within and between fields. The coupling of the professionals' expectations of satisfaction in work with the rising frustrations stemming from difficult mobility, second choice careers and lack of fulfillment can produce a potentially explosive situation. Unless the future world of work changes to meet the expectation of the rising number of professionals, or those expectations are modified, radical career change may become an increasing option. For a banker to turn waiter is a reasonable response to the discrepancy between high expectations and their lack of fulfillment in the work setting.

This analysis is only a bare outline of what some professionals now experience and what can be expected for the future. The shape of their present experience, as prognostic of the future, assumes clearer proportions if we attend closely to those back-page items about radical career changers. Their stories should have, I believe, front-page headlines, for they speak, right now, to at least as important an issue as war, taxes, and state visits. They speak to our common dilemma of how do we define our lives.

To make this statement has taken me about fifteen years of self-reflection about my own career which has surfaced as a research project. It is this study on radical career changers, like the banker turned waiter, to which I shall shortly turn.

But first, let me go back some fifteen years. At that time, I was just beginning my career as a teacher of psychology. I had read a similar news item about an eminent college professor turned construction worker. I didn't understand why anyone would give up such an esteemed position for so minor a life station as "construction worker." For me, my career contained infinite possibilities and challenges. I was well educated and felt in a position to exert control over my work, life and future. Why had this college professor given up the opportunities that now awaited me?

The simplest and most adequate explanation that I could provide to this question was that the professor had some "personal problems" which led him to this choice. This explanation of fifteen years ago still is plausible, but with one important reservation. Where I had implicitly attributed his radical career change to derangement, kookiness or craziness, I now see that this attribution masks the real issue. I have come to understand that while such changes are truly personal problems, they yet reflect universally shared problems about work and life. While one may question the rationality of changing a career, it is but one of many possible more or less reasonable solutions to the problems which all of us "normals" share. The fundamental difference between those of us "normals" who stay in the trajectory of our lives and careers and those who choose to change that direction, is in the solutions chosen, not in the problems themselves. For an individual to change the direction of his life and work, is to raise for each of us the question of what is the meaning of work and what provides the definition of a life. It is all too easy not to confront these issues by relegating the person to the category of "personal problem" and to the back page of our minds.

To say that the radical career changer speaks to a universally shared set of problems is by way of conclusion. I will develop the support for this statement through the stories of three people I interviewed who chose to change their career and life. These stories speak directly to the common problems of the meaning of work, responsibility, and choice. I've chosen to present these individuals' stories in the form of literary vignettes or portraits, rather than as quantified data or clinical description. The literary mode best conveys the richness and complexity of the issues involved.

Before turning to the stories, it is important to understand the context and method of this study.

The first research problem I faced was locating radical career changers, those individuals whose existence seemed only to surface occasionally as newspaper fillers. In talking with friends, it seemed that Santa Fe, New Mexico would be a likely place to find such individuals. For me and my friends, the name of Santa Fe evoked vague memories of some person who changed his career and settled out there. Santa Fe, and nearby Taos, also projected an ill-defined mystique of communes, artists, and "dropouts." Armed with little else than this description of a place where radical career changers might be found, and the name of one contact, I left in July, 1974 for the first of three one-month periods in Santa Fe.

My contact was a long-term resident of the area. He provided me with the names of three people who fit my criterion of a radical career change. This somewhat arbitrary criterion was that the individual had established a career of at least five years duration and had chosen to change. These initial three people provided me with the names of other people. In a snowballing fashion, I made contact and formally interviewed thirty people. By using an open-ended question format, each person created his own interview. The overall direction was the same: to describe what had led to their decision to change career and what were the outcomes of that choice.

To say that the sample size was thirty would be misleading. There were many informal, chance encounters in Santa Fe bars, restaurants or shops which provided additional information and confirmation. Often just a simple mention of what I was doing opened the door to new contacts and new stories. For example, while having a drink in a local bar, I described my research project to the bartender. This led to a two-hour Boccaccio-like discussion between me, the bartender (a former Broadway set designer with an M.A. from a major drama school) and one of the customers (a former head of an advertising agency, now director of a local art gallery). Although candor and openness were seldom a problem in the more formal interviews, these informal encounters were more direct.[1] Also these informal contacts tended to occur among groups of individuals; the resulting interchange was richer and more critical than what occurred in the more formal two-person interview setting.

The stories that emerged from the formal and informal contacts were of individuals ranging in age from thirty-two to fifty-six. All were well educated, holding at least an undergraduate degree, with many having postgraduate education. A broad range of former careers was represented: stockbroker, museum director, art school professor, social worker, TV producer, insurance salesman, among others—a range of careers not unrepresentative of well educated professionals and business people in any large metropolitan area. They had given up their professional careers for the narrow work options available in Santa Fe: construction worker, farmer, small business owner, and employee in the extensive tourist industry.

Let me begin my report on radical career changers with the story of Will, a thirty-seven-year-old former social services administrator turned jack-of-all-trades jeweler, construction worker, sometimes wel-

---

[1] I was initially quite surprised at the candor and ease with which the respondents talked about their careers and life. One interviewee, a thirty-four-year-old former social worker turned construction worker clarified admirably the reasons for this openness. He commented: "This place is like a giant encounter group. We've all been through similar things. Just along this road, there are four of us, each one has changed his career. We share a common experience so we can be open. But we've all been through it, so there's no reason to be guarded. I'm not living the past or feel funny about it anymore, so I can talk about it. But try getting my friends back home to talk meaningfully about their lives—you got a good case." His use of the term "encounter group" in relation to candor is an interesting one. The encounter-group movement legitimated openness, candor and sharing as part of attaining the values of personal happiness, self-growth and awareness. These projected values for a "good life," in turn, created the seeds of expectation and often dissatisfaction for which candor would then seemingly provide a solution.

fare recipient. His story dramatically underlines a common theme among the people I interviewed: At the time of decision, they perceived that they had no other real options but to change careers.

A Bit of Holland: Will's Tale

Will's homestead was coming into view. We were at the end of a long walk in a landscape so changing and unexpected that it filled most of our conversation and thoughts. Here, tucked away in an endless dry world set in barren hills, was this verdant green valley. It was criss-crossed by large irrigation ditches. There were cows munching on the lush grass. All it needed to be a replica of a Dutch landscape was sails passing on the canals in the fields. But there was one very major difference: it was still New Mexico—beyond the opulent green valley, that only man could have made, was the stark landscape that only God could have created—foreboding Badlands, set against the high snow-capped Truchas peaks.

But it was not this landscape that had drawn Will and his wife to the area. Rather, it was necessity, a cheap place to live. Will pointed out the character of the buildings as he originally found it. One of the three houses was still in its original condition—an adobe building crumbling in various quarters with vigas exposed. The other houses, after two years of hard work, were in much better shape. One house provided a living area, the other house a studio for his wife's sculpture and Will's workshop. Originally these buildings had been a school and administrative offices on a Spanish land grant. With the state government purchase of the land and irrigation of the area, the buildings fell into disrepair. Their remains were all that Will and his wife could afford after Will had left his job as an administrator in a small Oklahoma city. After buying the houses, they were broke.

"When I left my job I was completely disillusioned. I guess I had been disillusioned all along the way. It started with my graduate work in sociology. I really wanted to get a Ph.D. But it seemed to be more an exercise in academic futility than anything meaningful. So I stopped with a Master's, with a specialization in social problems. The first job I had should have told me what I could expect for a future, but I sort of buried my head in the sand and assumed it would be different. I spent a lot of time on that first job, and even more time on the job in Oklahoma, catering to directors who wanted the clients to be and act just like them. What I wanted to do was to provide services that the people needed and wanted. But what did I do—I spent most of my time being nice to rich people so they'd support the agency. What really started to frighten me was that I was getting to be like them. In this town in Oklahoma, most people spent their time drinking, hunting, and travelling. Everybody had a fair amount of money. It was a big oil town and everybody was on the make. I got to be on the make and I didn't like what I was seeing about myself.

"My frustration must have really shown itself because I came in increasing conflict with the Board of Directors. I realized what I was doing; I had advanced in the social services field and began to understand that it was all the same everywhere. The only hope was to get a job with a big public agency in a city so that I would be cut off from this fund-raising. I was going places, but I didn't like most of the places. Finally what put an end to this whole progression was the day when a couple of the directors came into my office, sat down, and noticed that I had the *New Republic* on my coffee table. This was a bit risqué for the arch conservative Birchites. I had had it by that point and by mutual consent, neither the Board nor I being too unhappy about my choice, I decided to leave.

"Leaving was a very risky business. I had to give up a home, a good job, and a steady income, but there was really no other choice." I tried to clarify his statement that there really was no other choice, since I felt that people always have options. But Will made a convincing case that he had no other real option but to change careers. At the age of thirty-five he could have theoretically gone back to school, re-tooled for a new career. The only career he wanted for the future was college teaching. But he'd have to return to academic futility. And it was a bad time to become a college teacher. He didn't feel like beginning over again from scratch. He had gone beyond that point. He could have taken another social agency job. They were plentiful at the time, but they all had the same problems he'd left. The only real option was to pull out and begin a new life, a life where he could be independent. This frightened him and his wife, but they decided to go ahead. "We had been raised in a depression mentality. Get a job with a big company, get your pay check on schedule and be secure. But we both saw the trap of this. I felt confined in my job, and I wanted out. Maybe I didn't have to go to the extreme that I did but I had no other choice. People thought I was absolutely crazy for doing it, but I think they're crazy for staying where they are. Some people said they wished they had the opportunity to do what we're doing. Well, they have the same choice. They'll have to suffer—hustling to eke out an existence. But too many people are frightened—that need for security. They have all sorts of excuses but it's really inertia and a lack of courage to do something. The thing that's really frightening is a lot of them don't really see what would be obvious to anyone had they examined their lives. They don't want to see the futility of their own existence, because to look at that would mean to confront themselves."

Will's wife came in bringing some beers. From the look of her hands and clothes she had been sculpting. She asked sheepishly, along with a touch of wryness, "Can I join in the conversation? I've never been taped. I never felt I'd be important enough. Anyway, it's really partly my story. I was involved in the risk and Will and I worked together fixing, growing food and making a life." Will and his wife were unusual in that they had one of the few intact marriages among the people I had talked with.

She said, "We chose this area because we had heard nice things about it. The only other place we considered was Appalachia since Will had done some of his Master's work there. But there were no jobs. Little did we know that there were no jobs here either."

Will chimed in: "I learned a lot about welfare and food stamps in the first couple of months we were here. They really make it hard for you to be on food stamps. It would cost me so much gas and so much time that I finally figured out that it was better to try to get any kind of work no matter how bad it was rather than spending all that effort and money trying to get help. I felt like a failure the first time that I went, especially at the point when they asked me about my level of education. But, it was really funny, I was sitting there feeling uncomfortable and got in a conversation with a guy. He was even better than I was. He had a Ph.D. This area is filled with people who have lots of education who are trying to make an existence. Welfare was sort of a fun place but I didn't really enjoy the driving, especially in bad weather."

Will's wife continued, picking up his lead: "We were stone broke when we came. What little money we had went into the house and the repair. We've been working hard on the house."

Will added: "It's important to have a house not only for the roof over our heads but as an insurance policy for my wife. When I got out here I tried to find any kind of job that I could do. I hadn't realized the skills that I had learned as a kid from my father. What I got into immediately was a lot of construction work, particularly the highly skilled parts. Later I worked in the cabinet shop. Then I got a job working at an art gallery buying rugs and jewelry. I learned that silversmithing was a very lucrative profession around here. All the tourists are coming in to buy Indian jewelry, and even though I'm not much of an Indian I can make something that looks pretty close if not better than what most of the local people can produce. But the gallery went out of business and I was out of a job again. So finally I put most of my time in on construction work and found a lot of people doing the same thing. I also found lots of kids who had never really worked to make a living. They really got me mad. The one thing that I learned, that's always been a part of me, is to do a good job. These kids would come in, learn the craft, do a slipshod job and then whoever was in charge or had vouched for them would be left holding the bag. I got burned too many times. I really wonder about those kids and what they're doing. They just come in telling how committed they are to all sorts of ideals and then disappear. They have a very short attention span, especially when it comes to work. There are some of them who have stayed and have really done a good job but on the whole, they're a bad lot. I hate to sound as conservative as the people in Oklahoma, but I've lived too long with a lot of bullshit and no output.

"I don't mind the work, so much. It's enjoyable and I feel happy with it, but it's only a way to sustain myself. I don't have any dreams about making a fortune or real fulfillment. It's like the garden outside. It's not that the land has some holy value to me. I enjoy working in the garden and it feeds us and that's good. But that's the end of it. I just like being on my own—that's what's important."

We had been so deep in conversation that I hadn't noticed that his wife had left the room. She came back in and said, "We'd like you to stay for dinner." I felt a little uncomfortable, although greatly pleased by the invitation, after hearing and realizing how poor they were. Perhaps recognizing my discomfort with this, she chimed in with a large smile on her face,

"There really isn't a great deal. It just came out of the garden. It's all vegetables. We hope you'll stay."

It was a delicious vegetable stew. Everything was very quiet and there was a sense to the atmosphere of the house that again reminded me of another bit of Holland. The Dutch have a word, which is very difficult to translate, as most important words are in a language. The word is *gezellig*. As close as one can approximate a meaning, it means a feeling of being at home, of a comfort you feel belonging in a place. Being in this house I felt at home in a world cut off from the rest of the world. It was a world of the pioneer that I learned about in reading children's books to my daughter. It was a world of strength and independence, of people making a new life for themselves cut away from the restraints of society. Even though Will and his wife's life were very much embedded in the life surrounding them, the world of work which supported them, their life was not defined by that. Its meaning was in the house and land, and in the freedom from the restraints, at least as much as possible, in our society. Driving back to Santa Fe, seeing the city lights in the distance, brought me sharply to the awareness of the separateness I had just shared in.

Will's feeling that he had no other option but to give up his career becomes more intelligible and sensible if the notion of career is broadened to include total life style. The unacceptable fund-raising aspect of Will's job might have been tolerable had it not intruded in his non-work life. The requirement to cater and pander to the agency's rich supporters created two problems for him: on the one hand it invalidated his desire to create a service for those who most needed it, those people who did not financially sustain the agency. So his work goals were frustrated. Moreover, in the course of creating an agency for his rich patrons, Will became aware that his life was taking on the cast of his patrons' lives. His world of living was being subverted by his work world, if indeed these two worlds are capable of being distinguished. In giving up a career that had produced frustration and promised little better, Will was also released from a life style which he found unacceptable.

For all the people interviewed, the decision to change careers involved far more than simply giving up the immediate activities involved in the work setting. For a fifty-five-year-old eminent TV producer turned school bus driver, his choice involved giving up an unacceptable future reality. The approaching slowdown in his work life, as he neared retirement, made his situation intolerable. He was willing to give up his successful career for the possible realization of his long-standing desire to work in the theater. For an art school professor turned dress store designer and owner, his work world initially presented few problems. But his work satisfaction was being eroded by his difficulties in living in a city where he felt alienated and unsafe.

For the respondents, all sectors of life interpenetrated; the work area could not be meaningfully disentangled from other sectors.[2] Consider the following statement by a forty-year-old stockbroker turned ice cream store owner:

> I was sitting in my car at a dead halt. It would take me, as usual, about an hour to go the four miles to the office. Why did I need this crap? So I made a lot of money. For what? To support a household that was more than I wanted and needed. So my kids could go to a good school. But I didn't like the values they were learning and the kinds of people they were becoming. My marriage was falling apart at the seams, partly because of the job, but mostly because of us. That traffic jam was really valuable. It gave me time to see with some perspective that my life was crumbling. That's when I seriously started thinking about what I could do about it.

For this person, as well as all of those interviewed, their growing awareness of the erosion of their whole life, what had previously seemed to be separable sectors of existence, gave them that critical distance, that point of examination, to look critically at their lives. This is the perspective from which Will indicted his friends back home for their refusal to confront life. He sees them copping out, taking the psychically easier strategy of maintaining the status quo and not dealing with whatever discomfort exists in their lives. The radical career changer recognizes, often painfully, that such a lack of confrontation does have an impact, however subtle. One extreme illustration of the impact of avoiding such dilemmas in living is provided by a thirty-eight-year-old former successful insurance agent turned construction worker:

> I was the great American dream. I had made my first million when I was thirty-two. The Junior Chamber of Commerce elected me Executive of the Year. But my life wasn't right. I couldn't figure it out: that's not to say I tried very hard. The booze made sure of that. No, I explained getting bombed all the time as just part of my job. A couple of drinks to make a sale. A little social drinking at night. Everyone around me was getting bombed too—that's a Texas habit. Also, I was breaking my butt working so that I could buy, buy, buy. I had everything and more than I or anyone could want, but I had to buy.
>
> I saw what was happening in those couple of months I spent alone in the desert. I went there to dry out and meditate right after I and some friends got involved in the Civil Rights movement back home. Our lives had been threatened and I saw the great American dream and me for what it was— not much. I pulled out and went to the desert to think. From there I understood that I was an alcoholic and a compulsive buyer because I had to fill a big hole in my life. The booze and the property made up for it but

---

[2] I can no longer avoid using the word "respondents." Although the word tends to depersonalize and objectify the lives of these very real people, it does allow for simpler writing.

not very well. I couldn't really make up for holding still, living with a frigid wife and working a job that was just simply ripping people off.

The interviewees saw from the critical distance of their crisis point what were the costs for living in a particular career and life situation. They found the price too high; a price inflated by a post-depression mentality, as so well described by Will. They were willing to take the risk of giving up a secure life of income, position and friends. There was more to this risk—there was the experience of guilt and degradation of being poor. Will graphically experienced this when he had to collect welfare. And for what? For the option of changing careers and the unknowns of Santa Fe. Such a choice was seen by the radical career changer's friends as crazy, as "something having gotten into their heads." But there was also ambivalence in some of their friends' reactions, a touch of envy often guardedly stated as "Sometimes I wish I could do what you're doing." This ambivalent reaction of friends back home is described by a statement of a forty-eight-year-old former well-established film maker turned farmer:

> Most of my friends thought I was out of my mind. I was at the top of my field—lots of money, two houses, everything. One of my closest friends, a top executive, kept on hammering at me. For all his arguments, he manages to come out every summer, sort of to check things out. He's been doing it for three years now. Finally, this trip he opened up. He'd like to come out for good. But he has all sorts of excuses. He wants something more from his life—he's not sure what it is. He can't define it, put words on it, and he's just not about to take the risk to find out what it is.
>
> Before I came out here, I didn't know what it was either. It only became clear when I took the jump. What I wanted was to be independent, free to do films as I thought they should be done, not to cater to producers or to the customers. I'm willing to be a farmer if that's what it takes to be free of that bullshit. Now, if I get a film job, I tell them, they don't tell me, what is right. If they don't like it, I come back and farm. That's what my friend probably wants in his own way, but he has to make the leap. But he won't—the gent doth protest too much.

This theme of freedom from work restraint is one aspect of the radical career changer's commonly shared concept of independence. For each person, the nature of that independence is different depending on the form of their work. What these differences share in common is a search to be a free agent, to be an individual capable of exercising control over his life. This aspect of independence is graphically presented in the next story of a forty-three-year-old embryologist turned potter.

Max, The Presence

"Well, if you want to know the real reason for coming here, it's this." Max stopped unloading his kiln, placed his large body in a ramshackle, no longer overstuffed chair, and proceeded to tell a story he obviously enjoyed. "When I was 17—let's see that was in 1949—I decided to see America. I was hitchhiking. One night I landed up in Santa Fe. I found this dance hall—it doesn't exist anymore. And there I met a very nice lady who danced with me for awhile. Then she provided me with my introduction to the joys of manhood. I've always had a soft spot for this place ever since.

"In a sense what I'm saying is that it really wasn't that important where I went. I just decided—it's now four years ago—that I had the option to do whatever I wanted. To go wherever I wanted. So I came here because this is where I first got laid.

"Why that thought—that I could do anything—came into my mind, I have no idea. I remember the day vividly. There I was deeply involved in my work and this thought came to me. That I didn't have to be here sitting and working. I was a free agent. What was weird was that I was very happy doing what I was doing. I really kept that idea away from me, treated it with forceps, examined it very closely. After awhile, I accepted it as part of me. I didn't have to be Max, the embryologist. I could be Max, the anything. So I'm now Max, the potter. It's really only me—Max."

There was a solidity to Max. Not so much for how he completely filled the ragged chair. Nor was it his large, graying beard. He simply sat as if he were there and knew he was. His involvement was total whether in our conversation or in the kiln, emptying which he was about to resume, or in selling pottery to the customers who just walked in.

He returned from his sale saying, "These little planters go like crazy. I have this image that all of America will die of oxygen depletion from too many vines in too many hanging planters. And I have contributed to this mass suicide. I really like to sell them, because I like to make money. I'm a potter but also I'm a businessman. I make to sell. I enjoy the problems of potting. I enjoy the doing. But I also like money.

"I took a financial risk coming out here. I came with $10,000 in mortgage money and a small income. All of that money went for buying this place and fixing it up. You know, the small amenities like electricity, plumbing, heat. I had a very good job as a research embryologist in a big hospital. So now I'm a potter. What's strange is that I live as well on my income here as I lived on three times as much before I left. It's not a cost of living difference. It's just that I've redefined what's important.

"It's the same thing that happened when I decided to come out here. I had my Ph.D. for ten years and was well known in my specialty. I had a job where I was completely free to do whatever I wanted. I was approaching my dream of being internationally known and respected. I had a long string of publications. I was invited to conferences all over the world—Tokyo, Paris, London. But never in the U.S. I finally figured that one out. But the most important thing was that I enjoyed my research. It wasn't work—it was a life. I'm really work-oriented. Here, I work even harder. I'm up at six and work all the time. Potting is now my life.

"What made me start really entertaining that strange thought was my NSF money ran out. The hospital I worked in offered me a regular position in medical research. I was a bit aloof in those days, looked down at applied research. So I decided to try out that thought and shop around for a new job in embryology. Would you believe it—the best I could do was some two-bit school in Florida. There were plenty of jobs then—I just wasn't being accepted.

"I couldn't understand it. I knew I was good. Why couldn't I get a decent job? My major advisor told me that a big shot in the field had been asked for a recommendation by most of the employers. He was submarining me by saying, 'His sexual behavior is extreme.' Where he got this from I think was from some party where he overheard me say to my wife, 'Let's split for the evening. That broad over there looks like a good piece of ass.'

"Finding that out about being submarined crystallized a lot of things. I saw my career in a new perspective. Like why I was internationally recognized but had never been invited voluntarily to a conference in the States. Oh, I'd call and push my way in, but they froze me out. I know I don't mince words. I say what I mean. That doesn't make you very popular. But yet my work was highly regarded. I enjoyed it. But my colleagues couldn't let me be.

"So four years ago, a couple of things were going. I couldn't find a job I wanted. Thanks to the submarine attack. I was alienated from my colleagues. My second wife took off for a whole set of reasons. I had no responsibility. So I took that little thought, that I'm a free agent, and came out here.

"I decided to make my avocation a career. I had studied pottery for two years while I was in graduate school. I had a small electric kiln and a potter's wheel at home. And my second wife—she was an artist—really helped along. I knew I wasn't destined to be a great potter, but I could make nice stuff that would sell. And it does. I make enough now to live comfortably—by my new standards.

"What's fascinating to me is that I approach pottery with the same style as I did embryology. First, stages of precision and detail, then floating creativity with the intermediate outcomes and then back to precision trying to pull it together again. I'm beginning to realize how similar things are—pottery and embryology, back home and here. It's still me.

"I remember when I first came out I thought I'd be different. I got into the hippie culture and was tripping a lot on dope. Then one night, a flash hit me, and I stopped. I was sitting on the floor with about ten people, getting stoned. I was feeling very high, grooving with the people. This was a nice place, I thought. People allowing other people to be. But then it hit me—I had the image of someone going up in flames, a giant immolation scene, and everyone would sit around saying 'Man, do your trip.' I wasn't into not-caring. A lot of kids are masquerading it as openness and tolerance. I care. I read everything. I care about the world situation. I work on a number of local projects. I'm involved. I was at home and I am here.

"New Mexico is a funny place. People here are more open and more accepting. They have a broad range of interests and concerns. But they are all detached from the world outside. Maybe this is because they cultivate themselves and relationships. But this seems at the price of being attached to the world. I try to do both."

Having been at Max's place over the space of three hours, I knew he was a success at least in the interpersonal world. People constantly floated through—one lady selling snow peas from her garden, another lady working with Max's equipment, another simply to chat. Max always continued with his work but managed to be involved, attentive—a good listener. Always completely there. Max's place had the feeling of being a haven for people finding their way. And Max's presence projected the image that a path could be found.

"Who knows. I may go back to embryology. I saw an advertisement for a job as chairman of a biology department. I didn't get it because the money didn't come through. But I had all sorts of fantasies about going back. Even though I like what I'm doing now, I can foresee reaching a point where I'll want to go back. Then, I will."

It was getting late, and we had tickets for the opera. Max went off to change. Almost in an instant he emerged wearing a pair of slacks rather than his baggy white shorts, a silver concho belt holding up his large paunch, an Indian design shirt instead of his ripped undershirt. His hands were now clean of clay and grime. Even his hair, what was left of it, and his beard, were combed. But he couldn't fool me or anybody else. I knew it was Max. And Max knew it was Max.

Why did Max find it so difficult to entertain the thought that he was a free agent, with the option to do as he chose? This thought intruded itself at such an inauspicious time: why should he want to do something else when he was happy with what he had? Even when the crisis in his career arose, this notion had to be handled with care.

For Max, as for most of us, the notion is problematic, since we see ourselves as being responsible individuals. Part of the value of work, as our society defines it, and as we introject it, is that it provides the basis for fulfilling our responsibilities—the feeding, clothing and sheltering of ourselves and our families. Why entertain the notion of free choice, many would say, since our responsibility makes this a hollow, theoretical option. The experiences of the radical career changer speak directly to the viability of free choice and how theoretical this option really is.

Responsibility weighed heavily in the respondents' consideration of changing career. But the emerging crisis in their lives made freedom of choice more than a theoretical option. They were forced to make a decision and in the process had to consider what is the nature and extent of their responsibilities. Often their changing familial situations also reinforced this reevaluation of responsibility. Many experienced family disruption and change along with their career crisis. The extreme of the situation is highlighted in the following statement of the fifty-five-year-old former TV producer turned school bus driver:

I was fifty-five. My kids were grown. My wife and I had recently broken up after some thirty-two years together. I had no responsibilities. No one really to support or take care of. And what did I have to look forward to? A future where I would be allowed to wither on the vine, what the government called "looking forward to retirement." So I packed my stuff in the car and came out to Santa Fe. I didn't know what I'd find, but I felt I could make enough money to do theater work. That's what I always wanted to do.

There is little direct or simple connection between familial disruption and the choice of radically changing careers. In some cases, the decision to change careers also led to a reevaluation of the family situation. In other cases, the spouse's unwillingness to accept a change of career led to a deterioration of the marriage. Or, most commonly, a decaying marital situation interacted with and was an integral part of the crisis in the work sector.

Whatever the extent of family responsibility, the respondents' decision to act on the notion of being a free agent raises the point that responsibility need not be constraining. From the respondents' perspective, responsibility is limiting only if one wants it to be: responsibility is often not a reason for lack of freedom, but an excuse. In Will's and Max's cases, their responsibilities were dealt with on a renegotiated basis, renegotiated in terms of how much was necessary for a reasonable, responsible life. While they maintained the ingredients of a responsible life—decent food, clothing and shelter—its quality and quantity were reevaluated. Admittedly, this renegotiation of necessity did not present insurmountable problems—Will and his wife have no children, Max is divorced and living alone. But to pass off the choice of changing a career as a function of lessened responsibility is to avoid a crucial issue, namely, how much does an individual or a family need in order to maintain a satisfactory and satisfying existence? Is an individual being responsible to himself or his family, if he provides them with little more than the bare essentials of living? It is not that the respondents have purposely chosen to live minimally. They have the taste, appetite, and often the desire for an expensive life from those previous years of affluent living. They were willing to live with a lesser material existence since their incomes allow for little else. Why? They felt there was a more paramount value than an affluent life—the value of greater freedom from external constraint which would allow them the freedom to be themselves. The cost of obtaining this freedom entailed more than a reevaluation of material possessions. It meant a reevaluation of how to measure their own personal value and the direction of their lives. Their new-found work could not provide an adequate measure since, in most cases, their work's major significance was to sustain the life that they chose to lead.

This presented a very difficult problem for the respondents: how to measure the success of a life when work is perceived as secondary to an evolving life style. Before changing their careers, the respondents, like most of us, used the available grading structure in work to evaluate the success of their life's direction. Getting a raise or promotion partially validates that one's work has been successful. But work interpenetrates and is not easily separable from other sectors of living; the spillover of moving through work's grading structure can also be found in other life activities. For example, such movement produces one basis for success in the family sector. The individual can use the increased benefits of his graded work to make a better life for his family. Work provides the wherewithal for acquiring more goods and experiences—travel, entertainment, property, schooling, etc. For the radical career changer work brought these benefits, and yet they were found to be empty. They did not bring personal satisfaction and even tended to erode the non-work world of family and interpersonal relationships.

Given the respondents' choice to leave their careers, and with the limitation of work possibilities in the Santa Fe area, they chose or were forced to redefine the significance of work as a measure of their lives. For Will, his work does not define his life. While farming is rewarding, it serves primarily as a means of obtaining food. Nor do Will's odd jobs define him. While the house provides the gratification of successful rebuilding, its major values are shelter and as an insurance policy for his wife. Work's main value is that it affords him the means to freely determine his life. In Max's case, the role of work as a measure of life is more complicated. For him, pottery is both his work and his life, as was embryology before. But pottery more effectively legitimates Max as an individual than did his former career. By being a potter, Max no longer has to deal with his colleagues' disconfirmation of his personality. Although Max is still constrained by potential disconfirmation—he has a buying public who must like his pottery in order for him to survive—he sees their judgment based more on his product than on his personality. Nor is Max's new buying public that significant to him in validating his life. Max projects a strong sense that he is striving to validate himself, to be personally satisfied with his life. This is the goal which his work and life as a potter hopefully will allow him to attain.

This theme of reevaluating the relative significance of work is a particularly strong one among the respondents. It is well summarized by a thirty-six-year-old Ph.D. computer scientist turned carpenter: "If I do go back to computer work, I will define my work, not let my work define me. That's what I learned out here."

The notion of "out here" is significant. There are certain values "out here"—in Santa Fe—which the majority of the respondents have found to replace work as the measure of their lives. Those who haven't found a new source of definition are searching for a new place to go.

One of the most dramatic measures that the Santa Fe setting provides is the mystique of the landscape and the Indian cultures that are embedded within it. It is this aspect that is illustrated in the next story.

A Man of Solitude: Mark's Story

It was that hat. How I coveted it. A real symbol of being a mountain man—strong, independent, capable of living with himself. It was brown, deepened in shade by years of grime. Two brightly colored bird feathers soared in different directions from the headband ribbon. But the *coup de grace* was the ragged hole in the crown. I imagined that it was made either by some passing arrows or the bites of a hungry wild animal. The front and back brims, bent forward, created a continuous flow of movement with the tie band, worn Mexican style, across the back of the head. Unfortunately, the hat was not on display in a store. It was on Mark's head. I had tried to negotiate for the hat but with no success. It was as much a part of Mark as I wanted it to be part of me.

His outfit was perfect in its imperfection. The hat, shading the dark sunglasses; the work shirt and pants; the whole body propped against the adobe wall. It said to the world that its owner had confronted his solitude.

We were at the corn dance at Santo Domingo. What a stunning sight—300 dancers and 50 singers, dancing in unison to an incessant, hypnotic drum beat, pulsating with the chant of rattles. But it was the clowns who were at the center stage. Their faces and bodies were dressed in white ash. Their heavy torsos moved constantly in and out among the dancers.

The next dance was just beginning. Mark was explaining the symbolism of the costumes and movements. He spoke in a slow, considered way—a straight line of feeling that seldom varied—a sense of solidity with a tinge of sadness. For Mark the dance was a world of indefinite subtlety, what seemed to the uninitiated as a scene of monotonous repetition. Mark knew the Indian world; he had been adopted by an Indian family—a payment for persevering in "being around."

Mark suddenly stopped talking and I stopped listening—the scene in front of us had been transfigured. The dancers and singers were still in the plaza. The clowns were still weaving through the lines. But the wind had come up, the bright sky had darkened, and an enormous cloud of dust enshrined the plaza. Through this fine gauze of unreality, the dancing moved into another dimension. And above the plaza, on top of the kiva, with its ladder extending heavenward, stood another line of clowns. They had magically appeared—their white faces and bodies floating above the cloud of dust. In a row, they looked like a long white sheet hovering against the angry sky. They seemed to be protecting the dancers, whose movements were encased in the shadows of dust.

The dancing continued. The sky cleared. The world returned to the expected. Mark and I left. We got into his VW bus, his home for the past five years in New Mexico. "I could live in a house. I get about $9000 a year from my stocks. I only spend about $2500. I don't need much. I live in the bus when I want to. Then I'm free to go. Each place is different. The whole rhythm of the earth changes in different places. The wind, the land, the plants, the sky. That's what brought me to New Mexico. I wanted to be free to follow it. Come on, we'll go up to Santa Cruz lookout. I'll show you what I mean. I lived there for six months."

We jolted along the Nambe road. Mark punctuated our silence with information about the geological formations, the plant and animal life and the shifting weather. It was a road I had travelled many times. It was always different. Each turn of the road unfolded a different facet of the landscape. The clouds and light called forth each part of the mosaic to take the lead. Sometimes it was the red of the coarse sandstone; sometimes it was the surreal shapes of the eroded cliffs or the massive green-to-black mountain peaks that served as their backdrop. Or sometimes it was the sky with its constantly shifting, moody clouds. At other times it was the silence that enveloped all. With Mark's tutoring the landscape was renewed in a different way. Mark said, as if reading my thoughts, "How can you get tired of this?"

Mark retreated into the landscape. He continued a little while later, picking up the thread of his last statement. "I've brought people up here to show them what New Mexico is all about. They're frightened of their souls. As long as they're in the car, it's O.K. It's familiar. But when they sit out, they can't handle it. I try to show them the rhythm of the land. It's so strong—you can't miss it. But they are afraid of being alone with it. But mostly they're afraid of being alone with themselves. I probably shouldn't expect it from them. It took me awhile to be able to deal with it."

Reaching the lookout, we walked out among the cacti to an unexcavated Indian ruin. We sat on a mound and looked at the peaks extending in layers, one above another. Mark sat at attention, tuning every sound and sight. I was interested in the landscape but most of my being was centered on Mark's past. He seemed willing to talk about where he had been. But he remained engaged in the landscape.

"I'd been coming out here since 1947. I made the decision to stay in '68, in just a couple of hours. It was at a time when my mind was quiet enough so I could listen to my heart. I was coming back from Esalen. I had been working with Fritz Perls and his people. I had to be back in Florida to run some groups. On the way I stopped in New Mexico. I decided then I had to be here. In this powerful landscape, I could be what I wanted and longed for in myself, what I wanted for my patients. Just to be myself, not what somebody else wanted me to be. But that meant a real risk. Not money, maybe losing friends. But really the risk was being alone. Alone with this landscape.

"My patients had that kernel of self in them. They would try to get to it. I would try to help them. But they were afraid of the risk. So they sucked on other people, on objects, to make themselves whole. They kept on showing up, trying to change. But they were always the same. There was too much danger in changing. That's why I gave up my practice. I wasn't very effective. Sure I was successful. I made a good living. But it wasn't accomplishing anything.

"So I went back briefly to Florida. Paid my bills, gave everything away—my books, records, all my possessions. I bought the VW bus and drove out here. Soon the bus got filled with other possessions, but they are from my life out here." I thought of the sense of comfort, of enclosure, in Mark's bus. It was peopled with his objects, his life. A stuffed bird, some sea shells, Indian blankets and books. Some of the books were about the birds, flowers, and geology of New Mexico. Others were strange and obscure treatises.

"Out here I'm free to do what I want. I read all the time. There is so much to learn. I move when I want to. And there is no one to tell me what to do or to think I'm strange or doing something unacceptable."

The wind and the light had changed. Mark suggested that we move to a place where we could watch the lake. When we arrived at our new location the surface of the lake was smooth. The wind from an impending storm soon ruffled the surface. "I see my life as a series of stages, each one necessary for the next. It's like the lake. It's like the land. It grows and evolves with its own logic and its own time dimension. You know your place, your relative worth out here." Mark moved his hand around, gesturing to the mountains, sky and the land.

"I dropped out of high school. My parents, who are old New England stock, thought I was crazy when I took off to Europe and started a racing team. I was good. I reached the point of being one of the top racers in the world. Then I got drafted. They tested me and found that I was bright. So I learned Russian and had a top-secret job listening in on the Russian's radio communications. I needed to keep racing, to keep me and my cars in top shape. I tried to get a dispensation to race—no luck. I had four Ferraris sitting in the garage.

"I saved a lot of money during my racing period. That's what I lived on after I got out of service and what I'm living on now.

"When I got out of service, I couldn't get started again in racing. My cars had lost their fine edge and racing had become a tough grind. I decided to finish school and I finally got an MA in psychology. I had the talent for it and liked it. But, like I said, after a while I realized I wasn't doing anybody any good and not me, in particular.

"The place that I'm at is good. But I feel a need to do something of value. I applied to medical school. I want to be a doctor very badly. They said I was too old. So I'm applying for doctor's assistant's training. If I get in, I'll start school in another year. It will be two years of grinding in the big city, but I can live with that. Then, I'll probably come back out here and work around. I can be of value. Also, it'll be a hedge against the stock market falling."

We sat together for awhile. Then I had to go home. Mark said he'd stay the night at the lookout. I wondered when I'd see Mark again. He floated through people's lives. I was sure that if I wanted to see him, he and his hat would be at some lookout or at an Indian dance. I had the strong feeling that we would meet again very shortly. I was right—I saw Mark, unexpectedly, a couple of nights later.

I had been with a group of friends who had first introduced me to Mark. We were in the center of a very high evening. About midnight, we decided to look at the stars from the lookout. As we drove up, we wondered where Mark was.

We parked the car and started out in a mock search for Mark. To our total surprise, we saw a hunched shape sitting on a mound among the cacti, silhouetted against the mountains. "It must be Mark," I thought, "who'd be wearing a hat in the middle of the night?" The moon was full, the sky was spilling over with stars. All was silent. We walked across the field to where the silhouette was camped. We were almost there, yet the silhouette didn't turn around, as if it were a boulder fixed in the endless landscape. When we stood in front of him, he lifted his head, took off his hat and smiled—a smile that almost gratefully said he was happy that we were there.

Mark's situation is almost pristine in its lack of adornment as to what is his measure. He has chosen not to use work or property as a means of defining himself. Instead he has chosen to use his continuity with Indian life and landscape as his scale. His personal growth, in terms of understanding and ability to survive, provide him with his measure.

There is almost a spiritual quest, a standing naked before one's Creator, that permeates Mark's story. He shares this aspect with another respondent, a thirty-two-year-old minister, who now works to survive in an isolated, New Mexico mountain community. He, like Mark, found that his attempts to reach and touch people had little hope of success. He points out, "My parishioners wanted me to take away their guilt, to make them whole. What they refused to do was to confront themselves and their lives." The minister chose to confront himself in the mountains, leaving behind a successful career. Survival has been difficult. There have been physical hardships. There have also been problems in psychological survival—difficulties in adjusting to the antagonisms of the local population and the humility of flipping hamburgers to exist. But, he feels he must define himself if he is ever to help others.

What is this definition of self that the minister is searching for? It is that same kernel of self that Mark was trying to get his patients to express and that he is still searching for in himself. It is the same self that Will argues that his friends at home refuse to confront. It is that same aspect which Max seeks in being himself.

Perhaps the simplest way to characterize this kernel is in terms of what is left for the individual when he shears away all the things which define, but are not the same as, self. It is self, not defined by property, work or family, but the individual standing alone confronting his own being and his own mortality.

This view of self is expressed in less abstract terms by the respondents when they speak of their interpersonal world in Santa Fe. They constantly point out that: "People in Santa Fe do not stand on formality or judge you by material signs of success. You're accepted for what you are and not what you've accomplished." "People here are willing to accept all ranges of interests and values. I feel free to be and explore what I really am." Admittedly such open acceptance can turn, as Max noted, to a lack of concern or disengagement from relationships. But this seems to be a minor aspect in the respondents' sense of community. They feel that they can share, be supported, and not be judged for their feelings and views about life. This feeling comes from the common, shared experience of having confronted major life crises and shifts, like divorce and career change. With this confrontation there is a sense of communicating more fundamentally, more openly about the problems of existence.[3] This ability to communicate and share about oneself is an aspect of their evolving sense of self, that kernel of being. It also forms part of their sense of independence, an independence to be oneself, to express and find that kernel of self in the supportive context of community.

Was it necessary to come to Santa Fe to find the kernel of themselves? Looking back, most of the respondents indicated that they could have found, in their original settings, expression for themselves, even a community of people to share it with, and less likely, independence within their career. But this was not what they initially sought when they chose to change careers. At the point of decision, the dominant motivation was to throw off the constraint of work and life style. For most, their goal was not positively defined but rather was an avoidance of what was wrong in their lives. They initially had little clear sense of what they were seeking except freedom from constraint. It was not independence to find self, but an exit visa from a dehabilitating environment.

The change of physical location was seen as an important step in removing these constraints. They assumed, in varying degrees, that being in a different place would make them different people.

Such an assumption is built into the fabric of "normal" living. This is especially clear in the area of travel. Traveling to new places tends to change the pattern of normal living and working. We become, in a sense, different people because the restraints and supports of our non-vacation lives are changed. On a holiday the house does not need repair, there is no fixed schedule of working, the budget is less oppressive. We seek to encounter novel situations and people when we travel. We are willing to engage this novelty since this forms part of the excitement and freedom of a holiday. Too much novelty is shielded off by traveling in the arms of American Express or by realizing that we will return, when the vacation is over, to the safety of the familiar. This

[3] It is not that the respondents spend a great deal of time discussing these issues. They assume them as one basis for relationship. The ability to assume certain things as given is part of the set of characteristics that the writer James Baldwin analyzed as "being home." He commented that "home" was a place where you didn't have to talk about things everyone already knew.

sense of security allows, in turn, a greater measure of freedom and independence to explore the new environment and ourselves within it. To the extent we are willing to engage this novelty, on its own terms, we can experience the wonder of being different people in a different place. Living in a new environment could offer us a critical perspective on who we are, that same kind of perspective that the respondents found through the crisis of career and familial disruption. However, most of us bracket new environments as episodic, a place where we are different only for a few weeks a year. But like Max's dealing with the idea of being a free agent, the idea of "different place—different people" is within us when the appropriate crisis may bring it to possibility.

Although the respondents could have stayed in their original environments, the realities of their past lives were too strong. In Santa Fe (or in any other place for that matter) they felt they might experience "different place—different people." In one sense things had to be different in coming to Santa Fe. For a person seeking to change his career radically, Santa Fe as an economic environment offers very little hope of recreating a former work world. Many respondents noted, with a note of wry pride, that New Mexico is the second poorest state in the Union. In this sense, a person had to change at least his scale of values because of the barrenness of the economic setting. Other facets of life also had to change with a shifting environment—different friends, different cultures require new responses.

For all the changes the new environment requires, there is also a continuity of self, as well as the structuring of the new environment to look like the old. Max's story underscores this point. For him, whether he is an embryologist or a potter, whether he lives in Santa Fe or in another place, there is a strong sense of his own continuity. This continuity of self, in a changed environment, was particularly underscored in the following experience with my friend Garry, a Pentecostal minister in Kenya. He was giving a sermon in a backcountry village and said, with a flourish of his arms:

> "We search for grace everywhere, but wherever you go Christ is always sitting on your shoulder. We just have to turn our heads to see him." He was dismayed when his audience started looking over their shoulders.
>
> As we were driving back to Nairobi Garry said: "I'll have to change that metaphor. It is such a simple idea and so hard to get across. It's only partly language. The Africans are too literal. They don't really understand English that well. But I've said the same thing to various Europeans and Americans. You know the ones who wander the exotic route—Ethiopia, Kenya, India, and then Nepal. They really think they're going to find salvation in these exotic places or in the consciousness of the primitive. They can't or maybe don't want to understand that they're the same people wherever they are. They carry themselves and Christ along with them

everywhere. Grace is no further than a turn of the head, not in an exotic somewhere. I wish I could find the right words for my sermon."

Whether one accepts the theological tone of this episode or not, Garry's message was clear—"different place—same person." Was Garry right in saying that we carry ourselves wherever we go? Or do places really make a difference? My answer to these questions lies between the extremes of "different place—different person" and "different place—same person." Our personalities are a complex of traits, some being more readily expressed in certain settings than in others. It is not that the environment creates different people, but rather the environment allows the same person to find freer, more open, acceptable expression for different facets of himself. This transaction between environment and self is like the light in the New Mexico mountains. The light calls forth a different part of the landscape, making the environment appear as constantly changing. Yet we know that the mountains (or in a parallel way, that kernel of ourselves within us) didn't disappear or change form. Another way to put the same thought is that Christ may well always be sitting on our shoulder, but he is easier to detect in some places than in others.

Some of the respondents had found their niche in Santa Fe. Aspects of the Santa Fe environment, like the powerful landscape, the sense of physical and psychological openness, the mix of cultures, have provided them with satisfaction. They are happier with the present trajectory of their lives than their previous one. That is not to say that they do not experience problems in living, the very same problems they experienced before, and the same that we all experience in our ongoing life. But given the respondents' redefinition of values, such problems as money, work, and responsibility seem less oppressive. A smaller percentage of the respondents are still searching for an answer to their lives. This is often expressed in a dissatisfaction with Santa Fe and a search for a new place. They are painfully aware that the facets of themselves which they found difficult to deal with in their original environment, have not changed or shifted in the Santa Fe setting. Some find not working in their former careers disconcerting and are considering returning. Others find the values that are part of the Santa Fe environment unsatisfying. Take one illustration: time is paced slower in New Mexico than in most other places in the United States. As one person put it: "When you have to wait ten minutes 'til the water comes out of the irrigation ditch and there is no way to make it come in nine minutes or eight minutes, then you adopt the attitude of mañana—it will wait." Those who are satisfied with Santa Fe find mañana time a joy—it allows a freedom in relationship partly because of the absence of pressure and the fast pacing of normal American life.

For the dissatisfied, it is a constant source of annoyance, a time perspective which never allows things to be accomplished.

Perhaps the only general conclusion that can be reached about the adequacy of the radical career-change solution is that it works for some but not for all. It is not a final solution—the problems of existence are still present, but they shift in priority and magnitude depending on the success of the solution. How different are the problems that the radical career changer has confronted and still experiences like choice, responsibility, the role of the environment and the meaning of work, from those which we "normals" deal with? We all share the same problems. It is the extremity of their solution that serves to highlight these often obscured common issues. These individuals show, in stark relief, how work can become a "vital lie" to use Ernest Becker's term. He notes in his book *The Denial of Death* (1973):

> I used to wonder how people could stand the really demoniac activity of working behind the hellish ranges in hotel kitchens, the frantic world of waiting on a dozen tables at a time, the madness of the travel agent's office at the height of the tourist season, or the tortures of working with a jackhammer all day on a hot summer street. The answer is so simple that it eludes us: the craziness of these activities is exactly that of the human condition. They are "right" for us because the alternative is actual desperation. The daily madness of these jobs is a repeated vaccination against the madness of the asylum. Look at the joy and eagerness with which workers return from vacation to their compulsive routine. They plunge into their work with equanimity and light heartedness because it drowns out something more ominous. Men have to be protected from reality [p. 186].

Becker's statement of work needs to be broadened to include the professional, not only the traditionally perceived dissatisfied blue- and white-collar worker. The radical career changer was a professional, being well educated and in the position seemingly of controlling his life. Yet he experiences the same problems as those Becker notes in the above quote. The reality Becker speaks of is the confrontation with the meaning of our own life, in that almost naked, spiritual sense characterized by Mark's and the minister's stories.

While such a confrontation with the kernel of ourselves has never been easy, it is even more difficult in contemporary times with the weakening of the usual social supports for meaning—the church, the state, and the family. The individual is thrown solely on himself for the definition of his life, to be bolstered only by such vague terms as "happiness" or a "good life." The individual, and not some ideology must provide the definition of these terms.

> . . . modern man cannot find his heroism in everyday life any more as men did in traditional societies just by doing their daily duty of raising children, working, and worshiping. He needs revolutions and wars and

"continuing" revolutions to last when the revolutions and wars end. This is the price modern man pays for the eclipse of the sacred dimension. When he dethroned the ideas of soul and God, he was thrown back hopelessly on his own resources, on himself and those few around him. Even lovers and families trap and disillusion us because they are not substitutes for absolute transcendence [Becker, p. 190].

Without elevating the radical career changer to the level of heroism, he does powerfully raise the difficult question as to how we are to define our work and lives. The crises in his life situation forced him to examine himself from a critical distance.[4] His stories, in turn, can provide us with a similar vantage point. To pass off the radical career changer or his solution as a function of a "personal problem" is to avoid uncritically the issues which he raises that are our common shared problems. The seeds of radical career change and Santa Fe are within all of us; to avoid them is itself a solution to these problems in the same sense that radically changing one's career is also a solution. To deny, to avoid, or to accept uncritically is as much a response to a life situation as is changing it. Is maintaining rather than changing a situation or oneself inherently more rational or sensible? To passively maintain "normalcy," the status quo, for fear of what a confrontation might bring may itself be just as mad as a radical change. There is an important truth in the philosopher Pascal's statement that "Men are so necessarily mad that not to be mad would amount to another form of madness."

---

[4] All of us experience some life crisis. Yet most of us do not take the extreme solution of radically changing careers or life style. What factors allowed the radical career changer to choose his particular solution has only been in part dealt with in this research. A separate study, using more personality-oriented techniques, would be required to answer, for example, why they experienced their crisis in a particular way or why they were willing to take the risk of change. We have dealt with these and other aspects of radical career change primarily in terms of group characteristics, not in terms of unique personal histories or style. These personal traits may also be common among the respondents, which might explain an important facet of their choice of solution. One such common trait was independently pointed out by three respondents. They suggested that coming from an economically secure home provided them with the psychological security and optimism to face the potential dangers involved in their change, with the resultant expectation that their lives would soon become secure again. The large majority of respondents did come from reasonably secure middle-class backgrounds.

IX
Career Change: An Autobiographical Fragment

A MAJOR, and certainly the most heroic, contribution of Freud was in asserting and demonstrating that his theory was not only for "them," the patients, but for the psychotherapist as well. Just as you do not need one theory for the oxygen atom and another for the helium atom, Freud developed a theory as applicable to one as to another human being. Whatever its shortcomings and distortions, none of its critics has questioned it on the grounds that it is applicable only to "them" and not to "us." The problem is no different when it comes to analysis and discussion of a problem of the culture of which one is part. Concretely, this book is about highly educated, professional people in our society. I am such a person. It would be fiction to write as if I were only talking about "them" and not myself. As I became interested in work, aging, and social change I was inevitably confronted with three major issues. First, I was becoming involved with a set of problems about "them" to which I was far from indifferent or neutral, and even if one made the invalid assumption that their problems were not my problems, we shared a common culture and to that extent I was not an impersonal observer or investigator. Could I under these circumstances maintain sufficient distance to describe, analyze, and understand with some "objectivity" an aspect of social reality? And if sharing a common culture was not problem enough, there was the additional fact of a sizeable age difference between me and many of them. The very fact that I was acutely aware of the implications of this age difference already reflected that we were living in a certain society at a particular time and not in much earlier times or societies where awareness of generational differences would have very different contents. Finally, and crucially, I was grappling with the problems of work, aging, and

189

social change in the most personal ways, and that is for a writer–
investigator a blessing and a trap—and a danger for the unsuspecting
reader who likes to believe that the author of a book like this is an
impersonal conduit of the "real world." Frankly, I was less concerned
for the unsuspecting reader than I was for my unsuspecting self, because I did not want to feel that I would end up deceiving myself (too
much).

There are no surefire ways of solving these issues, although some
people try to do it by resorting to procedures which too often trivialize
the problems they are working on or result in misdirected focus or
emphasis. These procedures are quite appropriate when there is general agreement that the questions being studied are well formulated
and their complexity recognized, so that there is conceptual control
against triviality and irrelevance. I am not dealing with questions of
this kind, although I believe that in the coming decades they will
increasingly force themselves into prominence and thereby gain in
sharpness of formulation.

The above is prologue to an autobiographical fragment. Its purpose
is less to tell the reader about myself but more to serve as a vehicle to
raise questions about career and career change. We are desperately in
need of systematic data which are minimally distorted by personal
experience and bias, but we need even more the security that such
data are being gathered because they will illuminate and not obscure
complexities.

1935 was midway in the Great Depression. My father was out of
work, and there were times when we did not know if there would be a
next meal. Going to college that year would have been an utter impossibility were it not, strangely enough, for the fact that I had had polio
and had just undergone corrective surgery. The operation was made
possible, first, as a consequence of a letter I had sent to President
Franklin D. Roosevelt and, second, through arrangements made by
the New Jersey State Rehabilitation Commission. It was the latter
agency who paid one-half of my tuition ($150) to a local commuter-type
university; the other half was obtained through a university loan to be
paid back after I had graduated. If I had been unable to go to college, I
would have done nothing; I literally could not have worked.

College was a magnificent experience, intellectually and socially. I
had wonderful teachers and made lasting friendships. I was politically
active and left wing (Trotskyite) and quite involved in a variety of
student organizations. I lacked certainty about many things, one of
them being what I would do when I got through college. For the first
three years I do not think I gave much thought to the matter. If asked, I
would say I probably would go to law school, but that had as much
economic reality as a check I would write to erase the national debt.

The fact is that I assumed that I would get a job, any job. Law school was not an interest, but it was about the only thing I knew and, besides, wouldn't it be nice not to have to look for jobs which didn't exist? There was a business school in the university, but I never gave it a thought. Given our economic plight, my physical limitations, and the "impracticality" of a liberal arts education, I am frank to say that I do not know why I did not major in business. There were precious few jobs in business, but that was not a factor to me. Those were the days when the first two years of college were largely prescribed in the liberal arts, and I could not get enough of them. The important point is that I saw college as a wonderful interlude, following which I would get a job somewhere, somehow—any job. This was not a depressing thought, because there were millions in the same boat. I had no great expectations, although expecting to get some kind of a job in those days was, I suppose, a form of great expectations. I well remember a long and earnest conversation with a friend who worked during the day and went to school at night. It was in that conversation that we arrived at $35 as the lifelong weekly salary for which we would settle.

I became interested in psychology. In the fall of 1938, with the encouragement of one of my two psychology teachers, I applied to graduate school. Coming from a small, barely accredited commuter college (University of Newark, now the Newark campus of Rutgers), and requiring a fellowship if I was to be in graduate school, and being Jewish, it was no surprise that I was accepted in only one of the fifteen schools to which I applied. As best as I could later figure it out, Clark University accepted me with a tuition scholarship ($300) because they were having trouble attracting students, that being the period right after the exodus of Clark's outstanding faculty under the leadership of Walter Hunter, and before the quality rebirth of the department after World War II. If I had been accepted in no place it would have been neither surprising nor depressing. I would have been disappointed but in the same way as when one does not win the weekly lottery. It would have confirmed my belief that we lived in an unjust and inequitable society where "them that has gets more," and "them what has not" looks on. I had my dreams, all quite bourgeois and un-Trotsky-like, but I never allowed myself to take them seriously except as a form of relaxation. I lived at a time of limited opportunity and of concern for having the bare essentials for living. The bright spot was my friends with whom and from whom I learned a great deal.

The one life–one career imperative, as I have discussed it, produced no conflict in me. Before the Clark acceptance I was headed nowhere career-wise. A job, any job, is not a career. I would have been delighted to experience the agonies the imperative produces. I was not even near the situation of many students today: prepared for a career but no opportunity to enter it. Nor was I like today's college graduates who came to college knowing they would need postgraduate training only to find educational doors closed to them. Career-wise I could only go up, sideways, or stand still. I could hardly go downhill.

I do not think it ever occurred to me to consider college irrelevant because it did not prepare me for anything, except for more education which I would have been happy to accept. So when I went to graduate school I was in heaven, and for the same reasons I loved college: the seminars and my new friends. I learned something about the contents of and research in different fields of psychology and concluded that my interests were in "working with people," and that could be in any one of many settings. My interests here were general; neither from within nor without was there pressure to declare a specialty, i.e., to say what kind of psychologist I would be. This is not wholly true because in the second of my three years in graduate school I found myself thinking about what would make me "marketable." I knew that most psychologists were in universities, and that would be my first choice. But getting a degree from Clark at that time was not exactly a door-opener. Besides, war had started in Europe, our draft had begun, the future stability of universities seemed bleak, and I was Jewish. (I always had known about discrimination, but it was in graduate school that I learned about how difficult it was for Jews to obtain university positions, and at Worcester State Hospital there were several truly brilliant Jewish staff psychologists who should have obtained a university position. After the war they received the university recognition they had deserved earlier.) My second choice was clinical psychology which at that time meant getting a job in a state institution or a child guidance clinic. Clinical psychology as we know it today did not exist in those days. Graduate schools did not prepare you to be a clinical psychologist. There was more truth than jest to the statement that if you got a Ph.D. and couldn't get a job, you became a clinical psychologist. To better my chances to get a clinical job, I managed in my last year to obtain extern status in Dr. David Shakow's psychology unit at Worcester State Hospital. For three days each week I attended various meetings, learned about psychological diagnosis and testing, and got the feel for a clinical setting. I learned a lot but did not find testing very interesting, but if that was a way to earn a living, I was willing to do it. What alternatives did I have?

Today's graduate student approaching the end of his training has a specialty, and at a depth far beyond anything I had. In terms of career opportunities, psychology today is a fantastically more differentiated field than it was before World War II. Today's student has a range of choice undreamed of in 1941–1942 when I received my doctorate. He also has a sense of career which I lacked. That is to say, he has a fair idea of where his working career will start and where it might take him over the next decade. If he goes into the university he knows what is expected of him if he is to be promoted up the career ladder. If he is headed for business or industry, or today's diversity of clinical settings, or governmental service, or special research laboratories, or the public schools, or a consulting firm, he has a mental map of how the starting point can lead to a number of end points. The map may be a vague one (and unrealistic for the individual), but it is a map which he knows others have projected and used. He knows that position *A* can lead to position *B* which can lead to position *C*, and so forth. Each job is a rung on a career ladder; each job will involve him in new activities. I had no such sense of career in graduate school. I thought in terms of a job, not a career. How could I think in terms of a career when I did not know the starting point?

I was not without great expectations if you included daydreams. I wanted to be another Freud, or a Henry Murray, or Gordon Allport, or a Köhler—depending on what book I was reading. Or an Itard. Or a J. F. Brown.[1] I wanted to help people and the world change. If there was anything I was clear about, in the gut sense, it was that people were capable of far more than society permitted them to realize, and that included me. I felt I could do great things, if I were given the chance, but I was quite vague about how I would or could do it. I was ambitious, and I knew I wanted to do things which the world and I would take pride in. But it all lacked specificity and direction. I was like a hitchhiker who wanted to be elsewhere than where he was and would take the direction of the first kind driver to pick him up. I was at the same time internally directed and very field-dependent, a strange combination of me and society.

Every value (e.g., autonomy, growth, authenticity) held by today's students was held by me; the big difference resided in the degree to which the society encouraged us to hold and act upon these values, as well as providing some of the means to do so. And when I say society, I mean it both in the abstract and in terms of its surrogates, e.g., parents and teachers. When everyone was security- and survival-oriented, how could they tell us "to do our own thing," "to realize our *full* potential," to seek "self-actualization," not to compromise with our destiny, or to suppress our dreams. And there were other factors: Hitler, Mussolini, and the Japanese militarists. The war had already started in Europe. On the day I finished collecting data for my dissertation, the Japanese bombed Pearl Harbor.

---

[1] Brown's two major books (1936, 1940) were atypical for the thirties. In his abnormal text (1940) psychoanalysis was the organizing theory; in his social psychology text (1936), he attempted to bring together Marx, Freud, and the Gestaltists.

My first job, obtained in 1942 via a Civil Service test, was at the Southbury Training School in Connecticut for the mentally retarded. It was brand new and in many ways a drastic departure, philosophically and architecturally, from tradition. It was traditional in that it was in the middle of nowhere—beautiful country but still in the middle of nowhere. Typically, the only thing really expected of me was to do psychological testing (Sarason, 1976). What else did a clinical psychologist do? The fact is that within very broad limits I had carte blanche to do what I wanted. The superintendent was a former educator who used Southbury to give full expression to his heretofore frustrated ambitions as an architect and aesthete. If he were not the old-line ethical person he was, he could have sold the Brooklyn Bridge several times a day, with the purchasers expressing their thanks on bended knees. So Mr. Roselle left me alone. There were no psychiatrists to remind me of status differences and to tell me what I could not do. Herman Yannet, the Medical Director, was a brilliant pediatrician interested primarily in research. He was supportive of whatever I wanted to do. So there I was, in a setting tailor-made for anyone treasuring the values of autonomy, growth, authenticity, and intent on indulging my curiosity. Crucially, Southbury permitted me to act on my belief that people were capable of far more than they and their society realized. The institution contained a population society had written off. I viewed the mentally retarded as I once did the "proletariat." The *meaning* of my work could not be discerned from what I *did* in an overt sense, but it was that meaning that not only powered what I did but made me a happy person. My friends could not understand how I liked working with "those cases" in the middle of nowhere, except for one friend: Esther, my wife-to-be, who in several crucial respects helped (and sometimes bludgeoned) me to move in new directions.

Southbury was the beginning of my career in the sense that for the first time I was able to clarify what I was like, could do, and wanted to do. I knew I was at point A, that I wanted to get to point B, and then C, and so forth. I no longer felt like a passive reed not kowing in which direction I would be bent by the next breeze. *I* was now in control of my own destiny, a very un-Skinner-like position, but then again Skinner has never understood the issues of will and freedom in the William James sense which Barrett (1975) has recently so pithily described. When I said point A and point B I was not referring to geographical points, because what I wanted to do and learn could be (could *only* be) found at Southbury. Literally, I was prepared to spend many years there. With Esther's help I had started a number of research projects, we were learning about and practising psychotherapy, I was being psychoanalyzed, we went to New York to learn Rorschach from Bruno

Klopfer, and I thoroughly enjoyed my intrusions into the different aspects of the institution's functioning. Besides, my starting salary was $2280, and I had received increases to $2850! (We did have an apartment on the grounds for $316 a year.)

Although in the middle of nowhere, Southbury gave me intellectual freedom and those conditions in which my values received expression. I was aware that Southbury could spoil me for other and better-paying jobs which began to come along as the armed services began to absorb a good portion of civilian health personnel. Where else could I learn as much and grow as fast? *The fact is that what I was experiencing at Southbury was what the post-World War II generations were taught to want and expect.* It was all right for my generation to want but not to expect such outcomes. I learned one other thing at Southbury that I was unprepared for, and which few psychologists (then and now) ever learn. I think it is true that nothing in my experience or education prepared me for what life in a complicated organization was like, especially in a geographically isolated one like Southbury (during a war-time period when cars and gasoline were precious commodities). Suffice it to say, such living is somewhere between a blessing and a curse. The nice distinctions between work and nonwork simply made no sense. I was at Southbury four years and midway in my stay the Peyton Place–Something Happened social dynamics began to erode the picture of paradise I have previously painted. This does not mean that I seriously thought of leaving, but rather that Esther and I began to feel socially confined and irritated at the ways in which organizational and social craziness intruded into our "work."

Getting a position in a university was not in my plans, because I did not see it as a realistic possibility and not because I had ruled it out. So when the opportunity arose in 1946 to go to Yale, I was pleased and excited. (Unfortunately, I cannot relate in this fragment how this opportunity occurred, but it is quite a story.) This raises an interesting and important question: was the switch from Southbury to Yale a career change or simply another job in a career as a psychologist? Phenomenologically, it was a career change. There was practically no overlap in my responsibilities in the two settings. The people to whom I would relate (e.g., faculty, students) were obviously different in terms of background and function from those of Southbury. At Southbury my working hours were set; at Yale I taught several hours a week, and how to spend the rest of the time was my responsibility. And Yale and Southbury were quite dissimilar on scores of dimensions. Yale was a new world and a new life for me. Yes, I would teach some of the things I had learned at Southbury, and I would continue to do research but in different ways and on different aspects of human functioning. Indeed, I did not have to restrict my research to mental retardation, and I did move in new directions. Therefore, to say that I had taken a new job *as a psychologist,* with the implication that there was significant overlap between the two jobs that did not involve a truly drastic change in how I thought and what I thought about, is to distort my phenomenology to fit pre-existing categories. I said earlier that it was not until I was at Southbury that I developed a sense of career, i.e., the future began to take shape, and I could begin to see the roads which would lead me to that future. I indicated what that meant, but there was more to it, e.g., getting more psychologists at Southbury, perhaps moving as chief to a better-paying and larger department in another institution, or even becoming head of such an institution (my masochism in those days knew no bounds!). I also toyed with the possibility of shifting to a state mental hospital in which there would be new opportunities to learn and grow—and gain more status and income. If I had gone in any of these direction, the overlap between any of them and Southbury would have been very significant. It would have been a move "up" in a familiar career pattern. Moving to the university was literally a new ballgame with new rules, traditions, functions, turf, and horizons. Soccer and football have a number of things in common, not the least of which is speed, agility, physical contact, kicking a ball, etc. But the soccer player has, so to speak, to start all over again when he wants to become a football player, and vice versa. (The one exception, of course, is the soccer player who becomes a place kicker in football—a function so specialized that it is mischievous to say he has become a football player.)

My purpose has not been to draw sharp distinctions but rather to suggest that what conventional thinking often regards as a stage in a career line or pattern—a line of natural ascent—may be phenomenologically the start of a new life or new career. And that is the point: the change may be powered by the desire for a new way of living and thinking, however much one's public label remains the same. I was a psychologist the day I left Southbury, and I was the "same" psychologist when I came to Yale, but the identity of public labels hid the fact that I was seeking rebirth. And here I must relate something which casts a different light over all that I have said so far. It is not only relevant to how one thinks about jobs and careers but also to the issue of candor and the one life–one career imperative.

When Esther and I left the chairman's home in a New Haven suburb, having come to final agreement about the offer and my acceptance, evening had come together with a spring mist which made the blooming dogwoods (in which the area abounds) look unusually heavy. We had about three blocks to walk to the bus. We never took the bus. When we left the chairman's house we said not a word to each other for about a minute, we just walked hand-in-hand. Then, as if by some prearranged signal, we turned to each other and shouted: "We are free!" That utterance was the first time I had allowed myself to say something out loud that reflected vague fears about spending our social lives in an institutional setting, and being intellectually confined by having to focus on a particular patient population. There was a part of me that knew that by coming to Southbury the confines of my career had already been determined: my positions might change, my status and income increase, I would write and do research, and I would try to branch out, but all of this would be as a clinical psychologist in a state institutional setting. When I day-dreamed about all the great and wonderful things I would do in my lifetime, the physical setting in which these would be done was a Southbury or one of its different kin. For the first two years at Southbury I enjoyed these daydreams. I was lucky, I had it made! I had *a* career line, thank God. I knew what my life would be like, and I liked the prospect. If anyone had told me that I was uncritically buying the one life–one career imperative, I would have signed his commitment papers. It was after a couple of years, and it was only in part a function of my marriage, that I would have fleeting and disquieting thoughts about what the long-term future looked like. But I never really allowed myself to pursue these thoughts. Where would it get me? Besides, wasn't I learning and doing a lot, and wasn't there a lot more to do? What more did I want? Sure, institutional life and work leave something to be desired, but you have to put these negatives in perspective. I never could bring myself to discuss this openly with anyone, particularly with Esther, who never hesitated to tell me how she regarded institutional living. I resented her putting into words what I feared to let myself think about. Why get upset about what you cannot alter? I saw the future and accommodated to it. So when we walked into freedom upon leaving the chairman's home, masculine me could for the first time acknowledge what I had previously allowed (= required) myself to believe was weakness and irrationality. I had been in prison and thought it was freedom.[2] Relative to any other institution I knew or heard about, I did have freedom at Southbury; relative to Yale it was a concentration camp.

It took more than a year to get used to my new freedom. I felt like a college freshman who, after years of having the school day structured for him, finds himself with a lot of "free time." I began to realize how well planted the work ethic was in me: you go "to work" in the morning and you do "work" until five o'clock and if in that interval you

[2] One of the things I first heard at Southbury, and later used myself was: "After you work with these children for five years you begin to talk like them, after ten years you begin to look like them, and after twenty years you are one of them!" Humor as a way of handling and masking anxiety is as revealing as it is effective.

didn't "do" work—the kind of activity that could be filmed and proved you were "working," and that proved to yourself that you hadn't goofed off—you felt and were guilty. You could enjoy this work, there was no law against it, but one of its essential ingredients was that you were satisfying an external criterion of worth. So when I spent evenings and weekends writing, that was "writing," not "working"! I coped well with my guilt, and it helped me understand how much a product of my culture I was. I came to understand that the prime function of a university was to create the conditions for its faculty to learn, change, and grow. Yale existed for *me* and the rest of the faculty. No one bothered me or even suggested that I do this or that. It took me six months to learn that I had "call" on various departmental resources and that the more you claimed "call on" the more it was interpreted that you had an active research program. It could also be interpreted as being pushy and imperialistic but at least it was in a worthy cause!

My experience at Yale was the reverse of that of many of my undergraduate students who left Yale for "the real world." As one student put it: "I bitched and yelled when I was here. It all seemed so irrelevant and theoretical. I couldn't wait to get out. But do I miss this place! I was more myself here." If Yale's primary function is the welfare of its faculty, it is a function only somewhat more exalted than its concern for its undergraduates most of whom understand this only after they have left. I understand freedom not when I lost it, but when I got it. I could write a large volume on universities in general and Yale in particular, and its contents would be far from a paeon of praise, but I would go to lengths to insure that the reader understood that the university is the most refreshing oasis of freedom in our society. It is by no means surprising that as masses of young people streamed into our colleges and universities after World War II they, directly and indirectly, absorbed values and outlooks which were much more those of the university than of the larger society.

The switch to Yale taught me much about myself. First, I had and needed to have a diversity of interests. Diversity of interest and stimulation was essential to my well-being, to the extent that if I felt a lack or waning of either, I would become uneasy. Not only did I have to feel that in the present I had diverse interests and goals, but it was also important that I know in outline the different things I wanted to be involved in and writing about in the future, e.g., five or ten years from now.[3] After thirty years at Yale it is hard for me to recall a day when on the way to the office I did not have the thought: "And what interesting things are going to happen today?" My days were unpredictable and interesting, to an extent I did not dream possible at Southbury. What I

---

[3] I am alluding here to the fact and denial of mortality, the dynamics of which I will take up in a later chapter.

am trying to say about my days is not unlike what I experience in writing. When I begin to write I have a pretty good idea of what I want to say, the ideas I want to put into words, and the organization of and interconnections among ideas. But shortly after I begin writing, the ideas and their interconnections begin to change and I end up with something discernibly different from what I initially planned. Writing is a form of exploration full of surprises (and tortures). In fact, I have gained the least in an intellectual sense, and found the task relatively uninteresting, when I was writing up journal articles based on empirical research; by the nature of the task and materials I had to be impersonal and do justice to data "out there." In more discursive writing I was playing with my ideas and I never quite knew where they would take me, where I would take myself.

Another thing I learned about myself—related to the first point as well as to the Southbury experience—was that I did not wish to remain with a particular issue, in research or otherwise, for an indefinite period of time. That is, when I began something new I already knew that there would come a time when I would want to move on to something else. Before moving on, however, I would have to make written sense of what I experienced. I became dimly aware of this when after two years at Yale I felt an internal compulsion to write a book reflecting what I had done in and learned about the field of mental deficiency. Put in another way: I needed to feel that I would be changing career every few years or so. The beauty of the university is that it permits and encourages such changes; the obstacles are usually internal and not external.

The two major things I learned about myself—the need for diversity of interest and stimulation and the opportunity to change career directions—are obviously not peculiar to me. On the contrary, as I pointed out in earlier chapters, they were and have increasingly become characteristics of people in our society, particularly those who are highly educated. In myriad ways we have been taught to hunger for new experience, whether it be for a new car, coffee-maker, home, exotic trip, clothes, drug, deodorant, the latest form of self-exploration, movie, or picture book on the new geography of sexual positions. We can scapegoat Madison Avenue for some of this, but it is my belief that Madison Avenue (and American industry) have followed wants as often as they have created them. The hunger for the new, exciting, and rejuvenating experience goes much deeper than Madison Avenue and requires a far more complicated explanation. The hunger goes beyond material things and can be found in our theories about how to raise children and to live our lives, about how we must encounter and confront ourselves so that we experience our protean nature and free ourselves from our procrustean bed. When, after World War II, Dr.

Spock's book became the child rearing bible, it was not because parents were truly ignorant of how to keep a child alive and healthy or because pediatricians did not exist or because help and advice from friends and parents were not available, but rather because they thought it contained the psychological formulas insuring two related things: the discovery, nurture, and expression of children's diverse capacities as well as providing the foundation on which they could scan and experience a very diverse world. Implicit in all this was that you had to avoid unduly imposing your tradition and cultural heritage on the child before he or she could comprehend what it was all about. My parents never read Spock but, like so many immigrants, they did not come to this country to recreate for their children the conditions of their own upbringing. If they did not find the streets paved with gold, they did see them as paved with opportunity for their children; and being Jewish made it very likely that the major thoroughfares would be called Learning, Education, Professions. I have discussed this in another autobiographical fragment elsewhere (Sarason, 1973).

None of this, of course, explains my great needs for diversity of stimulation and change. It explains in part my ambition, and I do not want to underestimate what it meant in my early schooling to be regarded as bright and encouraged by teachers to set my sights high. The Great Depression altered my sights, and when early in those years I came down with polio it must have been traumatic in the extreme for my parents. It was traumatic for me but, dialectically, it also created the condition in which fantasy could run riot, and in the two years when the upper part of my body was encased in a brace or cast, with my right arm held extended at shoulder length, I lived through at least a dozen different careers.

Earlier in this book I stressed how the one life–one career imperative can present problems to those who by objective standards are "successful." Before illustrating this in my own life I have to return to the question of what we mean by a career. One could say that coming to Yale meant embarking on a career in the university and that the criteria for judging success were two-fold. First, by virtue of my teaching and research I would be eligible for and achieve promotion to higher academic ranks: assistant professor to associate professor to full professor. If somewhere along this line I was not promoted or given tenure, I could try to go elsewhere and make it at another university, and if this happened I was still meeting the onward and upward criterion. If I made it at a less prestigious university than Yale, I and many others in the field would probably not view the accomplishment without some thought that I was not all that good. (Snobbishness is not in short supply in academia.) But if I made it no place and had to take a position outside the university, I and all others would view it as having failed in my university career. That is to say, the university has criteria by which it decides who is deserving of being a member, and if you don't meet those criteria a career in the university is impossible. Your career has been aborted. Implicit in the conception of a career is that one has "improved" one's status, e.g., objectified by a new title, or more underlings, or more income, or all three. A career is a ladder which has definite, albeit varying, rungs leading to an agreed upon, desirable elevation. One climbs the ladder, unless one falls or is pushed off. The length of the ladder varies from one profession to another, as well as in the stability of its construction and in the clarity with which society defines the ladder, but all ladders require climbing. Inherent in the concept of career, from both a subjective and objective perspective, is the onward and upward theme. Over the course of his lifetime an individual may be "doing" the same thing (e.g., a surgeon, psychotherapist), yet if at the same time he has experienced the sense of growth and increased worth he will regard himself as having a successful career, but only if there is some agreement from others. However, as the mid-life professionals related, you can be regarded by others as having a successful career and you may agree with them, even when your excitement and interest have waned or gone. Objectively you are successful; subjectively you are bothered. There can be, and often is, a disjunction between how society and the individual define and judge a career. Initially, the individual seeks a career and is prepared to climb the ladder, and there is no disjunction between his and society's definition of a career and the criteria of success. But for many individuals, there comes a time when this conception of career is experienced as confining and an unexpected trap. And if one no longer wants to climb that particular ladder, or if he is already on the roof of the house of success, climbing down or jumping off is dangerous. He has come to see that his conception of what a personal career *should* be differs from what he initially thought and bought.

Now for a personal example. Three years after I came to Yale I initiated research on anxiety in children. I did not have to do any research, but not publishing meant perishing, and dead people do not climb ladders. The problem I chose was of personal interest to me (and I mean *intimately* personal), and I believed it could be studied in a scientific manner. Please note that I said "could" and not should, because the fact is that I always felt uncomfortable with and not very competent in statistics and research design. But it went deeper than that. There was and is a fundamental mismatch between what gives me intellectual satisfaction and the requirements of systematic research. I was only dimly aware of this at the time, or, more likely, I rationalized the dissonance away. This was easy to do because the students who came to work with me were awesomely bright and caught up in the intricacies of statistics and experimental methodology. I learned from them. Within two years I had received a sizeable grant, hired several staff members, and there were usually two or three graduate students who were part of our group. And a marvelously compatible group it was, although quite diverse in talents and personality. We enjoyed and helped each other, and argued loud and long about important football games and politics. By conventional standards, we were very successful: at any one time several studies were in progress; journals, books, and monographs were written; we received increasing recognition; I was promoted to associate and then full professor and other members of the group received good positions. My guess is that a good part of whatever reputation I have in psychology is due to the wide recognition the anxiety project received. (I have done much since, but it has not had as wide a reception.)

Early on in the project, however, I became familiar with the mixed blessings of growth and the dubious virtues of progress. Take the dynamics of grant support, for example. It was in the early fifties that the federal government began really to support social science research, especially if it had a mental health theme. In academia it became a sign of professional worth if you received grant support because the project required the approval of an expert committee advisory to the government agency. (It was considered a sign of distinction to be asked to serve in such a capacity.) There was the additional factor that such grant support permitted you to hire the assistance you needed to carry out the project. There was also the consideration that since academic salaries are for nine months, the grant was a way of obtaining a pro-rated summer salary. I am saying explicitly that as in all other areas of human behavior the motivation for seeking support was plural; a combination of selfish and selfless factors. You didn't say this out loud, of course, because it would tarnish the public image of the scientist dedicated *only* to discovery of new knowledge. But you pay a price and that price begins, first, when you take on the responsibility of being an employer in the university, by which I mean that you have a responsibility to produce "results" at the same time that you have a responsibility for the development of your staff: graduate students or post-doctoral staff. The two responsibilities often clash, especially if the grant is for a short period of time and you have to begin getting ready for renewal of the grant. Of the thousands of new grants given during those years (or even today, for that matter) I would bet and give good odds that the number of grantees who did not plan or ask for renewal was not far above some two digit figure. The clash of responsibilities was a minor irritant to me, largely because the great bulk of our early studies came out pretty much as we expected, and I was not in the position of having to worry about whether we could justify a renewal application. Even in those early days I resented the pressure to produce by a certain time. Given my economic background and political persuasion, the thought that *I* was an employer was a source of personal embarrassment. Furthermore, I am one of those people who has difficulty asking anybody to do something for me, especially if I am paying them. My own diagnosis was (and my analyst agreed) that my desire to exploit was far from absent and, given a flourishing and masochistically tinged super-ego, I tend to go the opposite extreme. As I said, this was not *that* much of a problem in those early days of the project. But the price becomes higher when your. project grows in size and scope. Now I had more people to be responsible for and worry about: were they doing all that they could or should? Were *they* getting something which would further their development? When it became time for them to leave the project, would I be able to help them get a good job? If I dropped dead, who would look out for them? I had a wonderful bunch of human beings on the project, and the more I loved them the more worried I became about their future. One additional factor: I do not separate from loved ones easily.

What I have mentioned so far as sources of concern were there, but they really were not strong. Something else began truly to bother me, and it got stronger as this project went on over a twelve-year period. I was becoming a research administrator. *I* didn't do research, the others did. I no longer had any contact with research "subjects." At our meetings I gave out with my ideas, as did the others, and we would easily come to a consensus about the studies we should be doing. Increasingly, however, these discussions were about what the others wanted to do, and with few exceptions the directions they were taking were fascinating and creative and marvelous for the project. Every now and then at these meetings I would be confronted by the thought that I was not growing. I also found myself bored with discussions of problems of statistics, experimental design, and data analysis. Now, up until an event which took place at a certain moment in one of these meetings, I would have waxed ecstatic if someone had asked me if I liked what I was doing. I would have stilled that small voice in me that articulated doubts, and I would have done so as much to screen out these doubts to myself as to conform to the socially desirable response. How could I tell someone that maybe I was stale, that I had been fleetingly aware for some time that I ought to move on to other problems? How could I explain that it had nothing, absolutely nothing, to do with my friends on the project, and, indeed, if it were not for them (and some less selfish reasons) I would like to be dealt out of the game, like yesterday? And how could I get them to comprehend why there was a mismatch between Seymour Sarason—the person, social philosopher, and activist—and Seymour Sarason the professor and researcher? If I had difficulty comprehending, why should I expect others to? In the quiet of the night I knew I was flying under false colors, doing a creditable job but alienated from what I was doing.

My conflict came to a head during a meeting of the group. We were discussing results of two recently completed studies and enjoying the fact that the outcomes were far clearer than we had hoped for. It seemed as if whatever we did confirmed our ideas. At a certain point I heard myself say, quite smugly, "You know, I would be willing to bet that if we filmed high- and low-anxious kids drinking Coca-Cola, we would find significant stylistic differences." At that moment, I knew I was no longer thinking but mechanically grinding out variations on a theme. I knew I had to get out from the person I had fashioned for myself. It was not easy, because what was involved was not only facing the beginning of an end but also the start of a beginning. Beginning of what? As I look back on those days, I can well understand why such a crisis (in its dictionary sense: a turning point for better or for worse) can be devastating and slowly demoralizing for people who are *not* in the university. Bear in mind that what is at stake is radical: severing roots, thinking and doing new things, becoming again a neophyte, putting one's personal and professional security on the line, and there are always the consequences for one's family (and that may include one's parents if they are in one way or another dependent on you). The cogency of these considerations is proportionate to the degree of contemplated change. As a professor, however, in a university like Yale where professors have freedom the limits of which have really never been defined or tested, the crisis was not all that radical: my income and position were assured, and I was in a setting where the untraditional may be frowned upon by some but accepted by most in the name of freedom. After all, the university is a place where you pursue new knowledge and experience, no holds barred, and if that means starting a new life, that's playing by the rules of the game. That does not mean that others drop what they are doing and help you pursue your destiny—just that they do not put obstacles in your way. Yale is as tradition-conscious a university as you will find, sometimes exasperatingly so, but once you have become a tenured member of the faculty the bonds of tradition are surprisingly flexible. You could argue that the criteria by which people are evaluated for tenure insure selection of a tradition-bound faculty, but in my experience that is far from being a valid characterization. My purpose here is not to describe or diagnose Yale (which would mean being expert in the nature of institutional greatness and craziness) but to illuminate the differences between my crisis and those of individuals who do not have the institutional support I had. If my crisis centered around the possibility of leaving the university, then the differences would have disappeared. That was only a fleeting possibility, in large measure because I could not face *that* kind of full-blown crisis. So when I listened to mid-life professionals rationalize why they cannot change their life and career directions, I was sympathetic and considered myself lucky. And when I think what might have happened to me if I had stayed at Southbury or its equivalent, or if I had felt I had no options at Yale and had continued role-playing the dedicated researcher, I shudder. I also feel guilty, much like the survivors of the concentration camps (or wars) feel about those who died. I am aware that I may be overstating the difference, but my experience with mid-life professionals tells me otherwise.

At least three years before I terminated the anxiety project, I thought about what else I might do. Interesting but idle thoughts. How do you start a clinic that would be alternative in conception, function, and goals to the usual mental health clinic? How can I demonstrate that mental practices and the mental health industry were woefully inadequate to meeting the dimensions of the problems as *they* defined them? The Yale Psycho-Educational Clinic was being conceived, but there was no reason to believe that there would be a delivery. At that time, Esther was desirous of returning to work as a clinical psychologist and was running up against an insufferable degree of psychiatric preciousness and imperialism. She was unhappy and, therefore, I was unhappy. It is too long a story to tell here, but it was Esther's situation, together with my own and less personal reservations about the organization and thrust of mental health professionals, that finally forced me to begin to take the many steps leading to the creation of the clinic. To separate the creation of the clinic from my relationship to Esther is grossly to distort what happened. In fact, to try to understand what my work means or meant to me without comprehending its functional relationships to Esther and our daughter, Julie, is to miss the point that what I think or do is for them, not in the corny sense of the superior male protecting and providing for his family, but rather as a way of telling them what goes on in my head, i.e., it is a way of telling them about that character they live with. This is one of the major reasons I write. How else can I do it? This may seem to be begging the question: *why* do I have to do it? Regardless of the answer, it concedes the point that my work and relationship to Esther and Julie are not in different quadrants of living.

If the crisis I experienced was less difficult than for people outside the university, I do not take second place to anyone in knowledge of how starting a new life—and that is what the clinic was—can be stressful. Very little in my past experience was relevant for what I wanted to do. Indeed, the greatest intellectual problem was in making sure that I was unloading impedimenta from my clinical training and experience.

I had no models to guide me. The first two years had more than their share of crises. I summed it up in the dedication to my book, *The Culture of the School and the Problem of Change* (Sarason, 1971): "To my wife Esther, and dear friends Murray Levine and Anita Miller for their help and support, particularly during the first two years of the Psycho-Educational Clinic when it was not at all clear whether we would make it."

Was the clinic a new career for me? Can you say a new life in the mold of the same career? You can say it, but it makes no personal sense to me. My office was relocated to the clinic building; I initiated a large set of new relationships outside the university. If you filmed a typical day before and after the clinic started, one would discern little overlap between what I was doing on those days; and if my thoughts could be articulated for those two days the overlap would be even less. Again, I am less interested in sharpening a definition of a career than I am in understanding why people seek change, the degree of it, its effects on life style, and the internal and external obstacles to pursing change. These considerations are crucial to our sensitivity to the processes of social change because they go beyond global categorizing and behind the facade of conformity to custom. There is a strong tendency, especially among professionals, to see and report themselves in terms of familiar labels and in the light of consistency, even though these may be discrepant with what they are becoming or would like to become. Put in another way: we have so absorbed the one life one career-imperative that we report "career consistency" via labels or categories even though it does not reflect drastic changes in total living. It is like when I get questionnaires from professional societies asking me what kind of a psychologist I am. So, I may say: "I am a clinical psychologist." True and not true. I *was* a clinical psychologist but I no longer *am*. True and not true, because I would fight vehemently if I decided tomorrow to return to clinical work and someone said I could not. Or I could say: "I am a community psychologist" and the same hassles would ensue. The fact is that I resent having to declare myself, to accept a label which does violence to what I was, am, or would like to be. I am more than any one of these things; better yet, I want to be more than any or all of these things. *And that is what I have come to see constitutes the resentment which so many people feel but cannot or fear to articulate.* We are so many things, would like to be so many things, and could in fact be so many things, why must we confine ourselves or why does society confine us to a procrustean career bed?[4] After World War II, at first indirectly and then very directly, this was the message to which several generations of college students were

---

[4] When I say "could in fact be" I mean that literally. We all have our Walter Mitty fantasies, but we also have fantasies of change that are tied more securely to reality.

exposed, although society was and still is organized on the one life–
one career imperative. Take, for example, the "human-potential"
movement which spawned a galaxy of ideas, methods, and
gimmicks—and gives every indication of trying to disprove that we
live in a finite universe. The very name of the movement is testimony
to the emphasis on what people can be in contrast to what they are, on
actualization of self in contrast to accommodation to social norms, on the
seeking of change rather than on sustaining continuity, on wholeness
in living rather than segmented experience. If the pronouncements of
some (not all) of the leaders of the movement reminded one of the
biblical prophets proclaiming truth and condemning sin, if the movement took on the features of the Crusades by pronouncing anathema
on the infidels (a conforming society) and warring to save the precious
soul of man from imprisonment, if the gaudy excesses and flamboyant
rhetoric were of Barnum proportions, they nevertheless contained a
hard kernel of truth for the thousands upon thousands who came (and
keep coming) for insight and change, literally to be rejuvenated: to
experience again the lost sensitivity, exuberance, vibrancy, and open-
eyed wonder of children. The human-potential movement exploded
into the public eye in the early sixties, but if one traces the antecedent
training and experience of its leaders, one finds many of them coming
from one or another of the varieties of psychoanalysis that held center
stage for a decade or more after World War II. As I pointed out in
earlier chapters, World War II ushered in the Age of Psychology, and
the issues of the relationships between what man is and what his
potentials are, between what man needs and what society permits,
were put squarely on the table and there is no sign they will be
removed.

A final autobiographical note. In the interval in which I terminated
the anxiety project and began the clinic I made the resolve that the
clinic would only take a few years of my life, i.e., that there undoubtedly would come the time when I would and should say "no more." I
was not going to fashion my own prison. I was not far off in my estimate of the years I would be involved in the clinic, but I was completely wrong in thinking I could avoid the consequences of growth,
success, and new intimate friendships. The clinic involved far more
people than the anxiety project, and there were more who were or
became my professional peers. By its very nature (Sarason, Levine,
Goldenberg, Cherlin, and Bennett, 1966; Sarason, 1972) the clinic
would attract and select unconventional people who were seeking to
change the direction of their lives. Extricating myself from the clinic
was not easy, but it did not result in anything like a major personal
crisis. I really quit while I was ahead, and in no small measure that
was because I had learned something about myself in ending the
anxiety project.

X

The Community Mental
Health Center: An Example
of Professional Dissatisfaction

IN PREVIOUS CHAPTERS I have alluded to but not discussed what happens when the structure and content of a profession begins to change as a reaction to developments in the larger society. This issue was touched on when I discussed mid-life professionals, particularly physicians, who found themselves increasingly affected by governmental policy and programs. And the effects were invariably perceived as adverse. In the main, however, I have emphasized the dynamics and consequences of the one life–one career imperative independent of structural and content changes in the professions, and this as a way of disentangling a cultural factor from societal changes which do not confront that factor. That this particular cultural factor interacts with major societal changes goes without saying, but it is precisely because the societal change does not confront the cultural factor that the possibility exists that their interaction will have adversely multiplicative effects.

To illustrate the point, which is extraordinarily complex, I shall confine myself to a type of setting in which a number of professions are involved: the community mental health center in which psychiatrists, psychologists, social workers, nurses, and others have become increasingly involved in the last fifteen years. Although a relatively new type of setting, the community mental health center has complicated origins which I shall sketch briefly.[1]

[1] In a previous book, *The Psychological Sense of Community* (1974), I have discussed in some detail how the social movements of the fifties and sixties changed the mental health professions. In that book I described these changes, expressed my doubts about the viability of the community mental health center concepts, but I did not take up what all this could mean for career satisfaction for the professional.

Historical Overview

In a formal sense one can date the beginnings of the community mental health center from the initiatives of the Kennedy Administration. In truth, as was the case with so many of the innovations, issues, and upheavals of the sixties, the conceptual rationales was well as the coalescing of pressure groups began in the previous decade. In 1955, for example, by act of Congress, the Joint Commission of Mental Health was established to critically survey existing needs, resources, and practices in what was seen as the most staggering of health problems: mental illness in its various forms of severity. It was already recognized that most state hospitals were "snake pits" specializing at best in the maintenance of mental illness and at worst in its manufacture. The Joint Commission was comprised of knowledgeable, socially conscious mental health professionals who were very much influenced by experiences in World War II. In fact, it was during World War II that the mental health professions underwent revolutionary changes in conceptual rationale, therapeutic tactics, and growth. This was hardly surprising when one considers the contrast between practicing in civilian and military life, the requirement of the military to get the troubled soldier back into action, the overwhelming numbers who needed such help, and the ambience of crisis-facilitating change in thinking and action. For example, during World War II the professional imperialism and preciousness of civilian life were noticeably weakened. "Instant Professionalization" may be too strong a characterization, but it does convey the speed with which people were given professional labels and responsibilities which they never would have been given in civilian life. It was World War II which brought new blood and brains into the mental health professions, contributing in the aftermath of the war to a reexamination of needs, services, resources, inter-professional relationships, and the role of government.

That government (which almost always meant federal) should play a major role in initiating and sustaining new programs and services seemed obvious enough, even though this would represent a truly basic change in professional outlook and interrelationships. Up until World War II the federal government played practically no role, fiscal or otherwise, in the mental health area, which is another way of saying that what went on was primarily determined by the traditions, interests, and social views of professional organizations. Indeed, the professional organizations took pride in the degree to which they insured the professional quality and autonomy of its individual members from non-professional sources, and the thought that the federal government should be asked to become an important factor in professional affairs brought forth pronouncements of anathema. Although it would be an exaggeration to say that World War II produced a major change in outlook among the bulk of the members of professional organizations in the mental health area, one can say that many of their leaders and influential members—conscious of the scandalous inadequacies of the mental hospital, as well as of the equally scandalous discrepancy between the public need and available resources—were crucial in influencing federal action. The possible outcomes of such action were hardly explored, if only because mental health professionals were not very knowledgeable about the nature and processes of government. It is as if they saw government providing the funds for programs, the content and goals of which would be largely determined by what the professions thought to be right, proper, and beneficial for the public good. It was a view almost totally at variance with the realities of how public policy (in its political, legislative, and executive aspects) is forged and administered. There was little or no recognition that the forging of federal policy, far from being a process in which professional wisdom and foresight would be the main determinants, inevitably has to take account of considerations far afield of professional substance and that the entire process has, so to speak, a life or dynamic of its own, i.e., it becomes a force independent of "narrow" professional considerations (Sarason, 1976). In any event, the entrance of government (and on a grand scale) into the mental health field altered the professions in several ways: it became a large employer of mental health professionals (the largest, in fact, in its Veterans Administration); through its subsidies it indirectly but powerfully determined what mental health professionals could do; and it brought the mental health professions into the area of public debate. Up until the late fifties the governmental role did not seriously alter or conflict with what was then considered by the mental health professions to be in the public and professional interests. The main task in those days was to train more professionals and provide a better research base for service to troubled people. The Joint Commission report, mandated by the Congress and containing as it did radical recommendations deriving from its exposure of the inadequacies of mental health services, could not be ignored, and it served as a rallying point (within and without the professions) for meaningful change, i.e., change which would represent a real departure from past professional views and practice.

But a lot more was going on in the public arena at the time: civil rights movements and militancy, and the complex of issues labeled "poverty." That our society had long been aware of and tolerated discrimination and poverty goes without saying, but for the most part they had been regarded by most people as separate issues. Beginning in the fifties their interrelationships were not only emphasized, but the struggle for social justice and equality of opportunity gained a force and support it never had before. For my present purposes it is sufficient to summarize what a significant segment of society appeared to be saying: "We are not living in depressed times but rather in a period not only of unrivalled affluence, but also with the known potential to eradicate poverty and to destroy the barriers to equality of opportunity. We can no longer tolerate a situation in which health is a privilege rather than a right, quality education is a preserve of the rich, and equality of opportunity is empty rhetoric; because one is poor or a member of a disadvantaged minority it is adding insult to injury, adding immorality to injustice, to ask that he be satisfied with poor or even non-existent health services, to consign him to public clinics and hospitals which no one regards as humane or helpful. In their pursuit of self-interest and as victims of their social insensitivity the middle-class professionals have lost credibility, and it is asking too much to expect them to exercise leadership. The government of the people must take the moral initiative for the people. The professionals are not part of the solution but part of the problem. The time for the redress of grievances has come." Every major institution in our society was part of the indictment. The mental health professions were particularly vulnerable, given the indescribably non-therapeutic ambience of the mental hospital, and the custom of middle-class professionals treating middle-class patients for fancy fees per hour. As one militant of those days said: "Man, I can't even afford to buy a couch let alone pay to lie on it in a shrink's office."

There were more than a few mental health professionals who agreed with the indictment. They were less of a factor in what ultimately happened than the obvious fact that the forces of government were propelled to action. One of these actions was legislation creating the community mental health center, a facility funded by the federal government according to certain guidelines, and exercising responsibility and public controls by various federal–state interrelationships. At the heart of the legislation were the following features: everyone in a specified geographical area was eligible for service at the center regardless of income; it had to have a variety of services (e.g., walk-in clinics, facilities for acute patients, consultation to community agencies); and it must be staffed by a variety of professionals capable of providing differentiated services. The community mental health center was explicitly seen as a device to keep troubled people in their community and to reduce admissions to the state hospital, and because there had been an obvious social class and color bias in use of the mental hospital, the community mental health center became the vehicle to provide the quantity and quality of community-based service to disadvantaged groups that would negate that bias.

Role and Structural Consequences

Let us now look at the predictable consequences of this new type of setting for the professionals populating it. It needs to be emphasized that although I am restricting the discussion to one type of health setting, there is every reason to believe that it is far from atypical in regards to what has happened to many professionals in other health and non-health types of settings as well.

The most obvious consequence was that the professional became a cog in a very big wheel which I shall call the Federal, State, Local Complex (FSLC). Wheel is a poor metaphor to describe the situation, because a wheel has a recognizable center from which spokes radiate to a rim in a clearly geometric fashion, assuming, of course, that the wheel is intended to work. The dictionary defines a cog as "a subordinate person or part," presumably of a recognizable structure of some sort. A cog is not autonomous; its function is a prescribed one. Prescribed by whom? In the FSLC the prescribers are many, depending on whether the center is part of a general hospital or university medical center complex, so that when one says "local" it can have reference to several components. Not only are they many, but the different prescription writers prescribe for different things, although they may overlap. One might describe the situation in this way: there are a lot of decision makers, each of whom presumably is empowered to make decisions in circumscribed areas as described in the overall plan or administrative structure or chart. There are decision or policy makers on the federal level (legislative and executive), state (e.g., department of mental health), and local (e.g., hospital, university, regional health boards) levels. Please note that I do not include decision or policy makers within the community mental health center because I wish to emphasize the obvious fact that what goes on within the center is in part a function of what other decision or policy makers do. As any professional who has worked in these centers can attest, what these other decision makers decide can have pervasive effects on what goes on in a center. Now, it has long been considered a major hallmark of the professional that he primarily determines the conditions permitting him to apply his knowledge and skills to others in mutually beneficial ways. This has always been the ideal situation for which the professional would strive, even though he recognized that there was an inevitable discrepancy between the ideal and the real world, but if that discrepancy was not great, or it was temporary, it could be tolerated without serious damage to his sense of autonomy and professionalism. When it was more customary for the health professional to be in private practice, or part of a small and autonomous clinic, or a local hospital, it was not difficult for him to believe that he and not somebody else was determining what he did and the way he did it, even though to a dispassionate observer the discrepancy between the ideal and the real world might have seemed greater than the health professional perceived. Furthermore, on those occasions when the individual professional felt his autonomy or professionalism violated or threatened, it was more than likely that he could identify the source and deal with it personally and directly.

It is a very different ballgame for the professional in the FSLC. External to him and the center are numerous people or agencies who can make decisions or alter policies directly influencing some aspect of what he does and, therefore, how he experiences work. In this respect, the professional is a cog: a subordinate person who in significant ways has restricted control over the conditions and substance of his work. He may not perceive these restrictions and may see himself as a true professional using his knowledge and skills in ways most beneficial to those he seeks to help, giving him a sense of satisfaction and professional growth. Given the characteristics and dynamics of something like the FSLC, and assuming only a modicum of understanding of the economic and political features of our society, it is most unlikely that the professional will long hold the view that he is in control of things. It is far more likely that early on in his work in the center he confronts the reality that what happens in Congress, in the executive branch, in the state capital, in the local community, in a regional board meeting, or in the department of psychiatry of the medical school with which the center may be affiliated—what happens in these and other external settings mightily affect him. If the state makes changes in its Medicaid program, or the state or local department of public welfare alters its schedule for payments for mental health service, or if the state department of mental hygiene changes criteria for admission to the state hospital, or if the financial picture of the general hospital with which the community mental health center may be affiliated is altered—if any or all of these changes occur it has very direct bearing on what the center is doing because of the socio-economic characteristics of the population it serves. You do not have to be a psychologist or sociologist or expert in organizational behavior and the administrative sciences to conclude that the professionals in the community mental health center are more like atoms in a cloud chamber than sturdy spokes in a well-constructed, finely balanced wheel. This may strike some people as an extreme statement, in which case I would maintain, at this point in the discussion, that the question becomes not whether there has been a discernible departure from the traditions of professionalism, but rather how much of one. And that is the point: the professional in the community mental health center has become part of a "complex bigness" in which he is a very subordinate part and which puts predictable and unpredictable constraints on how he functions as a professional.

Let us turn to another consequence which is far more subtle but no less fateful because it involves a radical change in the substance of professional thinking and, therefore, practice. It is a change not only stimulated by events in the larger society but "willed," so to speak, by influential segments of the different mental health professions. What is meant by the *community* mental health center? The use of the adjective community was obviously not fortuitous or a form of window dressing or intended as a description of old wine in a new bottle; it was intended to herald a conceptual revolution in mental health services. Although different groups had different reasons for supporting the revolution (always a characteristic of intended revolutions), there seemed to be agreement on several points. First, there had to be a redistribution of mental health services so that their availability would be less subject to class bias. Second, given the disproportion between need and professional resources, the new centers would innovate in the development of new therapeutic services, i.e., even if traditional therapeutic services were maximally effective the resources to apply them on an enlarged scale did not exist and would not exist in the foreseeable future. (There were some professionals who seriously questioned either the efficacy or social utility of existing therapeutic techniques and looked to the community mental health center for new directions which ultimately would change the nature of services to all groups in the society.) Third, and quite crucial conceptually, the center had to view the troubles of the individual not only as idiosyncratic to him or as a consequence of familial dynamics, but also in terms of the nature and structure of his community (its assets and deficits, actual and potential) and *the center had to deal with those features of the community*. The mental health professional was not to see himself as only helping *individuals* but also interacting with the community with the aim of altering it in ways which would have two results: improving the psychological status of the individual patient and preventing other individuals from developing problems of similar nature and severity. The mental health professional had, so to speak, two patients: the individual and the community. Fourth, and derivable from the previous one, the community mental health center was not the preserve of the professionals in the sense that the private office was or, for that matter, the ways most health settings were. The center was intended to be in, for, and *with* the community to insure that community sentiment about needs and priorities would be represented. If in the early sixties this last point was stated vaguely and rhetorically, the social turbulence of the years to come transformed rhetoric into action as militant individuals and groups insisted on having a voice. Professional *noblesse oblige* took quite a licking.

The third and fourth points come to the heart of the matter because they required a radical change in how professionals thought and acted.

No longer were they only clinicians trying to do their best to help individuals who came to them with problems. No longer were they expected only to explore the psyche and change personalities. They were to depart from the stereotype of the "shrink" sitting in his office passively and patiently listening to words and occasionally responding in kind. Something more was required and that was that they *be* in the community gaining knowledge and making relationships in order, catalytic-style, to tap, create, and organize new vehicles or arrangements that truly reflected actual or potential problem-ameliorating and problem-preventing community resources. One might say that they had to blend in one role the knowledge and skills of mental health clinician, anthropologist, social activist, and community entrepeneur. After all, you don't get to know a community or have an influence on it by sitting in your office. Nor do you come to be seen as a person to be reckoned with by being boringly neutral in stance or irresponsibly irrelevant to the substance and dynamics of a community's problems. A center which says to the community, *"Bring* us your problems" is quite different from one which says, "We will *come* to you to find out how you see certain problems and what you see as possible solutions."

Just as the mental health professional did not know what he was getting into when he became part of the FSLC, he was equally naive in regards to the community game, especially in estimating the radicalness of the change in his professional relationship to people. The degree of required change, if the adjective *community* would stand for something new instead of more of the same, would be literally of revolutionary proportions, as I have said elsewhere (Sarason, 1974).

> To redefine the problem in this way would have required a very different stance in relation to the community. It would have meant taking a very different view of potential resources and how they could be located and utilized, and it should have meant that the center was not the responsibility of the professionals alone. Indeed, to redefine the problem along these lines would have required that the professionals *refuse* to accept sole responsibility; they would, obviously, be part of program planning and service activities but now in the context of a serious community problem which required wide community participation and acceptance. What happened, instead, was that the professionals defined the problem in their terms and as their responsibility, rendering it insoluble and setting the stage for future community disillusionment.
>
> But, some could argue, what does the community know about serious psychological disturbance? How can people be given responsibility when they have no familiarity with the complexities of etiology and treatment? Who is the community? How do you justify shared resonsibility when it can mean a lowering of the quality of service? Besides, aren't these new centers so new and such an obvious improvement over the mental hospital that we should refrain from being overly critical? Will they not evolve over

time into being truly community centers? One way of beginning to answer these questions is to distinguish sharply between matters which are community issues and those which are ordinarily considered professional, in the sense that they deal with the nature of service. Whenever there is a gross discrepancy between community needs and an available service, it is a matter of community policy, not professional policy, how the available service should be distributed and what alternative steps should be taken to meet community needs. To put the case in clearest form, if people considered professionally rendered psychotherapy 100 percent effective but knew that it would be made available only to a very few of those who needed it (either by definition or demand), it would be obvious we would then be dealing with a problem that belonged to the community and not to the professionals. How limited resources were to be distributed, how alternative approaches could be developed, what degree of compromise between alternatives and outcomes the community could accept—these would be issues for the larger community to confront and decide. These are not issues for the professionals to decide, and to the extent that they are taken over by the professionals as being within their prerogatives, it virtually guarantees that there will always be inequities in the distribution of services. There is one consequence to what I am suggesting: the process whereby a community accepts responsibility—which is another way of saying that it becomes more informed and sophisticated about the ins and outs of the issues—tends to increase the number of service alternatives which are possible and which the community is willing to support. It is a process whereby community change occurs through redefinition of its problems and solutions. And, needless to say, it is a process which can serve to strengthen and enlarge people's psychological sense of community. It is not a process without serious problems and pitfalls, and it is not one which assumes that a community has a kind of folk wisdom insuring an appropriate match between problems and solutions. It is, at the very least, a process which puts the responsibility where it belongs [pp. 189-190].

The concept of the *community* mental health center was a sign of the times in that it paralleled the articulation of similar values and actions in other spheres of society. Those were the days when all kinds of individuals and groups, in different ways in different places involving different issues, really began to imply: "No more! Life and living are too important to be left to the official policy makers and professionals. We the people want in on all important decisions affecting life and living. We don't want to be told what is good for us, we want to be part of the decision-making process. We don't want things done to us unless we have been part of that process. The superior wisdom of the professionals and official policy makers has led us to a sorry state. It's going to be a new ballgame and we will help determine the new ground rules." From the halls of Congress to the local community the message was clear: those who would be affected by any public policy should be consulted about that policy and its implementation. Whether it was pollution, building construction, destroying landmarks, model cities, the rights of human subjects, the rights of patients to be informed about possible consequences of any procedure performed on them, educational policy, or foreign policy, there was the mandate (official and unofficial) to end unilateral decision making. I am not talking about "participatory democracy," the flamboyant rhetoric of which was matched only by a naiveté leading to its quick exit from the social scene. Participatory democracy was a procedural fetish not to be confused with the upswell of feeling that things had gone too awry for public passivity in regard to policy matters to continue. The origins of the community mental health center have to be seen in terms of these more general developments. The professionals who flocked to the community mental health centers were sympathetic to the new values and orientation, but they were unprepared for their implications and consequences. For example, not only did their training not prepare them for the structural and skill changes the new roles would require, but it was an obstacle. When you consider how much of the training of mental health professionals was based on "intrapsychic supremacy" (i.e., fathoming the intricacies of the *individual* human mind, and all else was secondary), it should occasion no surprise that they should have had difficulty in a role requiring them to be part anthropologist, part sociologist, part political scientist, part economist, and a large part of community activist and catalyst. And when one adds to this the pedestal on which mental health professionals placed themselves, with the aid of educated segments of the population, it is no wonder that when they had to deal with other parts of the community whose militancy and suspiciousness were quite the opposite of the worshipping stance, they did not know how to step down from the pedestal, or step down graciously. What was required was not only to learn new ways of thinking and acting but to unlearn old ones, and that is never easy, especially when it involves a new professional role. It was not like when the new math or new biology or new physics were introduced and teachers had to learn not a new role but new content, i.e., their style of relating to children, running their classrooms, or their place in the school and the school system were not changed. And those educational innovations were failures (Sarason, 1971)! No, the professional in the community mental health center had to learn a new role in which he would relate in new ways with unfamiliar populations about matters of policy, internal and external. The task was not made any easier by the opposition of those members of the mental health professions who saw the community mental health center either as diluting quality of service or, because the centers were to receive federal and state grants, undercutting support for training in the more traditional roles. If in those days the professionals in the center felt kinship to Custer in his last stand, it was quite understandable. As their eyes opened to the realities of being part of FSLC, as the difficulties of working with community groups escalated, and as they sought to duck the potshots from their more traditional colleagues, the professionals in the centers could not be expected to feel their self-esteem maintained or increased.

I am not aware of any published study or even discussion of work satisfaction of staff in community mental health centers. Dr. Cary Cherniss (1975) at the University of Michigan has been conducting a series of such studies in connection with his interest in work satisfaction of that ever-growing group of professionals and non-professionals in public agencies. I have seen some of his data for the community mental health centers, and they confirm what was predictable from what I have said above. The most cautious interpretation of his findings is that the level of staff satisfaction, compared with national norms for male workers with fifteen or more years of education, is low. In regard only to professional staff the picture is not significantly better.

Over the past ten years I have had rather intimate experience with three rather large community mental health centers, and in two of these settings my observations started before the centers actually began functioning to the time they became organizationally "mature," i.e., with staffs ranging in size from 100–150. If up until five years ago I had been asked to characterize what I had observed, it would have gone like this: "It's not easy to generalize, because there has been a rather large turnover of staff due to a high level of organizational craziness and sheer ignorance of what was involved in creating a new setting. Not only were there different kinds of wars of imperialism—between psychologists and psychiatrists, between nurses and physicians of all varieties, between researchers and everybody else, between administrators and line staff, between nonprofessionals and professionals, between almost everybody in the center and "they" in the medical school department of which the center was a part, and between top center staff and militant community groups—but the center had no way of successfully thinking and managing the problems of growth. All of this had surprisingly little to do with financial resources which, if not unlimited, were certainly not paltry. Basically, everyone was in a new setting in which they were supposed to develop new roles or, at the very least, significantly alter previous roles."

I would not today change my response on which I have elaborated in my last two books (Sarason, 1972, 1974), but I would certainly give far greater importance to the FSLC than I did. I should have known better, a point I shall now document. Two years before one of these centers opened I was at a party at which was a professor who had just completed an arrangement by which the state would build and largely staff for the university a mental health center. He was quite proud of the arrangements for two reasons: it would provide his department with a large and differentiated training site, and it would pioneer in providing more service to more people in the community and decrease the size and plight of the state mental hospitals. As he was relating *his* hopes and plans I became uncomfortable at the way he was talking of *his* (= university) plans. The reason for my discomfort was that I had been an employee of that state for several years, and even after leaving its employ I continued to have close relationships with several of its central office agencies in the capital. Although I did not and do not regard myself as an expert on the functioning of state government, I do claim a good deal of experience, if not expertise, on how state human-services agencies and institutions are affected by being part of the state apparatus. For the reader who would like to be exposed in upsetting detail to what I mean I recommend Dr. Burton Blatt's (1970b) *Exodus from Pandemonium*, especially the chapter on how a central office of a state department of mental hygiene functions or malfunctions. In any event, in talking with my academic colleague I realized that he really had no understanding of what it meant to be related to, let alone dependent upon, the overt and covert complexity of state government. At that time the federal government was involved only to a small degree in community mental health centers, but it was not long before my colleague found himself very much a part of the FSLC. It is hard to say the extent to which the sustained upheavals of the first five or so years of that center were due to what I call organizational craziness (the base rate of which in most organizations is alarmingly high) and how much to enmeshment in the FSLC. But there can be no doubt that the role of the FSLC was and remains significant. The director of a community mental health center once put it to me this way: "It is a real question whether dealing directly with the feds and steds (the state equivalent of the feds) arouses stronger suicidal and/or homicidal tendencies than when you are the *indirect* object of their actions. When you deal directly with them you know you cannot win except by lying, in one of its more acceptable social isotopes. What makes it worse is that they are usually nice guys who would like to do the right thing, but they are so tied by those to whom they are accountable that they probably feel the way I do. My staff is affected by all this indirectly. That is, I pass along to them what we can do or not do, what our budget *may* be, whether it will go up or down or remain the same which means a cut, who had better put in for a research grant as protection, how careful we must be that we don't get caught outside of the guidelines, and let's make absolutely sure that we can say that we have a community base otherwise we are in trouble. They think I'm a liar and that I am pushing my weight around because I delight and specialize in turmoil as a way of giving expression to my sadism." If you can stand upsetting accounts I recommend an article by Dr. J. Herbert Fill (1974), who was New York City Commissioner of Mental Health for five years up until 1972, in which he describes one of his typical days. New York City is atypical only in the sense that what is true elsewhere gets magnified there. I think it is also true that officials in New York City talk and write more.

I could find only one formal study that addresses the question of how the FSLC affects a community agency: its staff and clients. The study was done by Sarata and Reppucci (1975) and is entitled *The Problem is Outside: Staff and Client Behavior as a Function of External Events*. The agency was not a community mental health center but a halfway house type of operation embodying some elements of a therapeutic community for pre-release adult offenders. One-half of the staff were non-professionals from the local community. The agency was funded jointly by the federal and state governments with participation from the local community. What is interesting about this study is that Sarata and Reppucci were not interested initially in "external events," but as contracted researchers their tasks were (a) to examine the in-program behavior of clients and its relation to recidivism, and (b) to examine the in-house decisions and processes involved in the development and implementation of a new program. In short, they were "internally" oriented. They collected a large amount of data about staff and residents. They were researchers, not part of the operations. It was not until data analyses were almost complete that they saw how certain external events were surprisingly related to some of their puzzling findings. Here is the brief history Sarata and Reppucci present:

> The history of central office's relations with CRP (Comprehensive Re-entry Program) can be divided into three distinct periods. During the first 2 months of operation, February and March, central office treated CRP with what might be characterized as "benign neglect." Relations were less than cordial since prior to opening the director and staff of CRP had come into conflict with various elements of the department—for example, the personnel office and other correctional centers—and CRP was generally viewed as a "decidedly unprofessional" operation. Similarly, the deputy commissioner to whom the CRP director was responsible, and others had expressed displeasure with the staff's appearance, that is, casual dress and long hair. However, in regard to the development of the program and the internal functioning of the center, CRP had been left to its own devices. They had contracted for staff training outside of the department and it was assumed that CRP would develop and articulate its own program. The commissioner had toured the facility on opening day and the deputy commissioner regularly met with the director for 1 hour each week. The director of programming had called CRP's director once to inquire about

"how things are going." Otherwise the central office was obvious because of its absence.

During the first week in April, the situation changed drastically. The deputy commissioner, wishing to "get a reading of the program," sent the director of prerelease programs to spend 2 weeks at CRP, "observing and evaluating the program's strengths and weaknesses." Later in April the department learned that the project might not receive funding for a second year. (Originally the department had been informally assured of a second year of funding and the possibility of LEAA not refunding the project arose from a change in funding policy and not from the evaluation of the project. The deputy commissioner learned of this possibility after having sent the director of prerelease programs to evaluate CRP. Thus CRP was informed that its existence after June 30 was problematic. Indeed, early in June the staff was informed that on the 14th of that month they would receive "2-week termination notices, to deal with the eventuality that the program is not refunded." Finally, CRP was informed in May that a drug rehabilitation program was also to be housed in the CRP building, in essence the clients and staffs from both programs would share the same quarters. This decision had been opposed by both staff; each felt that being new programs, they needed to develop fully their own procedures and identities. However, for administrative reasons, that is, the nonavailability of other space and a general shortage of funds, the deputy commissioner decided that the move would take place in June.

During the months of July and August, the central office again receded from the picture. The department had received a no-cost extension of the LEAA grant and was able to continue the program temporarily. A no-cost extension is authorization to continue spending—up to the amount originally allotted—even though the original period of funding has elapsed. Since the center had opened 5½ months late, they had considerable funds in reserve. The deputy commissioner went on vacation and the CRP staff had little contact with the central office, which turned its attention to other matters [pp. 93–94].

Sarata and Reppucci give compelling evidence for hypotheses about the relationship of changes between staff and client behavior, on the one hand, and the external events, on the other. In concluding their discussion of the implications of their findings, they said: "This study, which dealt specifically with the effects of central office behavior on the attitudes and behaviors of the staff and clients in a rehabilitative program, also reflects the processes by which the larger social context influences the functioning of rehabilitative programs. First, the actions of the Washington office of LEAA directly influenced the functioning of CRP. Today when federal funding is essential to the development of new programs in many fields, for example, education and mental health as well as corrections, this influence must be taken seriously." The community agency which Sarata and Reppucci studied was not a community mental health center, but their findings and reflections in every respect support not only my own observations, but the numerous reports I have been given by professionals in community mental health centers.

I do not wish to convey the impression that it is an established fact that most professionals in community mental health centers are dissatisfied, and that the FSLC is the culprit. That most of the professionals in the centers are a dissatisfied lot reflects my own observations and is consistent with ongoing studies, but a more substantially based conclusion will have to await the outcomes of many studies. Dissatisfaction can have diverse sources, but one of the blind spots in the theories and orientations of mental health professionals and organizational consultants—in psychology and psychiatry in particular and the social sciences in general—is their focus on individuals, groups, and circumscribed settings. They rivet, as Sarata and Reppucci initially did, on events and interactions internal to the setting and seem to regard external events as random nuisances. Consequently, they tend to see work satisfaction as due to a combination of personality and setting characteristics. There is, of course, truth to such a view, but it is a partial one, and the major implication of my argument is that the FSLC already has become a significant factor in these settings and there is every reason to believe that it is an inexorable one, the dynamics of which have hardly been conceptualized in the mental health literature. You can *see* individuals, you can *see* or assemble groups, and you can *see* the physical setting. You cannot *see* the FSLC. It has to be conceptualized as a system of different parts, functions, interests, and traditions before you can *see* how it intrudes into and affects individuals, groups, and the local setting. At the present time the FSLC is sensed by the professional as somewhere in the background but obscured by quotidian events and issues possessing a compelling immediacy which we can fit into our accustomed psychology of the individual and interpersonal relations. This is not without its virtues, because as the professional becomes increasingly aware of how his experience of work is determined by the dynamics of the FSLC, his picture of himself will undergo upsetting change.

Those who work in community mental health centers are part of a much larger sample of people in the public employ. One would expect that what I have said about professionals in community mental health centers would be no less true for that larger group of "public" professionals. Relevant to this is an ongoing study by Kane and Cherniss (1976) of a near total sample of employees in a particular state. I am grateful to these researchers for permitting me to quote from a letter to me summarizing their findings and impressions to date (italics are theirs):

The study concerns job satisfaction, work alienation, and attitudes toward work and life among over 700 public employees in the state of _____. Perhaps the most intriguing aspect, as far as our interest in professionals is concerned, is that the study has generated comparable job satisfaction data from a sample including large groups of workers from *all* occupational levels and categories, including professionals working in state institutions.

One of the most interesting findings is that there is virtually *no difference* between professionals and other occupational groups in levels of job satisfaction. The professionals are just as satisfied (or dissatisfied) with their work as anyone else. The myth that professionals find their work more satisfying simply wasn't supported. By the way, I came across a study done by Robert Kahn and some others here at Michigan over 10 years ago which, using a different measure of job satisfaction, came to the same conclusion. In their study, there also was no difference in job satisfaction between professionals, managerial groups, and others.

One of the things we've done in this study is to develop a measure of what we call "work alienation." This is operationally defined as "the percentage of higher order need fulfillment" a worker desires from work. In other words, it is the extent to which a worker seeks meaning, purpose, intrinsic enjoyment, and self-development from a job. A worker who doesn't expect the job to provide these is "alienated." We have found that there is virtually no correlation between "work alienation" and "job satisfaction." They are independent concepts. Thus, an "alienated worker," as we have defined it, is just as likely to be high in job satisfaction as to be low.

As one might expect, the professionals in our sample are more concerned about the higher order needs than are semi-skilled and other types of workers. As a group, professionals are more likely to say that they want a lot of meaning, self-development, and intrinsic enjoyment *from life*. However, professionals are just as alienated from their *work* as are the other workers. In other words, the *percentage* of meaning, challenge, and learning that the professional worker expects to get from work is not significantly different from this percentage for other workers.

We will have to await the completion and publication of the work by Cherniss and his colleagues in order to make a critical assessment of their findings and interpretations. It is unlikely, however, that such an assessment will change an unpleasant picture to a pleasant one.

The most comprehensive and systematic published studies of work satisfaction of professionals and non-professionals in helping services settings were done by Sarata (1972, 1975, 1976).[2] He compared the

[2] When Sarata surveyed the job satisfaction literature for the decade 1960–1970, he found very few publications having relevance for the human services area. I predict that by the end of the current decade the number of publications on job satisfaction of professionals generally and human services professionals in particular will be much greater. I am aware of ongoing or newly started research on this problem in various universities: Christine Maslach at Berkeley, Cary Cherniss at Ann Arbor, Steven Reiss and Gerald Senf at the University of Illinois (Chicago Circle), Gerard Rowe at the

employees of three relatively young state regional centers for the mentally retarded on various indices of work satisfaction. The three centers had different strategies for providing services, ranging from one with a community thrust to one which was a traditional, essentially custodial setting. Sarata predicted that work satisfaction would be highest in the center with the broad community thrust. This, in fact, was what he found. Equally interesting, Sarata found that for those who had the most direct contact with clients, almost always the non-professional employees, the most salient sources of satisfaction and dissatisfaction (mostly the latter) were client-related matters. In contrast, those with the least contact with clients, the professionals, had sources of satisfaction and dissatisfaction from elsewhere. Let us listen to Sarata's recommendations for administrative practices. Although he is talking about the mentally retarded, there are obvious points of similarity for those working with clients in community mental health centers, especially that significant number of clients who show lack of progress.

Implications for administrative practices. These findings would seem to have important implications for administrative practices. The data clearly indicates that for individuals currently employed in the field of mental retardation, satisfaction with the field is consistently high and only minimally correlated with agency-related matters. On the other hand, overall satisfaction is highly correlated with attitudes concerning agency-related matters and therefore is potentially alterable. Moreover, variables such as the amount of client contact and the lack of client progress, which are associated with differences in level of satisfaction, are associated with differences on the satisfaction-with-agency measure. Thus, the current data imply that administrative efforts to improve employee satisfaction should focus upon the employee's attitudes concerning the agency.

One specific approach for potentially increasing employee satisfaction involves the apparent lack of client progress. The gains made by retarded clients are often not readily apparent and therefore administrators should attempt to provide methods for systematically monitoring that progress which is made. Moreover, because progress is inevitably slow, employees must be aided to accept this as a given. Inservice training and staff meetings should include regular discussions of client progress and its influence upon employees. An employee's suggestion that a client is progressing

University of Connecticut. Dr. L. E. Thomas, also of the University of Connecticut, has organized a research group (R. L. Mela, P. I. Robbins, and D. W. Harvey) to study highly educated "corporate dropouts." Dr. Reppucci's (now at the University of Virginia) forthcoming book on a long-term intervention in a correctional setting contains some fascinating accounts and data on work satisfaction, as well as on how a human services agency is affected by being enmeshed in the Federal, State, Local Complex. If one included doctoral dissertations in progress, the number of studies would be far beyond what Sarata found for 1960–1970. It would seem that career satisfaction among professionals is "in the air" and being sighted by diverse investigators. The question is less why this is occurring than why it took so long for the problem to attract recognition.

slowly because of a deficiency in the agency should be seriously examined; it may be accurate. However, the current findings suggest that many employees adopt the general assumption that the lack of client progress is attributable to the agency or staff and that this type of reaction is associated with a lower level of satisfaction than is the recognition and acceptance of limited progress as a given. In short, the administrator should strive to create an atmosphere in which employees' frustrations concerning client progress is openly expressed and examined.

A second specific area upon which the administrator should focus is the work situations of HC group employees. Client-related matters are the most salient sources of satisfaction and dissatisfaction of HC group employees. The desirability of altering this situation is reflected in the lower level of satisfaction-with-agency reported by the HC group. One approach which administrators might consider is providing HC group employees with nonclient related responsibilities. For example, each employee might spend a portion of the work week engaged in training volunteers, doing community relations work or some other nonclient-related task. Such responsibilities not only provide an opportunity for specific "success experiences" but also provide increased variety, contact, and learning. Another approach would be redesigning agency procedures and job descriptions in ways which involve having employees functioning in several roles simultaneously and rotating responsibilities periodically.

Indeed, the general implication of these findings would seem to be that administrators wishing to increase staff morale should redesign agency procedures in light of staff needs. The development of operating procedures typically reflect three factors: (1) Historical precedents such as existing job specifications and the principle of hierarchical organization; (2) the perceived need to provide clients with a variety of essential services—many of which are provided by professional specialists; (3) fiscal consideration—i.e., providing essential services for a maximum of clients with a minimum of staff. The appropriateness of these concerns is not germane to this discussion. The point is that programs and procedures are developed without considering the needs and satisfactions of staff. Hence the almost universal view that staff morale is extremely low in agencies serving the retarded and other human services agencies is not surprising. The data reported here are consistent with the views of those writers who have suggested that the development of effective human service agencies can be achieved only if staff needs are integral to such deliberations. Some of the required technology is available (e.g., Hackman & Lawler, 1971), but the present lack of systematic research concerning work satisfactions in the human service fields must also be remedied.

There is much wisdom in what Sarata has said and in no way should the observations I will now present be interpreted as nihilistically denying what can be done in such settings if you hold certain values and they appropriately inform action and organization. The fact is that I was one of the advisors to Dr. Sarata in his study, and I was also quite knowledgeable about the three regional centers he studied. Indeed, I played a role in the creation of two of them. I have no doubt that Sarata's findings were valid for the time period in which he did the study. If he had done the study a year later or today, I would likewise have no doubt that differences among the centers would not exist and that the level of work satisfaction for professionals and non-professionals alike would be significantly lower than when the study was done. Here, too, I should have known better than to view the study as valid other than for the period in which it was done, because I was already well aware of the struggles that were taking place between central office and each of the centers, between central office and the state personnel and finance officers, and between central office and the new governor. Some of this was alluded to in a book (Sarason, Grossman, and Zitnay, 1972) describing the creation of one of these centers. But the full story, especially for the period after Dr. Sarata did his study, has yet to be told. Suffice it to say, it is one of the more seamy stories of how human services settings enmeshed in the FSLC are adversely affected by factors beyond their control.

It is unforgivable to view the FSLC as made up of wicked, power-hungry, insensitive mediocrities who spend their days developing new ways of administratively torturing the local setting, a point I have elaborated on elsewhere (Sarason, 1975). To take such a view is an insidious form of psychologizing that guarantees misplacement of blame and missing the trees for the forest. The fact is that the FSLC is a system comprised of parts each of which has a different history, tradition, perceived function, and style of operation. The state legislature is not the executive, and each has differentiated sections, many of which have different purposes, formal power, and informal influence. The same can be said for the federal government, and, needless to say, when it has formal relations with state and local government this organizational complexity threatens to get out of hand. To see this fantastic complexity in narrow psychological terms is to miss the entire point. Generally speaking, by virtue of their training, health professionals have no conceptual basis for comprehending what is happening or why it has happened, and, therefore, increasingly they adopt a paranoid stance as if the FSLC was organized to defeat *them*. If it were simply a matter of personal evil rather than of impersonal consequences of a fantastically complicated and inevitably compromised policy-making drama with a large cast on many stages, and with many directors, it would be easier to deal with. It is a drama (more like one written by Beckett than O'Neill) in which increasing numbers of professionals have a role—a new role subtly redefining their professional identities. For most the new role is a dissatisfying one. Acceptance of it was expected to be a self-fulfilling step on the road to personal growth and social authenticity. The expectations, today, are discernibly weaker.

Why has it been so attractive to be considered a professional? This begs the question: What are the criteria for professionalism? Extended formal education? Expertise? Specialization? Autonomy? Providing a socially needed service? All of these criteria have a surface plausibility, but I have always been nagged by the thought that there was a self-serving aspect to them, i.e., they are used as much to provide social approval and a sense of personal worth and distinctiveness as to reflect the emergence of new functions based on new knowledge. The attraction of a professional label is that it gives the holder a sign, literally and figuratively, that says to others: "I am distinctive. You should respect me for what I know and can do. I am not part of the mass. I am not interchangeable with others." Professionalism can be impersonally and "objectively" defined, but seeking to become a professional is quintessentially a quest for personal and social worth. According to census definitions and data, in 1890 3.78 percent of people between the ages of twenty-five and sixty-four were professionals. In 1920, the figure was 4.4 percent, and in 1960, it went to 12.99 percent (Veysey, 1975). This dramatic increase has many sources, and of the more significant ones is the belief endemic in our society that attaining professional status, having a professional label, attests to one's personal and social worth. Veysey (1975) has put it well:

> If one looks at the subject of the professions from the ground up—by perusing the pages of the United States census from 1880 forward which are devoted to categorizing and counting them—the inadequacy of the widely employed model of professionalization is apparent. All sorts of anomalies appear. Actors, for instance, are consistently termed professionals; so nowadays are funeral directors, yet the academicization of these groups has been relatively slight.
>
> Most key elements in widely used definitions of professionals turn out not adequately to distinguish them from other groups in the American population. The need for prolonged training is shared by artisans and craftsmen. Again, specialization is a tendency which has proceeded in many sectors of American society. Who could be more minutely narrowed in terms of function than an automobile assembly-line worker? Are the professions distinguished by a dedication to altruistic social service, as certain sociologists have claimed? Some of the most notoriously venal occupations are listed by the census bureau as professions. Even a few kinds of manual skills are rewarded with professional status—those of dentists, surgeons, and athletes, for instance. Yet businessmen are even now excluded because they deal with the buying and selling of material goods. In short, all sorts of hidden arbitrary assumptions are built into the very notion of the professions. Together they suggest that some degree of en-

hanced social status is the only true common denominator of the varied occupations that are given this label [p. 420].

To seek and attain enhanced social status may be the true common denominator, as Veysey says. When one considers how each new profession has had to struggle for its birth and existence against the objections of older professions, of academic conservatism, and of legislative and legal tradition, it should not be surprising that issues of enhanced social status mark the history of the different professions. Professional preciousness and imperalism (as found in the guilds of another era) is a social disease which fledgling professions resist only to manifest all of its symptoms once they have attained enhanced social status (a form of identification with the aggressor). From this standpoint, it is more correct to say that the common denominator among professions has two factors: first, to attain and maintain enhanced social status and, second, to make life difficult for any fledgling group the existence of which is perceived as diluting the established profession's status. Nowhere has this been more true than in the health fields, where so many new professions and accredited specialties have emerged, and the end is not in sight.[3] However, as I have tried to illustrate with the community mental health center, the fact that all health professionals are increasingly being drawn, willingly or not, into the FSLC makes enhanced social status a temporary source of satisfaction for the newer as well as the more established professions. Enhanced social status is a weak base for continued satisfaction when daily reality confirms that you are not in control over your destiny, that decisions affecting your work and life are made elsewhere, often by people and forces unknown and unknowable to you. The creeping sense of impotence, strange to professionalism however defined, has made professional work more problematic than ever. The degree and generality of this development are hard to gauge. There are no systematic data because, as I pointed out in earlier chapters, work satisfaction among highly educated, professional groups has not, unfortunately, been a fashionable area of investigation. I can only report that when I have presented my conclusions

---

[3] Someone once described the health fields in general and urban hospitals and medical centers in particular as one of the few unexplored jungles left on earth, populated by a bewildering array of old and new species of professionals of the hungry and devouring kind, each of whose concept of territoriality insures permanent war. The war, he went on to say, was somewhat internecine (e.g., the general practitioner vs. numerous medical specialists, the psychiatrist vs. all other physicians, the "Herr Professor" vs. his underlings, the public health practitioner vs. the clinical fraternity, the powerful surgeon vs. the powerful internist) but soon spread to those who heretofore were "allies" or "colonials," e.g., nurses (registered, practical, and others), hospital administrators, social workers, rehabilitation specialists, insurance firms, legislatures (spawning boards of one sort of another for purposes of planning and control), lawyers (specializing in malpractice), unionized hospital workers, and articulate representatives of ethnic and racial minorities.

to groups of health professionals they confirmed, with very few exceptions, the conclusion. One of them put it into words which, I think, had the virtue of unadorned, personal concreteness: "The other day I was talking to our plumber and I was aware that *I* was envious of *him* at the same time that he was envious of me, the big shot doctor. I kept asking myself: Why was I envious of a plumber? I didn't have to think long. The way I saw him he was far more in control of his work than I was. *He* decided what he would do and when, and he didn't have to check it out, as I do, with millions of sensitive souls each one of whom can make life very tough for me. And if I didn't like him or his work, he could say goodbye, or tell me to go to hell, and off he would go to someone else who has been pleading with him to come fix their pipes. He tells me what is wrong and how much it will cost, and I can take it or leave it and, of course, I take it and I am thankful to him. If I took a take-it-or-leave it attitude at the health center, I couldn't get done what I am supposed to do, and a lot of the time things don't go the way they should anyway. I have to touch more bases with more people than you can count, and I have to treat them the way I do my plumber. And that's only *in* the hospital! My plumber doesn't have to worry about what some idiot in City Hall or the state capital or Washington will come up with next. Today they change the rate for Medicaid patients, tomorrow Blue Cross says they are reducing payments for this or that, next week they will change the rules determining how long you can keep a patient in the hospital, and all the time I'm worrying if Congress will override the President's expected veto of this or that health bill. So who's better off, me or my plumber? If you asked my plumber, the damned fool would change places with me pretty quickly." This was said with humor, the kind of humor that allows a piece of personal truth to come out for public scrutiny. The speaker was a thirty-five-year-old physician who early on in medical school had eschewed the private office for a career in community medicine. By his own account, he had learned a lot and would go the same route again. However, he had already reached the point where there was a perceptible change in the balance between satisfactions and dissatisfactions, and the question had arisen: Should I get out? When, in private conversation, I asked him what change he was contemplating, he said: "If I knew the answer to *that*, the question would be *when* to get out, *not* should I get out."

It is misleading, I think, to attribute what I have described to unrestrained or thoughtless growth and bigness, although they are certainly factors. As important as these factors is the increase in the number of discrete groups or interests (professional, private, and public) seeking to influence and participate in policy formation and decision making. These groups are heterogeneous in role, purpose, tradition, and power. The role of some of these groups is formally recognized in legislation or through administrative regulations; those that are not so recognized attempt to exert influence by lobbying, political activity, and the use of the courts. The era is over when professionals and professional organizations are the major determiners of their own policies and practices. It was long recognized that war was too important to be left to the generals, and that principal has now been extended to professions serving the public welfare. Whether it be educators, physicians, architects, city planners, engineers, it has become accepted principle that far from being left to their own devices, they must be controlled by those affected by their activities. And behind this principle is public sentiment that professionals have put their own interests before the public welfare. For example, in a recent review of Auerbach's (1975) book *Unequal Justice*, an indictment of the American Bar Association, a law professor (Dershowitz, 1975) concludes:

> Auerbach's review of the failings of the elite bar during this century suggests that reform will not come by having law schools preach the ethics of the American Bar Association, but rather by restructuring the legal profession so that its ethics no longer remain the nearly exclusive preserve of a lobby group whose history is replete with bigotry, injustice and the expansion of professional prerogatives at the expense of the citizenry. Legal ethics committees should include lawyers who are not members of the A.B.A. as well as nonlawyers—perhaps philosophers and consumers of the law—who can view legal ethics from a *broader* perspective then that of the entrepreneurs of the law. I, for one, propose to have my legal ethics students read "Unequal Justice" before they read the A.B.A.'s Code of Professional Responsibility [*New York Times*, January 25, 1976].

The historical justification for this conclusion and recommendation in regard to law and the other professions I have mentioned is unassailable, but that should not blind us to the dynamics of "problem creation through problem solution." That is to say, in the understandable and justifiable quest to control "the expansion of professional prerogatives at the expense of the citizenry," the professional's satisfaction from his work has decreased, particularly that large number of professionals now part of the Federal, State, Local Complex. In noting this, I am in no way suggesting that we turn the clock back, and I am not asking for sympathy for these professionals on the grounds that they deserve special consideration. Although professionals are not small in number, their influence is out of proportion to their numbers. If it becomes increasingly the case that professionals experience a widening discrepancy in work between expectations and satisfactions, the negative consequences for their lives will have ramifications beyond the spheres of their individual existence. In earlier chapters I deliberately emphasized the dynamics and dilemmas of the one life–one career imperative in individuals who had experienced satisfaction and success in their professional work. In this chapter I have described a particular health service setting in which by virtue of a pervasive alteration in the structure of the professionals' role the confrontation with the one life–one career imperative will not have been preceded by a sense of accomplishment. One result may well be that the much spoken about mid-career crisis will occur significantly before the mid-career interval. There is a final consideration that cannot be ignored: to the extent that what I have described and concluded in this chapter has validity, it has obvious serious consequences for those whom these professionals serve.

Postscript

On February 23, 1976, this chapter was given as the keynote address at the convention of the National Council of Community Mental Health Centers and the National Institute for Community Mental Health. I had misgivings about delivering this as a keynote address. Such addresses are by custom supposed to be inspiring, uplifting, with onward–upward themes. Mine would be quite the opposite and might, I thought, engender a counter-productive response. I knew there was to be a question-and-answer period afterwards, via microphones placed strategically in the auditorium. It is somewhat of an exaggeration when I say that it was the first time I had ever observed a mass confessional, but putting it that way helps make the point of the experience. At least a dozen psychiatrists cornered me and in individual discussion gave me more lines and verses to add to my themes. When I looked at the convention program, I realized why I had gotten such a positive response. Here are some of the titles and descriptions of convention workshops:

Accountability: What Are the Hot Topics?

Analysis of counter-productive themes—situations where efficiency interferes with positive treatment outcome and creates larger rather than smaller costs to society.

Identification and discussion of conflicts faced by CMHCs in being accountable—with audience participation.

Programmatic Implications of CMH Standards

Open forum to discuss with center directors and others the possible impact on program organization and delivery of the Accreditation Standards for CMH programs in various settings. Will include considerations of rural/urban, free-standing/hospital affiliated, etc.

Peer Review: Overview

Workshop will consider goals and objectives of peer review, as well as the different models designed to monitor quality assurance, utilization review or cost containment. It will also provide an opportunity for discussion of such sensitive factors as costs, confidentiality, authority, selection of reviewers, educational benefits, consumer participation and guaranteeing impact.

Third Party Payments—Private

Seminar will focus on reimbursement from private sources—Blue Cross/Blue Shield, commercial carriers, HMOs, foundations. Each mechanism will be analyzed in terms of provider requirements, client eligibility, benefit package, rate schedule and risk factor.

Third Party Payments—Public

Seminar will emphasize how CMHC can receive reimbursement from public sources including Medicaid, Title XX, CHAMPUS, LEAA, VR, SSI and others. These sources will be examined through provider requirements, client eligibility, service and rate package, billing efficiency.

Contract Design and Implementation with State, Local Agencies and Corporations

Session will cover purpose and utilization of contracts, contract development, content and monitoring of contract performance. Emphasis placed on contracts with state and community-service providers.

Legislation on the National Scene

Workshop will review national legislation—pending and expected—with the focus on how center board members and staff can help get the NCCMHC message across.

Secrets of the Legislative Process

A frankly pragmatic exposé, revealing intimate, inside details of the legislative process and how to make it work for you; live-action citizen lobbying, notorious secrets of professional lobbyists. Rated (R) for reality.

Learning from Tragedies in CMHCs

Exploration of the professional liability, political, public relations, service delivery and human aspects of tragedies which have occurred in MHCs around the country. Emphasis is given to actions which can be taken to prevent tragedy or to minimize the consequences for the patient, staff, center and community.

CONFLICTS AND COMMONALITIES: CMH STANDARDS AND HEW REGULATIONS

Discussion of relationship and implementation issues of the Accreditation Standards, Medicare–Medicaid Conditions of Participation, and NIMH Regulations. Will be especially concerned with Third-Party Payments, surveys, etc.

PEER REVIEW: CRITICAL ISSUES

Workshop will examine critical issues involving accountability that reflects federal legislative and professional concerns at the national level. These developments, pressures and motivating forces will be discussed by the chairpersons of peer review committees of national professional organizations.

THE HIGH ATTRITION RATE AMONG CMHC DIRECTORS

For Center Directors and Citizen Board Members only. Meeting to exchange thoughts and observations regarding the high attrition rates of Executive Directors in CMHCs: namely, the political and policy problems Executive Directors encounter with staff, boards and other community providers. (Others are welcome as space is available.)

At the end of my stay at the convention, I concluded that in my address I had erred on the side of underestimating the seriousness of dissatisfaction in community mental health centers in particular and the health fields in general.

XI
The Frequency of Career Change

WHEN ONE BECOMES AWARE OF and accepts a set of new ideas, there is the tendency to overgeneralize their significance, i.e., to perceive the world in terms of the new ideas, to restructure perceptions, to reinterpret past experience, and to see an altered future. It is a mixed blessing. On the one hand, there is the possibility that the ideas have validity, if only to the extent that other people feel compelled to take them seriously; on the other hand, they may be so idiosyncratic (however compelling to you) that you are unaware you are applying them far beyond their merit and appropriate boundaries. At some early point in your thinking, you look for data to determine whether the new ideas have some foundations in the experience of other people. I was aware of this danger in regard to what I had come to see as the problematic nature of satisfaction from professional work. This was especially true in regard to frequency of career change, because if it was the case that the frequency was very low, it weakened but in no sense invalidated my arguments. After all, there are very real obstacles to career change. I was also aware that if the frequency was high, it did not necessarily follow that it reflected only dissatisfaction with work. As I have pointed out, you may seek change for positive reasons, i.e., you have been successful and satisfied but long for new challenge, stimulation, and meaning. But if the frequency was not small, it would be most unlikely if in part it did not reflect dissatisfaction. In the absence of data on the groups in which I was interested, I realized that I would have, at best, to seek data indirectly relevant to my needs. The first thing I did was to make a list of the people I had personally known who, in the past five years, had deliberately and discernibly changed the nature of their work. There were twenty-two names on the list.

This, of course, is hardly "data," because I may not have remembered some instances and, more important, since I did not make a list of *all* the people I know equally well, the list of career changers may be far less impressive than it seemed to me. But I was impressed. The next source of data was fortuitous. A student (Fountain, 1975) had completed collecting data for a dissertation on job satisfaction among high school teachers. As a group teachers rate their satisfaction from work significantly below the level of ratings of many other professional groups. Fountain interviewed fifty-two of the eighty-two teachers in a moderately large suburban high school, and to her surprise found work satisfaction to be higher than previous studies had found, a finding which considerably weakened the significance of certain analyses she had wished to make about the correlates of work satisfaction. Although unplanned, she broke her sample down into those who had always been teachers (N-35) and those who had had one or more previous careers (N-17). The percentage of career changes was surprisingly high. What was not surprising was that it was the career changers who had the higher level of work satisfaction. Unfortunately, because previous studies of teachers had not made comparable breakdowns, it could be argued that Fountain's sample was possibly an atypical one, and the findings should be discounted.[1] (In her exhaustive review of the literature on job satisfaction among teachers, Fountain found not a single study that had career change as a variable.)

We then began a search for existing studies relevant to two questions: What is the frequency of career change among highly educated, professional people? In other words, how many actually have changed careers? There was another question, of course: How many would like to change careers? To the first question, we could find no relevant studies. There are many studies, largely by economists, on frequency of job change (including drastic changes) in widely differing job groupings, but these primarily have involved blue- and white-collar workers, or managerial–executive types in business, finance, and industry. The frequency of such changes is by no means small, and they have usually been interpreted in terms of economic and related motivations. That is to say, the supply-and-demand characteristics of "the market," varying as they do from time to time, influence frequency of job change together with the desire to better one's social and economic

[1] In a very circumscribed study, three members of our project (Cowden, Fountain, and J. Sarason, 1974) studied the women in Terkel's book *Working* (1974). The women, as were the men whom he interviewed, almost always were blue- or white-collar workers. Of the forty-two women interviewed, thirty-five gave information relevant to job satisfaction. Twenty-four were clearly dissatisfied with their work, and eleven were satisfied. Two factors distinguished the two groups: the satisfied women tended to be older and to have had previous jobs which were dissatisfying and from which they made successful efforts to leave.

status. The absence of studies of professional groups outside of business, finance, and industry suggests either that their economic significance is considered small (despite their ever-increasing numbers), or that their work changes are also primarily determined by market factors, or that they are a different breed of person from the highly educated in business, finance, or industry. Or, it may be that, as I suggested in Chapter III, for historical–economic–competitive reasons the study of job satisfaction as a separate field of investigation was narrowly conceived because it was in the self-interest of business and industry to support such investigations.[2] Whatever the reasons, we could not find the kinds of systematic data on career change that would allow us to evaluate the hypothesis that work has become problematic for highly educated people in different professions. But in our search we did come across or obtain fragmentary data which suggested that our ideas had some validity.

Some Suggestive Leads

In 1965 Dr. Alan Entine, an economist with an interest in career change and development, directed at Columbia University what may well have been the first university-based program to help people change their careers. To be eligible for the program, the individual had to be at least a college graduate (although in exceptional cases this requirement could be waived) who had, formally or informally, acquired specialized knowledge and skills and had engaged for some years in what conventionally could be regarded as professional work. If accepted into the program, they would have the choice of entering one of several human-services professions, e.g., teaching, social work, hospital administration, library science. They received only partial financial support for the year or two they were in the "New Careers" program.

Not often does a modest educational experiment at a university attract national attention. Rarely does the public learn of the myriad innovative symposia, seminars, or workshops which are as much a part of today's campus life as undergraduates and final examinations. Yet "New Careers," a pilot program at Columbia University containing less than 40

[2] I have already indicated that I believe that all of the sources of career dissatisfactions for professionals in business, industry, and finance are, since World War II, also at play with professionals elsewhere, e.g., becoming part of large, impersonal, bureaucratized organizations, and being enmeshed in what in the Chapter XII I call the Federal, State, Local Complex (FSLC). It could be asked, therefore, why the abundant data from business, finance, and industry are not relevant for my purposes. They are, but that still requires being able to demonstrate with independent data that professional work outside business, finance, and industry has become problematic.

former businessmen and women, has received notice from major newspapers, national magazines, and network television. Moreover, the project has attracted more than 7,000 inquiries during the past year.

What stimulated this unusual interest? The New Careers Program opened the resources of a major university to mature, successful businessmen and women who wish to begin a second career in the non-profit, service-oriented professions. The program's goal is twofold: to help alleviate shortages of trained personnel in important areas of public service such as social work, library administration, and teaching; and to help qualified individuals find new careers which promise personal satisfaction and social usefulness.

Program participants receive counseling, guidance, and tuition assistance from sources which are not available to regular university students. Individuals who have made successful transitions to new careers include an interior designer who is now regional placement director of the Job Corps, a marketing executive who is director of public relations for a Maryland community college, an engineer who is a teacher of deaf children, and an advertising manager who is employed as a research librarian at the New York Public Library.

National interest in New Careers suggests that the program has uncovered a finding which is broader than the original scope of the project—countless Americans desire to change their careers in middle years. Not only do they wish to change from business to non-profit areas, but teachers wish to become stockbrokers, social workers would like to sell insurance, and farmers would like to join corporations. [Entine, 1967].

For a year or more after the program started and received quite a play in the national media, Dr. Entine's office would receive two or more calls on Friday afternoons from individuals around the country inquiring about entrance into the program. Seven thousand inquiries is no small number for one small program to receive. At the very least, it was quite surprising to Dr. Entine, who was unprepared for such a response, leading him to conclude that "countless Americans desire to change their careers in middle years." His experience with that program, its implications in terms of the potential size of the population such programs could serve, forced him, so to speak, away from a career in traditional economics to one in human resources and career counseling, with two consequences: he has probably had more experience than anyone else in dealing with people seeking career change, and he has had considerable experience as a consultant to public and private agencies seeking his advice in developing counseling programs to help people move in new career directions. I came to know Dr. Entine, his staff, and his work. Everything he has experienced since the New Careers programs confirms the initial impression that the number of highly educated people who would like to change careers is very large, although the number who actually take steps to do so is much smaller.

The reader will undoubtedly have reacted with nostalgia to that part of the quotation from Dr. Entine's article where he says that one of the goals of the New Careers program in 1965 was "to alleviate shortages of trained personnel in important areas of public service." Times have changed! In 1965 people were encouraged to move in new directions, as if there was some sensitivity to people's need to change their directions. And being older was not (for a time at least) an insuperable barrier. Today, some people are *forced* to move in new directions, even though they may be satisfied with what they are doing. The many more who would prefer to make a change consider themselves fortunate to be where they are.

In order to obtain data from large samples of highly educated, professional people, Dr. Entine and I got up a five-item questionnaire which we endeavored to mail to all faculty members in all parts (university, college, junior college, community college, professional schools) of three large state university systems. We did not ask for names or other identifying characteristics. The questions, which could be answered in a few minutes, concerned (a) whether the faculty person wished to change fields, (b) to what field or work he would like to move, and (c) factors constraining change. Neither Dr. Entine nor I are devotees of the questionnaire method for studying career satisfaction and change, but given our almost nonexistent research resources we thought that if we could give the brief and highly focused questionnaire to about 15–20,000 teachers in higher education we would get some idea of the numbers who would consider discernibly changing the nature of their work. Our choice of college teachers was not fortuitous, of course. In Dr. Entine's professional work a number of faculty members from his own (State University of New York at Stony Brook) and other parts of the state system had consulted Dr. Entine about changing their careers. Over the years I had known faculty members, at Yale and elsewhere, who had diminished interest in their work and fantasied about all sorts of things they would like to do (e.g., a professor of English literature who became a psychotherapist, a professor of psychology who worked in and wished to own his own restaurant, a world-renowned researcher who wanted to start his own florist shop, etc.). But the several score of instances about which Dr. Entine and I knew first-hand do not establish a trend, let alone a base rate. So we were willing to go the fast route to get a little data on many people. We went no place, as the following excerpt from a letter to me from an academic official of a large Midwestern state university system explains:

> While I am enthusiastically supportive of the idea of mid-career counseling and bringing into the open the kinds of consideration to which your questionnaire is addressed, I am more than dubious about its usefulness with the population to which it would be addressed. It is my hunch that

most faculty members would not only refuse to complete and return the questionnaire, but would protest as harassment even the distribution and the request that it be completed. I have much more confidence in a sampling technique, relying more on in-depth interviews than upon broadside questionnaires.

Ironically, I suspect that a very large number of faculty members would have an interest in confidentially expressing some of their hopes, fears and misgivings, and would be exceedingly curious as to how many others shared these feelings. They would find it too threatening to admit (even with the conventional assurance of anonymity) that they are not fully happy or perhaps fully effective in their present work. For example, how many Latinists have, at any time in the last three hundred years, been able really to confess that their field has lost significance? How many faculty members widely regarded as "dead wood" are able to admit, even to themselves, that they have lost interest or competence in their field?

It is possible that I am quite wrong, and that a new era of courage and candor is at hand. Perhaps Studs Terkel has opened the way by getting blue-collar workers to confess that they generally hate what they do. Perhaps our academic colleagues are professionally committed to scientific exploration of attitudes and perceptions, and are as willing to serve as subjects as they are to devise and carry out inquiries. However, my entire experience in academe leads me to believe that professional mores are such that approach through this questionnaire would be resented and rejected, and would be very unlikely to produce valid information. I suggest checking with some few others among academic deans and presidents to see whether their impressions confirm or counter my own.

This was the most astute of the three astute negative replies we received. The replies differed in several ways, but they were highly similar in several respects: (a) they agreed that the number of college teachers who had lost interest in their fields was large enough to be a matter of concern; (b) for a college teacher to admit, except under unusual circumstances of trust and confidentiality, that he or she would rather be doing something other than what he or she was doing required overcoming internal and perceived external threats and barriers of inordinate power, and (c) by implication, there was something wrong or unfortunate about those who wished to change. (This last point is significant, because it illuminates what I said in an earlier chapter about how we are made to feel that if we become increasingly disinterested in our work, there is something "wrong" with us. It is a variant of the disease of the clinician who is disposed to see pathology rather than health.) In another letter of refusal a point was made which casts a somewhat different light on the problem. Paraphrased (because the letter referred us to documents of several university committees) it went like this: "Along with other institutions of higher education we are now in a stable state system. There will be no significant growth of faculty and/or students. And yet we will continue to receive pressure to improve our teaching, to be more productive in research, to respond to community needs, and to be more responsive to national and international issues. The emerging combination of ease of travel and temporary relocation, specialized scholarship opportunities throughout the world, national and international social policy demands, consortia, and the international flavor of undergraduate education will involve more of our faculty in activities not associated exclusively with this university. The important question is: How can we facilitate a faculty member's moving in very new directions or, at the least, freeing him or her to assume more differentiated roles, so that with essentially the same size faculty we can fill existing gaps and meet emerging demands? We have reason to believe that a sizable fraction of the faculty would welcome the opportunity to learn new roles if it was not at an undue personal sacrifice and was in line with an explicit and positive university policy on career development and change." Although our efforts to obtain data from these universities were fruitless, it is noteworthy that our opinion that a sizable number of people in college teaching would like to make different degrees of career change was shared by others in universities.

Another way of attacking the problem is by studying applications to graduate and professional schools. How many "older" people are applying? Are they coming from other professional fields or careers clearly different from those they propose to get into? Ordinarily, when we say "older" we think of people who are at least in their thirties and have already "settled down" in some line of work. These criteria may have been appropriate when the number of choices available to a college student were far fewer than they are today and there was more general acceptance of the one life–one career imperative. If, as I have argued in earlier chapters, the imperative is less potent than before, we would expect not only that the point of decision will be postponed, but also that changes in career directions will occur much before "mid-career." *In fact, the weakening of the cultural imperative would suggest that the concept of the mid-career crisis as an experience tied to a particular age interval obscures the possibility that its dynamics have begun to be a lifelong characteristic.* When values such as authenticity, autonomy, self-expression, and new experience become dominant as forces in living, one should expect that they will change what people wish to experience in work and the length of time they will wish to remain with it. It also has to be recognized that from the standpoint of graduate and professional schools, "older" applicants tend to be anyone who is not coming directly from undergraduate school. This is an exaggeration, of course, but it makes the point that applicants who have been out in "the real world" after college tend to be perceived as having motivations that are obscure, if not suspect.

The point to be emphasized is that the turmoil which has come to accompany the process of career choice is also present in career maintenance or continuation. Consequently, in looking at applications to graduate and professional schools we have used age twenty-five as the beginning of the "older" period. In one such effort, we obtained and studied 1,568 rejected applications out of a total pool of 3,000 applicants to a law school for the calendar year 1973–1974. The applications were stored in large cartons in a basement, and we had the resources to go through fifteen cartons, no easy task considering the usual haphazard way in which material in an individual's folder is kept. We had no reason to believe that the cartons we chose gave us an atypical sample of rejected applicants.

From the sample of 1,568, there were 325 who were twenty-five years or older, representing 21 per cent of the sample. Depending on how one wants to define "older" their numbers are not insignificant. Most of the men in this group fell into the twenty-five–twenty-nine range and the women into the twenty-five–thirty-three range. In any event, many applicants are applying for admissions after a significant hiatus following graduation from college. Of the women, 26 per cent had been involved in teaching (only two women taught on the college level), whereas with the men 19 per cent had been teachers (half at the college- and half at public-school level). Another way of categorizing the previous experience of the group is in terms of pursuit of advanced education and training: 39 per cent of the women and 36 per cent of the men had pursued or were pursuing graduate programs of some kind. Some had not completed degree programs, some were in the process of doing so, and some had doctoral or master's degrees.

In reading these applications one is inevitably drawn to the question: why are these people changing to law? Are they *running away from* dissatisfying work or are they *going toward* something new and challenging? In the case of those who are in teaching, it is clear that they were dissatisfied with what they were doing. They said so. With others, the most frequent expression of motivation was that they wished to mesh their present work with legal training, i.e., to extend their knowledge, capabilities, and horizons (like the architect interested in the legal and architectural ramifications of city planning, or the Ph.D. psychologists wanting to combine psychology and law). But equally frequent in the statements of these "older" applicants is what may be termed the "need for meaning" or the "discovery of meaning," of which the following extracts are examples:

> My undergraduate grades appear spotty and undirected. . . . I used to be a cocky, vapid student, content that I was in a "good" school, occasionally getting good grades. Looking back on it all, I see that I had done nothing exceptional nor to be particularly proud of. I dislike talking of my

own maturing process, but I feel that I have come quite some way from being a callow youth. I only ask for fairness in evaluating my record. The lost sheep is to be more highly valued than the ones not gone astray. I have returned.

I want to obtain a measure of self-satisfaction and feel a sense of accomplishment when I evaluate what I have done in my lifetime. I would like to be able to look back on my life some day and feel that I truly accomplished more good than would be possible for an individual in an ordinary occupation.

. . . was a GS-9 Engineer and a Supervisor with up to eight people working under my direct supervision at one time. I decided that this was not how I wanted to use my life, however, and quit. I took a year off to study myself, what I had learned and where I was going. This application is the result of that year.

My delay in entering law school since college reflects no indecision on my part concerning the value of a legal education for my career. Such delay was originally necessitated by my military obligation. When discharged earlier than expected, a full-time job and part-time graduate school were begun. Work has aided in adding clarity to career goals.

I never appreciated life—its beauty, its significance, its possibilities— until I was faced with death. . . . I stopped and thought, "What is life? Why am I living it? What am I getting from it? What am I giving to it?"

What manner of man would apply to Law School at forty-nine years of age? Along the way, I have tried to serve others. . . . I now see an unusual chance to use the mature and active years still ahead, in which the balance can swing toward greater service. . . . I won't use the law training as long as my fellow students. I will use it, however, with a purpose and an appreciation that should bring credit to the Law School.

I don't want to die and have my cornerstone read that he was born . . . died, etc., etc. . . . I want to leave some deeds that have been beneficial to life and the world. I have a tremendous love for people, and I would love to aid them through understanding, knowledge, skill and a profession that serves a positive function in society.

What were some of the characteristics of the 172 applicants who were accepted? Twenty-two individuals, or 13 per cent, were over twenty-five years of age as compared with 21 per cent among the rejectees. Seventeen had completed or were near completion of a doctoral or master's degree. Only four of the twenty-two had any work experience outside the role of student or armed-services officer. The fields from which these "older" students came were quite disparate and in at least half of the cases the shift to law was a drastic one. In this respect they were similar to the rejected older students, but they were dissimilar in that most of them were entering law school directly from another educational institution. In fact, 80 per cent of the entire class were entering law school directly from another educational institution. This fact strongly suggests, as my own long experience on admissions committees indicated, that from the standpoint of this admissions committee there is a bias in favor of those who are proceeding directly from one part of the educational system to another, even where the parts are radically different. (Of the 20 per cent not entering directly from an educational institution almost half were entering from some type of compulsory national service, and apparently this was not judged adversely in terms of the applicant's sincerity of motivation to pursue a law career.).

Of the rejected applicants, 21 per cent were over twenty-five years of age, but since many of them were not coming to law school directly from an academic setting their chances for acceptance were much reduced. When I have talked with similarly older people who wished to change careers, I could always count on hearing from them that they did not stand a chance for admission because they were competing with students right out of college. They are right, of course, but the above findings suggest the additional factor that coming from "the real world" rather than from an educational institution is another strike against them.

In a study of applicants to a medical school, done for reasons unrelated to my purposes, 19 per cent of all applicants had advanced degrees: 6 per cent had the Ph.D., and 13 per cent were in various graduate fields. Of those with advanced degrees or graduate-school status the fields represented were engineering, law, divinity, the humanities, the social sciences, the physical sciences, biology, and "other." If one omitted those from biology, 12 per cent of all applicants, on the surface at least, are changing career directions. It was not possible to read the medical school applications and thus make a judgment regarding career change, as had been the case with the law school applications. Whether the "true" figure for frequency of career change in this pool of applicants is nearer 12 or 19 per cent I cannot say.

The figures from the law and medical schools, even if we had been able to base them on a large sample of schools are, at best, only suggestive of frequency of sought-after career change into these professions. I assume that there are more than a few people several years or more out of college who would like to enter these professions but assume, and correctly so, that their chances are virtually nil. I am not referring here to that large group of young people who did not get into law or medical school, many of whom will go through life pained by the knowledge that they could not enter the career of choice. Some of these young people reapply one or two more times and then give up forever. There is another large group who never intended to go to law or medical school but who, several years after college, find themselves desiring to do so at the same time they acknowledge that their chances for admission are virtually non-existent. We also studied applications to a graduate divinity school and here we found about 20 per cent seeking some degree of discernible career change. So, in three different schools we found by conservative estimates between 12 and 20 per cent of the applicants who seemed to be seeking career change.

An Analysis of Entries in *Who's Who*

Our final effort to obtain an estimate of frequency of career change involved entries in *Who's Who* for the years 1934–1935, 1950–1951, and 1974–1975. The substance of the entries permits one to describe and make a judgment about the different career directions individuals have experienced. The individual supplies the data in chronological form, giving the titles and duration of each position he or she has held. I shall describe below how we categorized the data, but first I must emphasize that I shall not defend the populations we used as being representative of a larger sample of some sort. As best as I can determine, individuals are selected for entry on at least one of several grounds: those holding important posts (elective or appointive) in the public arena; scientists in key positions in various types of organizations or who have received recognition from colleagues; college professors (especially from major universities); influential businessmen and bankers; artists, musicians, and writers; religious leaders; and other grounds not easy to label. I think it fair to say that extent of reputation, as well as success and accomplishment by conventional or popular criteria are the most frequent bases for inclusion in *Who's Who*. How many people are considered for entry but are not included, or how many people who are included do not submit entry data I cannot say. Obviously, the publishers of *Who's Who* believe they are including the cream of the crop of successful, important, well-known people, but, equally obviously, we don't know what the crop is and one can get violent reactions about a number of entries (or types of entries) both from individuals who have been included as well as from those who have not. Snobbishness is not in short supply in our society. Despite these legitimate caveats I concluded that for my limited purposes the study could be worthwhile. I was making no value judgments or projecting motivations into the career directions and changes of people. I only wanted to get an estimate of frequency of career change from published data about people the great bulk of whom were highly educated and professional. For 1934–1935 we took all entries whose last names began with C; for 1950–1951 we took the letter B; and for 1974–1975 we took the letter A. For each of these years we got a quick average of entries per page and multiplied by the numbers of pages for that letter of the alphabet. Surprisingly, by this method the number of entries for the three years was similar (2,353, 2,355, and 2,360), and to simplify calculations we used 2,360 as the denominator in getting percentages.

What constitutes a career change? For many entries this question was not difficult to answer, e.g., a banker becoming a minister, an accountant becoming a lawyer, a physician becoming a businessman. In these instances it is clear that the individuals have changed roles in that their responsibilities, tasks, and problems became drastically different from what they previously experienced. They had to think about new things, acquire specialized knowledge, interact with different kinds of individuals and groups, and literally change the scene of work. But what about a college professor who becomes an administrator in the university? When a faculty member rises from a lowly instructor to an elevated full professor, it would be hard to argue that any career change has occurred. He still teaches, does research and writing, interacts primarily with students and faculty colleagues, attends the same meetings and conventions, i.e., his status has changed, and many other things may have changed, but neither he nor others would say he has changed his career. But when he becomes an administrator he is no longer teaching, researching, and writing; he deals with new knowledge, problems and responsibilities. What he thinks about, whom he thinks about, and how he is perceived and perceives himself have changed. He is still in the university, he may continue to be a professor of this or that, but he is thinking, doing, and enmeshed in new things. Phenomenologically there has been a marked change. Indeed, his former colleagues (the word former signifies the change that has taken place) will usually perceive him as having changed the direction of his life, and some of the more snobbish ones will derogate his leaving the fold, i.e., he is no longer "one of us." That is to say, he may be regarded from their perspective as "downward mobile" even though from another perspective he has "moved up." (This is but another example of how difficult we make it for people departing from the one life–one career imperative.) Take, for example, a research chemist in industry who takes a position in the university. In a real sense he is still a research chemist, but now he is in a radically different social–work context, i.e., in a new culture in which he has assumed a new role requiring him to adjust to a new style of daily living. Others perceive him, and he perceives himself, as having made some kind of career change. Even if one defines career only in terms of what an individual overtly does in the course of a day, these individuals have changed their "work": what they expect of themselves and what others expect of them.

What about the lawyer who becomes a full-time, elected public official? It is true that many lawyers begin their career in law with an eye on public office. They may begin by being a member of a private law firm, but they are intent on moving to the public arena where they obviously do not practice law. However one describes what an elected public official does, it is radically different in most respects (not all) from what a lawyer in private practice does. Or take the lawyer who moves from a law firm to being head of a large company. He is still a lawyer, and he may even continue to use his legal experience, but to continue to categorize him as a lawyer is to use labels mischievously. I have no interest in defining or criticizing any definition of a career, but when such definitions obscure discernible changes in the substance and context of work, their usefulness must be questioned.

The categories below were not *a priori* ones. We read and recorded pertinent data from several hundred of the 7,068 entries and came up with categories which were as descriptive or as concrete as possible so that others can judge the degree and significances of the different types of changes.

A. Drastic horizontal change. Those who change from one professional field to another. Those who changed from one professional field to another for only one or two years were *not* included. Of those included, a small percentage worked in one field for several years before returning to school and afterwards entered a different field, e.g., a teacher with a B.A., who has taught for several years, then returns to school, earns an advanced degree, and then enters law or business, etc.

B. Lawyer to executive. The individual changes from practising law, privately or with a firm or business, to an executive position in the same or different business.

C. Lawyer to politics. The individual changes from practising as a lawyer to elective or appointed public office, e.g., senator, governor, mayor, attorney general, ambassador.

D. Lawyer to judge. Changes from practising lawyer to being a judge. (In a few instances the individual returns to the practice of law.)

E. Applied to academia. The individual changes from an applied job in any field (e.g., science, psychiatry, economics) to a teaching position in the same profession in a college or university. This category included applied to academia; applied to academia to applied; academia to applied; academia to applied to academia. Not included are (a) those holding applied jobs while working toward the Ph.D. and then getting a teaching job in the same field; (b) those holding an applied job for one or two years before changing to a teaching position; and (c) those concurrently holding academic and applied jobs.

F. Retirement from armed services to x profession. This was a very small category and includes those who after a long career in the armed services move to a very different position: business, teaching.

G. From the ministry to academia. This includes a change from a full-time ministerial position in any religion (i.e., actually practicing full time as a minister, priest, or rabbi) to a full-time academic faculty position in a prep school, college, university, theological seminary or divinity school. Not included were those clergymen who have not held full-time ministerial positions but who hold academic positions.

H. Vertical ministerial change. This is a change from ministerial or academic positions to an executive position in the religious organization, e.g., from priest to bishop, from a minister to executive position in a missionary organization of his religion.

I. Vertical change in academia. These are changes from a teaching to administrative position in an academic institution. Not included are those who progress from instructor to assistant professor to associate professor to full professor. Also not included are those who worked first in an applied setting, changed to teaching, and then moved into administration (these are included in category K).

J. Vertical rise and change in position within the same occupational area. These are changes from a non-executive or non-managerial position to an executive or managerial position. Examples: working as a chemist and becoming an executive in a chemical company; working as a reporter and becoming an editor on a newspaper; from practising as a physician to becoming head of a hospital; working as a clinical psychologist or psychiatrist and becoming superintendent of an institution. Not included were individuals who began their career in some managerial or executive position and moved to a higher one, or those who worked for a year or two in a non-managerial or non-executive position and then moved to managerial and executive positions. (No academics were included; they would be in I.)

K. Individuals who made more than one major change in the same general field. Examples: going from a position in an applied setting to a faculty position in a university to an administrative position in the university; going from practising lawyer to a judgeship to elective office; going from a full-time ministerial position to a faculty position to head of a divinity school; going from the practice of engineering to a faculty position to being head of a university or large consulting firm.

The categories are not overlapping: an individual is entered in only one category. Categories E, G, and I all involve academia, but we justified keeping them separate because G and I seemed to represent different patterns, and E turned out to have fewer entries than we expected. Table 1 presents the percentage for each category for each of the three years (the number of entries in each category expressed as a percentage of 2,360). The most surprising finding concerns the per-

TABLE 1. Career Change Categories (*Who's Who*). *Percentage In Each Category*

Year	A Horizontal Drastic Change	B Lawyer Executive	C Lawyer to Politics or Government	D Lawyer to Judge	E Applied to Academe	F Post-Armed Services	G Ministry to Academe	H Vertical Ministerial Change	I Vertical Academic Change	J Change Within Same Occupational Area	K More Than One Major Change
	%	%	%	%	%	%	%	%	%	%	%
1974–1975 41.8%	8.9	2.6	1.1	.9	6.9	.4	.8	.7	6.7	10.3	2.6
1950–1951 43.0%	8.0	1.2	1.5	1.6	4.6	.3	.8	1.5	6.4	13.4	3.6
1934–1935 39.0%	8.7	.9	2.8	2.2	4.2	.2	1.9	1.8	5.8	6.9	3.5

centages for category A, involving the clearest and most drastic type of change. We did not expect it to have the second highest frequency. Equally surprising to us was the overall frequency of one or another type and degree of career change. For each year the overall frequency is around 40 per cent. The difference between the overall frequency for 1939 (39.0 per cent) and those for 1950–1951 and 1974–1975 are small (4.0 per cent and 2.8 per cent), but given the large number of entries for each year the differences tend to statistical significance. Whether this is a real time trend we cannot say, although such a trend would be expected from all I have discussed earlier, but it would be best not to make much of this.

The most frequent question stimulated by these data has been: Is career change of varying degrees a characteristic of successful people? My answer to this question has been that we do not know why these individuals sought change or how they experienced it. The correlation between reputation, accomplishment, and status, on the one hand, and feelings of personal satisfaction and fulfillment, on the other, is probably far from perfect. So to make inferences from "success" to internal experience requires caution. This is analogous to our response when we learn that a millionaire committed suicide: How can somebody with so much money be so unhappy? Apparently, it is not all that difficult and a part of us knows that. Similarly, we know that the conventional criteria of success are not a surefire basis for predicting internal states of feeling. If I were forced to take a position I would say that most of the entries probably sought the change and experienced satisfaction as a consequence. It also would not surprise me if as a group they were striving, restless, ambitious, and cravers of new experience. I am reminded here of actors in a hit play. They enjoy their stage role, the accompanying acclaim, and the proof of their ability, but there comes a time (usually after a few months) when their enthusiasm dwindles; their interest in the play diminishes, sometimes to the point where their performance suffers. And they seek a new experience. In fact, many "stars" will only sign a contract which commits them to the play for a period of months, recognition of the fact that boredom and lack of challenge and new experience are not far down the road. And most actors try to avoid being typecast: the thought that they may play only one kind of role in their career is enough to drive them to despair. How many of our entries share these qualities I cannot say. From my standpoint, the major significances of the data are that career change of varying degrees and types are probably of frequent occurrence, and this seems to have been characteristic of our society for some time. It is safe to assume that the number of people who seek and achieve a change is far less than the frequency who would like to change, but take no steps to do so or who take faltering steps leading nowhere. Why some people depart from the one life–one career imperative while many more do not is an unknown and unstudied question. Just as there are many factors which can make a "successful" career an increasingly hollow experience, there are many factors which can make unsatisfactory work tolerable. As we saw in Chapter X, in the ongoing studies by Dr. Cary Cherniss of professionals and non-professionals, there is virtually no correlation between "alienation from work" and "job satisfaction." That is to say, an individual can report high job satisfaction at the same time that he feels alienated from his work, a paradoxical response illuminated by the finding that many individuals no longer expect much from their work. They are satisfied because they are getting as much from their work as they can expect, and their expectations are not high.

Implications

I did not present data in this chapter with the expectation that they establish a base rate for the frequency of career change (of different degrees) or the frequency for any one year or time period. To accomplish such goals would require resources of time and money which we did not possess. The major aims of this chapter were several. First, to suggest that getting satisfactory frequency data is necessary in order to judge the degree to which the one life–one career imperative has not only been diluted in strength but also to suggest that its dynamics and consequences are experienced fairly early in life. Second, such data would not only illuminate the degree to which a social change has occurred, as well as its pace, but has obvious practical implications for the formulation of public policy in regard to education, career counseling, and life planning. I shall have more to say about this in later chapters. Here it is sufficient to say that awareness or sensitivity to societal changes always occurs after the change has started, i.e., after its overt indicators have become sufficiently general to come to attention. Not infrequently, perhaps inevitably, we note the change under circumstances that are antithetical to attempts at dispassionate understanding, consideration of the implications of alternative actions, and clarification of the status of the values underlying the change as well as recommendations for further change. Third, I wanted to present the basis for the suggestion that the frequency of career change is not miniscule but seems of discernible proportions. When the data I have presented are taken together with the various kinds of interview material given in earlier chapters, they persuade me not only that career change is an issue for a significant portion of the highly educated, professional population but that it implicates the very nature of traditions and cultural beliefs inculcated in us as individuals and, therefore, in our major societal institutions. This is another way of saying that, whether we like it or not, we are the products of culture, a culture which like all others seeks continuity of traditions, values, and practices. And yet it is a culture which has always prized (more than rhetoric and much less than ideal) the values of change and innovation both on an individual and institutional level.

The opponent to the current scene and the changes which it reflects may claim that we have been hoist by our own petard. Those who favor the changes may with delight see the past interred and the present as harbinger of progress to a more sensible future. (And then, of course, there are those who do not give a damn and are prepared to make the best of the worst of all possible worlds either by ignoring it or creating a mini-world with as few points of contact with the surround as possible.) I shall reserve my views for the concluding chapter after I have taken up the relationships between work and aging. Any large-scale change in the nature and experience of work is accompanied by change in the experience of time. That is to say, how one experiences the passage of time obviously is part of one's sense of aging. How does one's experience of work relate to the experience of the passage of time and, therefore, aging? This question will be examined in the next chapter, not only because it is an important question, one of *the* important ones, but because it provides another perspective from which to view and make a judgment about social change.

XII

The Early Development of
the Sense of Aging

THE SENSE OF THE PASSAGE of time and the sense of aging are not identical, although as one goes through life they frequently are the warp and woof of one's experience. When you are waiting to meet someone who is late, the experience of time has a distinctive quality (depending, of course, on personality factors, relationship to the person, etc.), but it is ordinarily unrelated to the sense of aging. Usually, we think of the sense of aging—the sense that we are mortal, the life span is limited, there will be an end, and we are pointed and running or being pulled toward it—as highly correlated with chronological age. Young children, we say, have little or no sense of aging, but such an assertion has no validity from a clinical or theoretical standpoint. I can only refer the skeptical reader to Becker's *The Denial of Death* (1973).

A sense of aging develops early in life, although it is experienced fleetingly and takes quite a while for it to become an organizing and often agonizing magnet for experiences. When and how the sense of aging invades or merges into the sense of the passage of time, becoming a motivational dynamic altering the perception of the future by its shaping of the present, is only in part an individual matter. As I pointed out in Chapter V, events (war, atomic bomb, pollution) in the larger society have brought the two senses together for young and old alike, albeit with different degrees of force and consequences. If in an age in which dying and death have become impersonal affairs because they take place in a hospital room away from home and family, and the ambience of the funeral parlor prevents the expression of the depths of feelings, our highly developed mass media constantly remind us both of the countless ways in which our lives can be terminated and of the fragility of personal plans. If many people, particularly young ones, have decided that time is too precious a commodity to be wasted on a future which may never come, it should occasion no great surprise. You can muster "reasonable" arguments against such a decision, but that is precisely the point: for many people there is a chasm between reason and feeling. Perhaps more than ever before in history, the relationships between the senses of aging and the passage of time have become salient to a remarkable degree early in life. Let me illustrate this with my daughter (Sarason, 1961).

> Around the time Julie was five years of age she had already indicated indirectly but clearly that she had been thinking about the problem of death. She said, "When I grow up and get married I will live next door and then when you and Daddy die I will live in this house." Previous to this she had used the word "died," and certainly we had used this word in our conversations with her. For example, we were once examining a penny and I told her about Abraham Lincoln "who died a long time ago." Similar conversations had taken place in connection with the George Washington bridge over which we go frequently. I was aware during some of these conversations that she would become unusually silent whenever I used the word "died." On several occasions she asked questions about when people died, why they put them into the ground, etc. When I would answer these questions, she would listen quietly with a kind of frown on her face . . .
>
> For some time the number sixteen represented to Julie an unimaginably large quantity. To have sixteen of something, for something to be sixteen feet tall, to see sixteen things, to travel sixteen miles—this was her way of indicating "the most" that could be in this world. But there came a time when two lines of new knowledge converged to create a further problem: the first was that there were numbers which stood for amounts greater than sixteen, and the second was that her parents were much older than sixteen years of age. She not only resisted angrily any statement by anyone which in the slightest suggested that her parents were "old" but also began now to ask questions about the meaning of death [pp. 167–168].

What I have described is by no means remarkable, and it is narrowly psychological. But the reader may recall from Chapter V that it was Julie who at age six recommended to her parents that if we were to move to another house, it should be in Ireland on which, in case of world war, atomic bombs were least likely to be dropped. And like so many of her generation, the atomic bomb was only one of several similar sources of personal threat.[1]

If it is true that when we are young we live each day as if we are immortal, it is less true for recent in contrast to past generations. Their

---

[1] Although it is difficult to estimate their cumulative effects, on what basis can one dismiss the effects on young people of several days of television watching following the events after the assassinations of President Kennedy (including the killing of his assassin), Senator Robert Kennedy, and Martin Luther King?

sense of the passage of time and their sense of aging are no longer in totally separate psychological orbits waiting for marriage, parenthood, bodily symptoms, and the like to change the orbits because of a new force of gravity. In recent years I have been asking students this question: "I know how old you are in terms of chronological age. But how old do you feel or, for that matter, how young do you feel?" I do not defend the question either in terms of its clarity or its freedom from any "demand characteristics" (phrasing a question so that it suggests the answer you want or the answer considered desirable). The answers fall into two distinct categories. The first contains answers of which the following is a good example: "I feel older than I ever thought I would feel at this age, as if my best years are behind me and from this point on it will not be as good as it was in the past which as I look at it now was better than I then thought." Only rarely were these answers intended to convey depressive feelings about the present or future, but rather the anticipation that the chances were good that the future would be burdensome and the intervals between very infrequent high points would be experienced as undifferentiated in a negative sense. Although an extreme answer, the following one suggests a common theme in this category: "I feel as if from this point on it is all downhill. I feel like I think some really old people feel: I've had it."

The second and more frequent category would be typified by this answer: "I don't feel old but I sure don't feel young. I look forward to getting out of college (or graduate school) and getting into the real world, almost the way I felt about finishing high school and going away to college. With this difference: inside me is the feeling that I may not get the breaks and I will end up unhappy and bored and symbolically die well before my time." What was common to all answers was that the students were entering a period in which the passage of time would be experienced differently than before, and that one of the differences inhered in a dysphoric expectation. Not surprisingly, in the past two years the dysphoric element (mixed with anger) has become very frequent as the economic realities of a severe recession became obvious. One student said: "We were born ten years too late. We have to take what we can get, not what we want. Feel young? I feel old, old, old." I have no basis for saying that x number of students are organizing experience and expectations in terms of a young–old dichotomy. What I can say is that a sizable fraction of them fear being trapped in life, and the word "trapped," a frequent one used by students, conjures up not only imagery of confinement and impotence but of slow dying. As we (Sarason, Sarason, and Cowden, 1975) have commented elsewhere:

> What we are trying to say is captured in the title of a book written by an undergraduate, *Growing Up Old In The Sixties* (Maynard, 1973). When we

would ask students to write about "How young or old do you feel?" a surprising number said that they did not feel young but, rather (surprising to *them*), old. When we would interrogate them, sometimes in long no-holds-barred discussion, about how they would account for such a feeling—why they viewed the future so bleakly—they were not very articulate until they forced us (the interrogators) to face the fact that we grew up in very different times; that is, we grew up when it was possible to believe that society could be significantly reformed, whereas they were growing up when such a possibility was virtually nonexistent.

In light of the above, it was not surprising that so many students thought about and planned for a career with reluctance, anxiety, and even anger. As one student put it: "Why blame us for trying to postpone dying?" Or as another student put it: "Why should it be puzzling to you that we have serious doubts about striving for something that may kill us?" We make no claims about the generality of these feelings and attitudes except to say that we obtained them from undergraduate and graduate students in different universities. Obviously, there are many students who do not share these feelings and attitudes. Although it is important, it is not crucial for our purposes here to estimate the percentage of students who do have these reactions. Of the countless colleagues, at Yale and elsewhere, with whom we have discussed these matters, not one doubted that these attitudes were frequent. And, let us not overlook another obvious fact: the number of students who have dropped out of school and society not available to us for questioning [p. 586].

When I was a student I did not know about the mid-career crisis, and I did not know what a personal disaster old age could be. I had aged grandparents who were sick and dependent, but they were part of a family whose major aim was to love and protect them within the confines of the family. That is to say, I knew *I* had "aged" grandparents, but I did not think of or know about aged people in general, i.e., that they were a "problem" group. I read the newspapers every day and listened to the radio, but neither of them told me about nursing homes, the field of gerontology, senior-citizen housing, Medicare, the "golden years," retirement as a legally sanctioned form of human abuse, and the loneliness of many old people. This is now not only standard fare in all the mass media, but it is a dysphoric standard fare. Students today not only know about the scandalous conditions of nursing homes, they can see them on television. About the only thing I can remember learning about aging and old people was that they slowed up physically, memory for recent events was poor, and they could become childish. This was learned, I think, from a few pages in an introductory psychology text. Aging as a field of study has become more fashionable in the university, either as an area in its own right or as part of courses or programs concerned with public and economic policy. In the last decade, especially, students have become aware of and knowledgeable about aging in its social, familial, and personal aspects, and to a high degree. Is it any form of distortion or exaggeration to say that their heightened awareness has been infused with foreboding and cynicism? Is it unreasonable to assume that the development of the sense of aging has already begun in these young people, and that their sense of the passage of time, particularly their perception of how they might experience future time, has become related, albeit inchoately, to the sense of mortality, to the knowledge that time is a limited resource already beginning to run out and that postponement of gratifications is a risky business? It is not my intention to paint a gloom-and-doom picture, but rather to suggest that among the highly educated of recent decades wariness characterizes their outlook, and this wariness inevitably reflects and will influence the sense of aging and the passage of time.

Growing Up and Running Down

In all religions there is a ceremony or ritual signifying the end of childhood and the beginning of adulthood. In days when religion was more central to living, the ceremony was a momentous event for the individual, signifying arrival at a much desired status and the opening up of new vistas of sought-after responsibilities. Growing "up" referred not only to physical characteristics but to social–psychological ones as well. "Up" meant the accumulation of knowledge and experience, and the assumption of new responsibilities, out of which would be shaped an enduring personal perspective leading to the good life. Today, we see this no less clearly in our educational system: *Pre*-school or kindergarten, *first* grade, *second* grade, the years of *elementary* school, the *middle* school or junior high, *high* school, and then the different levels of *higher* education. What is significant is not only the "upward" trajectory suggested by the succession of adjectives–a succession of points in growing "up"–or even what it implies about the desirability and necessity of wanting to grow up, but rather the implication that the trajectory is not parabolic in nature, i.e., that process of growing "up" does not cease and begin to run "down." Indeed, every rationale advanced for prolonged education conveys the message that the experience of growth through formal education insures a similar experience of growth after formal education ceases. To get the most out of life requires that you get the most out of formal education. If this rhetoric obscured the realities, it probably was true that the rhetoric was quite persuasive up to the point when the individual's formal education ceased. If I put this in the past, it is because many people of recent generations no longer accept the rhetoric. The reasons for this are quite complicated, and not without an ironic twist. The fact is that students accept, on the deepest levels, the value of growth, of continuous growing up, but see two obstacles: the nature and structure of education, and society's demand to conform to traditional values of success in the world of work. Far from not wanting to grow up, younger people seem to want to be assured that the opportunity for growth will be available through life. One can, with justice, characterize the last fifteen years as the Age of Personal Growth: the active and often frenetic search for "growth experiences," for "consciousness raising," for "self-actualization," for probing and exploiting one's "human potential," for repeated "encounters" with self and others, for "peak experiences." The jargon multiplies, techniques appear with dizzying rapidity, and the supermarket of "growth" products overwhelms the consumer who comes back again and again to sample the different brands. This may sound like hyperbole, but my observations suggest it is not. One could argue that far more than need for growth is involved, and that is, of course, true. But the unambiguous emphasis on the importance of the experience of growth, the fear of boredom, the terror of entrapment, anxiety over perceived stagnation—to regard these as surface phenomena, as outcroppings of deeper levels of personality, is to miss entirely a very obvious fact: they are variants of society's message that education makes personal growth possible, that the more education one has the more will life be experienced as a satisfying growth process, and the individual has the right to experience life as vibrant living and not as a despairing descent to death. There is no message that one grows up as a preparation for running down.

It has long been the case that education as a door opener to growth was explicit in society's message to its youth, but growth as a continuous personal expansion of and probing into one's potentialities was a muted theme in the message. Growth was success, which meant status, material gain, and society's respect. That is to say, society defined growth by extrinsic criteria. There have always been articulate critics of the conventional criteria of success, but they were no more than a minority, sometimes respected but usually unheeded. As I pointed out in the beginning chapters, World War II set the stage for new values to emerge or become dominant and one of the major consequences was the emergence and dominance of the interrelated values of personal growth, authenticity, and new experience. And this was mirrored in the significance attached to education; the muted theme of lifelong growth began to come through loud and clear. Education was still seen as a necessity for the world of work, witness this statement by Vice-President Lyndon Johnson in a commencement address at Tufts University on June 9, 1963: "We have entered an age in which education is not just a luxury permitting some men an advantage over others. It has become a necessity without which a person is defenseless in this complex, industrialized society. . . . We have truly entered the century of the educated man." It was as President, in his first address to the Congress following the assassination of President Kennedy, that President Johnson said that our "complex, industrialized society" was riddled by problems and conflicts and that our overarching goal as individuals and a society involved human values, not material matters, ending with the words "We shall overcome." There was more to living than scrambling to achieve or protect material possessions. And what was this "more"? It was another "necessity": to liberate ourselves from stifling tradition and oppressive, self-defeating prejudice, and liberation was the primary function of education. Presidential addresses are noted for their inspiring rhetoric and glittering generalities and if I pay special attention to one such address, it is because it spoke to a time and circumstance which gave unusual force to values already occupying the minds of educated youth in particular and people in general. If anything was obvious, it was that to avoid being "defenseless in this complex, industrialized society" would require an education geared to more than the world of work. In fact, it would require a kind of psychological vaccine inoculating against the illnesses of a "complex, industrialized society," one of the major ingredients of which vaccine was an antibody to protect against invading, growth-defeating forces.

Growth vs. Aging

Emphasizing growth is the antithesis of a conscious concern about aging and death. More correctly, however psychologically related (in terms of a conscious–unconscious dichotomy) thinking about growth and aging may be, phenomenologically one tends to exclude the other. This is not always the case, to be sure, and depending on definitions or point of view you could argue that growth and aging need not be seen as polarities. You could say, for example, that one aspect of aging is the attainment of wisdom through a process of personal experience and growth and, far from fearing aging because it brings us closer to the end, we should embrace it for the truths it can reveal and the serenity which is a consequence of wisdom. Unfortunately, such a view of aging guides the lives of few people. In our society the word aging, far more often than not, connotes sadness, misfortune, obsolescence and other dysphoric feelings. I can say with humor that "I am getting older" or "I am not getting any younger" as long as I intend to convey that I am aware that by objective time I am at a different point in life from a year or five years ago. But I would be perceived as conveying a very different message if I said: "I am aging." More likely than not I would be interpreted as conveying one (or both) of two things: my physical capabilities are diminishing, or that the core of me as a person has "lost" something. Aging is loss, diminution, weakening, a loosening either of the bodily or psychological seams. I may not care if people know my advanced age (relative to my students!) as long as they have the sense, rightly or wrongly, to tell me that my appearance and thinking do not look and sound my years.

Consider the title of Simone de Beauvoir's book *Coming of Age* (1972). It is an excellent book which, however, perpetuates the convention that "age" is a latter-life phenomenon. This convention is even more apparent in the research literature on aging. With very few exceptions aging, in its biological and psychological aspects, refers to people in mid-life and beyond. There is recognition, of course, that aging is a developmental process, but in practice this recognition is a form of tokenism, a consequence of how our culture teaches us to think and in part a response to the fact that aged people are seen as a problem for society. Since research funds strongly tend to flow to recognized and compelling social problems, the perceived correlation between aging and adversity has been further strengthened.

If one were to take the developmental perspective seriously, where does one start and with whom? But there is a prior question: at what point in time in the history of a society is one raising and studying these questions? This is an unproductive question only if one assumes that changes in the society over time are unrelated to people's perception of themselves in time. Implicit in all that I have said in previous chapters is that there have been changes in people's expectations and ordering of values and these changes ineluctably affected, indeed defined, how time should be used and experienced. These changes have been pervasive in the society, but nowhere have they been more clearly expressed than in the outlook of the generations which poured in and out of our colleges and universities after World War II, and that is why I considered them a meaningful starting point for inquiry into a developmental conception of aging. If I am only partly correct in this way of thinking, it will at least have the virtue of bringing into focus a fact which, while obvious, has not received the attention it deserves: *Theory and practice in regard to the elderly are almost totally determined by the perceived characteristics of those who are now elderly. In three or more decades we will have the most formally educated aged population any society has ever had. There is good reason to believe that becoming aged will pose for them and society problems radically different and potentially more personally and socially disruptive than is the case with today's elderly population.*

Why give special importance in this developmental perspective to personal growth as a value? There are several parts to an answer. The first is that it is the primary and most frequently expressed value among recent generations. It may be, and usually is, articulated in vague, global terms, almost like a very hungry person who cannot say just what will "really" satisfy his craving. It is easy to respond to these phrasings as rhetoric devoid of shape, direction, and meaning, a flight from the responsibilities of maturity to the protection of naive idealism. I confess that the flowery rhetoric in which personal growth as a value is often couched brings to mind the quip: deep down he is shallow. But this would be to miss the point that this value informs the thinking and planning of many people who actively strive to engage in lifelong pursuits of which society approves and which it considers the hallmark of maturity. It is not a value expressed only by a minority of young people who, already convinced that the value is in jeopardy, either opt out of society or engage in seemingly endless forays for the peak experience defining growth. Nor is it a value treasured only by young people, a point I have stressed in earlier chapters.

The second part of the answer, adumbrated in the first, is that personal growth as a value is the litmus paper by which all major areas of living (work, sex, friendship, marriage, parenthood) are tested. If tentativeness has come to characterize relationships in these areas, it is in no small measure because growth and permanency of commitment are seen as polarities. "Stay loose," "keep your options open," "play it cool"—these cautions emerge from the feeling that society sets all kinds of booby traps that rob you of the freedom without which growth is impossible. The third part of the answer is in principle similar to Maurice Chevalier's retort to an interviewer's question about how it felt to be eighty years of age. "I feel fine, especially when I think of the alternative." Part of the motivating force of personal growth as a value is in its contrast to countless messages about alienation, stagnation, conformity, and entrapment, all of which are predictive of decline, disaster, and death. Growth is the reed one clutches to stay alive, to strive for a life in which self and external reality interact to produce the sense of challenge which, when met, produces new, sought-after challenge.

Finiteness is not a characteristic of this view of and dependence on growth. It is seen as an *endless* process, and with that we see the connection between the value, on the one hand, and aging, dying, and death, on the other. To emphasize growth is to fortify the tendency to deny death and its long prologue of aging in the sense of decline. The dynamic of personal growth as an overarching value is to lead one not to avoid getting "older" but to avoid "aging." If personal growth as a value has the function of denying death in the sense that you only infrequently think of *your* death, it is a function far less successful in the case of aging. But even that statement requires us to remember, as I pointed out in Chapter V, that events (war, atomic bombs, pollution) of recent decades have weakened the strength of denial. Similarly, these and other developments I have described have forced society to acknowledge "aging," if only as a kind of personal disaster that has rendered millions of people dependent, lonely, unproductive, miserable, discriminated against—all in those glorious "golden years." This has not gone unnoticed by younger people, and it has given added strength to the perceived validity of the primacy of personal growth as a value.

Work and Aging

It is in the process of career choice that the dynamics of the one life–one career imperative and personal growth as a value interact, occupying the psychological center stage, with aging in the cast waiting for the spotlight.

> *The process of making a career choice is the first significant confrontation with the sense of aging, involving as it does the knowledge or belief that such a decision is fateful because it determines how the rest of one's life will be "filled in."* It is a "moment of truth" kind of problem which makes for varying degrees of vacillation, postponement, and anxiety because the choice involves numerous factors: strength of interests, familial relationships and pressures, economic factors (personal and national), love and peer relationships, time perspective, and how one reads and structures the future. The need for independence and autonomy comes face-to-face with societal pressures to conform, not the least of which is that one feels one *has* to make a decision at a particular point in time. One can no longer sample from the smorgasbord of opportunity; one *must* choose and live with the choice. There are, of course, individuals, probably small in number, who long have known what they were going to do; they are viewed by some with envy, by others with derision, and by still others with an effete attitude that seems to be saying "anyone who willingly and joyously enters this real world with the expectation of happiness has postponed his moment of truth." However one conceptualizes the process of career choice, one cannot ignore that at this particular time in our society the process is for many suffused with dysphoric anticipations about what may be symbolically called *dying*. It is not only a matter of "am I making the right or wrong choice" but, for many, "will society allow me to be the kind of person I want to be, regardless of choice?" The locus of control is perceived as external rather than internal. This has probably been the case

for past decades, but it was accompanied by the belief that by striving, diligence, and maneuvering one could lick the odds. This accompaniment is much less in evidence today [Sarason, Sarason, Cowden, pp. 586–587].

The necessity to make *a* choice channels the power of the growth value into narrow confines, requiring the individual to construct plans and fantasies about how personal growth can be accommodated. In previous chapters I discussed the variety of factors which frequently (but not always) expose the illusory aspects of these constructions. The significant point to be made here is that this disillusionment tends to bring in its wake a sense of regret about "best" time, the anxious perception that the doors of opportunity have closed, and that dreaded feeling that one must confront a future relatively devoid of vibrancy. The strength of these consequences will depend on the quality and quantity of friendships, the qualities of the marital and love relationships, the satisfactions of parenthood, and the like. Many people will tolerate their disappointment in work because work becomes justified as a way to insure the happiness of loved ones, a resolution not without many future booby traps. What is perhaps more frequent, especially in the early years, is that the balance of satisfactions and dissatisfactions in work is not so great as to dash all hopes for growth or to propel one to drastic action.

We are a time-conscious culture. From our earliest days we are exposed to "time" words (e.g., today, tomorrow, now, then, later) and instruments of time. And by the time we learn the meanings of these words, and the use of the instruments, we have also learned that future time has many demarcation points, and the older the child, the more does future time take on the characteristics of a well-marked road telling us at frequent intervals when we will get to our destination. That our destination is death we will, of course, not say or recognize, and we strenuously avoid reminding our young about this, a function religion once discharged so well. When we get married, however, we can usually count on a friend or aggressive insurance salesman to remind us that life is fickle and finite, and shouldn't we protect those we love? The stimuli for thoughts of personal death are countless, although our capacity to ignore most of them is on the boundless side. Realistically (in an actuarial sense) death is a long way off for young people. What is not a long way off—indeed it is a here-and-now as well as a future possibility—is the potential abortion of the growth process. When I spoke in earlier chapters about great expectations I was implying that we see ourselves on the road of time and in traversing it the underlying assumption is "*first* A, *then* B, *after* which comes C, . . . " And in reaching and passing through each checkpoint in time we do so willingly, enthusiastically. We reach and strive for the future and the next checkpoint; we do not see ourselves dragging our feet. It is when (and if) we find ourselves no longer reaching for that future, but fearing it, that the "I have had it" feeling comes to the fore: that if that does not signify *the* end, it is prologue to it. The sense of aging is not a phenomenon of later life but develops in different ways in different young people, coalescing or crystallizing in clarity as its relationship to *the* end becomes undeniable.

This sounds all too somber and depressive and might lead one to question its appropriateness to people, say in their twenties. Let me, then, put my view in this way: it is not a matter of chronological age but when and how the individual, having gone through college or graduate or professional school, experiences his work in light of all he or she expected from it. The sense of aging, tied in as it is with the fear of stagnation and decline and anxiety about an unstimulating and finite future, is not born full blown one day or during a month or year, and its birthplace may or may not be in the arena of work, but wherever it is, it involves a threat to personal growth as a value. It may be a transient threat, and it may reflect idiosyncratic personal dynamics and/or a valid perception of external reality. The threat may have galvanizing effects of different sorts, and the threat may disappear. It is impossible to chart the possible vicissitudes. In some individuals in whom the personal growth as a value is less central than acquiring status or material possessions, the developmental picture will differ. In contrast to another era, those for whom it is central outnumber those for whom it is not, and it is this change in the scaling values that has led me to emphasize two things: the origins of the sense of aging have an earlier and different quality and context than before and, therefore, the experience of aging in its traditional sense will be markedly different. And if I have described work as probably the most potent source of the origins of the sense of aging, it is because of the ways in which our educational system in particular and society in general lead us to regard the one life–one career imperative as *the* basis for implementing personal growth as a value.

But the discussion thus far has been based on the implicit assumption that the individual has chosen or has entered the career of first choice. What about the large number of college students who could not enter the career of first choice? In the winter of each year we can count on hearing or reading in the mass media about the sizable disproportion between those who apply and those who are accepted in graduate and professional schools. And these familiar and upsetting ratios do not include what is probably a much larger group: those who for one or another reason would like to apply but cannot or do not. In terms of the present discussion, why this large group cannot or does not apply is of secondary importance. Of primary importance is the question: how many of them already see a future in which personal growth as a value stands little chance of being satisfied? How many of them (and now I include those who apply but are not accepted), like so many people in later life, look back at their past with regret and the sense of waste? I assume that some of them enter the arena of work and find their disappointment dissipating in surprising ways. But I also assume that for many, and probably most of them, it is a festering wound which they strive to heal. Wounds are rarely fatal or dangerous unless, of course, they are in a vital area, and I have been suggesting that threats to personal growth as a value are touching a vital area.

Support for what I have been saying comes from interviews with mid-life professionals described in earlier chapters. These individuals tend not to look back at the beginning of their careers with deep regret or with self-directed blame because they should have planned differently or should have been wiser, although these thoughts are never absent. It is rather that they are beginning to understand two things: the dynamics and consequences of the one life–one career imperative, and how inordinately difficult it was (and is) for them to attend to encroachments on personal growth and autonomy. Now they can label and categorize the events and situations that, subtly or otherwise, heralded their present feelings about the finiteness of life and a perceived downhill trajectory. Why isn't the sense of regret and self-blame stronger? Because it is obscured and diluted by the angry recognition that there was and is a disparity between society's rhetoric about growth and contemporary institutional realities. This is not to say that they passively acquiesce to a world they cannot change, although some do just that and "get my kicks where I can get them." Precisely because work is experienced in relation to all other arenas of living, many of these individuals find their marriages unsatisfactory, their children a burden, and their friends uncomprehending. And, let us not forget, when they see the young entering their profession, they see enthusiasm, drive, and growth. They tend not to see these younger people in the same society which had promised them more than it could deliver. They yearn for rejuvenation, to experience *again* that sense of youthful purpose and growth. It is a yearning signifying the emergence of the sense of aging in the conventional sense that you should or must confront the fact that your life trajectory has changed or may change. The mid-life or mid-career crisis is like social change in that we become aware of and label it long after the change process began. The mid-life or mid-career crisis is not so "mid," if it ever was only mid, and the sense of aging so central to the crisis similarly has its origins much earlier in life than we have been led to believe.

The major point to this chapter is not in the details of the picture I have sketched or in its dysphoric note. Although I am far from being a member of the Panglossian society, I do not count myself among those in the gloom-or-doom fraternity. There are times I feel like applying for membership in one or the other group, and the reasons for not following through will be given in the final chapter. Suffice it to say here, we are dealing with the "Broadway" problem: the death of the Broadway theatre has been announded many times, the death rattle has been heard in different decades, and all kinds of statistics have been amassed to prove qualitative and quantitative decline. Those who hold such a view fall into three groups: those who view Broadway's decline and certain death with despair; those who view it with satisfaction because Broadway has been a superficial, commercial center, basically against rather than for good theatre; and those who do not get terribly upset because they see the emergence of strong, regional theatres which will be the base upon which the renaissance of the theatre will be built. You can look into the future and see a bleak picture or you can see the present as a swirling of forces containing diverse qualities and potentialities hard to measure or weigh, and to which we are close and see with such custom-bound categories that we have to remind ourselves to be cautious about judging short- and long-term trends—especially, as we *do* know, when our view is powered either by extreme optimism or pessimism.

The major point in this chapter has been an obvious one: our traditional view of aging obscures the fact that the confrontation with mortality begins relatively early in life, and that the choice and experience of one's life work (as it was and still is in love and marriage) bring thoughts of aging into focus, a focus that initially is far from clear but rather quickly takes on a compelling clarity. The sense of aging does not erupt into awareness, just as the choice of work is not made at a particular point in time. It is in the nature of the sense of aging that it should have a dysphoric quality, particularly in its early phases. There are few young people who can accept their mortality with indifference. It is made the more difficult when one's work, long planned and sought, from which one has been led to expect the sense of growth and a continuous stimulus to zestful living is seen, if not as an obstacle, then as an obstacle course strewn with some potentially lethal mines. When great expectations founder on social realities, causing a polarization between self and society, and between one part of the self with another, the stage is set for the sense of aging to invade thinking.

What I have said has its counterpart on the biological side. Before World War II, biological aging in its pathological or disease aspects was primarily seen as a phenomenon of later life. There was the concept of normal senescence, i.e., beginning at the end of the second or in the early phase of the third decade of life, there is an almost imperceptible decline in vital function and not until the third or fourth decade could one discern the extent of the decline. Actuarially speaking, the pathological aspects of aging (heart disease, cancer, disorders of the eye, etc.) become increasingly frequent beginning in the fourth decade of life. But in the couse of countless operations on young people during World War II, it became obvious that many of these pathological conditions were already well developed, long before they were a "problem" to the individual and society. To see diseased hearts in "normal" youths should not have been surprising on theoretical grounds, but it took the conditions of war to force people generally and the medical profession in particular to take the obvious seriously. I have suggested that we do the same in the psychological domain. As I pointed out in Chapter V, our highly educated youth, precisely because of heightened knowledge of and concern about biological aging, have as a consequence shown a sensitivity to the psychological sense of aging. Whatever suggests either the lack of growth or the possibility of decline increases sensitivity to aging in all of its aspects.

XIII

Solutions and the Psychological Sense of Community

HAVING COME TO THIS CONCLUDING CHAPTER, the reader probably expects solutions, either an individual or a public policy of sorts. After all, I have maintained that the one life–one career imperative has become increasingly dysfunctional for highly educated, professional people, and I have attempted to describe how the imperative is deep within us and undergirds our educational institutions. In point of fact, the shape of possible solutions has already come into public discussion, and although they vary, they have in common the educational analogue of Medicare. That is to say, there should be a type of public insurance that would permit an individual, any time in his or her life, to receive financial support for x amount of time (usually no more than a year) to receive further education and training, regardless of practical utility. So, if a person wishes, say, to use the year to learn about archaeology, with no intention of becoming an archeologist, fine. If he or she wishes to use the year to become an archeologist, that is fine, although how one learns archaeology in a year is another question. If you take this type of solution seriously, you will quickly see that the complications are enormous from economic and educational standpoints. On the surface, an educare policy seems reasonable and feasible. It seems to be appropriately responsive to the values of personal growth, autonomy, and authenticity. It will permit people either without work or facing obsolescence in work to move in new directions, a kind of social safety valve having the additional advantage of "efficiency" in the economic use of human resources. And, finally, it would rescue many colleges and universities from extinction or drastic decline. Let us see what some, by no means all, of the complications might be.

The social security system was a response to the Great Depression. Among its immediate goals was to get the older person out of the work force, and to keep him out, i.e., to penalize him by reducing or eliminating benefits if he worked. Then, as now, the size of benefits was far below the level permitting even a modest level of subsistence. Although an educare policy would presumably not be based on a "putting out to pasture" philosophy, we can safely assume that the time and money supports to which an individual would have claim would be insufficient to allow most people to take advantage of them in terms of their individual goals. What if that assumption were not true, and people flocked to take advantage of educare? We would then be in the position that was predicted for Medicare, i.e., the goal of covering almost all the costs of older people's hospital and medical expense would become so high that in a short period of time the benefits would have to be decreased, which is what has happened and will probably continue to happen. There was another prediction for the fate of Medicare, and it was one that went unheeded: neither in terms of resources nor attitude were the health professions and institutions prepared to implement the spirit of the program. And that prediction, unfortunately, has also been borne out.

In the event of an educare policy, similar predictions can be made. For one thing, such a policy will assume that our educational institutions are prepared to alter existing programs, or to develop new ones, in order to accommodate to the new populations returning to schools. In light of their gloomy economic future, these institutions will be eager to welcome new students, but that is no assurance they will change their traditions, requirements, and standards to meet the needs of and constraints upon these new students. When economic considerations motivate institutional change and accommodation, there tends to be a wide gulf between the letter and spirit of change. We will be dealing with a situation quite different from that during and shortly after World War II when all of higher education willingly and enthusiastically altered customs and practices in order to meet society's immediate needs for quickly educated and trained personnel (and that required enormous governmental aid). In what we call peace time, that is unlikely to happen.[1] As a consequence, one can predict that an

---

[1] Occasionally, it does happen in peace time. For example, during the height of the population explosion, when the rate of building of new schools could not keep pace with the influx of students, and the need for teachers could not be met by sticking to the traditions of the teacher-training curriculum, all kinds of exceptions were made permitting people to be employed as teachers having only taken one or two summer courses prior to starting full-time employment. The situation was so desperate that many states gave their commissioner of education the power to allow a person to teach who had no professional training at all. I am not aware of a study of the quality of the teaching of these people, but my own rather extensive experience (as observer, helper, and consul-

indeterminate number of people would find their new educational and training experience a source of disappointment as they confront tradition-bound curricula and the obstacles of the accrediting process. *All the forces that have given such unreasoned strength to people's desire for professional or guild status, as well as to the wall–moat-building dynamics of professional organizations, may well be the most effective obstacles to implementing the spirit of an educare policy.*

There may be another consequence, a truly ironic one. It is safe to assume that if an educare policy is established, it will be intended to benefit people with the least amount of education, or those in blue- and white-collar occupations, or in professions of mid to low prestige. *If it turns out that the size and duration of educare benefits will be very modest, and insufficient to allow people to achieve their new educational and career goals, it could be that those with the most education, income, or savings will be the major beneficiaries, especially as men increasingly will be married to women of professional status.* Similarly, it could be women with a good deal of education and married to men of professional status who would benefit greatly.

Because an educare policy would presumably apply to the adult population, one must expect that its intended outcomes would be blunted by what is already pervasive in our society: age discrimination. Although in recent years there has been a slight tendency in professional and graduate schools to admit people with a hiatus of several years after graduation from college, it is still the case that the chances for admission of people over thirty are extremely small. As I pointed out earlier, many people over thirty who would like to change their careers do not take steps to do so because they believe, and realistically so, that their chances for acceptance are virtually nil. This situation will not change unless institutions of higher education are forced, for reasons of economic survival, to bring in new student (undergraduate, graduate, and professional) populations *and* permit part-time students. The latter recommendation has already been presented with eloquent force by a prestigious group of scholars and administrators (Educational Testing Service, 1973). As best as I can determine, their report has met with silence, testimony to the strength of the traditions of academia and professionalism. However, it is one thing to

---

tant) in schools (Sarason, 1966, 1971) during the fifties and sixties provides absolutely no comfort to those who hold that teachers without the traditional professional preparation would, as a group, be inferior to the traditionally prepared teachers. The disease or psychopathology of guildism (be it the medical, academic, legal, or educational varieties) lies in two "phobic" symptoms: fear of contamination by strangers, and a dread of experimentation. Aside from the ministry and the arts, all professions pray in the Church of Science and genuflect before Saint Experiment. I suppose it is another example of whose ox is being gored.

criticize the strength and rigidity of traditions, and quite another thing blithely to assume that recommended changes will be without some untoward effects. This point has been made in his accustomed telling manner by Robert Nisbet (1971) in *The Degradation of the Academic Dogma*.

What I have said illustrates an obvious point: in human society, particularly contemporary ones, efforts to solve a social problem always have intended and unintended consequences. It is not only because our understanding of the problem is usually incomplete, either because the problem was long ignored or because the pressure to act leaves little time for study or reflection, but also because of our inability to understand the relationships among problems and, therefore, how directing efforts to one problem will affect the others. We like to say with humor that everything is related to everything else, and many people say with seriousness that this is now one interrelated world in which what happens in one part affects all the others. We are never dealing with an isolated problem or, if we think we are, the effort to solve it inevitably has consequences for seemingly unrelated problems. So, when the scientific and technical problems involved in going to the moon were "solved" and as a society it was decided to go to the moon, several things became apparent. First, the billions that went into the moon venture very much affected how much money would be available for social problems. Second, venturing into outer space was very much a reflection of earthly foreign policy, especially in relation to Russia and our desire to benefit from the advantages of being Hertz rather than Avis. In fact, the accelerated time schedule of the entire space program had absolutely nothing to do with science or technology but to the narcissistic wound experienced by many people at the announcement in 1957 that Russia had successfully orbited a sputnik.

And then there was the "war" on poverty: much heralded, warmly supported initially by a majority of people, and powered by what seemed large amounts of money. It soon became apparent that not only was the war unlikely to be easily won, but that the strategy being employed was poorly thought through and beset with every problem that arises when agreement on values is followed by serious disagreement about consistency between values and actions. No one really expected that among those who were to benefit from the new programs there would develop a militancy about their role in policy formation and decision making. *Noblesse oblige*, like the *ancien regime*, was an early victim of the war. Similarly, there was a vast underestimation of what is obvious in our political system: there is a never-ending struggle between parts of the system (local, state, federal) as to who will have what degree of control over programs. Control means power, patronage, and a strengthened political constituency.

Some of the early programs were deliberate attempts to bypass political entrenchments and professional establishments that were seen as
parts of the problem rather than as vehicles for solutions or change.[2]
And that proved illusory. One of the intended outcomes of the war on
poverty was to engender great expectations. For the advantaged this
meant they would see injustice, discrimination, and inequality, if not
eradicated, devastated by the onslaughts of action powered by moral
fervor. For the disadvantaged, it meant that the gulf between rhetoric
and practice would be finally narrowed. In the face of disappointment,
great expectations had a different fate in the two groups. Busing,
segregated housing practices, ethnic and racial militancy, riots, the
Vietnam war, assassinations, increasing costs and taxes, a vigorous and
articulate student movement, the women's and gay liberation
movements—psychologically, economically, and politically the war on
poverty soon became related to everything else. And, as I said earlier,
even the space program, by virtue of its costs, began to be seen in
relation to earthly problems.

Let us take a less obvious example. Assume that there is agreement
that many of our public "humane" institutions (e.g., state hospitals,
institutions for the mentally retarded) are harmful and unnecessary,
and legislation is proposed to close them and develop in communities
more productive and less dehumanizing programs. ("Deinstitutionali-
zation" has, in fact, entered the arena of public debate.) What are some
of the obstacles to such a policy? First, a lot of people currently employed in these institutions would see their jobs vanish. Second, many
highly paid and influential professionals in the state's department of
mental health would become unnecessary or irrelevant to the new
programs. They would have been rendered obsolete. Third, emptying
buildings on which bonded capital costs have not been amortized
would mean that the state would have to pay for the new programs at
the same time it would be legally bound to continue to pay bond
holders. The financial community would not have a neutral stance.
Fourth, the existing institutions are big business, i.e., they purchase an
enormous amount of food, clothing, equipment, transportation, etc.,
etc. Many businesses, large and small, depend on the existence of
these institutions. Fifth, it is probably true that the state is the most
consistent and largest "purchaser" of new buildings, i.e., the state's
construction industry also depends on institutional building and
renovation programs. Sixth, the idea of community-based and com-
munity-contained programs is relatively new, and one would encounter

[2] The interested reader should consult Marris and Rein (1969), Moynihan (1969), Ryan
(1971). I am not suggesting that the war on poverty was a dismal failure, and this is not
the place to discuss my conclusions. Suffice it to say here, the outcomes were of the
intended and unintended varieties.

opposition on many grounds: fear, zoning restrictions, professional conservatism, and political rivalries. These are only some of the predictable consequences. Some of the unpredictable consequences would become evident as soon as the proposed change in public policy would become a focus of the political–legislative process; others would arise in the process of change and implementation.

One could multiply the examples, but it would add nothing to what should be obvious, particularly for those people who propose major changes in public policy. Any change will have percolating, not encapsulating, effects. The public and private domains overlap. And, crucially, there are no solutions in the sense that you can solve a social problem without creating new ones. Ordinarily, we are unaware that we use the word solution in the sense that "four divided by two is two" is a solution, and that solution was valid yesterday and will be valid today and tomorrow. And so, when we say we are going to solve the reading problem, or poverty, or mental disorder, or juvenile delinquency, we, without having to reflect, use the word solution in the same way we would use it in questions like: How do we solve the problems of going to the moon? We used to think in this way about solving the cancer enigma: find *the* etiological basis for cancer and we automatically will have solved *that* problem. But cancer, we find, does not have a single cause and, fatefully, there is good reason to believe that human behavior, social organization, and the fruits of technological progress (so-called) are part of the problem. For example, if heavy cigarette smoking plays a role in the etiology of cancer, our concept of solution has to be quite different from when we were dealing with polio. You can outlaw cigarette smoking, but then you have to deal not only with its predictable and unpredictable psychological and social consequences, but the serious economic dislocations that would follow. And, as was true with Prohibition, we can expect massive law-enforcement problems. In the realm of human or societal affairs there are no solutions in the popular natural science sense. To understand this may be the beginning of wisdom, but it cannot be an excuse for inaction or the acceptance of the status quo. Just as the knowledge we are going to die someday is no excuse to end it all now, that knowledge should in some deliberate fashion inform our days. But "inform" is not a once-and-for-all solution, but a constant dealing with the interaction between the predictable and unpredictable consequences of informed action.

Any public policy directed to improving the quality of the work experience is at best empty rhetoric and at worst unimaginable ignorance if it has not confronted the fact that the problem of work inheres in the nature of our society and culture. This is but another way of saying that it is a problem because what we have long thought to be

natural, right, and proper—so skillfully taught and learned that it required no thinking—is no longer perceived as such by many people.
There has been a reordering of values that has made a gulf between
needs, on the one hand, and custom, practice and organization, on the
other. The conflict between the new and the old has been joined. The
change process is well on its way. Precisely because what is at issue is
the viability and flexibility of centuries' old values and categories of
thought, it is unlikely in the near future that a public policy on improving the quality of work will emerge or even be given serious attention.
But the conflict and the social change will continue until its pervasiveness becomes so obvious that public policy will only legitimate that
which has already taken place. Depending on the occurrence of major
political–economic crises, other outcomes are possible, but they, too,
will have both intended and unintended consequences.

Women and Work

When we think of solutions, we think in terms of what should or
might be done, i.e., by doing something now we can bring about a
desired state of affairs in the future. Insofar as changing the experience
of work is concerned, there already is an ongoing change that will
undoubtedly have more of an impact in the future than it has had to
date. I refer to the changing role of women. It is only in the last two
decades that pressure mounted for untrammelled, unambiguous
equality for women in all respects, embedded in law for the purpose
ultimately of being reflected in the society's thinking and customs.
Law reflects a spirit and its letter states expected practice, but in the
case of full equality of women, like that of racial minorities, it takes
decades for spirit and practice to be joined in the minds and hearts of
people, and it probably will take more than decades. It should be a
source of instructive chagrin that on the announcement of the 1954
Supreme Court desegregation decision many people reacted as if, finally, a moral cancer had been cured. From a judicial decision or legislation to changed customs and habits of thinking is a long road, more
like a long, winding tunnel where the light at the end is not visible. If
it is such a long tunnel it is not only because, in the case of blacks,
whites have to undergo major changes, but blacks must change as
well, comprised as they are of diverse groups disposed in different
historically determined ways to assimilate and accommodate to new
opportunities and roles. It is precisely the same with women. We are
far more aware of how men and a masculine-dominated society must
change, and we know that these changes will occur at different paces

depending on which groups of men and institutions one looks at. This is no less the case for women.

Women should not restrict themselves to the traditional "career" of wife and mother. That message is increasingly accepted by men and women alike. The intriguing question concerns the possible consequences of this acceptance for the one life–one career imperative. The desired answer according to a "theory" of the women's movement is two-fold: at the same time that women enjoy the full benefits of equal opportunity in the world of work, men will be relieved of economic and psychological burdens constricting their flexibility to move in new career directions. In the course of our formal interviews and informal discussions, we have found evidence that this is already taking place. One clear cluster of instances is mid-life men who have or are in the process of drastically changing their career directions, and this was possible in large part because their wives were working, although in about a third of the instances, the women were not professionals. (Far more frequent, of course, are women who were able in mid-life to move into a professional career because their professional husbands could "support" them.) Another cluster is comprised of professional men who worked in "big business" or industry and found themselves without employment as the economic downturn accelerated. These men were married to professional women working full or part time, by virtue of which the men did not feel under pressure to take whatever position came along. More relevant, some of these men used the opportunity to seek to move in new career directions; in a sense they welcomed having been forced, as one said it, "to see that I had options which I always thought were dreams." In the past several years, the mass media seem to have made it a point to describe professional men who, faced with loss of jobs, abandoned their professional careers to start florist shops, cultivate a farm, open a restaurant, activities they had secretly yearned to engage in, but did not have the courage to take seriously until unemployment stared them in the face. Common to these accounts are the desire for the autonomy expected from their careers but not found, and the willingness of their mates to collaborate in the new venture. Finally, I have known young couples who entered marriage crystal clear, at least on a verbal level, that in the event that one of them wished or needed to change directions, or to get further special training, it was the obligation of the other to provide support, economically and psychologically.

At the very least, these instances reveal that attitudes toward the interrelationships between marriage and work are undergoing change. As one young woman said: "Marriage and work are not in different ballparks. They are in the same one." They never were in different ballparks, but if they were considered in the same one, it reflected more how language and labels determine thinking and perception than it did personal experience. These attitudinal changes represent a potent challenge to the one life–one career imperative. Earlier in this book, I pointed out that our society has made it easier to change marital partners than to change careers, although the dynamics for both changes are identical. It is not surprising, therefore, that changes in attitudes toward marriage are beginning to have repercussions in the world of work. If marriage is not viewed as an inevitable tie, and work is no less important than marriage, and if personal growth is the value by which to judge the satisfactions both of marriage and work, it becomes obvious that the imperative is an obstacle to be overcome. Two things are hard to judge. The first is the strength and pace of attitudinal changes among women, and the second is the degree of shift among men both in regard to the imperative and their acceptance of the changes in women. And judging these developments is not made easier by such imponderables as the frequency and depth of economic downturns and the speed with which colleges and universities recognize and adjust to the fact that in a very few years the absolute numbers of entering students will begin to decline precipitously, a decline already familiar to those administering our public elementary and high schools. How will colleges and universities justify partially used facilities? How many will be faced with extinction? Many of these institutions have already begun to set up or enlarge their divisions of adult or continuing education. Career change programs are the "in" thing. As best I can judge, these programs are geared largely to mid-life women seeking to enter or re-enter the world of work after years of marriage and child rearing. They are far less appropriate to professional men and women seeking a serious degree of career change. For such people, the obstacles to career change are many and real, and they are not overcome by taking a course or two a year.

The women's liberation movement is radical in that it purports to expose and strike at the root of the matter which, simply put, is that our society has been organized by men on the basis of values and assumptions justifying the view of women as inferior beings capable of being socially productive only as willing and dependent servants of men and, worst of all, preventing women from recognizing or questioning the values giving rise to such a view; and in victimizing women, men have victimized themselves. The liberation of men depends on the liberation of women. As in all radical movements, accepting the message is only the first step in the change process, and it is followed or surrounded by a variety of didactic techniques the purpose of which is to broaden and deepen the individual's understanding of how he or she had been imprisoned in a web of values and assumptions blinding one to the true state of affairs, i.e., the difference between appearance and reality. This is in principle identical to what Marx sought to achieve. It was not enough to tell the prolatariat they were "the prisoners of starvation, the wretched of the earth"; they had also to be educated (=consciousness raising) as to why and how they had been brainwashed to accept such a condition, and what they needed to know if they were to break free from the chains of oppression. Central to Marx's thinking was the relationship between the content and structure of a person's mind, on the one hand, and the person's relationship to work (the modes of production), on the other, and in the case of most people that relationship could best be characterized as one in which the person was degraded to a "thing" whose distinctive human qualities in no way were stamped on his work. And Marx was clear on another point: the liberation of the proletariat would bring about the liberation of the capitalist who by virtue of being in the role of oppressor had also been robbed of a good deal of his humanity. Like Marx, there is a segment of the women's liberation movement that sees personal growth as possible only in the context of major political–social change.

The changing role of women will have enormous consequences for men and women alike. It will have great impact on the economy, marriage, child rearing, and aging. However, we can make the mistake of overlooking that the character of all of these changes will not simply be a function of the changing role of women, but rather of an interaction between these changes and other powerful forces. The women's liberation movement is just that: *a* movement. There are other forces a good deal more powerful and established. Among the most potent of these is one described in Chapter X, in which I illustrated not only the accelerating trend for the professional to work as a member of a group in a discrete, socially complicated setting—a remarkable change from the old conception of the autonomous professional—but also how the character of these settings is determined by the fact that they are (formally or informally) related to and affected by a larger system of which they are a part. The bureaucratization of professional work, long a feature of the business, financial, and industrial organization, has already occurred. From my perspective, this is the decisive factor over the long run, for men and women alike. Should this trend continue, as appears to be the case, one of its likely consequences will be to downgrade the importance which individuals give to work. That is to say, work will become less and less *the* organizing center in living. In the case of the professional person, the predictable emphasis on leisure-time activities will not be due to reduced need for the person's services, but rather as compensation for dissatisfactions. This is the significance of the finding by Kane and Cherniss that among professionals in the public arena, there is no correlation between job satisfaction and feelings of alienation: the individual who reports a high level of job satisfaction will, as likely as not, report feelings of alienation from work. It is as if one should not expect much from work, and should look elsewhere for personal growth and expression. The less one expects from work, the less the disappointment.

We are already well into the era when all segments of society are experiencing work in big, bureaucratic organizations. If the one life–one career imperative has begun to lose its force, it is not only because new values have collided with the imperative, but also because these values can find so little fulfillment in an arena of work where one's fate is determined by forces and decisions beyond one's control. There are no grounds to believe that as women increasingly become part of the professional work force they will avoid the dissatisfactions men report.

There have been numerous calls for a public policy to improve "the quality of the experience of work" but, as I have emphasized, the population which I have discussed has not been an object of concern. There is now no public policy to change the experience of work for anyone, but this may not long continue. However, if such a public policy should emerge, we will be faced with a process which, by the very fact that it will be taking place, will not only change the character of the problem for which solutions are sought, but also bring in its wake intended and unintended consequences. When a society recognizes a problem to the point where it is prepared to act, a dynamic is set in motion that alters perception of possibilities for action. What heretofore was taking place "naturally" now becomes subject to new forces of change.

It used to be that a primary function of women was a centripetal one, i.e., to be an organizing and socializing force instilling and nurturing the "sense of family," coping in the process with all the divisive factors that dilute the sense of belonging and willing reciprocity. In earlier times, when the inexorable consequences of the Industrial Revolution were only dimly sensed, the sense of family was supported by a sense of belonging to a large collectivity. As that sense of community became more fragile, and in many places disappeared, rootedness in the nuclear family became the most reliable bulwark against loneliness in an impersonal social world. In recent times, as the nature and structure of marriage and the family have changed and the sense of family has become more fragile, loneliness–alienation has come to be seen as a force affecting all arenas of living. Work has been no exception, especially when it exposes rather than seals over the longing to belong. In the opening chapters of this book, I emphasized that the boundaries of the experience of work are far greater than the boundaries of the work arena, and that the fabric of the experience of work is

given shape and substance by needs, the strength of which is determined by characteristics of the larger society as well as by idiosyncratic ones. In the following and concluding section, I turn to a need
which in our society is as unsatisfied as it is insistent.

The Psychological Sense of Community

As individuals we are inevitably alone. By words, gestures, and
touch we communicate our internal states to others, but rarely, if ever,
does it go unrecognized by us that these vehicles do an injustice to the
complexity of our feelings and thoughts. I can say "I am very happy"
and you may, watching me, say that you know what I think and feel,
but a little reflection tells us that our agreement has to do with labels
which stand for but incompletely express the experience itself. There
are times, and they are rare, when two people sense that their internal
states are fleetingly identical, and this is in part because so much of the
time we are keenly aware that communication is, at best, partial, even
if we wish it otherwise. A good deal of the time, of course, we deliberately insure a wide gulf between words and feelings.

Ordinarily, the knowledge of our inevitable aloneness is not, or
need not be, troublesome, particularly if we are part of a culture organized to provide us with structure and relatively clear guidelines for
thinking and action. A monk who has taken the vow of silence may feel
less alone than other people, because he willingly accepts the structure of his days and the communion he feels with a tradition, a history
and a divine presence. Indeed, because he regards his internal states
as no secret to his God, his silent but verbal prayers probably express
these states rather well. He is alone, but that does not necessarily
mean he is deeply lonely. Loneliness is that poignant feeling that what
is inside us has no avenue for expression, that our need for close,
supportive relationships is unsatisfied, and that the boundaries of our
inevitable aloneness have unnecessarily widened considerably. The
psychological sense of community is a response to the knowledge that
you are part of a network of relationships, reciprocal in nature, and
possessed of qualities that prevent or dilute or shorten the disintegrat-
ing effects of severe or prolonged loneliness.

The sense of community is a psychological phenomenon, but its
presence or absence is a manifestation of political–economic structure
and organization and their underlying values. This is the case whether
one is dealing in a general way with an entire society or a particular
institution within it. No one has described better than Robert Nisbet
(1969) the history of the "quest for community" over the centuries in

Western society. He weaves in the most masterful way an ever-changing tapestry depicting how changes in the sense of community varied with interrelated changes in religion, the role of the state, political–economic structure and organization, the family, and work and labor. And if the sense of community becomes even more fragile as the tapestry he weaves unfolds, and we cannot avoid recognizing how we are the products of the tides of history, we at least know that what we long for as individuals is a general phenomena. Our loneliness' is psychological, to be sure, but to see it only as psychology is an egregious form of ignorance, because it transforms a complicated social–historical process and problem into an individual one, the crowning achievement of trivialization. It also contributes to the popular belief that history has no living descendants, that the past literally is absent from the present.

The tie between the psychological sense of community and the experience of work is intimate and complex. Let me illustrate this with some examples. A number of years ago some colleagues and I (Sarason, Levine, Goldenberg, Cherlin, and Bennett, 1966) wrote a book on our work in schools. It was an exploratory effort to understand the culture of the school: how it was organized, how its structure and organization were perceived and justified, its response to change, how all of this influenced the ways different groups comprising the school experienced their work and each other, and, crucially, the nature and consequences of the relationships between a school and the larger system of which it is a part. A chapter (written by Dr. Murray Levine) in that book drew many spontaneous letters of praise. It was entitled "Teaching Is A Lonely Profession." The major thrust of the chapter was that teachers felt alone and lonely, even though their days were spent in one of the more densely populated settings in our society. It was obviously not a matter of a hunger for sheer human contact, because there was contact virtually every moment of the day. Neither from their students, other teachers, principals, and diverse types of supervisors did they feel that sense of reciprocity permitting them to give and seek help, to be candid without producing estrangement, and to feel an integral part of group tradition and mission. They were alone with themselves and their problems, and they were lonely. Elsewhere I (1971) have described why such feelings have to be frequent by virtue of the weight of tradition, the training of teachers, the conception of the role of a teacher, competitiveness within and between levels of organization, the process of and criteria for teacher evaluation, and architecture. I cannot elaborate here on these factors and their interrelationships, but if anyone has doubts that the loneliness of teachers is not a consequence of the characteristics of school tradition and organization, I can only suggest that such a person attend a series of school faculty meetings. (Or, more practical, dispassionately observe PTA meetings, one of the more effective concoctions developed to prove man's inhumanity to man.) Perhaps an example from the university will illustrate an aspect of the point in brief fashion. One of the more frequent complaints heard from university faculty and administrators is how uncommon it is for faculty members to have close working relationships with each other. By and large, university faculty are "loners," and although I suspect the level of their feelings of loneliness is less than that of school teachers, the difference would not be found to be striking. Now, in regard to major universities, let us ask two questions: who tries to "make it" at these universities? On what basis do the universities select their permanent faculty? In brief, the answer is: *individual* performance. The traditions, organization, practices, "rewards and punishments" of these universities define conditions guaranteeing a faculty who are unlikely to create or possess other than a superficial psychological sense of community.[3] It is not a psychological matter alone. Indeed, if one views the psychological sense of community as an individual or personality characteristic, one is truly missing the trees for the forest. So, if school teachers experience an unwanted loneliness in their work, it must be put into a larger context. The experience of work and the psychological sense of community are always inextricably related, and when the latter is weak or absent, dissatisfaction with "work" tends to be high.

Of all the words that have overwhelmed our language in the past three decades, few can compete with "communicate." Its obsessive popularity is not fortuitous, of course, and neither is its etymological relationship to the word "community." The significance attached to "good" communication—and the recognition that "poor" communication is the rule and not the exception—is the most powerful evidence of the weakness of and the hunger for the sense of community. "If only people can learn to communicate with each other." That hope is probably articulated thousands of times a day, and among those who utter it most frequently are professionals who earn their livelihood trying to deal with dissatisfaction in work settings. It is a hope expressed not only about work settings but about all arenas of living. And therein lies the significance of the emphasis on communication: the desire to expe-

[3] The university tends to select people who prefer working alone, but my observations suggest that it does not take long before their hunger for a sense of community becomes sufficiently strong to create a conflict between the overlearned and much rewarded preference for aloneness, on the one hand, and the need to dilute strong feelings of loneliness, on the other. By that time, however, habit has usually done its job too well to succumb to other styles of work relationships. It is true, but no surprise, that teachers and university faculty rarely comprehend how the stage for conflict was created in the distant past and although the scenery has changed, and there are new characters in the drama, the plot and outcome are still recognizable.

rience a psychological sense of community has become stronger as the centrifugal social forces in our society have whirled with increasing speed.

If the absence of the psychological sense of community is a symptom or outgrowth of the nature of our society and of its major institutions, to what extent can we expect to create and maintain that sense as an integral part of our experience of work? Putting the question that way is misleading, because the experience of work involves settings physically outside those of work, and the sense of community one can experience in the work setting cannot be expected to be unrelated to one's experience in others.

If the absence of the psychological sense of community is a symptom of the nature of our society and its major institutions, to what extent can we expect to create and maintain that sense as an integral part of the experience of work? For an answer to this question, we turn to the second example, which involved an attempt by Dr. N. Dickon Reppucci and his colleagues to introduce sanity into a situation of total organizational craziness.[4] It is impossible here to do other than list a few of the characteristics of the setting to which Dr. Reppucci and colleagues devoted four years, and a few of the outcomes.

1. The setting was a state facility for juvenile offenders. When a new superintendent and Dr. Reppucci entered the scene, the goings-on in the institution were front-page news in the newspapers, state police patroled the grounds, brutality was rampant, everybody was victimizing everybody else, and the governor and central office were forced to action.

2. From the beginning, Dr. Reppucci knew (it was not an assumption) that the nature of the setting was determined by, among other things, its being part of the state's administrative apparatus, and by the attitudes of the local community and the larger society to juvenile offenders. Granted that the nature of the setting was a reflection of internal factors, it was still true that the institution was a reflection of society and society's way of dealing with this particular population.

3. The intervention strategy had three goals. First, to deal with and change the relationships among the institution, the state system of which it was a part, and the surrounding community. Second, to create the conditions and begin a process by which all who populated the institution could experience a sense of community. (To say that the

[4]This project is being written up for publication in book form. It has been reported in several preliminary reports containing description and results (Dean, C. W., 1971; Dean, C. W., and Reppucci, N. D., in press; Reppucci, N. D., 1973; Reppucci, N. D., Saunders, J. T., and Wilkinson, L., 1971; Saunders, J. T., Reppucci, N. D., and Wilkinson, L., 1971; Wilkinson, L., and Reppucci, N. D., 1973; Wilkinson, L., Saunders, J. T., and Reppucci, N.D., 1971).

relationships between the boys and the staff and between different factions of the staff were hostile and self-defeating is to indulge in understatement.) Third, to reach a point when the public would comprehend why this and similar institutions are unnecessary.

4. Over a period of four years, the institution became dramatically different from what it had been. Extensive longitudinal data support the conclusion that among the clearest findings was the positive change in staff's experience of work and relationships with each other.

5. At all stages of the intervention the two major obstacles encounted by the intervention team were the state apparatus in which the institution was embedded, and public attitudes toward offenders. The former was not only more intractable than the latter, but also the barrier to reaching the public. Despite the pleadings of the intervention team and the institution's staff, the state proceeded to build an expensive and unnecessary maximum security building.

6. By the three-year mark, the tensions between the institution and the state apparatus heightened, to the point where it became obvious that the days of the intervention team were numbered. The team bowed out, as did the superintendent, and after they left the slide downhill began, so that two years later dissatisfaction was rife. This was another example of what I described earlier in connection with Sarata's study.

The answer to the question, then, is that it is possible to improve the experience of work by engendering a sense of community. With this addendum: the effort will constantly encounter obstacles and probably defeat, because it cannot deal with or influence "the larger system" to which, whatever else may be the bases on which it is organized and functions, the psychological sense of community is foreign. And if we were to pursue how that part of the state apparatus is in turn controlled by other systems, we would find the experience of work in that part is no less negative than it is now in the institution. What I have described is no less true for teachers in a school, just as it is identical to the experience of work by staff in the community health centers (Chapter X).

It might seem from the first two examples that I am concluding that what is inimical to the psychological sense of community, and therefore to a positive experience of work, is the ever-growing size, complexity, and interrelationships of work settings, instilling in us the feeling that we cannot control our individual fates, that we are unable to imprint our stamp on our work, that we experience our work as labor. There is, of course, a good deal of validity to this conclusion, but it is an incomplete and oversimple conclusion. *What gets overlooked in such an explanation is that in the values that determine the choice of and expectations from work, the value of the psychological sense of community is either not present or low in priority.* One of the major themes of this book has been the reordering of values brought about by World War II. Personal growth as a value, the emphasis on new experience, personal authenticity—these are not incompatible with valuing the psychological sense of community, but the fact is they were not grounded in or explicitly related to the sense of community. It is not fortuitous that the major psychological theories which have dominated the scene since World War II have been either quintessentially a psychology of the individual, or of interpersonal relationships hardly reflecting the nature, social fabric, and political–economic structure of our society. They have been ahistorical theories, almost as if the goal of developing a once-and-for-all explanation of human behavior was incompatible with an attempt to understand behavioral permutations over time in a particular society. Whether it was psychoanalysis or existentialism or Skinnerian versions of the determinants of behavior, society was a relatively undifferentiated backdrop, a vague abstraction in contrast to the marvelous complexity of the individual mind. It really should occasion no surprise that generations brought up on an individual psychology, in a society that has always lauded individual achievement, should look at work primarily in terms of individual needs and expectations. The rugged individualism of the nineteenth century justifying the activities of the robber barons is not different from the call of the sixties to "do your own thing" as an expression of personal growth as the overarching value in living. Granted that their social consequences were different, the emphasis on individualism was similar. Both honored the rhetoric of community by ignoring it.

The third example gives a different view of the tie between the experience of work and the psychological sense of community. In the nineteenth century, as in the 1960s, there was a dramatic increase in the creation of communes having the goal of instilling a deep sense of community among its members. They differed widely in the impetus forcing them to communal living, but they differed far less about the nature and obligations of their relationships with each other. Work was important, and in many of the communes individual interest and talent were taken into consideration, but its ultimate significance lay in what it meant for group cohesion and survival. In fact, one can speculate whether the distinction between work and labor was a meaningful one in many instances, because whatever one did was a willing offering to (or had personal meaning for) a "larger cause." Unlike the laborer who cannot identify his interests, talents, and desires with his activity and its products, the commune member who was engaged in what we would call labor derived satisfaction from his perception of what he contributed to a quality of communal living. Most communes were failures, and I have discussed this in an earlier book (Sarason, 1972). However, one of them, the Oneida Community (Robertson, 1970, 1972), lasted for several decades and no truly satisfactory explanation for its longevity has been presented. But in 1975, Levine and Bunker reprinted John Noyes's 1876 monograph *Mutual Criticism*. It had long been recognized that Noyes, who founded the Oneida Community, was a fascinating person with great intellectual gifts. *Mutual Criticism* demonstrates Noyes's astounding conceptual and technical accomplishments in instilling and sustaining the sense of community. From one standpoint, *Mutual Criticism* is the best group-dynamics manual ever written. Such a judgment, however, glosses over the fact that for Noyes the principles of *Mutual Criticism* were a glue keeping *all* aspects of an entire community together. They were principles that superseded, controlled, but did not eliminate personal growth as a value. Indeed, Noyes's "Perfectionism" not only permitted but encouraged individuals to follow their varied interests and to give expression to their talents.

> As Noyes points out in *Mutual Criticism*, individuals living together will inevitably rub each other the wrong way. In many communities differences between people lead to gossip, back biting, avoidance of relationships, or open enmity. A second and equally important use of criticism was to bring such interpersonal differences into the open, and to help settle them. In one notable example, criticism was employed to solve a problem among the group of musicians. Oneida had developed a musical body of considerable merit. The group had developed out of the interests of those who sang and played for their own amusement, to a nearly professional body which gave public performances. After a number of years, it became apparent that the musical group had developed interpersonal difficulties affecting their ability to work together. Noyes noticed one of the young women had become quite withdrawn. After talking with her, she confessed she was angry with another girl who was recognized as a better singer than she was. Noyes called the entire group together, and soon' elicited from each frank confessions of the ill feelings stemming from competitive jealousies among them. Further discussion pinned the problem not to music itself, but to the fact that there was competition related to solo performances in front of outside audiences. Once having identified the problem, which Noyes labeled "prima donna fever," the group all offered suggestions for controlling the problem. Each vowed to try to control feelings of jealousy and carping criticism of musical performance. Each also agreed to offer themselves for criticism to help overcome the personal flaw that entered into the group problem [Levine and Bunker, p. XVI].

Noyes is one of a long list of people who understood that there were predictable tensions between the individual and the community, and the task was to avoid resolving them by weakening or destroying either individual needs or group values. He saw with amazing clarity that every problem of the individual had repercussions for the community, and vice versa, and only when members of the community thought and acted on the basis of this insight could the needs for belonging and growth be harmonized. His genius lay in the recognition that agreement on values was no guarantee that action would automatically reflect these values, and means needed to be developed continually to confront, clarify, and harmonize action with values.

The psychological sense of community alters one's perception and experience of work. In our society that alteration tends to happen *after* rather than before dissatisfaction with work. When a person becomes aware that he cannot continue to make a strong commitment to work, that an impersonal society has rendered him impotent and dependent, and has frustrated the desire for personal growth, the resulting alienation and loneliness bring to the fore the absence and need for a sense of community. This does not mean that the need for a sense of community was weak or absent, but rather that it was not a value governing career choice and expectations. That the need for a sense of community is deep and strong in all of us in this society requires no discussion or proof here. At the same time in the sixties that "doing your own thing" was so popular, communes were mushrooming, and people were giving up careers to start small shops and businesses promising them greater autonomy and more satisfactory human relationships. It is impossible to overestimate the hunger for a sense of community. One could argue that our society is no more congenial to the need for community than it has been to personal growth as a value. That is a valid argument, and there is no point in trying to counter it with vacuous expressions of hope. That the desire for community amounts to a hunger is far better than if it were weak. That there is reason to believe that the highly educated segment of our society is experiencing a degree and quality of work dissatisfaction long recognized by them as the fate of the less advantaged, is cause both for hope and fear. Hope because it is an influential segment in our society and it could become a force for positive change; fear because when cynicism and disillusionment invade the minds of that segment the consequences can be quite negative.

Social change cannot be judged by our personal conception of time, because we see and judge the substance and pace of change in terms of our life span, i.e., judge it by its effects on us. Because we are never neutral in such judgments, we usually either overestimate or underestimate the pace and consequences of the perceived changes. We hear ourselves saying that "a change has taken place" and fail to see that our language is describing a static process and not a continuous one. So when we say "a change has taken place" we tend not to recognize that that change has already been incorporated and been changed. Social change is a never-ending process which at any one time we describe in terms of what we see and think we know. And it is not until a later point in time that we look back and find that the earlier description or diagnosis was, at best, only partially correct, because we were not sensitive to or even aware of social phenomena and consequences predictive of what we later found out.

We are now beginning to understand the consequences of the reordering of values during and after World War II. We are also beginning to understand as never before that we have been victims, willing ones for the most part, of a cult of efficiency and growth that seemed to be based on the attitude that if something could be done, it should be done. The myth of unlimited resources has been exposed. And as a society we have barely begun to confront the fact that our autonomy has been curtailed in an increasingly interrelated world. If I am unable or unwilling to indulge in futurology, I am able to assert that fateful for that future will be how these swirling, new and old social forces of change will shape the strength and substance of people's sense of community. If our need for that sense remains unconnected to and does not inform the major arenas of social living, we will at best see again that the more things change, the more they remain the same, and at worst see the boundaries of loneliness enlarge.

Bibliography

AUERBACH, J. S. *Unequal Justice*. New York: Oxford University Press, 1975.

BARRETT, W. *Irrational Man. A Study in Existential Philosophy*. New York: Anchor Books, 1962 (paperback).

—— "Our Contemporary, William James." *Commentary,* 60 (No. 6), 1975.

BECKER, C. L. *The Heavenly City of the Eighteenth Century Philosophers*. New Haven, Conn.: Yale University Press, 1932.

BECKER, E. *The Denial of Death*. New York: Free Press, 1973.

BECKER, H. S., B. GEER, E. C. HUGHES, and A. L. STRAUSS, *Boys in White*. Chicago: University of Chicago Press, 1961.

BECKETT, S. *Waiting for Godot*. New York: Grove Press, 1954.

—— *Endgame*. New York: Grove Press, 1958. (London: Faber & Faber, 1958).

BELL, D. *The End of Ideology*. New York: Free Press, 1965 (paperback).

BERG, I. *Education and Jobs: The Great Training Robbery*. Boston: Beacon Press, 1971.

BERNSTEIN, R. J. *Praxis and Action*. Philadelphia: University of Pennsylvania Press, 1971.

BESTERMAN, T. *Voltaire*. New York: Harcourt, Brace & World, 1967.

BLATT, B. *Exodus from Pandemonium*. Boston: Allyn & Bacon, 1970.

BROWN, J. F. *Psychology and the Social Order*. New York: McGraw-Hill, 1936.

—— *The Psychodynamics of Abnormal Behavior*. New York: McGraw-Hill, 1940.

BUXTON, C. E. *Adolescents in School*. New Haven, Conn.: Yale University Press, 1973.

CHERNISS, C. Personal Communication, 1975.

CHINOY, E. *Automobile Workers and the American Dream*. Garden City, N.Y.: Doubleday, 1955.

COLEMAN, J. S. (Chairman) *Youth: Transition to Adulthood*. Report of the Panel on Youth of the President's Science Advisory Committee. Chicago: University of Chicago, 1974.

COWDEN, P., P. Fountain, and J. Sarason, *Career Change and Job Satisfaction.* Unpublished paper, Work and Aging Project, Yale University, 1974.

DEAN, C. W. "From a Superintendent's Perspective." Paper presented at the American Psychological Association, D.C., 1971.

———, and N. D. Reppucci, "Juvenile Correctional Institutions." In D. Glaser, ed., *Handbook of Criminology.* New York: Rand-McNally (in press).

DE BEAUVOIR, S. *The Coming of Age.* New York: Putnam, 1972.

DEGRAZIA, S. *Of Time, Work, and Leisure.* Garden City, N.Y.: Doubleday Anchor, 1964.

DERSHOWITZ, A. Review of Jerold S. Auerbach's *Unequal Justice. New York Times Book Review,* January 25, 1976, sec. 7, pp. 1–2.

DEWEY, J. *Art as Experience.* New York: Minton, Balch & Co., 1934.

DOLLARD, J. *Criteria for the Life History. With Analyses of Six Notable Documents.* New Haven: Yale University Press, 1935.

EDWARDS, L. P. *The Natural History of Revolution.* Chicago: University of Chicago Press, 1927.

ENTINE, A. D. "At Mid-Life They Return to College and Change Careers." *Journal of College Placement,* April–May, 1967, 50–57.

ESSLIN, M. *The Theatre of the Absurd.* New York: Doubleday, 1969 (Anchor Books paperback).

FILL, J. H. "An Epidemic of Madness: The Confessions of a Perpetrator." *Human Behavior,* March, 1974, 40–47.

FOUNTAIN, P. *What Teaching Does to Teachers.* Unpublished doctoral dissertation, Yale University, 1975.

FREUD, S. Analysis of a Phobia in a Five-Year-Old Boy. *Collected Papers,* Vol. 10. London: Hogarth Press, 1955.

GREEN, T. *Work, Leisure and the American Schools.* New York: Random House, 1968.

GURIN, T., J. Veroff, and S. FELD. *Americans View Their Mental Health.* New York: Basic Books, 1960.

HACKMAN, R., and E. LAWLER. "Employee Reactions to Job Characteristics." *Journal of Applied Psychology,* 1971, Vol. 55, 259–286.

HARRIS, C. *One Man's Medicine.* New York: Harper & Row, 1975.

HEILBRONER, R. L. "The Human Prospect." *The New York Review,* January 24, 1974, 21–34.

HUBBELL, J. B. *Who Are the Major American Writers?* Durham, N.C.: Duke University Press, 1972.

JASTROW, J. *The House That Freud Built.* New York: Greenberg, 1932.

JOINT COMMISSION ON MENTAL ILLNESS AND HEALTH. *Action for Mental Health.* New York: Basic Books, 1961.

KAHN, R. L., D. M. WOLFE, R. P. QUINN, J. D. SNOEK, and R. A. ROSENTHAL. *Organizational Stress.* New York: John Wiley, 1964.

KANE, J., and C. CHERNISS, Personal Communication, 1976.

LANGER, W. C. *The Mind of Adolf Hitler: The Secret Wartime Report.* New York: Basic Books, 1972.

LEMASTERS, E. E. *Blue-Collar Aristocrats.* Madison, Wis.: University of Wisconsin Press, 1975.

LEVINE, M. "Teaching is a Lonely Profession." In S. B. SARASON, M. LEVINE, I. I. GOLDENBERG, D. L. CHERLIN, and E. M. BENNETT. *Psychology in Community Settings: Clinical, Educational, Vocational, Social Aspects.* New York: John Wiley, 1966.

———, and B. B. BUNKER, Introduction to *Mutual Criticism,* by J. H. NOYES. Syracuse, N.Y.: Syracuse University Press, 1975.

MARRIS, P., and M. REIN, *Dilemmas of Social Reform.* New York: Atherton Press, 1969.

MAYNARD, J. *Looking Back: A Chronicle of Growing Up Old in the Sixties.* New York: Avon Books, 1974 (paperback).

MICHENER, J. A. *The Drifters.* New York: Random House, 1971.

MILLER, A. *The Death of a Salesman.* New York: Viking Compass Books, 1958.

MOYNIHAN, D. P. *Maximum Feasible Misunderstanding: Community Action in the War on Poverty.* New York: Free Press, 1969.

NATIONAL COUNCIL OF COMMUNITY MENTAL HEALTH CENTERS, AND THE NATIONAL INSTITUTE FOR COMMUNITY MENTAL HEALTH. *Proceedings of Annual Meeting.* Denver, Col.: February 22–25, 1976.

NISBET, R. *Social Change and History.* New York: Oxford University Press, 1969.

——— *The Degradation of the Academic Dogma.* New York: Basic Books, 1971.

NOYES, J. H. *Mutual Criticism.* Oneida, N.Y.: Office of the American Socialist, 1876. Reprint ed. and Introduction by M. LEVINE and B. B. BUNKER. Syracuse, N.Y.: Syracuse University Press, 1975.

O'TOOLE, J. (Chairman) *Work in America.* Report of a Special Task Force to the Secretary of Health, Education, and Welfare. Cambridge, Mass.: M.I.T. Press, 1973.

——— (ed.) *Work and the Quality of Work.* Resource papers for *Work in America.* Cambridge, Mass.: M.I.T. Press, 1974.

PHILLIPS, C. *The 1940s. Decade of Triumph and Trouble.* New York: Macmillan, 1975.

PLANT, J. S. *Personality and the Cultural Pattern.* New York: Octagon Books, 1966. (Originally published in 1937 by The Commonwealth Fund.)

POMEROY, W. B. *Dr. Kinsey and the Institute for Sex Research.* New York: Harper & Row, 1972.

REPPUCCI, N. D. "The Social Psychology of Institutional Change: General Principles for Intervention." *American Journal of Community Psychology,* 1, 1973.

————, J. T. SAUNDERS, and L. WILKINSON, "The Prehistory, Port of Entry and the Mandate for Change." Paper presented at the American Psychological Association, Washington, D.C., 1971.

ROBERTSON, C. N. (ed.) *Oneida Community: An Autobiography, 1851–1876.* Syracuse, N.Y.: Syracuse University Press, 1970.

———— *Oneida Community: The Breakup, 1876–1881.* Syracuse, N.Y.: Syracuse University Press, 1972.

ROGERS, C. R. *Counseling and Psychotherapy: Newer Concepts in Practice.* Boston: Houghton Mifflin, 1942.

RYAN, W. *Blaming the Victim.* New York: Pantheon, 1971.

SALINGER, J. D. *Nine Short Stories.* New York: Bantam Books, 1964.

———— *The Catcher in the Rye.* New York: Bantam Books, 1968.

SARASON, S. B. "The Contents of Human Problem Solving." Paper presented at Nebraska Symposium on Motivation, 1961.

———— *The Culture of the School and the Problem of Change.* Boston: Allyn & Bacon, 1971.

———— *The Creation of Settings and the Future Societies.* San Francisco: Jossey–Bass, 1972.

———— "Jewishness, Blackishness, and the Nature–Nurture Controversy." *American Psychologist,* Nov., 1973, 28, No. 11, 962–971.

———— *The Psychological Sense of Community. Prospects for a Community Psychology.* San Francisco: Jossey–Bass, 1974.

———— "Psychology to the Finland Station in The Heavenly City of the Eighteenth Century Philosophers." *American Psychologist,* November, 1975, 30, No. 11, 1072–1080.

———— "Community Psychology and the Anarchist Insight." *American Journal of Community Psychology,* September, 1976 (in press).

———— "The Unfortunate Fate of Alfred Binet and School Psychology." New York: *Teachers College Record,* Columbia University, 1976 (in press).

————, F. K. GROSSMAN, and G. ZITNAY, *The Creation of a Community Setting.* Syracuse, N.Y.: Syracuse University Press, 1972.

————, M. LEVINE, I. I. GOLDENBERG, D. CHERLIN, and E. BENNETT, *Psychology in Community Settings: Clinical, Educational, Vocational, Social Aspects.* New York: John Wiley, 1966.

————, E. K. SARASON, and P. COWDEN. "Aging and the Nature of Work." *American Psychologist,* May, 1975, 30, No. 5, 584–592.

SARATA, B. P. V. *The Job Satisfactions of Individuals Working with the Mentally Retarded.* Unpublished doctoral dissertation, Yale University, 1972.

———— "Employee Satisfactions in Agencies Serving the Retarded." *American Journal of Mental Deficiency,* 1975, 79, 434–442.

———— "Job Characteristics, Work Satisfactions and Task Involvement as Correlates of Service Delivery Strategies." *American Journal of Community Psychology,* 1976 (in press).

————, and N. D. REPPUCCI, "The Problem is Outside: Staff and Client Behavior as a Function of External Events." *Community Mental Health Journal*, 1975, 11, (1), 91–100.

SAUNDERS, J. T., N. D. REPPUCCI, and L. WILKINSON, "Toward the Development of a Rehabilitation Program." Paper presented at the *American Psychological association*, Washington, D.C., 1971.

SCHAEFER-SIMMERN, H. *The Unfolding of Artistic Activity*. Berkeley and Los Angeles, Calif.: University of California Press, 1948.

Scholarship in Society, A Report on Emerging Roles and Responsibilities of Graduate Education in America. Princeton, N.J.: Educational Testing Service, 1973.

SELZER, R. "The Art of Surgery." *Harpers*, October, 1975, pp. 38–34.

SKINNER, B. F. *Walden Two*. New York: Macmillan Co., 1948.

―――― *Beyond Freedom and Dignity*. New York: Alfred A. Knopf, 1971.

TERKEL, S. *Working*. New York: Pantheon, 1974.

VEYSEY, L. "Who's a Professional? Who Cares?" (Review of *Advocacy & Objectivity: A Crisis in the Professionalization of American Social Science, 1865–1905* by M. O. FURNER). *Reviews In American History*, December, 1975, 3, No. 4, 419–423.

WILKINSON, L., J. T. SAUNDERS, and N. D. REPPUCCI, "The Development of a Behavioral System for an Established Institution: A Preliminary Statement." Paper presented at the 5th Annual Meeting of the Association for the Advancement of Behavioral Therapies, Washington, D.C., 1971.

――――, and N. D. REPPUCCI, "Perceptions of Social Climate Among Participants in Token Economy and Non-Token Cottages in a Juvenile Correctional Institution." *American Journal of Community Psychology*, 1, 1973, 36–43.

WILLS, G. *Bare Ruined Choirs: Doubt, Prophecy, and Radical Religion*. New York: Doubleday, 1971.

WIRTZ, W. *The Boundless Resource*. Washington, D.C.: The New Republic Book Co., Inc., 1975.

WOLF, T. H. *Alfred Binet*. Chicago: University of Chicago Press, 1973.

Index

295